AF708908

Visual Delights – *two*
Exhibition and Reception

DATE DUE

DISCARD

Demco, Inc. 38-293

ENTERED MAY 9 2006

COLUMBIA COLLEGE LIBRARY
600 S. MICHIGAN AVENUE
CHICAGO, IL 60605

Visual Delights – *two*
Exhibition and Reception

Edited by Vanessa Toulmin and Simon Popple

COLUMBIA COLLEGE LIBRARY

British Library Cataloguing in Publication Data

Visual Delights – *two*
Exhibition and Reception

A catalogue entry for this book is available from the British Library

ISBN: 0 86196 657 0 (Paperback)

Published by
John Libbey Publishing, Box 276, Eastleigh SO50 5YS, UK
e-mail: john.libbey@libertysurf.fr; web site: www.johnlibbey.com

Orders: **Book Representation & Distribution Ltd**. info@bookreps.com

Distributed in North America by **Indiana University Press**, 601 North Morton St, Bloomington, IN 47404, USA. www.iupress.indiana.edu

Distributed in Australasia by **Elsevier Australia**, 30–52 Smidmore Street, Marrickville NSW 2204, Australia. www.elsevier.com.au

Distributed in Japan by **United Pubishers Services Ltd**, 1-32-5 Higashi-shinagawa, Shinagawa-ku, Tokyo 140-0002, Japan. info@ups.co.jp

© 2005 Copyright John Libbey Publishing. All rights reserved.
Unauthorised duplication contravenes applicable laws.

Printed in Malaysia by Vivar Printing Sdn. Bhd., 48000 Rawang, Selangor Darul Ehsan.

Contents

Introduction

> There always are, always have been, always will be, people who are willing to be 'entertained', i.e. amused, by a 'show' of some kind. Not only willing are they, but eager for such amusement. And they will travel miles and part from their money with no other object to view.[1]

This collection of essays is drawn from the second in the series of the Visual Delights conferences, held at the University of Sheffield in July 2002. This tri-annual event is an exploration of the different audiences, media technologies and exhibition contexts enjoyed by popular cultural forms in the period leading up to the First World War. The Victorian and Edwardian periods are rich in detail for historians of popular entertainment incorporating magic lanterns, fairground shows, magic, the development of circus and of course the cinematograph. Additionally the overlap between photographic history, printing technology and the development of the popular press has resulted in a rich vein of archival material that records these shows. Although now important archival resources, there were originally ephemeral pieces of advertising often mass produced solely for the purpose of attracting an audience in the ever competitive world of popular entertainment. These performances could be found on the fairground arena, within a travelling or fixed circus, in a show of optical and scientific wonder at permanent halls or on the high street. Everything and anything was presented under the banner of education and entertainment. Many of these areas have developed their own individual histories and bodies of work that have explored the chronological development of these performances without emphasising the cross-fertilisation that occurred at the time.

The conference attracted an extremely rich variety of papers and performances exploring the dominant popular cultural forms of this era and approached them from a fascinating range of methodological perspectives. A dominant sub-theme was the development of representational strategies related particularly to notions of gender. In addition the Bamforth Photographic and Film Company of Holmfirth was celebrated with a day of performance and presentations dedicated to celebrating the rich visual history of the company from the 1840s to the 1960s. The Bamforth

Day was held in the firm's original cinema built in 1913 and the local setting of the magic lantern slides, films and postcards was keenly received by both the conference audience and the local participants.

All of the essays presented in this book are strongly indicative of the diversity of focus and approach evident at the Visual Delight conferences and demonstrate the exciting potential of intermedial and intertextual readings of popular cultural forms offered by many of the authors. Their specific approaches are often rooted in well established disciplinary traditions but one of the great successes of the conference series has been the opportunity to experience and assimilate complimentary methodologies and critical strategies and thus create new and inclusive readings of many early popular cultural forms. We hope that this experience is replicated by reading the selection of papers contained in this anthology and taken from the second event held in 2002.

As part of the ongoing process of developing new readings of popular cultural forms the journal, *Living Pictures; The Popular and Projected Image before 1914*, which supports the conference series has been re-titled and re-launched. *Early Popular Visual Culture* is a peer-reviewed, academic journal dedicated to stimulating research and interdisciplinary studies in relation to all forms of popular visual culture pre-1930. The journal will develop the approaches developed in the *Visual Delights* conference series in examining the use and exploitation of popular cultural forms such as (but not limited to) cinema, photography, magic lanterns and music hall within the fields of entertainment, education, science, advertising and the domestic environment. In common with the conference and these proceedings the journal will also be concerned with the evolving social, technological and economic contexts which such popular cultural products have inhabited and defined. Both the journal and the conference series are providing historians of visual culture and performance histories an arena in which inter-disciplinary approaches will provide an empirical and analytical body of use to the variety of research communities that study this rich historical period.

Vanessa Toulmin and Simon Popple
May 2005

Note

1. Goodrick, G. J., *Tableaux Vivants and Living Waxworks with Directions for Stage Management*. London: Dean and Son, 1895.

1

Vision and Touch: Photography and Women's Popular Culture in the Nineteenth Century

Patrizia Di Bello

> Every day the urge grows stronger to get hold of an object at very close range by way of its likeness, its reproduction.[1]

The development of photography in the nineteenth century is often discussed in terms of theories of vision and the gaze. According to this logic, photography is conceptualised as a tool of knowledge and as an instrument of the gaze, working in the interests of those in power.[2] This is partly a response to the technical characteristics of the medium, and to how photographs are made. The act of taking a photograph is set up through the agency of the photographer, who is engaged in framing its subject matter spatially and temporally through decisions about camera viewpoint, exposure and focus; but the process itself takes place without the direct intervention of the photographer's hands. Unlike a draftsman, who has to use his hands to record on paper the image formed by the camera obscura, the photographer lets photographic technology, a mix of optics and chemistry, take its course, allowing the subject to image itself on the light sensitive surface. During subsequent processing, good darkroom techniques (for example, the use of tongues) ensure that hands do not touch the photographic image, only its borders.[3] As Walter Benjamin describes in his essay on 'The Work of Art in the Age of Mechanical Reproduction':

> photography freed the hand of the most important artistic function which henceforth devolved only upon the eye looking into the lens.[4]

Photographic prints, however, are used – looked at, distributed, captioned, catalogued and stored – in ways and social contexts that often involve not only gazing but also holding and touching; this is especially true of images circulating as mass culture and in the private sphere. As Linda Williams points out:

> the mass produced image, whether lithograph, photograph, or stereograph, is accessible to handling in a way that painting, for example, is not.[5]

Elizabeth Edwards, writing about 'Photographs as Objects of Memory', emphasises the sensual, tactile experience of photographic prints as three-dimensional objects. She argues that the photograph's availability to being 'handled, framed, cut, crumpled, caressed, pinned on the wall, put under a pillow, or wept over',[6] is crucially important to its role as a privileged conduit of memory.

Making wider claims for the importance of considering photographs as tactile rather than purely visual objects, Geoffrey Batchen argues that:

> photography is privileged within modern culture because, unlike other systems of representation, the camera does more that just see the world: it is also touched by it.[7]

Drawing on Roland Barthes's identification of the 'noeme' of photography as the way in which its sensitive surface is touched by the same rays of light that had touched the world,[8] Batchen argues that what he calls 'Vernacular Photographies', objects integrating photographic images with three dimensional, often hand-made arrangements, reciprocate not the visual but the tactile gift of the photograph.[9]

In this essay, I want to consider the dynamics of vision and touch in two nineteenth-century images: *Her Majesty the Queen with the Princess Beatrice on Her Knee (From a Photograph published by A. Marion and Co., 152, Regent-street.)*, a wood engraving which was published on the front cover of the *Lady's Newspaper and Pictorial Times*, 14 March 1863 (Fig. 1); and the carte-de-visite that was probably its original, taken by Chèmar Freres, Photographers to the King, in Brussels, and here collected in an anonymous nineteenth-century album of cartes-de-visite of assorted European Royals (Fig. 2).

In both, Queen Victoria is seated behind her young daughter, holding her on her knee and encircling her with her arms, one hand touching hers, the other clutching the girl's dress. Beatrice, sitting on her mother's lap, is in turn holding a small photograph of Prince Albert. We cannot actually see this, only a rectangular flat object, containing a darker oval shape. But reading this shape as a photograph would have been obvious to viewers at the time, and perhaps now as well. What else, but a photograph of the beloved departed, could be gazed at with such melancholic intensity by the widow and her daughter? Keen readers of women's magazines of the time might even recollect the portrait photograph of Prince Albert, a head-shot in an oval frame, distributed free with one of the first issues of the *Queen*, a similar, rival magazine before it merged with the *Lady's Newspaper*.[10] In both photograph and engraving, Queen Victoria is represented sharing with us not the look of the photograph, but its nature as an object: a small thing to be held close to one's lap, and looked down at, like a child.[11]

Prince Albert's death in 1861, twenty-two years after photographic systems were first announced in England, coincided with the beginning of the carte-de-visite craze in England, and might even have contributed to it. In the week after his death, orders for his carte-de-visite portrait, published like this by Marion and Co., were reported in the photographic press to have been 'no less than 70,000'.[12] The Queen herself, already fond of photographic images, used photography extensively as part of her elaborate rituals of mourning, both private and public. She slept with a

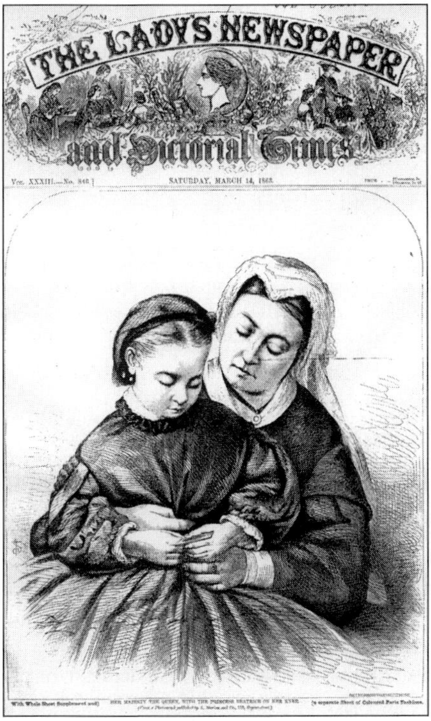
THE LADY'S NEWSPAPER and Pictorial Times

Vol. XXXIII.—No. 846. SATURDAY, MARCH 14, 1863.

Fig. 1. 'Her Majesty the Queen, with the Princess Beatrice on Her Knee. From a Photograph published by A. Marion and Co.' Front page of the Lady's Newspaper and Pictorial Times, *14 March 1863. 30 x 24 cm. British Library Newspaper Library.*
[By permission of the British Library.]

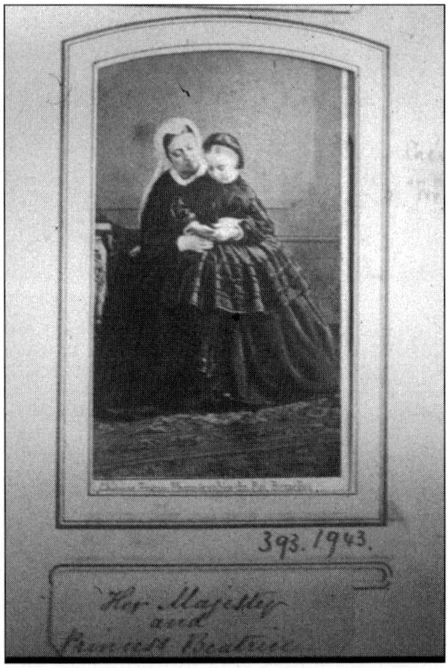

Fig. 2. Chèmar Freres, Brussels, 'Queen Victoria and Princess Beatrice'. Carte-de-visite, 1860s. 10.5 x 6 cm. Victoria and Albert Museum. [Copyright V&A Images.]

photograph of Albert pinned above his side of the bed. Presents of mourning jewellery – rings, bracelets and pins – adorned with miniature photographs of the Prince, were distributed amongst family and courtiers for years after his death.[13] For her official diamond jubilee photograph, in 1897, Queen Victoria decided to pose wearing a mourning bracelet with an oval portrait of Prince Albert, and holding his photograph framed in a travelling case.

The Queen had posed holding photographs of the Prince even before his death. In a photograph taken at Buckingham Palace in 1854, she posed holding one of *Prince Albert* taken in May 1854. In *Mourning Group*, a photograph by William Bambridge taken at Windsor Castle in March 1862, Prince Albert is represented twice, as a marble bust and as a photograph. The group is ignoring the bust, rendered a ghostly apparition by the photograph's poor tonal range; it is the photograph in Queen Victoria's hands, big enough to be legible as a portrait of Albert, that is the focus of attention.

In her study of *Royal Representations*, Margaret Homans shows how Albert's death resolved the particularly difficult political and cultural position of Victoria. She was a reigning Queen in an age that denied women political representation, who became popular by presenting herself above all as a woman, embodying values of domesticity not always consonant with life at Court and the monarch's political role.[14] In a double strategy of both remembering and forgetting Prince Albert, Queen Victoria started to invoke him as the will behind her every action, even when she was doing things he had expressly asked her not to do, such as building monuments to him. In representing herself as his widow, the Queen successfully incorporated the image of her absent husband into that of herself, turning her wifely deferral to the wishes of her husband, even after his death, into a metaphor for the Monarch's deferral to the wishes of her Parliament. Homans argues that the gender of the sovereign for most of the nineteenth century was instrumental to the survival of the British monarchy, at a time when many other were in crisis. The Queen came to represent the government like other women represented their husband when out in society. Being a widow resolved any potential conflicts between her role of representing her husband, and that of representing her government. But for both Queen and society women, representation rested on their appearing in person, and widowhood rendered Queen Victoria's representational duties problematic.

The engraving of *Her Majesty the Queen with the Princess Beatrice on Her Knee* was published in the *Lady's Newspaper* more than a year after the death of Prince Albert, and four days after the marriage of the Prince of Wales to Princess Alexandra on 10 March 1863. The Queen was very reluctant to appear in public, and was still refusing to hold levees and drawing rooms, important events in the upper-class social calendar, legitimising the status of the political and aristocratic elite.[15] Her mourning was creating something of a constitutional crisis: was the Queen fit to hold her position while secluded in deep mourning, away from the public representations the Monarchy was expected to perform? And if she was, was that not a sign that the Monarchy itself was no longer actually performing any function, and that it was therefore redundant?

At the wedding of the Prince of Wales, the Queen had been conspicuous by her refusal to lighten her mourning, and to join in the wedding banquet. After the ceremony, she had instead retired to her privacy and sadness, with the sole comfort of Princess Beatrice. In this sense, this image illustrates what the Queen had been doing while not at the wedding celebrations: mourning her husband in the company of her youngest daughter. It is a typical example of what Margaret Homans and Adrienne Munich have identified as Queen Victoria's strategy of not appearing in public in her body but as a representation.[16] As the Queen herself pointed out in various of her letters and diaries, Royal public appearances were mostly for the benefit of the privileged few: those who could expect to be invited at a Royal wedding, or introduced at Court during drawing rooms. Photographs and magazines, on the other hand, could be purchased by most, if not all, her subjects. The Queen thus makes up for the lack of her appearance in public as a body, by appearing in public as a representation. Any loss of popularity due to her continuing seclusion was in the long run more than compensated for by the greater 'exhibition value' (in Walter Benjamin's term) of her mechanically reproducible image. In an emerging celebrity culture, fuelled by the development of mass communication media such as photography and illustrated magazines, Queen Victoria used them to modernise the representational duties of the Monarchy, and to make them all the more powerful through cultural rather than political means. She demonstrated that she could perform as both (public) Queen and (private) woman by appearing in public not through her presence at public events, but through media representations. In doing so, she transformed the Monarchy into the celebrity of celebrities, and democratised its appeal by making it appear for the benefit of all its people, not only the elite.

Queen Victoria often expressed her discomfort at taking part in public events without Albert. As she explained in a letter to Lord Russell, then Prime Minister:

> That the public should wish to see her she fully understands, and has no wish to prevent ... but why this wish should be of so unreasonable and unfeeling a nature, as to long to witness the spectacle of a poor, broken-hearted widow, nervous and shrinking, dragged in deep mourning, alone in State as a Show, where she used to go supported by her husband, to be gazed at, without delicacy of feeling, is a thing she cannot understand, and she never could wish her bitterest foe to be exposed to![17]

Without the support of her husband, exposure to the public gaze is cruel and abjecting. But to show herself in a photograph, dressed as a private woman, is not. Yet photographs and magazines circulated in the public sphere – were exhibited and sold through window displays. But beyond the moment of window shopping, these images were consumed in the privacy of home, as Victoria herself seems to be doing in *Her Majesty the Queen with the Princess Beatrice on Her Knee*. Mediating her public appearance thorough the representational means of photography seems to restore to the public gaze the delicacy of feeling it loses when the Queen is forced to appear 'alone in State as a Show'.

The Queen's renegotiating of public and private, delicate and indelicate modes of being looked at, mirrors the way in which readers of women's magazines were renegotiating private and public modes of looking. Through buying them, women could take part in the range of public arenas represented by women's magazines: parliamentary debates and art exhibitions, society gossip and news from abroad, as well as the latest fashions; and could do so from the comfort and privacy of their homes. This is not to suggest that women did not go out in public in person, but that, as Lynda Nead points out:

> it is possible to conceive a variety of ways of accessing the public world and a number of different public arenas in which women could be involved.[18]

In these photographic and engraved images (Figs. 1 and 2), Queen Victoria is performing the privacy of her mourning for the benefit of her public, who can in turn enjoy a public image, available in news-stands and shops, in their own private space of home. Both images are visually structured through a series of curves, beginning with the ovals of the head-dresses and the downcast eyes, then down along the puffy sleeves and the gathers of the dress, and up from the curves of the skirt, towards the centre of the image: a small photograph surrounded by female hands. But, too small and undefined, the photograph cannot sustain the viewer's interest for long, which is then guided to the outer edges of the image by an outward ripple of curves – hands and cloth and shoulders and frames – which seem to emphasise the Russian-doll construction of the image: the child holding the photograph, the mother holding the child, the frame of the image holding the mother. The effect is completed by the hand of the viewer, also a feminine hand, holding the page of the magazine she is looking at, or the photograph as she slips

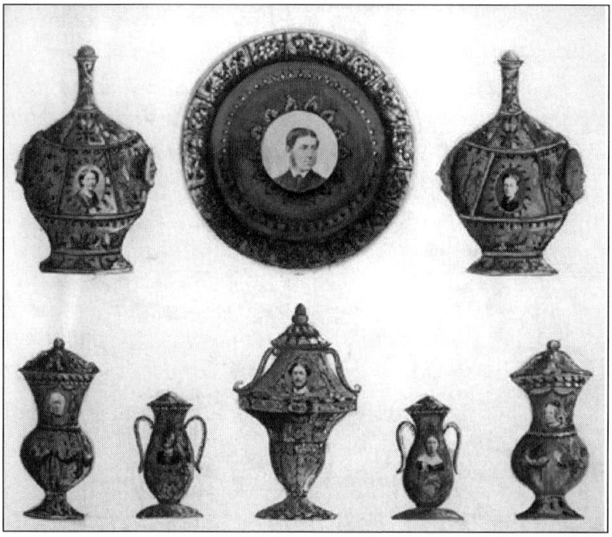

Fig. 3. Page from Georgiana Berkeley's Album, 1860s. Cut out albumen prints, watercolour, pencil and ink. Musée d'Orsay. [Photo RMN/Hervé Lewandowski.]

it into her album. So what we have here is a series of gazes, female gazes, mediated by touch.

While theories of the gaze have tended to focus on its masculine connotations, touch has been most consistently associated with femininity. As we can see from a study by Louise Vinge of the representation of the senses in literary texts from antiquity to the Renaissance, touch was the sense most often associated with women and feminine activities like weaving.[19] By the late eighteenth century, domestic ideology increasingly separated genteel femininity from commercial and professional activities performed for monetary remuneration, and gave women's handiwork within the home an important role as an accomplishment signalling to society the status of the family.[20]

In nineteenth-century feminine culture, women's touch became endowed with almost magic powers to bring harmony within the home and in the relationships between family and friends. Often described as a lady's touch, it had the power to personalise bought, possibly machine made goods, into signs of human care. In Sarah Ellis's writings, which were widely circulated at the time as manuals advocating domesticity, women's hands changed the meaning of objects, from commodities valued by price, into fetishes endowed with affective powers.[21] Re-made by the hands of the women of the house into freely bestowed gifts, objects in the home were cleansed of the alienating relationships engendered by the factory and the market place. This female touch around the home made itself tangible and visible in a myriad small gestures – pouring tea; cutting flowers; arranging furniture and knickknacks; hand-making items, or embroidering, painting or otherwise marking the surfaces and edges of purchased objects. We find a visual echo of these activities in the recurring representations, in women's albums of the 1860s, of personal or domestic items personalised by the addition of photographic portraits (Fig. 3). In the album page, the machine made object is the photograph, personalised by the hand of its owner by being dropped into a hand-painted surround representing feminine objects. It seems to illustrate not only real or fantasised

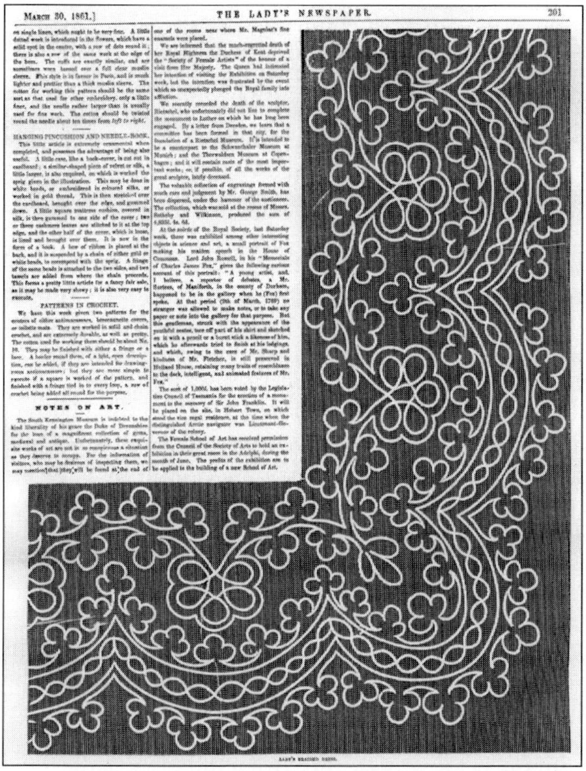

Fig. 4. Embroidery pattern for a 'Lady's Braided Dress' and 'Notes on Art', the Lady's Newspaper and Pictorial Times, *30 March 1861. 33 x 26 cm. British Library Newspaper Library. [By permission of the British Library.]*

objects, but also the complex relations between objects and people as arranged and manipulated by the hand of an accomplished woman.[22]

Like many other aspects of femininity, this special tactile engagement with the world of objects was supposed to be both an innate attribute of women, and a skill to be learned. Instructions on how to perform feminine and genteel handiwork were an important feature of nineteenth-century women's magazines.[23] But the lessons, and the magazines containing them, had to be not only useful, but also a pleasure. They were thus illustrated, often lavishly, with patterns and diagrams for embroidery patterns, lace borders, fretwork frames, fire-screen, and a variety of other decorative projects to wear or for the home. The illustrations seem to be there as an appealing feature in their own right, not just as useful diagrams (Fig. 4). Their linear simplicity invited the viewer to fill them in mentally, by fantasising about colours and stitches and actual fabrics and materials, according to personal tastes. Verbal instructions were not always clear or easy to follow, but geared towards evoking the pleasures and satisfactions of making such objects, as a fantasy rather than an actuality of making:

> A New and Easy process of Painting in Oil Colours: A Recreation For The Boudoir. By Georgiana C. Clark. This new process, by which even those totally unacquainted with art may make pleasing pictures, and those with a little skill charmingly furnish a boudoir or dining room, has its basis in photography. Pleasing likenesses of relatives and friends may be executed and

> perpetuated. [...] Not only may ladies or young persons by cultivating this really pretty art preserve for themselves the likenesses of relatives and friends, but they may make a variety of charming pictures to decorate their rooms or to give away as remembrances and tokens of friendship. By using the photochromatic or diaphanous process, photographs can be painted quickly and with an extreme appearance of finish. [...] The photograph is first rendered transparent as glass and the colour simply laid on in dead colouring at the back, the shadows, lights, and varied tone of a finished picture being communicated by the photograph itself. [...][24]

The quantity of ambitious projects featured each week, way beyond what anyone could possibly produce, suggests that they provided not only choice and variety, but pleasurable forms of looking and fantasising. These pleasures and fantasies were not only visual (or textual) but evoked tactility: manipulating, marking or making things, even if only at an imaginative level.

In the engraving of *Her Majesty the Queen, With the Princess Beatrice on Her Knee*, the connection between vision and touch is presented in the context of an established relationship between the two, in which tactility is what gives meaning to the objects that could be seen in a house arranged by genteel feminine hands. For the viewers of this image, the photograph that Beatrice is holding is defined not by its subject, which we cannot see, nor by the photographer who took it, whom we don't know, but by who the women are. Queen Victoria here is exemplary, not only of widowhood or motherhood, but of feminine ways of looking at photographic images: closely, with a gaze defined by her gender and by her touch rather than by the realism of the image or by the value of the photographer. A miniature could also be so held, but in a photograph the touch of the hand holding it mingles with the image as a direct trace from the beloved body, bypassing the work of the hand of the artist. This connection between sitter and photograph was noted in the nineteenth century. In one of the first articles on photography, 'Photogenic Drawing, or Drawing by the Agency of Light', Sir David Brewster discusses not only the role that photography will come to play in the development of knowledge, but also:

> in the narrower, though no less hallowed, sphere of the affections, where the magic names of kindred and home are inscribed, what a deep interest do the realities of photography excite! [...] The picture is connected with its prototype by sensibilities peculiarly touching. It was the very light which radiated from its brow – the identical gleam which lighted up his eye – the pallid hue which hung upon his cheek – that pencilled the cherished image, and fixed themselves for ever there.[25]

In women's magazines, lessons on how to look at visual signs were an important aspect of the construction of genteel femininity. A lady was expected to know not only how to look good herself, but also how to look at paintings or art objects in exhibitions, performances at the theatre, and picturesque scenery in foreign locations. Fashion plates constructed looking at images as a fashionable feminine activity. Two examples, (Figs. 5 and 6) one from 1849, the other from 1861, can be seen to illustrate the difference between looking at paintings and looking at photographs. Painting is looked at with a certain distance, emphasised by the mahlstick, even when the picture is made at home, by a friend. The painting has

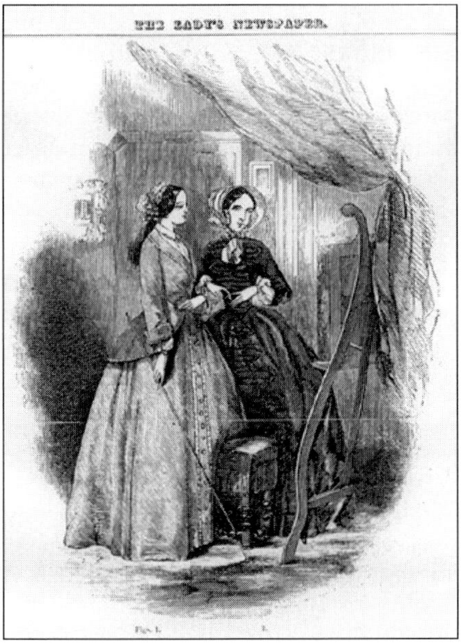

Fig. 5. 'The Paris and London Fashion', the Lady's Newspaper and Pictorial Times, *10 November 1849, p. 265. 22 x 17 cm. British Library Newspaper Library. [By permission of the British Library.]*

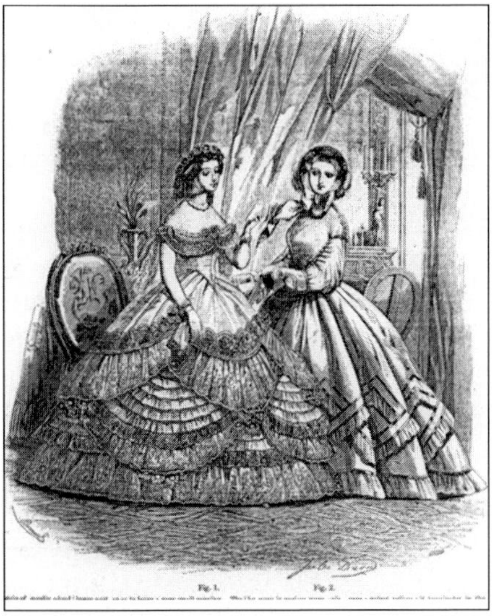

Fig. 6. 'London and Paris Fashions', the Lady's Newspaper and Pictorial Times, 12 January 1861, p. 20. 22 x 19 cm. British Library Newspaper Library. [By permission of the British Library.]

been made by hand, but its aesthetic touch is best appreciated by moving away from the work to gain detachment and perspective. Here the two women seem to be re-enacting at home the museum's injunction 'Do Not Touch', while holding instead each other's arms.[26] Photography and other forms of mechanically produced visual culture, on the other hand, engender a closer and more intimate form of looking, mediated by touch. The young woman in a 'Ball Costume' is holding and looking closely at what looks like a carte-de-visite, which has perhaps just come out from, or is destined for, the carte-de-visite album held open by the lady in an 'Out-door Dress'. This intimacy can render the relationship with the image more casual, but also more intense. Prints and photographs were more easily integrated into the tactility of other feminine handiwork; this could personalise images with informal playfulness, even those that were commercially distributed, like cartes or engravings of celebrities, but also invest them with the emotional charge of fetishised relics of loved ones.

Femininity, vision, touch and modernity

Iris Marion Young, in her investigation of female body experience, analyses her own pleasures in looking at fashion photographs in contemporary magazines in terms of a tactile gaze. Working through Lacanian-based discussions of the photographic gaze operating in advertising and fashion imagery, she argues that, however much she too responds with 'the desire to be that sexy woman',[27] a sexiness she can evaluate by adopting a male gaze, these analyses cannot adequately account for her pleasure in clothes. She exemplifies these pleasures using her memories of playing with paper dolls and drawing, colouring, and cutting their clothes, one form of Victorian *decoupage* that has survived into the twentieth century. Marion Young turns to Luce Irigaray's essay on female sexuality, 'The Sex Which Is Not One'. In this analysis, the male gaze is a distancing sight in which the subject stands separate from the object; it is a patriarchal seeing aimed at knowing objects in order to master them with the mind's eye. This male gaze is contrasted with women's pleasure in touch. In Irigaray's much-quoted formulation:

> the prevalence of the gaze [...] is particularly foreign to female eroticism. Woman finds pleasure more in touch than in sight and her entrance into a dominant scopic economy signifies, once again, her relegation to passivity: she will be the beautiful object.[28]

Young makes a qualified use of Irigaray's notions of feminine tactility to analyse her own pleasures in clothes, as objects and as images, in terms of a feminine touch which immerses 'the subject in fluid continuity with the object' (182). For the touching subject, the object touched reciprocates the touching, 'blurring the border between self and other' (182). This feminine way of looking at images, evoking fantasies of tactile sensations, is 'a mode of vision [...] that is less a gaze, distanced from and mastering its object, but an immersion in light and colour,' (182–183) and by implication, in texture.[29]

This description of an observer immersed in sensations, blurring boundaries between subject and object of vision, is consonant with Jonathan Crary's description of the modern observer, plunged into bodily sensations by modes of vision that no longer follow the conceptual model of the camera obscura, in which vision mediated by perspective and geometry can objectify and master a distanced world out there. The object of modern vision, in contrast, is not the world out there, but the inner world of the body as a subjective producer of visual sensations.[30]

Let's consider again the engraving of Queen Victoria on the cover of the *Lady's Newspaper*. No claim is made for this image as news, as a depiction of an actual event. As the caption makes it clear, the engraving is a representation not of the Queen, but of a photograph of her, here rendered in flat linear patterns that need to be filled in with details, like embroidery patterns, by the fantasy of the viewer, or by purchasing the actual photograph. The photograph itself is not a representation of Queen Victoria at a public event, nor an intrusion into her privacy, but the result of an event staged for the specific purpose of producing an image: Queen Victoria visiting a photographic studio, and re-enacting her privacy for the benefit of the public, in a pose which actually shows very little of her, the princess or Prince Albert. What we see mostly are signs: mourning clothes, melancholy poses, a photograph. This cover of the *Lady's Newspaper* might seem an example of a realist image: an engraving of a recognisable Queen Victoria, backed by the documentary evidence of photography, in a context that suggests references to news as factual writing; but on further analysis there is no reference to a reality out there that the viewer can objectify and master through the illustrated magazine, only references to other signs. The Queen herself is there as a sign, legitimising the currency of other signs of Sovereignty, and of desirable femininity, by appearing in effigy on coins and stamps, and on the masthead of the magazine.

Like other optical toys described by Crary as instruments of the modernised observer, cartes-de-visite, the albums in which they were pasted and the magazines in which they were reproduced, functioned as viewing devices that were both optical and tactile, and operated on the body of the individual through both these senses. Crary's argument emphasises how, in the modernised observer, sight is associated to touch in a fragmented or contradictory relationship. Discussing, for example, the stereograph, he points out how it operated in a breach between vision and touch. The system (stereographic card and viewer) visually suggested a three-dimensionality that was contradicted by the tactile experience of the cards as flat, and created an image dislocated from the tactile and pleasurable experience of handling the cards, slotting them in the stereoscopic viewer, and then bringing this closer to the eyes, again and again. The machine transformed the viewer into the producer of a 'tantalising apparition of depth' (132). The content of the images was less important than the routine of moving from one card to another and producing the same effect.

In the magazine cover, Her Majesty and Princess Beatrice seem to demonstrate a similar dislocation. They are looking at Prince Albert, but the Queen is holding the child's dress, in a gesture that seems to signify at once, the distress she feels at not being able any more to lean on her husband, and the comfort she draws from the closeness of the child's body. Beatrice is holding the photograph, her finger just feeling the edge where the mount drops into the glazed surface of the albumen print. The observer of the magazine, meanwhile, is looking at this image while holding the rough paper of the magazine and being reminded that she too could purchase and hold this photograph, or commission one just like it for her own album. Further tactile and visual fantasies are promised, urging us to move further on into the magazine to enjoy the whole sheet supplement (usually an embroidery pattern) and the coloured Paris fashions. What we have here is not the touch of doubting Thomas, using his fingers to ascertain the objective truth of what his eyes tell him but he can't quite believe, but a touch emphasising the corporeal subjective reality of the observer. The viewer is invited to identify with the Queen and the child's tactile sensations: the warmth of the child's body encircled by the mother's; the smooth coldness of photographs, evoking perhaps the coldness of distance and death; the soft texture of cloth compared with the stiff card in which the photograph is mounted. But the sensation of her own fingers, as she handles the limp, absorbent newsprint paper, emphasise the reader's distance from what is being represented in the images, a distance or dislocation that opens up the possibility not so much to know or control, but fantasise and desire. This embodied gaze, at once evoking and dislocating tactility, fragments the senses and ultimately emphasises not the coherent reality or realism of the images, but the power of the body to create sensations.

My qualified use of Crary, emphasising touch and the gender of the observer, is inspired by Linda Williams's use of Crary's work in her essay on 'Corporealised Observers'.[31] Like Williams, I have been interested not in theorising an abstract notion of the gaze, as inherently male or not male, but in exploring historical instances of how women looked at images. Women's magazines can be seen as an apparatus constructing an historically specific, female and tactile gaze. Women's albums and other handiwork, can be seen as examples of how women imaginatively manipulated photographic prints as tactile objects.

In the obscene photographs discussed by Williams, the indexical nature of the photographic sign enhances the erotics of a gaze, presumed to be male by most writers on nineteenth-century pornographic photographs. In the images I have been discussing the photographic enhances the subjective sentimentality and tactility of a mode of looking constructed as feminine by the culture of its time. The gaze here both exercises power over the Queen, demanding and obtaining her tactile visibility, and gives her power as the original of her own reproductions.

If, in Crary's and Williams's terms, vision was modernised in the nineteenth century into a fragmented, subjective experience by new technologies and visual entertainment machines which were operated by and operated on the body of the observer, my argument is that women's magazines and albums were part of this process. These new instruments for vision, which also activated a dislocated, subjective and corporeal touch, upset the stable references of the camera obscura with an unstable and promiscuous range of effects. The modern feminine observer was immersed into a 'corporealised immediacy of sensations',[32] looking at and fingering images, to gain not so much rational and objective knowledge but subjective and emotional experience. The focus of the experience is not the reality of the referent causing the sensation (in this case, Prince Albert for his wife and his daughter, or the Queen for the readers of the magazine) but the feminine body's vulnerability to sensations; a sensitivity that when channelled through the culture of domesticity, gave women the power to change the meaning of goods simply by touching and rearranging them.

Williams develops her argument about the dislocated corporeality of the viewer of pornographic pictures, using stereoscopic viewers, peep boxes and other pre-cinematic viewing machines. She argues that the pleasures, for the modernised user of pornography, are not only visual, but also tactile. Touch and vision are dislocated or, in her terms, 'unloosened', because the observer is looking at a photographic image of a naked body, but 'cranking' the viewing machine and, ultimately, him or her self by masturbating.

My argument focuses on the more genteel and ladylike pleasures of looking at and touching photographs of loved ones, cranking up emotional rather than erotic desires by holding photographs, turning album pages, leafing through a magazine, and perhaps further re-touching these images by cutting and pasting them into albums, colouring them or painting watercolour borders around them. The point of these mixed media techniques is not to look old-fashioned, but rather to mark specifically feminine ways of using mechanically produced and reproduced images; making visible as cuts and streaks of paint the role of touch in the pleasures of looking at photographs. This is not strictly a form of touching oneself, but at the same time all touch has a reflective element, is about feeling not just the world out there, but oneself touching it.[33] Socially and, to an extent conceptually, looking at a photograph of one's departed husband while clutching one's child is different from looking at pornography and clutching one's genitals, which Williams discusses. I would argue, however, that the dynamics between vision and touch in her material are not so different from those animating the dynamics of vision and touch in nineteenth-century feminine culture. Rather than erotic and constructed as male, the pleasures here are sentimental, producing not orgasm, but a gush of visual and tactile fantasies, sensations and meanings that are constructed as feminine, and thoroughly modern.

Notes

1. Walter Benjamin, 'The Work of Art in the Age of Mechanical reproduction', in *Illuminations*, (1955) tr. Harry Zohn, (Bungay, Suffolk: Fontana/Collins, 1982), pp. 219–253, p. 225.
2. See for example John Tagg, *The Burden of Representation* (London and Basingstoke: Macmillan Education, 1988) or Suren Lalvani, *Photography, Vision and The Modern Body* (New York: State University of New York Press, 1996). More generally, most histories of photography begin with a discussion of the optics of the camera obscura, and other devices to frame vision, used before photography. On the hierarchy of the senses in contemporary culture, privileging vision, see Christian Metz, 'The Imaginary Signifier', in *Narrative, Apparatus, Ideology*, Philip Rosen ed. (New York: Columbia University Press, 1986), pp. 244–278.
3. Julia Margaret Cameron was famously incapable of refraining herself from touching the plates during processing, one of the technical limitations her work has been accused of. For a discussion of this mode of photographic tactility, see Carol Mavor, *Pleasures Taken. Performances of Sexuality and Loss in Victorian Photographs* (Durham and London: Duke University Press, 1995).
4. *Illuminations*, p. 221.
5. Linda Williams, 'Corporealized Observers: Visual Pornographies and the "Carnal Density of Vision"', in *Fugitive Images: From Photography to Video*, Patrice Petro ed. (Bloomington and Indianapolis: Indiana University Press, 1995) pp. 3–41, p. 17.
6. Elizabeth Edwards, 'Photographs as Objects of Memory', in *Material Memories. Design and Evocation*, Marius Kwint, Christopher Breward and Jeremy Aynsley eds. (Oxford and New York: Berg, 1999) pp. 221–236, p. 226.
7. Geoffrey Batchen, 'Vernacular Photographies', in *Each Wild Idea* (Cambridge, Mass. and London: MIT Press, 2001) pp. 56–80, p. 61.
8. Roland Barthes, *Camera Lucida* , (1980), tr. Richard Howard (London: Fontana, 1984).
9. For another reading of Barthes's as a tactile conception of the photography, see Kathy O'Dell, *Contract With The Skin. Masochism, Performance Art and The 1970s* (Minneapolis and London: University of Minnesota Press).
10. On these women's magazines, see Margaret Beetham, *A Magazine of Her Own? Domesticity and Desire in the Woman's Magazine, 1800–1914* (London and New York: Routledge, 1996) and Erika Diane Rappaport, *Shopping for Pleasure* (Princeton and Oxford: Princeton University Press, 2000).
11. For a full discussion of the conceptualisation of the photograph as a child, see Lindsay Smith, *The Politics of Focus* (Manchester and New York: Manchester University Press, 1998).
12. Andrew Wynter in *Photographic News*, 28 February 1862, p. 104, quoted in Frances Dimond and Roger Taylor, *Crown and Camera: The Royal Family and Photography 1842–1910*, (Harmondsworth: Penguin, 1987), p. 22. On the role of Royal photographs in the dissemination of the carte-de-visite, and their contribution to the nascent celebrity culture, see also Nancy Armstrong, 'Monarchy in the Age of Mechanical Reproduction' in *Nineteenth-Century Contexts* 22 (2001), pp. 495–536; and John Plunkett, *Queen Victoria: The Monarchy and The Media* (Oxford: Oxford University Press, 2003). On Queen Victoria's passion for photography, see also Helmut and Alison Gernsheim, *Queen Victoria* (London: Longmans, 1959)
13. My discussion of Queen Victoria's mourning is based on: Adrienne Munich, *Queen Victoria's Secrets* (New York: Columbia University Press, 1996); Margaret Homans, *Royal Representations: Queen Victoria and British Culture 1837–1876*, (Chicago and London: University of Chicago Press, 1998); Elizabeth Longford, *Victoria RI* (London and Sydney: Pan Books, 1983); Giles St Aubin, *Queen Victoria. A Portrait*, (Sevenoaks: Sceptre 1992).
14. Homans, *Royal Representations*.
15. Leonore Davidoff, *The Best Circles: Society, Etiquette And The Season* (London: Cresset, 1986).
16. Homans, *Royal Representations*; Munich, *Queen Victoria's Secrets*.
17. Homans, *Royal Representations*, p. 64.

18. Lynda Nead, *Victorian Babylon. People, Streets and Images in Nineteenth-Century London*, (New Haven and London: Yale University Press, 2000) p. 70.
19. Louise Vinge, *The Five Senses. Studies in a Literary Tradition* (Lund: Royal Society of Letters, 1975).
20. See, for example, Anne Bermingham, 'Elegant Females and Gentlemen Connoisseurs. The commerce in culture and self-image in eighteenth-century England' in *The Consumption of Culture*, Bermingham and Brewer eds. (London and New York: Routledge, 1995), pp. 489–513.
21. Sarah Ellis, *The Women of England* (London: Fisher, 1839; various subsequent editions 1839–1895).
22. For a fuller discussion of this and other mixed-media women's albums see my 'The Female Collector: Women's Photographic Albums in the 19th Century' in *Living Pictures* 1:2 (2001) 3–20.
23. I have looked at the *Lady's Newspaper and Pictorial Times* (1847–1863); the *Lady's Own Paper* (1866–1872); the *Queen*, (1861–1970); and the *Englishwoman's Domestic Magazine* (1852–1871).
24. The *Lady's Own Paper*, 24 October 1868, p. 258. The instructions do go on, but do not become much clearer, being mainly concerned with the mixing of colours to obtain, for example, flesh tones.
25. David Brewster, 'Photogenic Drawing, or Drawing by the Agency of Light', *Edinburgh Review*, 76:154 (1843), pp. 309–344, pp. 330–331.
26. For a discussion of museums as sites conserving the artistic touch by frustrating the viewer's desire to touch, see Susan Stewart, 'Prologue: From the Museum of Touch' in *Material Memories. Design and Evocation*, Marius Kwint, Christopher Breward and Jeremy Aynsley eds. (Oxford and New York: Berg, 1999), pp. 17–36.
27. Iris Marion Young, 'Women Recovering Our Clothes', in *Throwing Like A Girl and Other Essays in Feminist Philosophy and Social Theory* (Bloomington and Indianapolis: Indiana University Press, 1990), pp. 177–188, p. 120. Further references to this edition are given in brackets after quotations in the text. For a different feminist reading of vision, touch and clothing, see Francette Pacteau, *The Symptom of Beauty* (London: Reaktion, 1994).
28. Luce Irigaray, 'The Sex Which Is Not One' in *New French Feminisms*, Elaine Marks and Isabelle de Courtivron eds. (New York and London: Harvester Wheatsheaf, 1981) pp. 99–110, p. 101. On Irigaray, see Elizabeth Grosz, *Sexual Subversions* (St Leonards, NSW: Allen and Unwin, 1989).
29. For a different account of women's tactility, associated with fetishism, see Emily Apter, *Feminizing the Fetish. Psychoanalysis and Narrative Obsession in Turn-of-the-Century France* (Ithaca and London: Cornell University Press, 1991). Marion Young is focusing on the pleasures of looking at photographs of clothing in fashion and adverts, and does not pursue an analysis of the tactile pleasures involved in handling actual cloth. For a different deployment of Irigaray's theories to read fashion photographs, see Silvia Kolbowski, 'Playing with Dolls' in *The Critical Image*, Carol Squires ed. (London: Lawrence and Wishart, 1991).
30. Jonathan Crary, *Techniques of The Observer: On Vision and Modernity in the Nineteenth Century*, (Cambridge, Mass.: MIT Press, 1990). Further references to this edition are given in brackets after quotations in the text.
31. In *Fugitive Images*, Petro ed., pp. 3–41.
32. Williams, 'Corporealized Observers', p. 7.
33. My understanding of tactility is indebted to: M. Merleau-Ponty, *Phenomenology of Perception*, tr. Colin Smith (Routledge: London 1962); Didier Anzieu, *The Skin Ego*, tr. Chris Turner (New Haven and London: Yale University Press, 1989); Steven Connor, 'Integuments: The Scar, The Sheen, The Screen', *New Formations* 39 (1999) 32–54.

2

Joseph Burton Wallett: 1835–1916 The Life of a Travelling Photographic Artist

Ann Hartley

When Joseph Burton Wallett was featured on the front page of the *World's Fair* on his birthday, 16 May 1908, as 'one of the oldest Photographers on the road', he claimed to be 76 years of age (Fig. 1). He was, in fact, 73, having been born in 1835, in Boston, Lincolnshire. He was baptised as Joseph Burton, son of William Burton, gentleman's coachman, and his wife, Sophia (nee Dickenson), at St Botolph's church on 18 May 1835. His brother, Reuben Nathaniel (a musician and

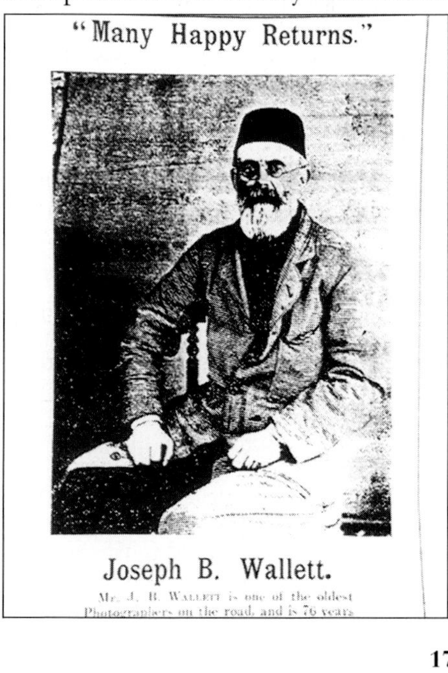

Fig. 1. Joseph Burton Wallett on his 76th (73rd) birthday. Front page of 'World's Fair' 16 May 1908. World's Fair was established in 1904 by Frank Mellor in Oldham as the newspaper for the fairground community. It includes reports on recent fairs, details of forthcoming events, classified advertisements, obituaries, etc.. The publication is the chief medium of communication for members of the Showmen's Guild and is still published weekly from Oldham. In the photograph Joseph appears to be wearing his working clothes and the edge of a backdrop can be seen in the top left of the image. [Courtesy of World's Fair, Oldham.]

general labourer who never left Boston), was born five years later, but of the two, only Joseph attended the National School in Boston where he was admitted at the age of nine on 22 July 1844.[1] Most of the children attending the school were sponsored by the vicar or the headteacher but Joseph was recommended by Mr Henry Edmund Pack, of Pack and Clayton, Linen and Woollen Drapers, High Street, Boston and was perhaps fortunate to be still at school in 1851 when he was nearly sixteen, two years after the death of his father, when his mother's circumstances must have been much reduced.

On 23 March 1856 Joseph married Eliza Clark Squires, daughter of Frederick Squires, wheelwright, at Spilsby Register Office. Both gave their residence as Alford, a small town about 23 miles north east of Boston. A daughter, Sophia Eliza, was born the following January in Bardney (about 10 miles east of Lincoln) but died three weeks later. At the time of the 1861 census Joseph and Eliza were in Coningsby, Lincolnshire. By 1866 Joseph had taken 'Wallett' as his middle name and moved to Leeds where on 2 July at the Parish Church he was married for the second time to Mary Emma Storman, daughter of Zachariah Storman, a Polish immigrant. Since Eliza was still alive, this marriage clearly was bigamous.

Three children were born to the couple – Ellen Sophia Burton in 1867, Joseph Reuben Wallett in 1870, and Albert Burton/Wallett in 1871. In February 1880 Mary Emma died in Aberford, West Yorkshire. Just over a year later in the 1881 census Joseph described himself as a 'widower' but by 1891 he and his first wife, Eliza, were back together again and living in Normanton, near Wakefield, where they were based for the rest of their lives.

So, what do we know of Joseph's working life? At the time of his marriage in March 1856 at the age of 20 he described himself as an 'Artist'. When his daughter, Sophia Eliza, was baptised at Bardney on 29 January of the following year the parish register states more precisely 'Portrait Painter'. Just over a month later on 3 March 1857, at the civil registration of the birth and death of the baby, he was designated 'Photographic Artist'. He was still using the term 'Artist' at the time of the census in 1861 and in 1866 at the time of his second marriage, but from 1867 he was more consistently a 'Photographer' and in 1880 a 'Travelling Photographic Artist'. His son, Albert, described him as 'formerly a Photographer (Master)' when he registered Joseph's death in 1916.

It is likely that Joseph was trained initially as a portrait painter, being apprenticed privately by family arrangement. The most prominent portrait painters in Boston at the time were William Willoughby, Jabez Barwick and John Wells. Joseph's adoption of photography as a career probably occurred in 1856 or earlier and may have been a natural progression from the colouring-in of photographs, demand for which had increased in the mid-1850s after the widespread adoption of the wet collodion process, invented by Frederick Scott Archer (1813–1857) in 1851 and to which many artists were forced to turn with the rise in popularity of the photograph and the decline in portrait painting.

The method of photography first offered to the public in Britain was the daguerreotype perfected in 1839 by Louis Daguerre in Paris and introduced to this country by Richard Beard in 1842. The noted daguerreotypist, Oliver Sarony (1820–1879), a Canadian who worked as an itinerant here from 1843 to 1857,

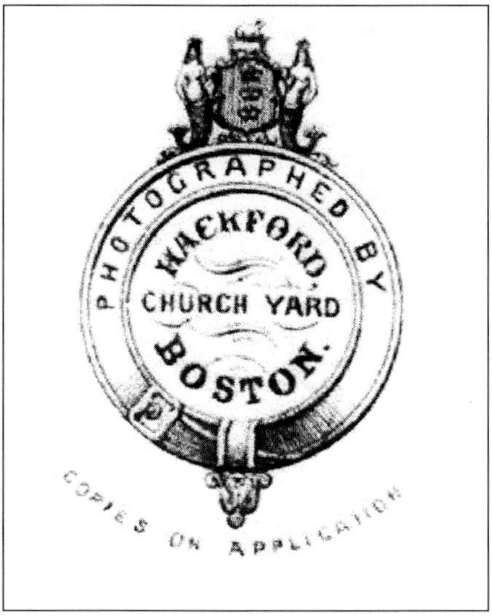

Fig. 2. Hackford Photographers, Boston, Lincolnshire. Trade Plate c.1860. Edward Chapman Hackford became Verger of St Botolph's Church in 1849 and in 1851 was living in Church Street, a few doors away from the Burton family. The Hackford's photographic business was established in 1855 and for over 100 years they owned the Church Key photography studio and curio shop in Church Close, just opposite St Botolph's.

had visited Boston in 1853 and trained several others in the art of the daguerreotype, including Peter Fields who remained in the town, and Henry Vauban, who, with partners, later opened studios in Epworth, Thorne and Alford.[2] While it is possible that Joseph was actually taught by Sarony, it is perhaps more likely that he worked for one of Sarony's pupils, possibly for Vauban at the studio in Alford, the town where he was resident at the time of his marriage in March 1856. A chance meeting with Sarony in 1850 had led to John Beattie, a Scot, also taking up photography.[3] Beattie travelled initially in the eastern counties of England, visiting Suffolk, Norfolk, Lincolnshire and Yorkshire, and may have been another contact for Joseph Burton.

Boston town itself, however, was not short of photographic pioneers and several residents and visitors had set up studios prior to 1856, including Edward Cooke, the Hackfords, Charles Ingamells, George Massingham and William Veal.[4] One of the most influential as far as Joseph was concerned may have been Edward Chapman Hackford, an artist and photographer, and resident of Church Street where Joseph himself was living in the late 1840s and early 1850s. Edward Hackford had been a cabinet maker prior to his election in 1849 as Verger of St Botolph's church, in succession to his father, John. The Hackford's photographic business was established in 1855 at 30 Church Street, later becoming the Church Key Studio which survived until 1935 (Fig. 2).

It is also just possible that Joseph was initially a daguerreotypist (the patent on this method having expired in 1853) but the chances are that the first technique that he learnt was the collodion wet-plate process. Indeed the word 'collodion' was the only one remembered in the family in relation to their ancestor's work! Joseph may even have taught himself, as by 1857 cheap instruction manuals were available and all the necessary apparatus, including the camera, could be bought for the sum of five guineas.

Scott Archer's process involved coating a plate of glass with a layer of collodion (gun cotton dissolved in ether) containing potassium iodide, the plate being dipped into a solution of silver nitrate and exposed while still wet. After exposure it was developed, fixed and washed. Because of its simplicity, speed and cheapness the method, which was free of all patent restrictions from 1854, revolutionized photography and brought it within the reach of the working man. The cost of a portrait fell from a guinea for the smallest daguerreotype in 1849, to one shilling for a glass positive in 1857.

High-class photographers regarded the wet collodion process as inferior and turned from the daguerreotype to producing fine quality albumen positives. For the majority of commercial photographers, the itinerants who went from door to door in search of orders or who set up booths in fairgrounds and on beaches, or adopted a pitch at a public house or railway station, glass positives (and later ferrotypes) soon replaced the daguerreotype and dominated the market from the 1850s to the mid-1880s. Their greatest advantage was speed of production, essential for a transitory visitor to a fairground or racecourse. Because all the processing stages of the glass positive had to be carried out on the spot, the photographer also needed a mobile darkroom as well as a camera. Those at the top end of this market had large portable studios in which they lived and worked, whilst at a lower level those without such transport devised many contraptions for transporting the bulky apparatus such as expanding suitcases, backpacks and carts.

It is unlikely that Joseph himself had a living van in the 1850s and his early travels were probably made by rail. By 1849 Boston was part of an extensive railway system with links to London via Spalding and Peterborough; to the Midland counties through Lincoln and Newark; and through Louth to Hull and all parts of Yorkshire. The station at Alford, half a mile west of the town, was close to his wife's family home, and passenger trains ran six times daily 'to all parts'. The Great Northern Railway passed through or near other places where Joseph visited; there were stations at Bardney and nearby Southrey and although Coningsby did not then have its own station, it was only a mile and a half from the halt at Tattershall.

It is not out of the question, however, that Joseph made use of the region's important inland waterways network during his time in Lincolnshire. Boston and Bardney are on the river Witham which is navigable to Lincoln and which had links with various canals. Coningsby is near the banks of both the Bain and the Witham rivers, and of the Horncastle canal. Packet boats ran daily from Boston and there were regular weekly services from other towns and villages.

So, other than his home town of Boston, we have evidence of Joseph in three locations in Lincolnshire: Alford, Bardney and Coningsby. Alford was a small town with a weekly market, and fairs for cattle and sheep on Whit Tuesday and in November. In 1841 its population was 2,262 and White's Lincolnshire Directory of 1856 informs us that the town had been considerably improved in the 19th century, especially since the opening of the East Lincolnshire Railway. 'The market place ... is a fine open area, and the town has now a clean and respectable appearance, and contains several excellent inns, well-stocked shops, and commodious residences'. A Mechanics Institute had been erected in 1854 and there was a library, a newsroom and a lecture hall. Bardney and Coningsby were both large, predominantly rural villages with the usual range of village trades. They were similar in population size – Bardney with 1,329 inhabitants in 1851 and Coningsby with 1,938 in 1861. Coningsby had a large number of cordwainers, tailors and drapers and also boasted a mineral spring, enterprisingly called the 'Spa'.

We do not know how long Joseph was based in any of these places or whether he visited them repeatedly but he was in Alford long enough to make the acquaintance of and marry Eliza Squires, daughter of the wheelwright. The marriage took place in Spilsby, rather than Alford, but this may have been because of a desire to marry away from home in a register office, possibly because they were both so young

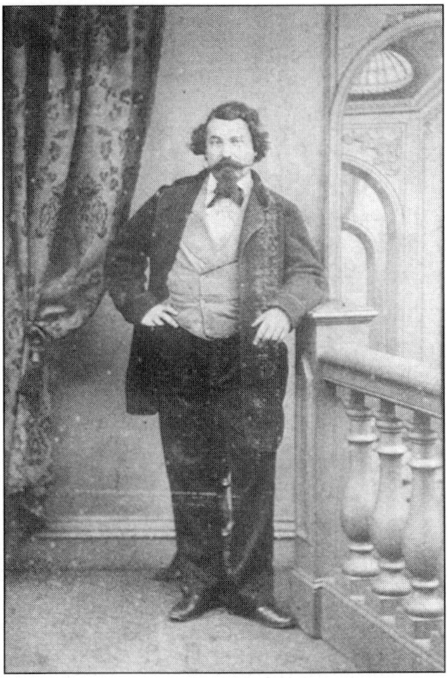

Fig. 3. Zachariah Storman: born Krakow, Poland in1813, died Leeds 1877. Photograph (carte de visite) taken by Edward Boot in the 1860s. Joseph B. Wallett married Zachariah's eldest daughter, Mary Emma, in 1866 at the Parish Church in Leeds. Zachariah came to England in the late 1830s and, amongst other occupations, operated as a tobacconist from no. 20 Central Market, Leeds, assisted by his stepson, Thomas Read, who later became a musician. Edward Boot was born in Leeds about 1825 and began as a general dealer in Central Market. He was in business as a photographer at no. 20 from about 1855 to 1870.

(Eliza was 18 and Joseph gave his age as 21 but, in fact, he was only 20). The couple were in Bardney for at least 5 weeks from the end of January 1857 to the beginning of March, but this length of stay may have been forced upon them by the premature birth of their baby.

At the time of the 1861 census Joseph Burton, 'Artist' and Eliza were listed as 'visitors' in the household of Margaret Clabrough, proprietor of a 'Berlin wool and fancy repository' in High Street, Coningsby. The term 'visitor' (rather than boarder or lodger) as used by the census enumerator might indicate that Joseph had a previous acquaintance with the Clabrough family and was staying in Coningsby on only a temporary basis. The mention of fancy goods might also hint at early connections with the fairground community, but a search of the rest of the Coninsgby census does not reveal any travellers or showmen in the vicinity other than the usual handful of licensed hawkers. Nearby Horncastle, however, was the site of the largest horse fair in the country in August each year, with smaller fairs on the fifth Thursday in Lent and in June and October.

Joseph's move to Leeds may have taken place earlier, rather than later, in the period between 1861 and 1866. Leeds had been in the forefront of photographic activity from the establishment of a daguerreotype studio there in April 1842. From this time until the late 1850s there was a period of intense experimentation by many amateurs and the Leeds Photographic Society was founded. This was followed by the establishment of increasing numbers of commercial studios in the late 1850s and 1860s[5] where Joseph may have sought employment. Sarony himself, in partnership with Dickinson, had opened a studio in Leeds in 1862 at 15 Park Place and this establishment continued until 1866 when it was taken over by John Hobbis.[6] By the early1860s at least 20 photographers were working in central Leeds, several of them in the courts or yards off Briggate and Boar Lane, in close proximity to the Temperance hotel in Dickenson's Court, Briggate, occupied by the Storman family. One photographer, Edward Boot, operated from 18 Central Market, almost next door to the tobacconists run by Zachariah Storman, Joseph's new father-in-law. Indeed, about this time, Zachariah visited Edward Boot's studio and had his full-length portrait taken (Fig. 3). The large number of photographers in Leeds reflected the enormous increase in their number nationally which had taken place in the 1850s between the census years. In 1851 there were 51 photographers in England, and by 1861 nearly 3000.

When Joseph married Mary Emma Storman in Leeds in July 1866 he gave his residence as Harewood Court. We can only wonder whether this address was correct as almost every other detail he gave about himself was untrue. Curiously he used the name Joseph 'Wallett' Burton, and even more curiously stated that his father was 'George Wallett' Burton, Grocer. The most blatant lie was the claim that he was a bachelor!

Conditions in Harewood Court off Harewood Street in the centre of Leeds would have been typical of the crowded and insanitary yards of mid-nineteenth century Leeds and there would be no space to park a van. It was probably only after his marriage that Joseph acquired a living van at a time when many portable studios were coming onto the market as earlier photographers left the road and opened up permanent studios in the larger towns. Some of these carriages were truly magnificent and were elaborately fitted out with both living and working areas. John Beattie's wheeled studio measured 30 feet by 9 feet with three rooms, including a living room and bedroom, and had actually been constructed for him in Leeds at a cost of £200. Sarony also had a 'monster carriage, the length of which is 32 feet, and is divided into three compartments; the height of each room is 12 feet and the whole is beautifully fitted up, and admirably adapted for Photographic and domestic purposes'.[7] Joseph's van would have been more modest in scale similar to the one shown in Fig. 4 or that advertised in The Manchester Examiner in 1860: 'To Photographers – To be sold at great sacrifice a well built one horse caravan, 18ft by 9ft with complete fittings for carrying on the business … . It cost about 100 guineas and to be sold for 25 guineas'.[8]

Ellen Sophia, the first child of Joseph's marriage to Mary Emma Storman, was born in October 1867 at Wharf Street, Leeds, home of her grandparents. In August of

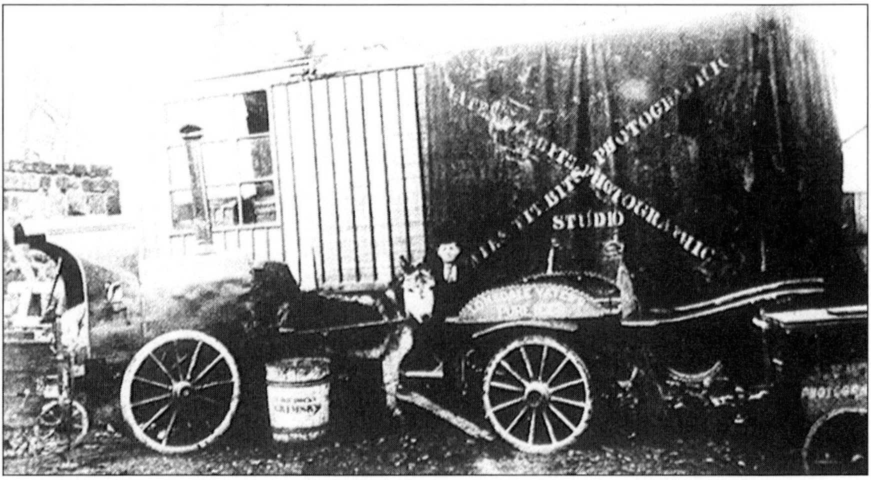

Fig. 4. Mr Yates' photographic studio and miscellaneous transport. Harrogate. Taken about 1890. [Courtesy of North Yorkshire County Library.]

the following year the family were in Oulton, five miles south east of Leeds. Here tragedy struck and Frederick William Storman, the nine-year old illegitimate son of Mary Emma, was killed in an horrific accident involving a stationary engine at a stone quarry. Oulton, with a population of just over 2,000 in 1871, was similar in size to the Lincolnshire towns and villages frequented by Joseph. The surrounding district was largely agricultural but many of the population worked in the extensive stone quarries in the township. Nearby Woodlesford had a station on the Midland Railway Company's line and here stone quarrying was augmented by earthenware manufacturing and brewing.

Incidentally, it is at this time in 1868 that Joseph first uses 'Wallett' as a surname, the reason for which has been the subject of much family speculation. An advertisement in *The Athenaeum* of March 1860 for the lease of a 'photographic carriage' requested applicants to apply by letter, stating 'real' name and address.[9] Is there an implication here that it was the norm for itinerant photographers to adopt a pseudonym? Or could the use of the name be related to Joseph's bigamous marriage and desire to hide his origins? The latter seems unlikely as he married both the first and second time as 'Burton' and only assumed 'Wallett' as a surname two years after the marriage to Mary Emma. Both his wives were known as Wallett and both were buried with that name.

But why this particular name? 'Wallett' is a very uncommon surname and most Wallett families originate from Shropshire and the West Midlands. Was it a name that occurred in Joseph's ancestry, that of a grandmother or other relative? There certainly had been 'Walletts' in Lincolnshire but those families had almost died out by the mid-1700s.

All three of Joseph's children became actors with small travelling companies in their late teens and Mary Emma Storman had come from a theatrical family. Could Joseph be linked in some way with William Frederick Wallett, the Queen's Jester, a well-known nineteenth century comedian and clown who had appeared before Queen Victoria in 1844? William Frederick Wallett had been born in Hull in 1813 and did, in fact, have a brother called George Wallett, born about 1815 who was also a comedian and who had Lincolnshire connections. Had Joseph met or admired George and adopted him as a father figure? Lincolnshire also figures strongly towards the beginning of the Jester's own autobiography – Market Rasen, Gainsborough and Alford were amongst the places he visited early in his career.[10] Intriguingly, two separate branches of the family descended from Joseph Burton Wallett each possess memorabilia of the Jester, including a circus poster featuring the Jester performing in Nottingham in 1890 and sent through the post by the Jester himself to Zachariah Storman the younger, Joseph's brother-in-law, at the 'Hope and Anchor' public house in The Calls, Leeds.

A second child, Joseph Reuben Wallett was born to Joseph and Mary Emma on 19 March 1870 in Rothwell, near Leeds. No precise location is given on the birth certificate but the following year at the census taken on 2 April 1871 the family are again in Rothwell, in Oulton Lane, enumerated between the households of William Hartley of the 'Bowling Green' public house and Edward Parker, brewer. The 'Bowling Green', now demolished, was some distance off the main Oulton Lane and it seems likely that Joseph was living in the yard of the inn, although there is no mention of a caravan as such. Again, Rothwell (population 3,755 in 1871) was

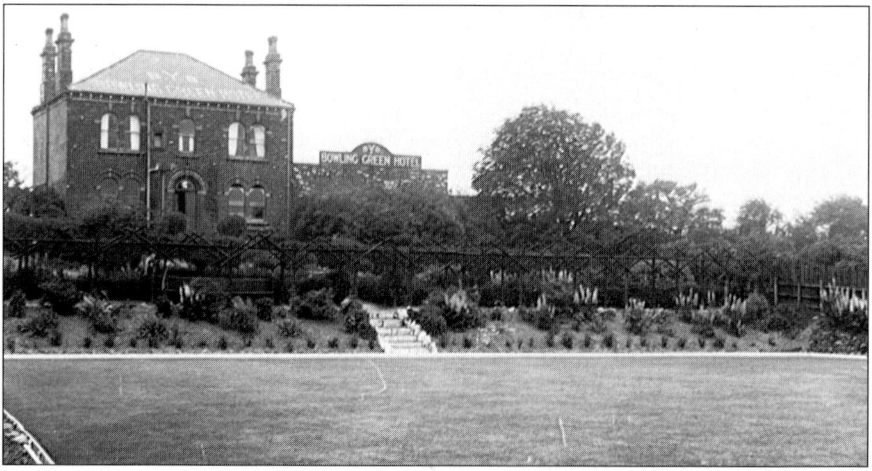

Fig. 5. The Bowling Green Hotel, Rothwell, known later as 'The Rabbit Trap' (photograph taken about 1910). Joseph B. Wallett's family was enumerated here in the 1871 census and the hotel was described as 'the New Public House in the field near to Mr Brown's Lodge gate in Oulton Lane'. Rothwell Feast was held around Easter every year, at first on Commercial Street (the main shopping street), later being moved to a field behind Shearman's Shop, just across the road from the Bowling Green. Like Joseph, the Shearman family originated from Lincolnshire and in 1871 Joseph Shearman had a market garden at the top of the lane leading to the Bowling Green. [Courtesy of Rothwell and District Historical Society.]

a semi-rural area, with varied industries including coalmining, matchmaking (one firm alone employing two hundred hands), rope, twine, basket, and gluemaking. There were corn mills and several market gardens. Possibly Joseph went there at the same time each year for a period around Rothwell Feast which traditionally took place on Easter Monday and Tuesday. The imposing presence of the Bowling Green Hotel, however, does suggest that Joseph may have obtained custom from a more up-market clientele than simply those who visited the fairground (Fig. 5).

It is not until the inquest held on 18 February 1880 on the death of Joseph's wife, Mary Emma, that we get more information on the family's way of life.[11] Mary Emma was found dead in bed in the caravan in Lotherton-cum-Aberford on the morning of 17 February and her death was registered by Joseph Wallett 'Travelling Photographic Artist'. The inquest was held the following day at the Boot and Shoe Inn by Thomas Taylor, the Coroner for Yorkshire. Joseph Wallett gave evidence as follows:

> I have not any fixed place of abode. I live in a caravan and travel about. I am a photographer. Deceased was 38 years old and my wife. She had been in the habit of accompanying me ... she helped me. We came from Leeds on the evening of Monday the 9th inst. with our three children. I put up in Mr Joseph Barker's yard in Main Street. Lotherton ...

His eldest daughter, Ellen Sophia stated 'I am nearly 13 years old. Deceased was (my) mother. I have travelled about with her'.

The only photograph taken by Joseph Burton Wallett known to have survived dates from this period (about 1880). The image comes from the Storman family album and shows three unidentified individuals possibly members of the Read family of

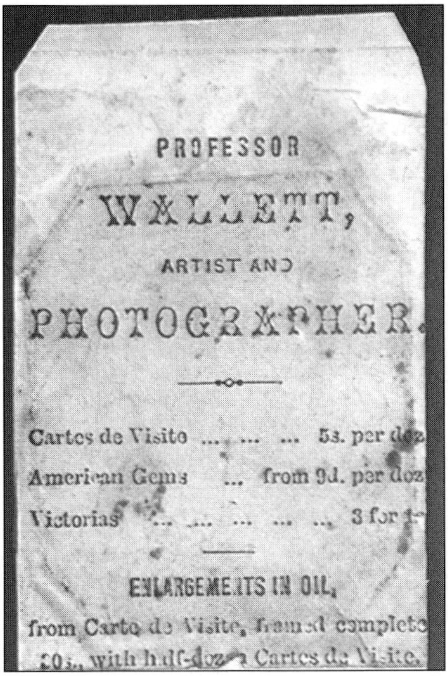

PROFESSOR

WALLETT,

ARTIST AND

PHOTOGRAPHER.

Cartes de Visite ... ... 5s. per doz

American Gems ... from 9d. per doz

Victorias ... ... 3 for 1s

ENLARGEMENTS IN OIL,

from Carte de Visite, framed complete

20s., with half-doz. Cartes de Visite.

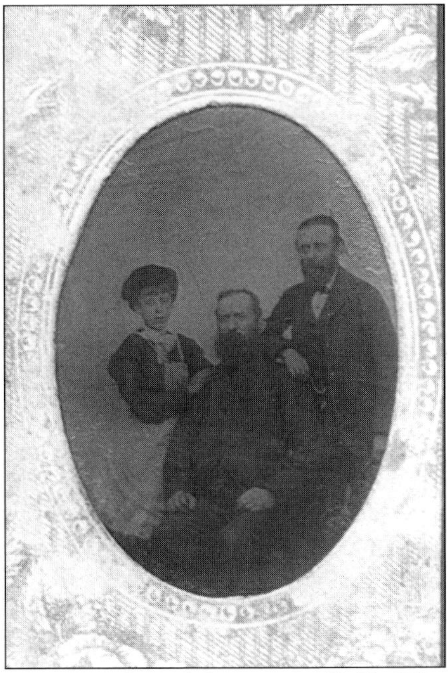

Fig. 6. Ferrotype taken by Joseph Burton Wallett dating from about 1880. The metal plate measuring 1$^{9}/_{16}$“ by 1¾” is slipped between a decorated piece of thin card with an oval aperture and the backing label which advertises Joseph's services. The aperture measures 1$^{5}/_{8}$“ by 1¾” and is intended for a ferrotype of the 'Victoria' size. The whole mount has been cropped, possibly to fit into a container other than an album. The subjects of the photograph have not been identified but the fact that they are touching indicates a close family relationship. The absence of any accessories also indicates that the photograph was taken in the open air in front of a simple backdrop. The product is typical of that of an itinerant of the period and is almost indistinguishable from a studio portrait. [Storman Family Photographs.]

Clitheroe, Lancashire, relatives of Mary Read the mother of Mary Emma Storman. The photograph is a rectangular ferrotype (or tintype) with the corners snipped off, mounted behind a piece of thin card with an oval aperture displaying an image measuring 1$^{5}/_{8}$“ by 1¾”, a size known as a 'Victoria'. The backing of the mount displays Joseph's name (and here he has elevated himself to 'Professor' Wallett, Artist and Photographer) and lists his services: Cartes de Visite 5 shillings per dozen, American Gems from 9 pence per dozen and Victorias 3 for 1 shilling. He also offers 'enlargements in oil, from Cartes de Visite, framed complete for 20 shillings, with half-dozen Cartes de Visite' (Fig. 6).

Although the ferrotype had been developed as early as the 1850s and remained popular in America, it had almost gone out of production in Britain by the 1870s. However, the process had a sudden and quite short return to popularity between the late 1870s and early 1880s with the establishment of the American Gem Studios. To enable them to fit in the standard album, postage stamp size 'American Gems' or 'Gem' portraits were inserted in carte de visite size cardboard mounts carrying a tiny oval aperture. The production of the ferrotype was similar in principle to that of a glass positive except that the glass backing was replaced by a thin sheet of iron covered with black enamel. The gems were produced by a multi-lens camera and after processing the thin tin plate was simply divided up with scissors. The standard gem camera was usually fitted with nine lenses and gems usually retailed at 9 for 7 and a half pence, rather than 9 pence per dozen. Joseph's cartes at 5s per dozen were somewhat more expensive than the 3/6d charged by some of the highstreet studios, but his enlargements in oils at 20 shillings suggests an appeal to the price conscious market as these were usually offered at 30 shillings and were the area in which such portrait photographers could make most profit.

While the ferrotype still demanded the same processing stages as the glass positive, the process had certain advantages which appealed to the itinerant. Exposure and development were quicker and the portrait could be produced even more speedily on a 'while you wait basis'. In addition the metal plates were cheaper and lighter than glass and more robust. In 1891 prepared ferrotype dry plates became available and this was soon followed by the introduction of cameras with built-in processing facilities where the exposed plate could drop directly into an internal developing tank through a light-tight seal. Such advantages meant that the ferrotype continued to be used by itinerants at fairs and at the seaside until well into the twentieth century. Most ferrotypes, however, were of poor quality and the method was regarded with contempt by the more upmarket practitioners of the craft.[12]

After the death of Mary Emma, Joseph appears to have given up travelling for a time. Just over a year later at the time of the 1881 census he is living in Ratten Row, Aberford (just across the road from the churchyard where Mary Emma was buried) as a widower with his three children and a photographer servant, William Gray, aged 35 years. Aberford at the time was a large village but with a population of under a thousand and without a railway station. Some employment was provided by collieries in the nearby Parlington township but the main focus of the village was the provision of hospitality for the many travellers who passed through on the Great North Road (subsequently the A1). Joseph would have had a continuous supply of potential customers, and evidence from the inquest report on the death of his wife indicates that he had planned a stay of at least a week in the area, even though it was the coldest period of the year.

Joseph presumably needed help with the photography after Mary Emma's death and this may have prompted him to take on William Gray as his assistant. William was born in 1844 in Markham Clinton, near Tuxford, Nottinghamshire (just off the Great North Road), son of George Gray, agricultural labourer, and Sarah Hewitt. Contact with him may well have been made on a family visit to Lincolnshire. One of William's major roles certainly would have been to act as a tout, accosting passers-by and encouraging them to enter the booth or caravan to have their 'likeness' taken. It would be of interest to know whether Joseph's cousin's husband, Richard Shearstone, who gave his occupation as 'Canvasser for Portraits' when he married in Huddersfield in 1896, worked for one of the highstreet multiples such as A. and G. Taylor, or whether he, too, had a direct working relationship with Joseph.

At the time of the 1891 census Joseph's elder son, Joseph Reuben aged 20, was acting as his assistant and they were living in a 'Photographer's Van' in Talbot Street, Normanton near Wakefield. His daughter, Ellen Sophia, had gone to live with the Stormans in Leeds in her early teens and was already married to an actor. The younger son, Albert, had also left home to work as a fancy goods salesman and was courting Mary Ann Seed, daughter of John Seed, owner of one of the largest fairground bazaars in Yorkshire. The suprising situation revealed by the 1891 census entry is that Joseph is living again with his first wife, Eliza Squires, whom he had married in Lincolnshire in 1856!

Normanton is 12 miles south east of Leeds and 3 miles north east of Wakefield, and between 1851 and 1891 its population had expanded enormously from 495 to more than 10,000 inhabitants. The town was an important junction of three railway routes, those belonging to the North Midland, the Manchester and Leeds, and the York and North Midland Railways, all of which had opened in 1840. A hotel and refreshment rooms were established in 1842 and the station rebuilt in 1871. After the opening of the new route to Scotland via the Settle and Carlisle railway in 1876 the corridorless trains stopped at Normanton for half an hour, long enough for a meal – and possibly for a visit to the local photographer? The other major industry influencing the growth of Normanton in the nineteenth century was coal mining. New pits sunk in the late 1850s and 1860s attracted many immigrant workers and resulted in the establishment of secondary industries, shops and many other local facilities.

Talbot Street, Normanton, runs south from the railway station and there are several gaps between the houses and a large yard at the back of the Talbot Hotel, any one of which could have accommodated the photographic van. The 1901 census return, however, reveals that Joseph and Eliza's caravan was by then parked on the 'Feast Ground' together with caravans belonging to his son, Albert Burton (general dealer), and to William and John Griffiths (stall keepers at fairs), Henry Testo (cinematograph exhibitor) and George tucker (travelling showman). There were, in fact, lodging in Normanton at this time a large number of performers and their families and it seems likely that the town was host to a travelling show. The visitors included actors, music hall and variety artistes, musicians and vocalists, a professional change artiste, and Frank Pirie, choir and diorama comedian with Horace Gibb, travelling diorama lecturer.

Glimpses of the old market and fairground can be obtained from the pages of the *World's Fair*, the newspaper for the fairground community.[13] On 2 February 1907, in the 'Grounds to Let' section, Fred Denison of Talbot Street advertised the Normanton Market and Fairground with stalls 'covered and lighted' and a 'good Saturday pitch for market salesmen'. Two weeks later he was trying to attract bookings from travellers intending to come to the carnival at Heath, near Wakefield on Easter Sunday. In May 1907 there was an advertisement for the 'New Market' on Saturdays and Mondays on the fairground with a 'good pitch for Cinematograph or other show'. In August the fairground was described as the 'finest pitching ground in Yorkshire'. There was probably some justification for this latter claim as on 4 May 1907 *World's Fair*, had a long report on its front page of the visit of the enormous travelling company of Lord John Sanger and Son's Circus to Normanton. 'The huge marquee was erected on Mr F. Denison's Market and Fairground and was visited by big crowds, over 2,000 visiting the circus in the afternoon, and at night by a huge crowd of 5,000'. The circus featured the athlete, Cyclo; the Maro Troupe of equestrians; Coleman's elephants; Pimpo and Zampo the Clowns etc., the whole culminating with an 'admirable representation of Dick Turpin's ride to York'. There was also an 'excellent collection of wild animals in the menagerie'.

Events such as this which drew large crowds, together with visiting fairs and theatres and later the cinematograph shows would have provided Joseph with much of his business in Normanton. The fair was held the week after Easter and in 1907 the first Normanton Winter Carnival was established. At quieter times there were other local fetes and carnivals such as the following which were advertised in just one edition of the *Wakefield Express*: 'Crofton Sports and Gala 22 July 1893, Calder Grove Feast 31 July, Outwood Church FC Athletic Festival 5 August, Pontefract Show next Thursday, and the Patients' Annual fete at the Asylum this evening'!

Joseph is said by the family to have had a Bioscope and 'other shows' and to have 'dabbled in all sorts of things'. His relationships with the Romany community were good and he regularly traded horses with them and allowed them to pitch their camp on a piece of ground which he was said to own. (An important Horse Fair, Lee Gap Fair, was held annually on St Bartholemew's day, 24 August, at West Ardsley, not far from Normanton).[14] Family tradition describes Joseph as a 'fairground photographer' but only the largest photographic enterprises, such as those owned by Caddick, Fossett and Gunthorpe, received a mention in the 'Around the Fairs' column of *World's Fair*. Joseph would be one of the many single or two-man operations who passed unrecorded each week. Enumerated in the 1881 census, for example, is a fair in Grantham, Lincolnshire, and of the thirty five vans listed, five were occupied by photographers, their families and assistants. The birthplaces of the heads of these households i.e. Leicestershire (two), Derbyshire, Kent, and Essex show just how far they had travelled from their home towns.

Joseph led a more settled life in his later years. His caravan was based in Normanton from at least 1891 until his death in 1916. We know from the feature in the *World's Fair* in May 1908 that he was still 'on the road' at that time and was then one of the oldest travelling photographers. Indeed in April 1927 when the *World's Fair* featured the coming-of-age of Albert's son, John Albert Burton ('cinematograph bioscope operator at the 'Palace' in Normanton'), the latter was described as 'a grandson of the late Joseph Burton, better known as Joe Wallett, who was at one time the oldest photographer in Yorkshire'. John Albert Burton apparently remembered seeing Joseph as an old man with a long white beard in the caravan in Normanton. Here he would be given a sweet from a collection around the oil lamp which lit the van.

By this time, just prior to the First World War, Joseph was living alone in the van and times were becoming increasingly difficult for him with advancing age and the increased popularity of other competing attractions, such as the cinema. In September 1908, just months after Joseph appeared on its front page, *World's Fair* had a long article about Mr William Spilsbury age 68, a travelling photographer who had been found dead in his caravan in Derbyshire. 'Poor business of late' had resulted in him committing suicide by taking 'cyanite of potassium', a substance used by itinerant photographers for fixing ferrotypes. It was reported that he had even tried to persuade his housekeeper to take it with him the week before.

It is possible that the continual use of such toxic chemicals may have had a cumulative effect on Joseph's brain for on 1 January 1916 he died of senile decay in Wakefield Union Infirmary at the age of 80 years. He was buried with Eliza in an unmarked grave in Normanton cemetery. Six months later to the day, on 1 July 1916, his grandson, Jack Roberts, was to die in France on the first day of the Battle of the Somme at the age of only nineteen.

Whether Joseph had connections with showmen and performing artists prior to leaving Lincolnshire is not known, but as time went by he became increasingly associated with the fairground community. There had always been a strong link between photography and acting and to quote a comment in the *Photographic News* of 1885 'It was a common thing, in the old glass positive days, for a man who practised cheap photography in the daytime, to appear at night at a music hall, generally in the capacity of an acrobat'.[15] The adoption of multiple occupations by the fairground photographer was a necessity, as not until the use of luxograph powder in the 1880s could he take photographs during the dark evenings when the fairground would be at its busiest.

Joseph's three children carried on his itinerant life-style until at least the end of the nineteenth century, moving around with small theatrical companies. Ellen Sophia, his daughter living in Leeds, was no doubt influenced by the Storman family's own theatrical bent and in 1890 had married an actor, Jonathan Roberts, who styled himself the 'Great Charles Hilt'. Jonathan was a 'comedian' until 1893 at which time he gave his occupation on his daughter's birth certificate as 'photographer (master)', having learnt his craft from his father-in-law. By all accounts, some of his activities were irregular, to say the least, and accepting money for pictures taken without film in the camera was not unknown. Joseph Reuben (his father's assistant in 1891) painted scenery for the theatre but again was described as a master photographer when he married in Coventry in 1899. Albert also travelled with the performers but on at least one occasion struck out with his own theatre company to Dublin where he is said to have swum the river Liffey to escape his creditors. He eventually settled for the life of a fancy goods salesman, working for his own father-in-law, John Seed, on the fairground bazaars and operating a set of steam swings.

At the beginning of his life as an itinerant photographer Joseph probably travelled by rail, taking advantage of the huge expansion of the network in the mid-Victorian period. By the 1870s, or earlier, he was living and working in the photographic van where he spent most of the rest of his life. He seems to have had a regular annual route around the West Riding of Yorkshire, his stopping places coinciding with the visits of fairs and other large events. There are hints, however, that in the first few decades he returned at intervals to his second wife's family home in Leeds (by 1866 the Stormans had moved to Wharf Street off The Calls in Leeds, where they manufactured boots and slippers), using it as a base for the birth of two of his children in 1867 and 1871, and also for travelling out to surrounding towns and villages. A pitch near a public house or railway station would have provided a regular supply of customers on a daily basis and horse dealing would have been an additional source of income. His possession of a bioscope show indicates that he also turned his hand to 'fashionable' novelties to supplement his income from photography. His clientele appear to have been mainly the industrial working class of small towns and large villages (Fig. 7).

Early itinerant photographers such as Beattie regarded themselves as more enterprising and superior to those who established fixed studios in the high street. However, as photography moved down the social scale to become a part of popular entertainment, it is perhaps inevitable that the status of its practitioners should also decline, and travelling photographers came to be regarded with contempt and to

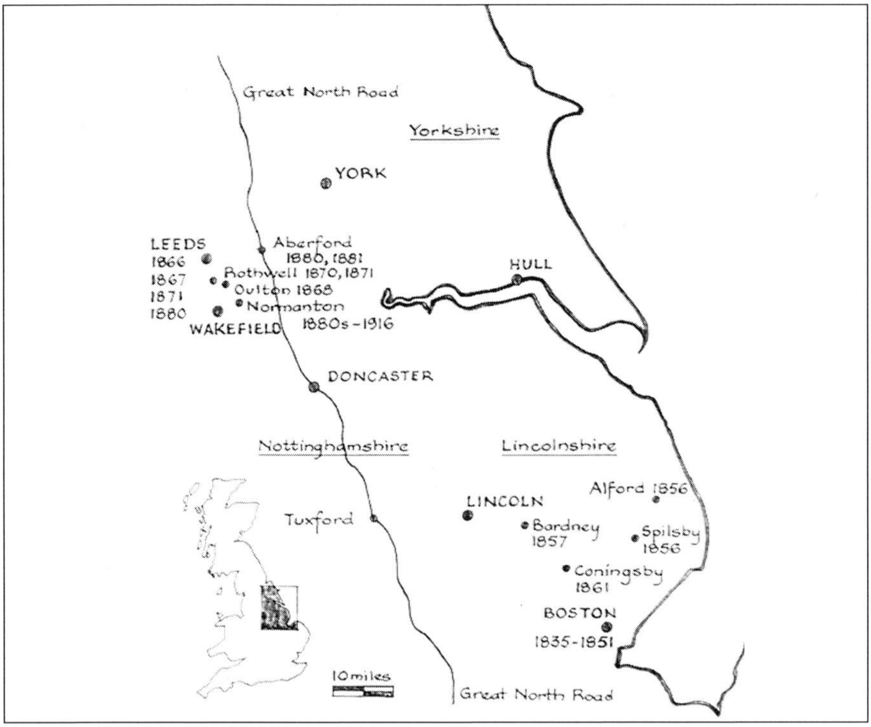

Fig. 7. Sketch map showing places associated with the travels of Joseph Burton Wallett. Born in Boston, Lincolnshire in 1835, he was an itinerant photographer by early 1856. After spending at least six years working in the area south of Lincoln, he had moved to Leeds by 1866. He appears to have spent the rest of his life travelling in the West Riding of Yorkshire, being based in Normanton near Wakefield probably from the late 1880s up to his death in 1916. His assistant in 1881, William Gray, was born near Tuxford and Joseph probably made contact with him on one of the family's return visits to Boston.

be stereotyped as down at heel and not averse to petty criminality. Joseph's adoption of the title 'Professor' is surely in the best traditions of the fairground huckster through the ages. It was also in character for a man who was essentially theatrical in his family life, who, if his change of name, invention of a father, and bigamy were anything to go on, was not particularly observant of the law. We must not, however, judge him too harshly. Although operating on the margins of society, no tales of trickery have been handed down through the generations – unlike stories of his son-in-law, Jonathan Roberts, who was undoubtedly a rogue. Joseph was not one of those showmen or entrepreneurs who jumped on every bandwaggon to take advantage of the latest craze and turned their hand to photography as yet one more speculative enterprise, but a man who made an early transition from portrait painting to photography and who stuck with the craft for the rest of his long working life. He was at best a romantic in a commercial age, at worst an opportunist.

Joseph Burton Wallett apparently never appeared in any trade directory and only one photograph taken by him is known to survive. Yet well-documented evidence for his life as a photographer points to his consistent activity over a period of at least sixty years from the mid-1850s to the First World War. This period spanned almost exactly the heyday of the travelling photographer and Joseph would have witnessed all the changes in the process from the daguerreotype to the collodion process through to the carte de visite, the ferrotype and the roll film. The events of his life have been reconstructed from oral tradition and from sources used by the family historian. To the photohistorian he has remained invisible, yet he must have been one of a substantial group of photographers who maintained the early itinerant lifestyle without ever having a fixed studio, even in the winter months. Joseph was one of many enterprising young men who launched themselves into the exciting, expanding industrial society of the mid-nineteenth century on the 'new' photography boom, but who fell victim to the very same speed of technological change which had been their inspiration. It is both sad and ironic that his long life, marked by a spirit of initiative and industry, should have resulted in such meagre financial reward and led only to a workhouse hospital and an unmarked grave.

Acknowledgements: Audrey Linkman's book *The Victorians: Photographic Portraits* (Taurus Parke Books, London 1993) provided much of the background for this article and I should like to thank her for help and encouragement and for drawing my attention to other sources. I am grateful to Julie Layton for information about the Jester's family, and to Roy Hackford and the late John Orange of Boston for details on the Hackfords. I would also like to thank Michael and Gillian Roe for the loan of Storman family photographs and Frank Trowell for help with Fig. 7.

Notes

In addition to the sources listed below, much of the family detail in this account has been obtained from birth, marriage and death certificates; parish registers; trade directories; and the 1841–1901 census returns.

1. Boston National Schools Admission Register 1815–1856. Lincolnshire Archives.
2. Keith I P Adamson, *Photographers in Victorian Doncaster 1842–1900* (Doncaster: Doncaster Museum Service 1998) and Personal Communication.
3. Audrey Linkman, 'A Roving Scot: Itinerant Photography in the Heart of England in the 1850s', *Scottish Photography Bulletin* No.1 (1992): 3–15.
4. Keith I P Adamson, 'Professional Photographers in Lincolnshire', *Photohistorian Supplement*, No. 99 (1998): 12–24.
5. *Early Photography in Leeds 1839–1870* (Leeds: Leeds Art Galleries, 1981).
6. Keith Adamson and Adrian Budge, 'Professional Photographers in Leeds 1842–1900', *Photohistorian* Supplement No. 60 (1983): 6, 10.
7. *The Lincolnshire, Boston and Spalding Free Press and Eastern Counties Advertiser* (11 July 1854): 4, col. 3.
8. *The Manchester Examiner*, (5 May 1860):3, col. 4.
9. *The Athenaeum*, No. 1688 (3 March 1860): 286.
10. 'Death of Mr W F Wallett', *Nottingham Evening Post* (14 March 1892).
11. Inquest Report on the death of Mary Emma Wallett, 18 February 1880. West Yorkshire Archive Service.
12. Audrey Linkman, 'Cheap Tin Trade: the Ferrotype Portrait in Victorian Britain', *Photographica World* No. 69 (June 1994): 17–28.
13. The *World's Fair* newspaper published in Oldham, 2, 16 February; 4, 25 May; 24 August 1907.
14. Michael E Ware, *Historic Fairground Scenes*, (Moorland Publishing 1977).
15. *The Photographic News*, Vol. 29 No. 1408, (28 August 1885): 552–553.

3

Cheap Fiction, Popular Periodicals and Early Film Dramas: Some Continuities and Exchanges

Gerry Turvey

The 'cinema institution' put in place before the Great War was the latest addition to a lower class field of commercial popular culture that had been under construction since the introduction of cheap reading matter in the 1830s and whose forms and institutions operated as an emergent, alternative culture.[1] It was 'emergent' in so far as it developed to cater for the growing leisure interests of a new lower class urban population and 'alternative' in that its values and preoccupations were different from the dominant culture of better established classes. Its components multiplied through the nineteenth century as a succession of commercial ventures emerged to provide entertainment for the new consumers. Together, they constituted a rich intermedial and intertextual field ranging from penny blood fiction, through the music halls and melodrama theatres, to the mass circulation newspapers, periodicals and comics of the 1890s. In turn, the whole field was characterised by various complex systems of borrowings, exchanges, continuities, correspondences and duplications conducted between its component parts. Cinema, as a late addition, was, in consequence, able to draw upon the resources, established practices and traditions of a broad-based popular culture.

My particular concern is with the film dramas of the British and Colonial Kinematograph Company (B&C) in the years between 1909 and 1913 when they were moving from producing primarily topical materials to fiction filmmaking and when the form of the 'film-drama' was undergoing development. B&C responded to the latter challenge by, in part, adapting the conventions of the cheap sensation fiction that had been launched some eighty years earlier. Various characters, images, genres, narratives, themes and subjects from this tradition had become embedded in popular culture and the popular imagination and were taken up and reworked in popular film. Such familiar characters and story-lines facilitated ease of recognition and comprehension in the difficult years when filmmakers were finding their way towards a form that would articulate increasingly complex narratives[2] and could be used to promote a film's popularity. Here, B&C was drawing on a particularly fecund 'undergrowth of literature' that had proliferated in a socially disreputable realm of publishing operating at some distance from the firms that dealt with the more middlebrow novels of the circulating libraries and who printed those texts criticism was elevating into the literary canon of 'great works'.[3] Within this populist publishing tradition, there were three significant 'moments': the appearance of the 'penny bloods' in the 1830s and 1840s, their displacement by 'penny dreadfuls' in the 1860s and 1870s and the rise of the mass-circulation 'miscellany' periodical in the 1880s and 1890s.[4]

The penny bloods and serial productions

The penny bloods were launched by Edward Lloyd in the late 1830s. They were eight pages long, sold at a penny, took the series form and followed the adventures of particular featured characters. Popular story lines could be extended indefinitely and sales of hundreds of thousands and, on occasion, millions was not impossible. This series-issue policy offered a precedent that could, in turn, be adopted by B&C to generate film series presenting such recurring characters as the female thief Three-Fingered Kate (seven releases between October 1909 and October 1912), Dick Turpin (five films between July 1912 and August 1913), the Spanish bandit Don Q (four films released in 1913), the Master Crook (three films between December 1913 and July 1914) and their highly popular and long-running naval hero Lieutenant Daring (thirteen films between September 1911 and June 1914). For both nineteenth century publishers and twentieth century filmmakers, the series – offering regular characters in a succession of more or less self-contained new stories – was an astute business strategy designed to encourage a guaranteed market for their products by bringing the customer back for more of the same. In fact, as Alex Marlow-Mann has pointed out, B&C dominated the early British series market as five of the nine series issued between 1909 and 1916 were produced by the company.[5]

Lloyd's bloods were also mixed-media products because the printed text was always illustrated by a 'fierce plate' or engraving, invariably of a violent or lurid nature. Similarly, his successors, like the Aldine Publishing Company (formed c1888), would place an enticing colour picture on the front cover of their small-format 'libraries'. These illustrations were a device consciously deployed to solicit the attention, willingness to buy and desire of the customer. However, they also provided a repertoire of visual images with an established currency within popular culture that B&C and other film producers could readily take over. More than this, the iconic nature of the new medium of film meant that an exclusively visual imagery could displace the earlier printed texts – a fact B&C took the opportunity to exploit in its advertising. Thus, in promoting their first Dick Turpin film, they declared:

> Dick Turpin is coming ... what is *reading* about him compared to actually *seeing* him ... See the wonderful chase across country ... You will hold your breath in suspense.[6]

The subject matter of Lloyd's bloods was a matter of plagiarisations and bowdler-isations of Dickens's early novels, reworkings of themes from Gothic fiction and tales of pirates, bandits, outlaws, highwaymen, criminals and the underside of London life. Several of the latter subjects were taken up in B&C's early film dramas. More particularly, Lloyd and the tradition he founded featured certain seminal figures who subsequently reappeared in B&C's films. This, I am suggesting, was not a case of direct influence but a consequence of the way particular characters, stories and images, circulating ceaselessly in the field of popular culture, were readily appropriable.

Lloyd's first blood in 1836 was *Lives of the Most Notorious Highwaymen*. It was an instant hit, going to sixty issues, and established the highwayman – in particular, Dick Turpin – as the most popular subject in cheap fiction. The Turpin story's greatest success, however, was Edward Viles's *Black Bess, or the Knight of the Road. A Tale of the Good Old Times* which ran for nearly five years from 1863. In 1869, Turpin's life was again investigated in Percy St. John's fantastic series *The Blue Dwarf* and Aldine dedicated a 'library' to him in 1901. These retellings took their cue from Harrison Ainsworth's 1834 novel *Rookwood* which recast Turpin's legend as that of an essentially good man driven to crime by harsh circumstances. In his pathbreaking investigation of these texts, E.S.Turner hinted at the potentially critical perspective such tales of villainy may have offered their lower class readership. He claimed the public:

> 'Wanted to read about fiery individualists, men of spirit who defied harsh laws and aggressive officialdom, even though they finished at the end of a hempen rope' and that readers were especially tolerant 'towards any malefactors who could be shown to have been forced into wrong-doing through deprivation of parents, miscarriages of justice, or the activities of oppressive guardians, grinding employers, rascally landlords or lecherous squires'.[7]

Similarly, in developing Turner's account, Louis James suggested the bloods were often involved in the development of anti-hero characters and that, in them, '[p]opular aspirations were expressed through figures opposed to established order'.[8]

B&C's Turpin films adopted the characters, themes and conventions of such populist accounts unproblematically. They had already entered the cinema in the spring of 1906 with Lewin Fitzhamon's one-reel *Dick Turpin's Ride to York* for Hepworth and with a shorter version of the same event from the Warwick Trading Company.[9] Like their literary predecessors, B&C's film series eschewed the cause-and-effect logic of classic narrative to opt for discrete episodes and spectacle. Each film in the series stood alone and each was made up of its own succession of more or less discrete events and adventures. Hence, in *No.4: A Deadly Foe, a Pack of Hounds and Some Merry Monks* (released January 1913), Turpin escaped a king's officer, hid in a monastery, assumed monkish disguise, was rescued from a second capture and ended up pursued by a pack of foxhounds. At the same time, the whole series had an overall logic, beginning in episode one with Turpin's turn to crime and his acquisition of Bess and ending in episode five with the ride to York and her death. In the first episode, which the *Bioscope* observed had no particular plot and so served as a sort of preface or introduction to the series,[10] Turpin was presented as the son of a poor country family who had tired of the 'smooth and peaceful life of a son of the soil' and had drifted into crime by first stealing a cow and then cheating the owner of Bess.[11] Spectacle depended upon authentic period costume, the beauty of the English countryside, the fact the films were made in some of the locations originally associated with the highwayman, upon disguises and escapes, fights and chases and, most importantly, on masterly horsemanship.

Contemporary commentary received them in the spirit established by the nineteenth century literary series. One shrewd *Bioscope* review acknowledged the prior history of the tales to argue there was, perhaps:

> No hero in the annals of British real life romance more dear to the heart of the great British public than that renowned champion of the highways, Dick Turpin...[T]ime and the popular imagination have worked wonders with his character and the quondam criminal is now a knight of chivalry and honour ... in Turpin we have the ideal hero for the writer of romantic novels, dramas – or, picture plays.[12]

Another commentary revealed something of the vigorous intermedial history of the Turpin legend:

> Those of the older generation will remember with what enthusiasm the equestrian representation of this piece was received at Ginnett's Circus, as well as at Hengler's. Since that time the ride to York has scored a signal success as a music-hall sketch and whenever it has been played it has drawn crowded houses.[13]

Central to the Turpin legend, therefore, was Black Bess and the famous ride to York. Consequently, the fifth and longest of B&C's series was a protracted representation of this spirited event.[14] The *Bioscope* claimed to be 'particularly impressed by the admirable horsemanship to be seen in the film', declaring '[n]o 'western' picture, played by cowboy actors on the American prairies, has given up finer riding or more thrilling pursuits'.[15] The *Kinematograph Monthly Film Review* was similarly impressed and invoked cinema's photographic realism to support its claims for the film's advantage over print:

> The story of Dick Turpin and his wonderful ride to York will never fail to hold the imagination...[But h]ere we have the real thing. No longer do we have to imagine the incidents of that great ride...We see them enacted before our eyes.[16]

Throughout the series, authority figures behaved villainously and were treated disrespectfully – for example, a hostile Sir Robert Walpole was almost slain by Turpin in a duel and the Bow Street Runners were regularly thwarted. At the same time, coaches were robbed and society beauties danced with; rural inns provided sustenance; and the companionship of the highwayman's gang was relished. Thus, B&C's Turpin series celebrated the alternative cultural pleasures presented by a carefree law-breaker disdainful of authority and loyal to his close friends.

The company's rapport with the world of popular publishing was further demonstrated in *The Pictures,* the 'Illustrated Weekly Magazine of Fiction for Lovers of Moving Pictures'. This early fan magazine was put out by the Moving Pictures Sales Agency – the company responsible for selling B&C films – as a method of promoting the pictures and production companies they were handling through the telling of the stories of their films. At the end of their 'novelisation' of B&C's third Turpin release the magazine printed a note observing, 'Further adventures of Dick Turpin appear in the "Turpin Library", issued by the Aldine Publishing Co., Ltd.'

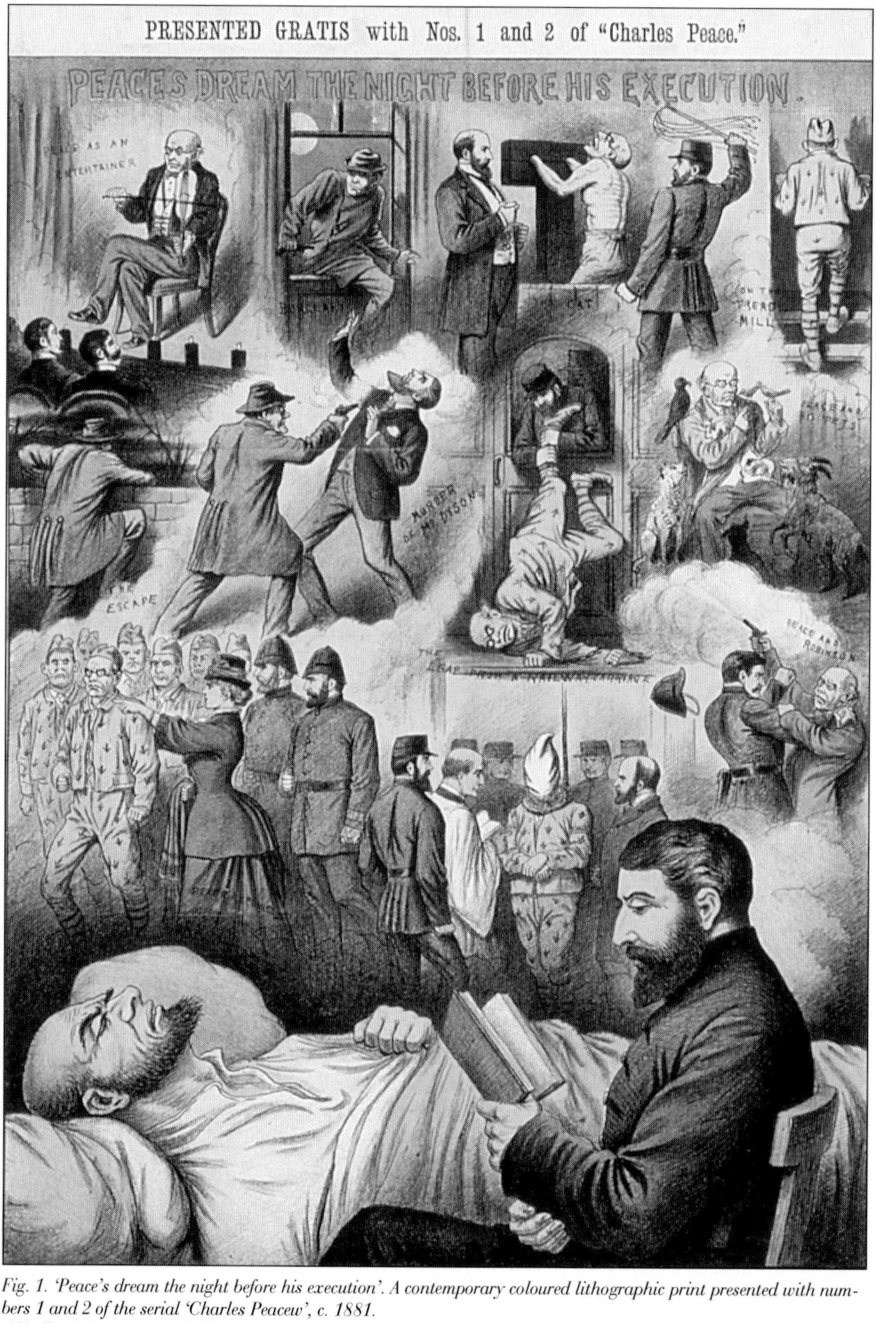

Fig. 1. 'Peace's dream the night before his execution'. A contemporary coloured lithographic print presented with numbers 1 and 2 of the serial 'Charles Peacew', c. 1881.
[Sheffield Museums and Galleries.]

– thereby establishing a direct intermedial correspondence between the worlds of cinema and cheap fiction.[17]

The second major outlaw hero of nineteenth century fiction was Robin Hood. He broke through to success with Pierce Egan's *Robin Hood and Little John* in 1839 and generated his own multi-series publishing phenomenon which included a Robin Hood Library from Aldine in 1901. B&C also took him up and released *Robin Hood Outlawed* in October 1912, in the middle of the Turpin series. This film was clearly intended as the first in a new series and audiences were alerted to watch for future announcements – although, in the event, no further releases appeared.[18] Nevertheless, like the first Turpin film, this episode was designed to set up a succession in so far as it dealt with the Earl of Huntingdon's outlawing and his assumption of the Robin Hood identity as well as introducing key characters in the legend. The Aldine connection again appeared in *The Pictures* when, after the story of the film, it was noted that:

> The Aldine Publishing Co., Ltd., are shortly reissuing their Robin Hood Library, a series of penny books published weekly, which will each contain a long complete story of the Sherwood Forest Outlaws.[19]

Aldine re-released fourteen issues between September 1912 and May 1913 but made no reference in their texts to B&C or their films. However, as the firm had been deeply in debt since 1906, the tentative association with the expanding film company may have had value mainly for Aldine.[20]

A more contemporary villain to enter the popular imaginary was Charles Peace who was executed in 1879. At once, a penny series running to one hundred issues called *Charles Peace; or, The Adventures of a Notorious Burglar* detailed his thefts, murderous behaviour, disguises and reckless attempt to escape the law. Peace's facility for disguise was also featured in two British films of 1905, one from William Haggar and the other from the Sheffield Photographic Company,[21] and B&C returned to the topic in July 1914 with *The Adventures of Charles Peace, King of Criminals*. The film followed nineteenth century precedents by offering a catalogue of sensational episodes from Peace's criminal career. It showed him house-breaking, wounding a policeman, killing a man and unsuccessfully diving from a train window to avoid going to trial.

Another figure with a certain notoriety in nineteenth century popular fiction to appear in a B&C film was Guy Fawkes. He had featured in G.A.Sala's series-issue *Guy Fawkes; or, Gunpowder, Treason and Plot* in the 1880s and B&C took him up for release in November 1913 as *Guy Fawkes and the Gunpowder Plot*. The idea of such a narrative had already been adopted in the second Turpin episode in August 1912 when Dick, in a moment of royalist impetuosity, foiled an attempt to assassinate George II and blow up his parliament.

The 'miscellany' periodical, Don Q and Three-Fingered Kate

Thus, a gallery of characters (like Turpin and Peace), a series of story-lines (like the ride to York, the Gunpowder Plot and the outlawing of Robin Hood) and a set of thematic preoccupations (like anti-authoritarianism) had been carried over from nineteenth century cheap fiction into the films B&C were offering mass audiences before the First World War. In particular, an emphasis fell on transgressive behaviour and individuals defying the law. This was also the case with B&C's series on the Spanish bandit, Don Q, released through 1913. The films were taken from stories written by Hesketh Pritchard and his mother Kate that had first appeared in *Pearson's Magazine* between July and November 1903. *Pearson's Magazine,* however, belonged to a rather different area within the field of popular printed matter than the penny bloods. The 'miscellany' periodical selling at a penny a copy was developed in the 1880s and 1890s by the rising media tycoons George Newnes, Alfred Harmsworth and Cyril Pearson. The pioneering journal was Newnes's *Tit-Bits*, first published in 1881, which provided the model for Harmsworth's *Answers* of 1888 and *Pearson's Weekly* of 1890. The target audience, like that of the earlier bloods and later popular cinema, was artisans and clerical workers and the miscellany orientation provided a mix of competitions, jokes, short stories, series, serialised fiction and factual accounts which, in several ways, continued the preoccupations of the old bloods. Thus, *Pearson's Weekly* was obsessed with stories of crime, policing and detection, both factual and fictional. *Pearson's Magazine*, selling monthly at price sixpence and presenting itself as the 'most artistic and up-to-date magazine of today',[22] was, like Newnes's *The Strand* (founded 1891), a rather more up-market periodical printed on better quality paper and employing higher status writers and artists. Even so, the latter ran Conan Doyle's Sherlock Holmes detective stories and the former offered the lawless bandit Don Q and both, as did the earlier bloods, explicitly combined text and illustrations.

By the time of B&C's adaptations, Don Q had become, like Holmes, an established fictional character. In 1904, the year after their magazine appearance, the original stories had been published in book form as *The Chronicles of Don Q*. This was followed by a second book in 1906, *The New Chronicles of Don Q*, and a third in 1909, *Don Q's Love Story*, which returned to his early years to explain how he had become a bandit.[23] Promotion for the film acknowledged these literary connections by declaring 'the stories were written by Hesketh Pritchard, have been read by one million people in Britain and translated into half-a-dozen languages'.[24] The original tales were illustrated by Stanley L.Wood who drew the Don as bald, thin and hook-nosed, wearing a wide-brimmed black hat and a loose black cape and B&C consciously transposed this imagery into its films.

Don Q continued to inhabit earlier fictional traditions of outlawdom, cruelty and violence and the *Bioscope* was enthusiastic about the transfer of the stories to the screen whilst recognising a significant intermedial shift into a different form when it observed that the:

> Adventures of Don Q have achieved such wide popularity with the readers of the monthly magazines, that it was inevitable that he should be introduced to that vaster public which elects to take its literary and dramatic recreation in the *tabloid form* of the picture play.[25]

Here, the writer, seems to be admitting to an eclipse of the printed text by its visual realisation and, in a sense, to the displacement of words by a set of animated 'fierce plates'. Consequently, this commentator found the picture play to be 'far more complete in its appeal to the imagination' than the original because of the presence of the romantic cliffs, caverns and moorlands of the Peak District and because of the way the bandits were 'so effectively posed amongst their wild surroundings, that they create a more vivid impression of reality than could be conveyed by pages of descriptive writing'.[26] Don Q remained isolated in this mountain retreat, which other men might enter only on his terms, and there he would outwit enemies and defy authority and the agents of the law so that, like Dick Turpin, Robin Hood and Three-Fingered Kate, the lawless Don constantly triumphed over his adversaries.

B&C's first film series, however, had introduced the adventures of a *female* thief, Three-Fingered Kate, and the success of her films helped establish the company as a producer of film dramas. This time, however, the character of Kate was originated by the company itself. Yet she too had nineteenth century antecedents in the strong and resourceful women of the cheap fictions. For example, the success of Viles's Dick Turpin stories in 1863 encouraged, the following year, the short-lived *May Turpin, the Queen of the Road, A Romance* and, in the 1880s, there was a series with the catch-all title of *Joanna Polenipper, Female Horse Stealer, Foot-Pad, Smuggler, Prison Breaker and Murderer*. Earlier still, heroines of penny-issue fiction had evidenced what Louis James has called 'tougher sensibilities' as they assumed male attire and acted with traditional masculine decisiveness and Peter Haining has observed how, in the 1840s, stories directed to lower class women readers had heroines:

Changed in character from the delicate swooning, incredibly naive maidens of the Gothic novels to young women actively seeking love and not entirely tied to the commands of home and parents.[27]

Kate was heiress to this tradition, as were her contemporaries *Galloping Gloria, the Lady Turpin* and *Grace Daring, the Girl Chauffeur* in a Harmsworth comic paper of 1912, *The Penny Wonder*. Further, Kate's manual distinctiveness had its own recurrent imagery in commercial culture. There was a precedent in *Three Fingered Jack, the Terror of the Antilles* in the 1880s and, contemporary with Kate, there was a three-fingered villain in the serial story, *A Strange Sin*, running in *Pearson's Weekly* in the autumn of 1911 whilst the first issue of the *New Nick Carter Weekly*, published by Harmsworth in 1911, presented an image of detective Carter studying a miscreant's three-fingered hand print on a robbed safe.

In the films, Kate was an enterprising and successful robber whose quick-wittedness and astute planning allowed her and her sister Mary to live as independent women in some wealth and luxury. So, at the moment the company's comic films were sending up the suffragettes, the Kate series was glorifying the autonomy of a New Woman. Further, Kate's first daring illegalities appeared three years before the plucky but put-upon 'serial queens' entered the American cinema in mid-1912 – though her return after a twenty month lay off in August of that year may have been B&C's response to the arrival of the new genre. In her first four films, she was assisted only by Mary but, on her return, she became leader of a criminal gang that included subordinate males. In all but one of the films, her main antagonist, whom she regularly outwitted, was the private detective, Daniel 'Sheerluck' Finch. The echo of Sherlock Holmes's name was, of course, deliberate as Doyle's fictional character had achieved ready recognition in popular culture – as the artist Jack Yeats's comic-strip *Chubb-Lock Holmes*, appearing regularly in Harmsworth's *The Funny Wonder* comic, confirmed. Kate remained resolute in her pursuit of 'the good life' and in her films illegal machinations usually triumphed. Except for episode four, where she was handcuffed and arrested, Kate remained un-captured, despite a careless tendency to leave her own incriminating handprints all over the place. Her series evidenced such gothic devices as trap doors, secret sliding panels, concealed tunnels, a machine for pumping a disabling gas into a particular room and a false clock for concealment. Yet the films also put on display luxurious modern home interiors, fast cars, revolvers and elegant contemporary fashions. Kate's victims were, of course, the prosperous upper classes. Each film involved a chase and, except on one occasion, her ultimate evasion of her pursuers. Each hinged on her cleverness and capacity for ingenious trickery, especially in matters of disguise. As the *Bioscope* observed 'Dame Nature, having reduced the number of Kate's fingers, has, as a compensation, sharpened her wits' and the series took pleasure in the sustained success of this female rogue.[28]

The penny dreadfuls, Lieutentant Daring and middlebrow fictions

B&C's fifth and final series, from early 1914, featured The Master Crook who, like Don Q and Kate, was an invented character rather than one drawn from folk traditions, like Turpin, Hood and Peace, but who, whilst outside the law, was not, like his predecessors at B&C, anti-authority. In this sense, he expressed the company's general policy shift to more polite fictions – a process of 'bourgeoisification' – and was probably also a response to the stricter supervision of film content introduced with the setting up of the moral guardianship of the British Board of Film Censors early in 1913. He also represented the transfer into film of a relatively new character-type, this time from the realm of middlebrow fiction – the 'gentleman thief'.

Raffles was the invention of E.W. Hornung, Conan Doyle's brother-in-law, and had made his fictional debut in 1899. Julian Symons has identified him as the 'last flicker for a long time of the criminal hero tradition'[29] but, unlike the figures discussed above, he was an English gentleman produced by the public school system who belonged to a leisure class and who kept himself in luxury by his expertise as an 'amateur' cracksman. Consequently, as Symons further observed:

> Hornung never sees Raffles as an enemy of the class in which he had been brought up, as an earlier writer would have done, but as a man who adheres to the standards of his class even though he is a crook.[30]

Similarly, in contrast to the traditions of Robin Hood and Dick Turpin central to lowbrow fiction, Colin Watson has argued that:

> What [Raffles] really personifies is... something inimical to the principles of justice, of the righting of wrongs, with which the rebel heroes of England have always been associated. Raffles is himself a product of privilege; he is unconcerned with justice.[31]

B&C's new protagonist was a man of this type as the *Bioscope* was well aware when it suggested:

> Raffles and Jimmy Valentine will find that they have a serious rival in the Master Crook, who, with his charm of personality, his impudent bravado, and the ingenuous simplicity with which he outwits the most astute of his antagonists, beats them on their home ground.[32]

So, whilst the physically impaired Three-Fingered Kate intruded disruptively into established worlds of traditional wealth, the suave, dress-suited Master Crook, with his servant, cigars and comfortable rooms, inhabited those same social environments with ease. As the *Bioscope* review continued:

> '[t]he Master Crook, who lives in great splendour, appears to be a gentleman of considerable means' and, as there was no evidence he made a living from his nefarious practices, 'apparently he carries out his exploits merely for the fun of the thing, and to prove to his less gifted [criminal] confederates how easy it is for a man of more than common intelligence and audacity'.[33]

Thus, the culturally subversive charge of some of the earlier series was dissipated in the Master Crook's embrace of a more snobbish set of values. In this context, however, it is worth noting B&C never made a series featuring that other bourgeois hero flourishing in popular fiction since the 1890s, the crime-prosecuting detective.

In his first film, the Crook used his illicit skills to rob a Regent Street shop window for the sheer joy of outwitting the police – later returning the stolen pearls – before applying those talents to help detectives capture a violent and ruthless criminal gang. As the *Kinematograph Monthly Film Review* noted:

> 'It would be hard to say that [the film] places the commission of crime on a pedestal' because its conflict was 'between two classes of "crooks", in which the subtler ingenuity of the "master" proves more than a match for the more cumbersome methods adopted by the more degenerate fraternity'.[34]

On his third appearance, the Crook used his abilities to have money and jewels *returned* to a wealthy banker and his wife. Here, traditions of criminal anti-authoritarianism have not only been infected by the snob-appeal introduced by Raffles but have been subverted by their inversion. Furthermore, the Crook readily succumbed to pious sentimentality, as when he rescued a blind girl from criminal involvements and had her sight restored or when he allowed himself to be outwitted by a winsome waif selling fruit on the street. Further, at the end of his exploits, he returned to the isolated comforts of his bachelor rooms, thereby avoiding the companionable groups so congenial to Turpin, Robin Hood, Kate and even the sinister Don Q.

Finally, there was B&C's greatest series success, Lieutenant Daring.[35] He had a direct cinematic predecessor in Clarendon's Lieutenant Rose, whose own series had begun in February 1910, but he too had significant antecedents in nineteenth century cheap fiction. These were in the 'penny dreadful' magazines of the late 1860s and 1870s. The dreadfuls were directed to a more juvenile reading public as the older audience for the bloods had been drawn towards the racier Sunday newspapers and the newer mass-circulation periodicals. They were eight pages of double-column, small-type print with a vivid, action-packed illustration on the cover.[36] The prime mover here was the publisher Edwin James Brett. His most celebrated publication was *Boys of England*, 'A Young Gentleman's Journal of Sport, Travel, Fun and Instruction'. This was a miscellaneous mix of series stories dealing with youthful characters that ran from 1866 to 1899. In contrast to the earlier bloods, John Springhall has argued:

> The narrative formulas of penny dreadfuls *reinforce[d]* rather than subvert[ed] existing social and political structures ...[37]

Patrick Dunae, in his analysis of how the dreadfuls developed in the 1890s, maintains that:

> Although the newer periodicals co-opted the aggressive spirit that had

> [initially] characterised the penny dreadfuls, that aggression was redirected into outlets which a new generation of conservative critics found acceptable...themes expressed in the old dreadfuls had [by the last decade of the century] been tamed, politicized, and redirected to serve the needs of empire.[38]

This also appears to be the responsibility assumed by the Lieutenant Daring films, in contrast to their companion B&C series.

If Turpin and Robin Hood were the heroes of the bloods, *Boys of England*'s Jack Harkaway, whose tales ran for over twenty years from 1871, was the most famous and most imitated figure from the dreadfuls. His career began at public school, went on to a double first, cricket and rowing at Oxford and then opted for travel and adventure in most parts of the world. As Louis James has observed, the racial and ethnic stereotypes of Harkaway's fictions proposed that Russians were loutish, Spaniards cruel, the Chinese wily and non-white savages treacherous and that, in his stories, the exploits of 'Tom Brown's heirs reflected the violence and brutality of an expanding empire'.[39] This was also the world inhabited by B&C's dashing naval lieutenant whose imperialist conceit led him to triumph over Algerian brigands and South American ruffians, to avenge an insult to the Union Jack from Corsican bandits, to defeat a cowardly North American boxer and Yankee jewel thieves, to aid a foreign president in quelling a rebellion and to defend a missionary's home from the revolt of black plantation workers in Jamaica. The *Kinematograph Monthly Film Review* declared of such films that the public delighted:

> to see a sailor get in and out of tight places and to nonchalantly make his way through innumerable and in many cases apparently insurmountable difficulties.[40]

The *Bioscope* suggested:

> The gallant young officer...has no equal as a man possessed of a ready wit and *bull-dog determination* to carry to the finish any proceeding on which he sets his mind...Englishmen and women delight in being shown the qualities which have won for England's sea-dogs a name at once so greatly feared and respected.[41]

At the same time, James noted, Harkaway was often accompanied by a loyal black servant who would frequently rescue him. In an echo of that scenario, black Jumbo in *Lieutenant Daring and the Ship's Mascot* (released May 1912) was forced to run for naval bluejackets to aid his hard pressed master. Even so, unlike the series featuring successful rogues, Daring's films portrayed a particular kind of public school, gentlemanly 'virtue' that, by the end of each film, had to emerge triumphant.

These patriotic films, inflected by the late nineteenth century literature of empire, were a great success and, in a journey that reversed the trajectory of Don Q from the pages of *Pearson's Magazine* to the films of B&C, Daring's cinematic adventures were reworked in short-story form in the mass-circulation *Pearson's Weekly*. In November 1912, after the release of the first six films, the magazine announced:

> Frequenters of Picture Palaces all know Lieutenant Daring. He is probably the most popular of all cinematograph heroes. By special arrangement we are able to narrate these new stories of his adventures.[42]

Thereafter, *The New Adventures of Lieutenant Daring* ran through twenty-one original episodes. Also, in 1912, the stories of the films themselves were being told in *The Pictures*. This provided further evidence of intermedial connections when, in September, its editor admitted:

> When we say that *Pearson's Weekly* is enterprising and excellent, we don't write at random. We learned our business under its brainy and tactful assistant-editor ... and spent several happy years sub-editing it.[43]

Five of Daring's exploits, however, involved spies and these films were taking up another set of characters and themes circulating, this time, in the domain of middlebrow fiction from the 1890s. The basic formula of the early spy novel was developed by William Le Quex, whose *Fatal Fingers* was adapted as a film by B&C in 1916 and whose dire predictions were rehearsed as 'The Great War in England of 1897' in Harmsworth's *Answers* of 1893.[44] He helped establish the convention – redolent of the values of Raffles, the Master Crook and Harkaway – that distinguished between the gentlemanly English 'secret agent' and the devious alien 'spy'. Daring, of course, was a gentleman pitted against foreign others. David Stafford has argued that the duel between these two figures 'symbolised a conflict of values that lay at the heart of Edwardian society' and that the victories of the former provided:

> A deeply conservative reassurance to those troubled by the emergence of that industrial and urban society which so obsessed the pessimists of Edwardian England ...[45]

The spy as 'gentleman patriot' acted to defeat not only threatening foreigners but also home grown social disorders and political unrest. Given the currency of such fictions, it is unsurprising B&C imported aspects of them into its films. Hence, Daring put down labour unrest in colonial Jamaica but concentrated on defeating enemy agents operating on British soil. Such acts of patriotic establishment Englishness meant the Daring films were articulating a set of socially dominant values that had been reinvigorated in recent middlebrow fiction and in particular areas of late nineteenth century popular publishing. These ran counter to the alternative and occasionally subversive value system that had been voiced by mid-century lowbrow fiction and B&C's earliest series films.

Like its rival film companies, B&C was involved in sustained borrowings from and exchanges with other media within the field of commercial cultural production and in reworking those borrowed materials to develop the new form of the film drama. As a consequence of these complex processes, the company's films in these years were pulled in contradictory ideological directions – directions that were both challenging to established authority and supportive of traditional order.

Notes

1. The terms are those of the 'cultural materialist' perspective developed by Raymond Williams and given an initial schematic formulation in 'Base and Superstructure in Marxist Cultural Theory', *New Left Review* No.82 (1973).
2. This issue was introduced into discussions of early cinema history by Charles Musser in 'The Nickelodeon Era Begins: Establishing the Framework for Hollywood's Mode of Representation', *Framework* Nos. 22–23 (Autumn 1983).
3. The phrase is taken from the title of Gillian Freeman's account of the literary underworld of sexual fantasy, *The Undergrowth of Literature* (London: Panther, 1969).

4. For my account of the penny bloods and penny dreadfuls I have drawn on: E. S. Turner, *Boys Will Be Boys* [published 1948, revised 1957] (Harmondsworth: Penguin, 1975); Louis James. *Fiction for the Working Man* (Harmondsworth: Penguin, 1974); Peter Haining, *The Penny Dreadful* (London: Victor Gollancz, 1976); Peter Haining, *Terror! A History of Horror Illustrations from the Pulp Magazines* (London: Souvenir Press, 1976); Victor E.Neuberg, *Popular Literature: A History and Guide* (Harmondsworth: Penguin, 1977); Kevin Carpenter, *Penny Dreadfuls and Comics: English Periodicals for Children from Victorian Times to the Present Day* (London: Victoria and Albert Museum, 1983).
5. In fact, Marlow-Mann lists only eight series for this period, having overlooked B&C's *The Master Crook* series. He also undercounts the Dick Turpin and Don Q films. See: Alex Marlow-Mann, 'British Series and Serials in the Silent Era' in Andrew Higson (ed), *Young and Innocent? The Cinema in Britain 1896–1930*, (Exeter: University of Exeter Press, 2002).
6. *The Pictures*, II: 33 (1 June 1912): back page, their emphasis.
7. Turner: 52.
8. James: 198
9. *Dick Turpin's Ride to York*, script and direction by Lewin Fitzhamon for Hepworth, released May 1906; *Dick Turpin's Last Ride to York*, (probably) directed by Charles Raymond for the Warwick Trading Company, released April 1906.
10. See: 'A romance of the great gay road', *The Bioscope* (16 May 1912): 463.
11. 'Dick Turpin on the films', *The Kinematograph Monthly Film Review* No.3 (July 1912): 97.
12. 'Dick Turpin: Walturdaw's latest all-British 'exclusive'', *The Bioscope* (10 July 1913): 140.
13. 'Britain scores again', *The Cinema* (9 July 1913): 44.
14. Episode five was nearly two reels long whilst all the others were just over one. The first four films were numbered 1–4 for their releases but, because number 5 was an 'exclusive' to Walturdaw as renter, the numbering was dropped. Rachel Low correctly appreciated the Turpin films were 'not so much complete stories as one long meandering series of incidents' but wrongly believed 'these rather shapeless ... films were *remade* as one long exclusive feature ... [with] a great improvement in general dramatic effect'. (201–202, my emphasis) This error is a consequence of her particularly heavy reliance on *The Bioscope* – and overlooking of other trade periodicals – for this period in her history. *The Bioscope*'s rather muddled account of 10 July 1913 could, read on its own, have mislead her. See: Rachel Low, *The History of the British_Film, 1906–1914* (London: George Allen and Unwin, 1973).
15. 'Dick Turpin: Walturdaw's latest all-British 'exclusive'', *The Bioscope* (10 July 1913): 140.
16. 'Dick Turpin's ride to York', *Kinematograph Monthly Film Review* No.16 (August 1913): 163.
17. *The Pictures* II: 48 (14 September 1912): 14.
18. 'Tales of "Robin Hood" filmed/No.1 – "Outlawed"', *The Film Censor* (4 August 1912).
19. *The Pictures II*: 47 (7 September 1912): 4. The magazine's story-version of the film was titled, *Robin Hood Outlawed: An early adventure of the historical hero.*
20. W.O.G. Lofts, 'Success and Failure: A Short History of English "Penny Dreadful" Publishers', *The Dime Novel* 46: 1 (February 1977).
21. *Charles Peace*, directed by William Haggar for Haggar and Sons, released September 1905; *The Life of Charles Peace* directed by Frank Mottershaw for the Sheffield Photographic Company, released November 1905.
22. Advert in *The Newspaper Directory* (1903): 291.
23. K. and Hesketh Pritchard, *The Chronicles of Don Q* (London: Chapman and Hall Ltd., 1904); K. and Hesketh Pritchard, *The New Chronicles of Don Q* (London: T.Fisher Unwin, 1906); K. and Hesketh Pritchard, *Don Q's Love Story* (London: Greening and Co. Ltd., 1909).
24. Advertisement in *The Top Line Indicator* (13 November 1912): 4.
25. *The Bioscope* (21 November 1912): 599, my emphasis.
26. Ibid.
27. James: 198; Haining, *The Penny Dreadful*: 134.
28. *The Bioscope* (7 October 1909).

29. Julian Symons, *Bloody Murder: From the Detective Story to the Crime Novel: A History* (Harmondsworth: Penguin, 1974): 93.
30. Ibid.: 95.
31. Colin Watson, *Snobbery With Violence* (London: Eyre and Spottiswoode, 1971): 50.
32. 'The Master Crook', *The Bioscope* (20 November 1913): 791.
33. Ibid.
34. 'The Master Crook', *The Kinematograph Monthly Film Review* No.21 (January 1914): 35.
35. Kate was B&C's first series and Daring their second, appearing some 23 months after her debut. Series three, Dick Turpin, followed after another eleven months.
36. Sales were promoted by competitions and the other standard sales gimmicks of the late nineteenth century. In some cases they climbed to a quarter of a million copies and it has been estimated that each copy could have been read by up to nine readers. The term 'penny dreadful' was not widely used in commentary on popular publishing until the 1870s.
37. John Springhall, '"A Life Story for the People"? Edwin J.Brett and the London "Low-life" Penny Dreadfuls of the 1860s', *Victorian Studies* 33: 2 (Winter 1990): 225, my emphasis.
38. Patrick A.Dunae, 'Penny Dreadfuls: Late Nineteenth-Century Boys' Literature and Crime', *Victorian Studies* Vol. 22 (Winter 1979): 150. See also: Patrick A.Dunae, 'Boys' Literature and the Idea of Empire, 1870–1914', *Victorian Studies* Vol.24 (Autumn 1980).
39. Louis James, 'Tom Brown's Imperialist Sons' *Victorian Studies* Vol. 17 (September 1973): 99.
40. *The Kinematograph Monthly Film Review* No. 1 (July 1912): 99–100.
41. *The Bioscope* (30 October 1912): my emphasis.
42. *Pearson's Weekly* (3 September 1912): 263. Alex Marlow-Mann claims the practice of 'tie-ins' between the film and print media was not widely exploited in British cinema at this time and suggests Don Q's link to a Pearson periodical was the only exception. Clearly, he was wrong in the case of B&C for they cultivated tie-in relations with *Pearson's Weekly*, *Pearson's Magazine*, *The Pictures* and even with the Aldine company. See: Marlow-Mann.
43. *The Pictures* (14 September 1912): 31.
44. Harmsworth's newspapers and periodicals were vociferously anti-German and obsessed with threats of invasion as well as being militantly pro-Empire.
45. David Stafford, 'Spies and Gentlemen: The British Spy Novel, 1893–1914', *Victorian Studies* 24: 4 (Summer 1981): 509.

4

Popular Sensations: Institutional Modernity and the Textual History of *The Long Strike*

Joe Kember

The popularity of sensational elements in nineteenth-century theatre and early film has led some recent critics to reinterpret the connections and influences between these media. In one recent study, Ben Singer has traced the concept of melodrama across turn-of-the-century media and demonstrated the close relationship of this genre with conditions of industrial modernity. Singer describes this relationship as one aspect of an overarching 'modernity thesis' in which the popularity of melodrama, while reflecting many causes, derived in part from its capacity to capture the sense of upheaval and vulnerability experienced by the masses in a world of unprecedented cultural discontinuity and social atomisation'.[1] In response to David Bordwell's critique of the modernity thesis in relation to film, he writes:

> Movies were responsive to developments in cinematographic technology, stylistic and generic cycles, industry practices, shifts in cinema's social functions, and so on. All the modernity thesis aims to do is add 'environmental context' or 'sensory experience' to that list. There is little point in speculating on relative degrees of influence among all the determinants (assuming we can even identify them), but it is fair to say that proponents of the modernity thesis think it is worthwhile to explore the possibility that the emergence of urban modernity – arguably the most momentous social transformation in human history – had some degree of impact on an art form that developed within this context.[2]

Singer argues that, among several equally valid critical approaches to early cinema, the correspondences between cinematic and metropolitan experiences offer a convincing rationale for interpretation of widespread popular representations of melodramatic, spectacular, or traumatic events.

The development of the modern metropolis and new technologies of transportation and communication have proven pertinent in accounting for sensational aspects of *fin-de-siécle* representations. The mental and physical dangers posed by cultural and technological trends in the city seem to offer an analogy, and perhaps an explanation, for the anxieties registered at this time on the stage and the screen, and within literature and the periodical press. Early film studies, in particular, has pursued the spectator of early film from the penny gaff and Music Hall into the urban landscapes of the early twentieth century, contextualising early film as a manifestation of much broader cultural anxieties.[3] Selected elements associated with the fiction of Baudelaire and Poe, the sociology of Georg Simmel, and the critical theory of Walter Benjamin particularly, have all contributed to an understanding of early film in terms of the disjunctive metropolitan experience of space and time.[4] Centred by the active and subjective constructions of a wandering spectator figure, labelled the *stranger* by Simmel and the *flâneur* by Baudelaire, the substance of modernity is here articulated as a series of neurasthenic attractions that accost this urban subject on every street, in every arcade, at every shop window:

> Lasting impressions, impressions which differ only slightly from one another, impressions which take a regular and habitual course and show regular and habitual contrasts – all these use up, so to speak, less consciousness than does the rapid crowding of changing images, the sharp discontinuity in the grasp of a single glance, and the unexpectedness of onrushing impressions. These are the psychological conditions which the metropolis creates. With each crossing of the street, with the tempo and multiplicity of economic, occupational, and social life, the city sets up a deep contrast with small town and rural life.[5]

It is easy to understand the attraction of Simmel's 1903 prognosis for the city-dweller to historians and theorists of early film. Among several justly celebrated contemporary pieces, it goes some way to explain the early film's fascination with the hustle of street-level actualité footage, with panoramic views of cities, with local films, and with phenomena like 'phantom rides'. These can be considered as consolidations of ways of seeing and experiencing the world that had become implicit to metropolitan life. For Lynne Kirby, following Wolfgang Schivelbusch among others, the train and the cinema are even to be understood as 'two great machines of vision that give rise to similar modes of perception'.[6] Furthermore, discursive constructions like 'the rapid crowding of changing images, ... the unexpectedness of onrushing impressions' are ideally tailored to discussion of a cinema of attractions. Another recent commentator has described the experience of travelling and spectatorship in the period as essentially the same phenomenon: 'The film 'viewer' is a practitioner of viewing space – a tourist'.[7] Such assertions preserve much of Simmel's sociological insight and are also strongly suggestive of the spectatorial attitude assumed within the cinema of attractions.

This perspective tends to confirm the argument that 'in certain salient respects cinema is *like* modernity'.[8] As a result of studies that favour high modernist discourses of fragmentation and distraction, our understanding of early film's place within its heterogeneous cultural context has certainly improved. But this model of cinema as an expression of spectatorial distraction and metropolitan anxiety, if rigorously applied, sometimes threatens to mistake conditions of modern industrial capitalism with the emergence of twentieth-century cultural discontinuities. Modernity was not only an agent of fragmentation and disjunction, but also a unifying force, as seems amply demonstrated by the example of the development of cinema. Modernity was also characterised by the unifying, totalising operations of highly structured and efficient institutional frameworks. As modern sociologists such as Anthony Giddens have convincingly shown, institutional conditions are directly interlaced with the 'environmental context' and 'sensory experience' privileged by Singer's description of modernity. 'It has become commonplace to claim that modernity fragments, dissociates,' writes Giddens, 'yet the unifying features of modern institutions are just as central to modernity – especially in the phase of high modernity – as the disaggregating ones'.[9] Within conditions of modern industrial capitalism, institutional structures were not only the product, but also the premise for cultural conditions of modernity.[10] It therefore becomes problematic to address instititutional and cultural aspects of early film history independently.

In part, modern institutions associated with the developing film industry have escaped prolonged critical attention within early film studies because they were not often explicitly recorded or theorised within artistic, philosophical, or academic discourses at the turn of the century. They were formulated, by and large, within the more gradual and less visible development of nineteenth-century institutions of popular entertainment and within the consolidation of distinct models of professional praxis associated with these institutions.[11] However, this is not to say that institutional conditions remained entirely untheorised by practitioners within the entertainment industries. The profession of acting, to take a relatively well-known example, was thoroughly examined by a series of theorists throughout the nineteenth century.[12] By contrast, the acutely self-conscious and professionalised forms of writing associated with late nineteenth-century stagecraft in the UK have been acknowledged rather inconsistently. Yet, within such writing the consolidation of theatrical institutional frameworks within a modern industrial infrastructure is explicitly theorised. Furthermore, the closely related development of a definitively modern form of expertise and self-reflexivity from audiences is thoroughly explored.[13]

To be clear, this understanding of nineteenth-century institutions and of their definitively cynical or 'knowing' spectators has appeared in a number of contexts concerned with Victorian traditions of British showmanship, Music Hall and meta-theatre.[14] I simply wish to return this idea to the centre of the debate concerning modernity and melodrama in popular entertainments, especially in the context of melodramatic and sensationalist theatre and cinema. The following case study of the various performances of Dion Boucicault's melodrama *The Long Strike* between 1866 and 1912 in the theatre, variety theatre, and cinema will therefore argue that the success of each adaptation rested on its fulfilment of very narrow institutional objectives. In each case, instead of focussing on the sensational impact of *The Long Strike* on its spectators, I will emphasise the idea of popularity within the 'popular sensation'. Not only were sensation scenes among the biggest draws at the Victorian box-office, but they were also 'popular' in the political sense of opening up a democratic space for spectators. In this space, spectators were expected and even encouraged to cynically apply their own expertise and knowledge concerning melodramatic convention and spectacular effects. In doing so, they brought to bear highly institutionalised conventions and routines of reading spectacle – everyday routines that were themselves characteristic of conditions of modernity at the turn of the century.

Dion Boucicault and the theatrical institution: *The Long Strike* at the Lyceum

Dion Boucicault offers a logical starting-point for such an analysis. More than any of his contemporaries Boucicault enacted and articulated a thoroughly pragmatic approach to stagecraft, to audiences, and to the theatrical institution at large. Within his extensive contributions to periodicals and in lectures and classes delivered on both sides of the Atlantic, Boucicault developed a consistent model for melodramatic writing, staging, and acting. In doing so, he also reinforced his ownership of this model, advertising a popular image of himself as the master of Victorian melodrama. Indeed, Boucicault perpetually dramatised his public identity – often in the third person – to the extent of disguising his authorship of his celebratory 1883 autobiography under the assumed name, Charles Lamb Kenney.[15] As a premier exponent of a definitively modern celebrity culture, Boucicault recognised that he was powerfully placed within the Victorian theatrical institution to capitalise upon its functional approach to melodramatic productions. He saw at least 200 of his plays produced (one critic at least credits him with a hand in more than 400) between his London debut in 1841 and posthumous final production in 1891.[16]

Among his productions were many adaptations of French plays and of English and French novels. Frequently, these were the most popular and enduring of his productions. *The Corsican Brothers* (based on a French dramatisation of a Dumas novel, *Les Frères Corses*), *The Octoroon* (based on Thomas Reid's 1856 novel *The Quadroon*), *The Colleen Bawn* (based on Gerald Griffin's 1829 novel *The Collegians*), and *The Long Strike* (adapted from Elizabeth Gaskell's *Mary Barton*), for example, were among his greatest successes of the 1850s and 1860s. Typically, Boucicault would emphasise the melodramatic content of these earlier works, add at least one sensation scene to the piece, and mount the whole with music and spectacular effects: fires, ghosts, explosions, and the *mise-en-abyme* scenic backdrops that had long been the standard fare of stationary panoramas and dioramas. Within the periodical press, Boucicault regularly defended his practice of pirating these texts. 'The great value of our drama,' he claimed, 'lies not in the stuff borrowed, but in the use it is put to'.[17] Putting material to effective melodramatic use on the British stage, regardless of the original provenance of this material, thus became central to Boucicault's identity as a dramatic author.

Boucicault's concern with establishing himself as a popular author was driven by the financial return he looked for from his plays. He would jealously protect all profits accruing from his occasional hits, and the pages of *The Times* are littered with references to court proceedings against British and American theatre managers over copyright infringement. In America, where no copyright laws for plays existed when Boucicault arrived in 1853, it became essential that the author should be afforded the sole right of allowing plays to be represented. A brief statute was passed to that effect, under Boucicault's influence, in 1856.[18] Still more important were the alterations made generally to theatrical practice. Up to the 1850s in Britain, authors would commonly receive as little as thirty pounds royalties per week for plays that might yield a good deal of money for theatre managers and the star actors within those theatres' stock companies. Furthermore the presence of such stars within the play tended to eclipse the significance of the author. Boucicault reports that he received a fee of only £300 for *The Corsican Brothers*,[19] a play that proved so popular in the season of 1852 that it gave rise to a whole new genre of what Michael Booth calls '"cloak and sword" melodrama'.[20] Narrating his return from America in 1860 following the phenomenal success of *The Colleen Bawn*, Boucicault makes his financially driven model of theatrical authorship quite clear:

> He [Boucicault] refused to allow 'The Colleen Bawn' to be played on royalty or fees. He engaged four comedians, Mr. John Drew, Mr. Sloane, Mrs. Sloane, and Mrs. Hudson Kirby, and instructed them in the principal characters. He offered the play as the star, supported by this group of American comedians ... The play became the thing, and the author received half the gross receipts ... The leading dramatic authors, perceiving the very large profits accruing from this new method, began to secede away from the Dramatic Authors' Society, and to follow the new method, under which the name of the author of the play was starred and his importance recognized.[21]

Regardless of hyperbole, Boucicault's desire that the author of the play should take up a position before the footlights, in advance even of the positions of the actors and the characters they represented, is here powerfully countenanced. Justifying his substantial fee as the author of the piece, Boucicault appeals to Shakespearean legitimacy, claiming that 'the play's the thing.' In spite of the growing currency of star discourses in the theatre, Boucicault claims that the theatrical author, like the literary author, could be the main attraction. Labouring under a metaphor immoderate even for the author, it was his wish 'to obtain for the dramatist not only the place of honor at the entertainment, but the largest share of the loaves and the fishes'.[22] Under the 'new method,' star billing for actors became a valuable commodity, but the dramatist, as the author of the work and proprietor of its actors, became a natural object of public interest.

In common with this cultivation of authorial status came a concern that the plays should initially find large target audiences across as broad a market as possible. This was a market that would, in turn, visit the theatre when a Boucicault production was playing. Boucicault cultivated an acute consciousness of his audience and sought on various occasions to define it within the theatrical institutions of London and New York. In fact, his model appears rather inflexible, failing to distinguish between alternative locations and changing very little over time. During the seventies and eighties, as the proportion of his failures slowly grew, he took to explaining its place in his theory of contemporary drama more frequently.[23] The following from an 1877 article entitled 'The Decline of the Drama' is representative of the strand:

> During the last hundred years the mind of mankind has been eagerly devoted to the application of scientific discoveries to useful purposes, and particularly to the unification of political and commercial interests ... Even the spiritual world has been staked out into claims. The ghosts that visited the couch of Richard were spirits in which the Shakespearean public devoutly believed. Ghosts are now secured by patent and produced by machinery by Doctor Pepper. Such is the positive generation that calls its drama into existence,

> requiring the mind of the dramatist to be practical, utilitarian, to be in sympathetic accord with the minds of the people. He must not consider anything too deeply; his audience cannot follow him. He must not soar; their prosaic minds, heavy with facts, cannot rise. He cannot roam; their exact information turns him back at every step. I earnestly believe the human mind always maintains the same average level. There is always a Homer, a Virgil, a Dante, a Shakespeare in existence, but mankind is pleased not to call them forth ... Such crops of great artists or great poets are not freaks of Nature but the necessary results of human demand.[24]

The dramatist exists here as a function of his audience, and Boucicault, in defence of his own pragmatic approach to the stage, the spectacular effects, and stock melodramatic plot-lines he continually resorted to, intimates that his 'practical, utilitarian' work was the inevitable product of 'prosaic' late nineteenth-century theatrical spectatorship. These were spectators that demanded the efficient and practical exploitation of the capacities of the stage. The audience, he argued, was more interested in the achievement of a competent 'ghost effect' than in the appearance of the ghost itself. Boucicault's cynical spectator was actively engaged in matching its tightly scripted expectations of a reality effect with the stage's spectacular deployment in meeting those expectations. And behind that deployment was the figure of the author, held by the audience as the agency responsible for proceedings on-stage.

By 1889, recalling an anecdote intended to shed some light on contemporary tastes in the London and New York theatres (and, perhaps, to defend his model of the theatre against the literary demands of the 'New Drama'), Boucicault made precisely the same point. 'At a dinner party which took place in 1866,' he writes:

> The question was discussed as to the value of the literary merit of a play that had recently been produced. One side maintained that the literary element in a drama was rather an impediment than an assistance to popular success.[25]

In order to resolve this dispute, according to Boucicault, it was necessary for him to write three plays: a society drama relying mainly on what he called its 'literary treatment'; a sensation drama relying purely on spectacular effects; and somewhere between these, what he called a 'domestic drama'. In fact, all three are better described as melodrama in the nineteenth-century stage tradition, only with greater or lesser reliance on spectacular stage effects. Boucicault's prediction was that the success of the play would increase proportionately as did its engagement with spectacle, regardless of any other qualities the plays might possess. Predictably enough, and regardless of the actual result, Boucicault's anecdote concluded that he had been completely correct in this prediction, and that his assumptions about the tastes of his audience had been fully exonerated in practice.

The society drama was a piece entitled *The Two Lives of Mary Leigh* or *Hunted Down* – and concerned a troubled wife who is blackmailed by her villainous first husband, whom she had believed dead.[26] The spectacle piece was *The Flying Scud*, a racing drama whose plot primarily consisted of the four-legged hero of the title being repeatedly 'nobbled' by a Captain Goodge, in an unsuccessful attempt to wrest both financial success and the girl from a rather haphazard hero. The play was chiefly noted for the spectacle of a horse on stage, and for the race itself, run at the back of the stage with cut-out animals.[27] The domestic drama was Boucicault's adaptation of Gaskell's *Mary Barton* and her short story, *Lizzie Leigh* – though the precise contribution of the latter is far from clear. Several versions of *The Long Strike* are in existence, but in what follows I will be focusing primarily on the first version to be put into production in September 1866.[28]

All three of the 'wager plays' were produced between August and October of 1866 in London, and a few months later in New York, but the results were not exactly as Boucicault reported. *The Long Strike*, as Richard Altick indicates, was, on opening, at least as successful as *The Flying Scud*, and went on to remain in popular repertory for the next twenty years.[29] Intended as the season opener for the London Lyceum, *The Long Strike* marked the beginning of the hundredth season on which entertainments had been held at the site.[30] The manager and producer, Charles Fechter, was so concerned that the play should be successful on this night that he even sent a copy of it to his friend, Charles Dickens, for his comments. The play was performed under the conditions Boucicault had established with *The Colleen Bawn*, the author providing the company (including himself and his wife) and taking the largest proportion of the receipts. Throughout the Lyceum production, Boucicault was careful to exploit and further promote his increasingly eminent public image. The opening night, *The Times* reported, 'was filled by an audience fashionable above the general average of playgoers, and distinguished by the presence of many literary celebrities'.[31] It was imperative for both Fechter and Boucicault that this first night should have the desired impact on such an influential audience. Boucicault's own promptbook for the play indicates that he was obliged to make many alterations in the course of rehearsals, before he was satisfied with his adaptation.

An unfinished and undated manuscript by Boucicault entitled *Mary Barton*, with characteristics of both the novel and the first version of the play indicates something of Boucicault's cribbing from Gaskell's text.[32] Probably a first draft for *The Long Strike*, much of the plot remained unchanged. Indeed, all versions of the play contain snatches of dialogue – usually from the romantic plot of the novel – that are reproduced verbatim. The version produced at the Lyceum Theatre on 15 September 1866 differed, however, in several respects. Many of the novel's characters are disposed of, or re-named, while others become condensed into new individuals who drive the plot rapidly forward with a greater economy. The first half of the novel, with its predominant concern with the condition of manufacturing labourers in Manchester's slums, was excluded. The industrial strike, which begins half way through the novel is here merely the initial motivation for the chiefly romantic problems encountered by the central characters. These changes were geared toward emphasising the melodramatic content of the plot, while troublesome social and political issues associated with the novel were disregarded. In place of social realism, then, there was a commitment to what *The Athenaeum* called a 'picturesque reality,' to dramatic efficiency, to continuity of action, and to full exploitation of the capacities of the deep Lyceum stage.[33]

Boucicault's most significant addition to the plot, for which he received immoderate critical praise, was its sensation scene, which was innovatively staged as a telegraph office. In this scene, Jane Learoyd (Mary, in the novel) and the lawyer Moneypenny (a comic interpretation of the novel's Mr Bridgenorth) attempt to

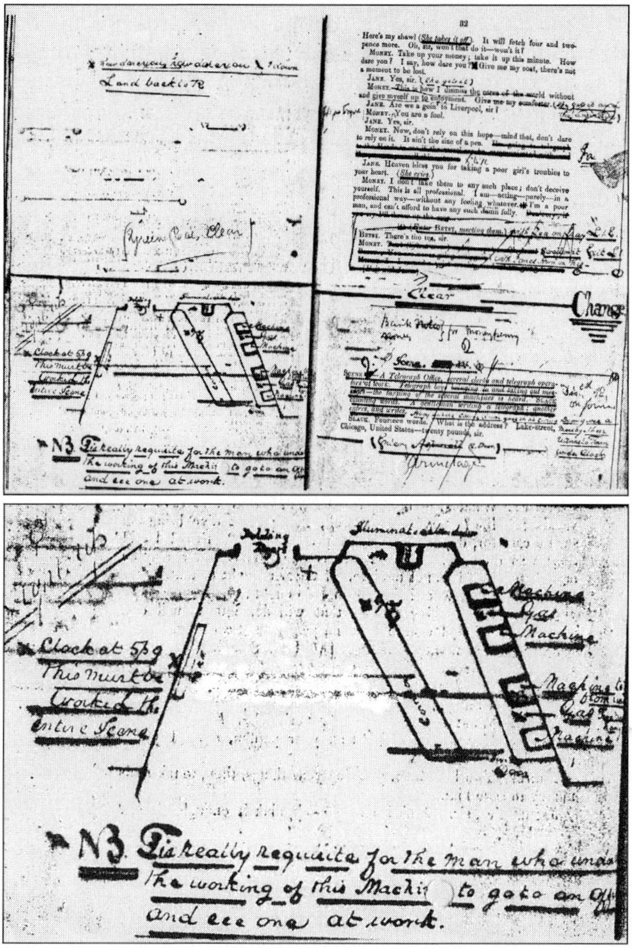

Fig. 1 (above and below). Charles Bennett's promptbook for the Lyceum production of The Long Strike *including sketch of the stage and stage directions.*

contact Johnny Reilly (Will Wilson) in order to provide the last-ditch alibi for Jem, the condemned hero of the piece. But Johnny is about to set sail for the Americas, so Jane and Moneypenny must reach him before he leaves. The suspense builds as they wait, at length, for an answer. This was the dramatic centrepiece of the play and it was crucial that the scene exploited every available part of the Lyceum stage, which rose high above the pit and opened immediately onto viewing galleries on both sides. The stage included real telegraph machines to the left of the stage, with gas lights above, and incidental actors of whom the stage manager, Charles Bennett, noted 'Tis really requisite for the man who undertakes the working of this machine to go to an office and see one at work' (see Fig. 1). The stage buzzes with this scripted activity while Jane and Moneypenny standing at the counter, mid-stage, wait breathlessly for Jem's alibi. At the back and to the left was an illuminated view of Manchester at night as viewed through a window. On the right was a very large stage clock, which Bennett indicated must be cranked throughout the scene. While the characters waited the clock ticked loudly and exaggerated the effect of passing time. Eventually, against all hope, the machine began to work. In this scene the narrative of the play pauses and, in a frame-breaking tableau, Moneypenny, Jane, and the audience wait together, with growing hysteria, for the machine across the counter to start tapping.

These details suggest that Boucicault was correct in his diagnosis of the modern theatrical audience. The telegraph scene lends credence to his conviction that successful stagecraft was adept at satisfying the demands of a 'positive generation' of theatregoers even in the exceptional circumstances at the Lyceum on the opening night of *The Long Strike*. Furthermore, the scene supports a general description of late nineteenth-century melodrama not only as sensational, but as 'deliberately self-conscious and self-reflexive' in its use of sensation.[34] Indeed, Boucicault firmly underlined his own mastery of melodramatic effect within the 1866 production by appearing in the linchpin role. He played Johnny Reilly, the Irish sailor with Jem's alibi, whom Jane desperately tries to contact in the telegraph office. Boucicault's performance was pivotal to the functioning of the plot – the denouement arrives at exactly the point Johnny arrives on the stage. Not only did the role enable Boucicault to use his best brogue, but, as *The Times* acutely noted:

> If he is not seen often, and never stays long, he always pops in just at the time when his place in the story makes him certain to produce a sensation.[35]

The turning point of the sensationalist narrative thus revolved visibly around the play's author, allowing audiences to apply their knowledge concerning Boucicault to the masterful staging of the play.

In the growing wave of publicity and cult of personality that Boucicault typified, this metatheatrical understanding could be deliberately cultivated. Audiences quickly acquired expertise concerning theatrical conventions of spectacle and firmly expected it from the most famous sensation-monger of them all. Boucicault's highly efficient exploitation of the sensation scene was one aspect of an intricate contract established with audiences, actors, the Lyceum, and the theatrical institution in general. It was, indeed, among the most familiar and comfortable of the attractions the Lyceum had to offer. However, in New York, where the play opened at the Olympic Theatre six weeks later with an entirely new cast, the comparatively minor role of Moneypenny came more clearly into its own.

Variety theatre and film: *The Long Strike* adapted

In this version, Moneypenny was played by the character actor J.H.Stoddart, who, in spite of methodological misgivings, developed what he called a 'nervous, crabbed, and fidgety' mannerism for Moneypenny, which 'made the character stand out,' and brought to the scene a comic emphasis, counterbalancing the powerful suspense of the London version (see Fig. 2).[36] *The Long Strike* played for two months at the Olympic, with Stoddart at the top of the bill, and then toured all the New England cities with great success for the remainder of the season. Next year he joined Lester Wallack's theatre in New York, and was engaged twice that summer to play the same part with some of the most famous performers of the day. Each performance yielded for Boucicault – then in England – a substantial dividend, chiefly because of the copyright laws he had himself helped through in the US a few years earlier. It was equally profitable for Stoddart, who was eventually tempted to leave Wallack's famous company, to star as Moneypenny under less famous management. By 1873, now under his own management, he had bought the American performance copyright for *The Long Strike* from Boucicault and undertook to rake in all the profits of his own stardom. He was to play the role at least 200 times in the next twenty years.[37]

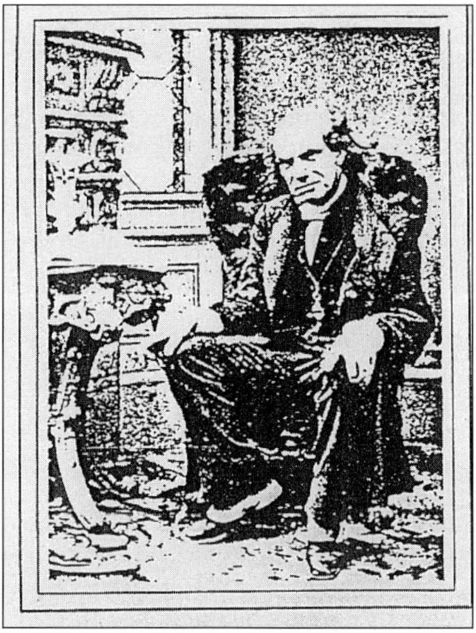

Fig. 1. J.H. Stoddart as Moneypenny.

Boucicault's anecdote on the 'wager plays' obscures the conspicuous success of *The Long Strike* in the US for rhetorical effect in order to lend credence to his conviction that audiences were more impressed by the overt spectacle of *The Flying Scud*. However, his belief that audiences were pragmatic and cynical, typified in his anecdotal and self-mythologising writings for the periodical press during the 1880s, was borne out by the long runs of *The Long Strike* in the UK and US and in the success of the play's sensation scene. As the play worked its way via Stoddart's frequent productions into the popular consciousness in and around New York, and as the telegraph scene in particular was marked for what G.C.Odell called 'one of the greatest of all trick melodramatic devices,' the presence of new localities, new audiences, and alternative institutions quickly made itself felt.[38]

Stoddart began to perform the telegraph scene separately – often on benefit nights in New York – which tended to call on the most popular and conventional of variety performances.[39] As early as 1872 the scene was performed in musical programmes at the Brooklyn Academy of Music. Variety bills across New York began to pick up on the trend – though it is uncertain whether the services of Stoddart were required in all of these performances. In 1886 the entire play was produced at the Novelty Theatre in Williamsburgh, sandwiched between performances by 'McIntyre and Heath's Minstrels.' In the Spring of 1890, the bill at New York's Grand Theatre featured the Boom Burlesque Company, Whallen and Martell's Mammoth Combination, Bert's Creole Burlesque Company, *The Long Strike*, and then The Union Square Speciality Company.[40] The play, and particularly the telegraph scene, now featured as variety turn – albeit predominantly in those theatres most given to occasional runs of variety and the most gentrified of the vaudeville houses.

Vaudeville performances tended to be arranged via booking agencies, which would find and fill empty slots in theatres as and when they came up. Each variety bill would be assembled carefully, typically with circus acts to open and capture the audience's attention, a number of 'headline acts' for the close, and a dramatic piece in the meantime for contrast.[41] The telegraph scene seems to have been a particularly popular selection in the New York area where, independently of the rest of the plot, it functioned effectively within a variety aesthetic. However, even in this definitively sensationalist environment, the success of the performance depended on the knowing audience's recognition of the scene, and especially of Stoddart. It became a trademark role that, like a successful showman, gave the actor an institutionally consolidated identity of his own. This was marked most obviously by Stoddart's purchase of the US rights to *The Long Strike*, but it was also manifested on each occasion that the scene was performed. Like Boucicault, Stoddart encouraged his audiences to entertain a degree of intimacy with his most celebrated role, thus instituting a range of comfortable and familiar relations at the heart of an entertainment apparently characterised by fragmentation and contra-contemplative distraction. This was the foundation of his acquisition of a rather parochial version of theatrical stardom within the New York area. It was also the gesture that allowed audiences to gain a knowing and appreciative expertise concerning this kind of stardom and to be able to implement it as the primary attraction of the role's performance.

Unsurprisingly, given the success of the Moneypenny role in the US, it was preserved by a 1911 Essanay film of *The Long Strike* and again by an IMP film of 1912. These films painstakingly duplicated the eccentricities of the character, though Stoddart was not involved in their production. The surviving fragment of the IMP film demonstrates that the melodramatic plot remained principally unchanged from later versions of the play.[42] However, the configuration of the play's chief attractions now responded to yet another, radically different, institutional environment. Once again, we can identify in this text the existence of a wide range of sensational attractions embedded in a melodramatic narrative. Once again, audiences witnessed the spectacular display of the latest technological wonders in a manner that fully exploited the representational capacities of the medium. But, as in all previous productions of *The Long Strike*, these attractions were coordinated and unified by a coherent institutional blueprint. On this occasion, Carl Laemmle's IMP company and director, Herbert Brenon, sought to satisfy the contrasting demands of an international marketplace.[43]

In response, perhaps, to sympathy for labour activism among many of its intended audiences, the film sees a reversion to the politicised perspective of Gaskell's novel.[44] It also rejects Boucicault's famous telegraph scene, perhaps because the telegraph no longer represented a significant novelty. In an apparent reversion to the plot of the novel, Jane now travels to the dockside where she chases a boat carrying Johnny, and Jem's alibi, away. In this version, however, she is accompanied by the now popular figure of Moneypenny, derived from the play. Significantly, the two chase after the massive steamship, 'Columbia', in a hired tugboat.[45] This action enables the film to further exploit widespread popular coverage concerning the construction of spectacular super-liners in the early 1910s. It also enables Herbert Brenon, who now played the linchpin role of Johnny Reilly, to dive over sixty feet from the deck of the Columbia, safely carrying the alibi back to dry land (a contribution well publicised in the press). This spectacular stunt replaces Boucicault's appearance in the telegraph scene as the turning point of the film's narrative and is cleverly cross-cut with the action of the courtroom, where Jem is awaiting his death sentence. The cross-cut action is resolved in the final scene, when Johnny Reilly arrives in the nick of time at the courtroom, and breathlessly delivers his alibi.

In large part, the selection of material from the stage and the novel is geared toward the most efficient exploitation of the capacities of the screen. The telegraph scene – a neat melodramatic trick device, which foregrounded the roles of Moneypenny and Jane – would have been problematic without sound, and might simply have reminded audiences of the fixed tableau dramatisations that had characterised one-reelers in previous years. Instead, the screen is occupied with dramatic and spectacular action continually intercut with images of Jem's trial in progress. The film thus participated in the development of the uniquely cinematic form of narration that would ultimately become definitive of the American cinema. However, *The Long Strike* was also careful to duplicate many of the attractions associated with earlier versions of the text. In addition to the reappearance of Moneypenny, the centrality of a sensation scene, and the likely cultivation of working class audiences interested in its representation of industrial action, the film also solicited the attention of the middle-class audiences that were increasingly drawn to the photoplay within the new picture theatres. A two-page March 1913 advertisement for *The Long Strike* in a British trade journal does not include any reference to Gaskell, or indeed to Brenon, but prominently announces that the film was 'Adapted from the Famous Drama of Mr. Dion Boucicault' and that 'the entire production [is] worthy of its great and popular author.'[46] The association with Boucicault's theatre and with his model of an ideal audience remains relatively strong.

In fact, a great number of Boucicault adaptations had been produced from as early as 1903, with *The Shaughraun*, *The Octoroon*, and *The Colleen Bawn* particularly popular. A few days after the release of *The Long Strike*, the IMP company released their tenth feature – adapted this time from *Kathleen Mavourneen*, another perennial Boucicault favourite. This certainly speaks for Boucicault's popularity, which endured well into the twentieth century, but it also suggests that his model of nineteenth-century spectatorship for melodrama retained much of its currency in the 1910s. IMP's *The Long Strike* certainly participated in the gleeful presentation of sensational attractions for the consumption of modern audiences. But it did so within an institutional context with which audiences had a long and comfortable relationship. Their familiarity with institutional frameworks associated with the legitimate and variety theatres thus contributed to the consolidation of an increasingly centralised and powerful model of institutional cinema. Above all, productions such as *The Long Strike* were interpreted, as in nineteenth-century theatre, by audiences that demonstrated a knowing and discriminating attitude to their own spectatorship. In a limited but important sense, the cinema thus opened up a Benjaminian democratic space, in which spectators were enabled to apply their own expertise and thus find a reflection of their own knowledge within the film.

We can identify within Brenon's film, as in all previous versions of *The Long Strike*, the existence of a wide range of attractions embedded in a melodramatic narrative. Once again, audiences witnessed the spectacular display of the latest technological wonders in a manner that fully exploited the representational capacities of the medium. The film thus fully realised one version of the modernity thesis, demonstrating that in one key respect, cinema is like modernity. However, I would add, that as in the entire history of the text of *The Long Strike*, it is like modernity in much more than its sensational impact on spectators. Each version of the text fully demonstrates the capacity of successful competitive institutions like the Lyceum theatre or the IMP Company to predict the demands of its knowing and sophisticated audiences. If we are to expose both the institutional and the human dimensions of the early twentieth-century entertainment industry, we must keep sight of this idea. By the end of the nineteenth century, distractive entertainments were mostly produced by institutions that required cultural continuity and economic security and that developed systematic routines of production, exhibition, and reception in order to achieve it. Acknowledging this fact reminds us that popular entertainments around the turn of the twentieth century represent the adaptation of long standard institutional practices to modern technologies, environments, and cultures. Within this process, fragmentation, distraction, and sensation were knowingly played out by entertainment institutions and their audiences.

Notes

1. Ben Singer, *Melodrama and Modernity: Early Sensational Cinema and its Contexts* (New York: Columbia University, 2001): 294.
2. Singer: 128.
3. For analysis of this movement, see Tom Gunning, 'Film History and Film Analysis: The Individual Film in the Course of Time', *Wide Angle* 12:3 (1990): 4–19.
4. Edgar Allan Poe, 'The Man of the Crowd,' in *Selected Writings*, ed. David Galloway (Harmondsworth: Penguin, 1967): 179–188; Charles Baudelaire, 'The Painter of Modern Life' in *The Painter of Modern Life and Other Essays*, trans. and ed. Jonathan Mayne (London: Phaidon, 1964): 1–40; Georg Simmel, 'The Metropolis and Mental Life,' in *Sociology of Georg Simmel*, trans. and ed. Kurt H. Wolff (London: Collier-Macmillan, 1950): 409–424; Walter Benjamin, *Charles Baudelaire: A Lyric Poet in the Age of High Capitalism*, trans. by Harry Zohn (London: Verso, 1983); Walter Benjamin, 'The Work of Art in the Age of Mechanical Reproduction,' in *Illuminations*, trans. by Harry Zohn (New York: Schocken, 1969): 219–253.
5. Simmel: 410.
6. Lynne Kirby, 'Male Hysteria and Early Cinema,' *Camera Obscura* 17 (1988): 113.
7. Giuliano Bruno, 'Site-Seeing: Architecture and the Moving Image,' *Wide Angle* 19:4 (1997): 17.
8. Singer: 102.
9. Anthony Giddens, *Modernity and Self-Identity: Self and Society in the Late Modern Age* (Stanford, CA: Stanford University Press, 1991): 27.
10. For further key texts, see, Anthony Giddens, *The Constitution of Society: Outline of the Theory of Structuration* (Cambridge: Polity Press, 1984); and *The Consequences of Modernity* (Cambridge: Polity Press 1990).
11. See, for an example of institutionally-based research, Richard Brown and Barry Anthony's book length account of documentation pertaining to the British Mutoscope and Biograph Company: *A Victorian Film Enterprise: The History of the British Mutoscope and Biograph Company, 1897–1915* (Trowbridge: Flicks Books, 1999).
12. In the British context, see especially, Gustave Garcia, *The Actor's Art: A Practical Treatise on Stage Declamation, Public Speaking and Deportment* (London: T. Pettitt, 1882).
13. See Giddens (1991): 133–143.
14. See, for example: Peter Bailey, *Popular Culture and Performance in the Victorian City* (Cambridge: Cambridge University Press, 1998): 128–150; Joe Kember, '"It was not the show, it was the tale that you told": Film Lecturing and Showmanship on the British Fairground', in Simon Popple and Vanessa Toulmin (eds), *Visual Delights: Essays on the Popular and Projected Image in the 19th Century* (Trowbridge: Flicks Books, 2000): 56–64; and Katherine Newey, 'Melodrama and Metatheatre: Theatricality in the nineteenth-century theatre', *Journal of Dramatic Theory and Criticism* (Spring 1997): 85.
15. Charles Lamb Kenney, *The Life and Career of Dion Boucicault* (New York: [np], 1883).
16. Richard Fawkes, *Dion Boucicault: A Biography* (London: Quartet, 1979).
17. For Boucicault on the prevalence of 'stolen' French plays through the 1840s and 50s, see 'Early Days of a Dramatist,' in *The North American Review* 148 (May 1889): 591.
18. On the 1855 Dramatic Author's Bill see Richard Fawkes, *Dion Boucicault: A Biography* (London: Quartet, 1979), pp . 91–92.

19. Boucicault, 'Leaves from a Dramatist's Diary', *The North American Review* 149 (August 1889): 228.
20. Michael R. Booth, *English Melodrama* (London: Herbert Jenkins, 1965): 166
21. Boucicault (August 1889): 232.
22. Boucicault (August 1889): 233.
23. For an overview of Boucicault's theories on contemporary drama see, Cleveland Harrison, 'Boucicault's Formula: Illusion Equals Pleasure,' *Educational Theatre Journal*, 21 (1969): 299–309.
    Particularly relevant among Boucicault's numerous articles on this are 'The Decline of the Drama,' *North American Review* 125 (September 1877): 235–245; 'The Art of Dramatic Composition,' *North American Review* 126 (January 1878): 40–52; 'Mutilations of Shakespeare: The Poet Interviewed,' *North American Review* 148 (February 1889): 266–268; 'Theatres, Halls, and Audiences,' *North American Review* 149 (October 1889): 429–436; and 'The Future American Drama' *Arena* 2 (November 1890): 641–652.
24. Boucicault (September 1877): 239.
25. Boucicault (August 1889): 234.
26. *Hunted Down* or *The Two Lives of Mary Leigh*, prompt copy (1866). This copy available at the Boucicault archive at the University of South Florida (USF), Tampa.
27. *The Flying Scud* or *A Four-Legged Fortune*, prompt copy (1866), in the archive at USF. For brief descriptions of the play, see G.C. Odell, *Annals of the New York Stage*, 14 vols. (NY: Columbia University, 1936) 8: 134; and Booth: 168.
28. At USF there are two prompt copies, one from the 1866 production at the Lyceum and the other from an 1869 production at the Adelphi. There are also fragments of a manuscript entitled *Mary Barton; a Drama in Four Acts*, and a translation, dated 1873, entitled *La Greve de Manchester* signed by Eugene Nu.
29. Richard D. Altick, 'Dion Boucicault Stages *Mary Barton*', *Nineteenth-Century Fiction* 14: 2 (September 1959).
30. *Athenaeum* 2030 (22 September 1866): 376–377.
31. *The Times*, (17 September 1866): 8.
32. For detailed work on the alterations and similarities to Gaskell's plot, see Altick (1959).
33. *Athenaeum* 2030 (22 September 1866): 376.
34. Newey: 85.
35. *The Times*, (17 September 1866): 8.
36. J.H. Stoddart, *Recollections of a Player* (NY: The Century Co., 1902): 145.
37. Stoddart: 145.
38. Odell, vol. 8: 140.
39. On 25 November 1890, Stoddart was even called upon to play the telegraph scene at the benefit for Boucicault's widow, Agnes Robertson Boucicault. A famous actress in her own right, she had played Jane Learoyd in the Lyceum production alongside her husband.
40. Odell, vol. 14: 763.
41. Albert F. McLean, 'US Vaudeville and the Urban Comics,' *Theatre Quarterly* 1:4 (October–December 1971): 48.
42. At the National Film Archive, London. This German copy, titled *Freund in der Nott* is the only extant version and 730 feet of the reported 2029 are all that remain of it.
43. Jack Lodge, 'The Career of Herbert Brenon', *Griffithiana* 57–58 (October 1996): 7–9.
44. On this aspect of the film, see Steven J. Ross, *Working Class Hollywood: Silent Film and the Shaping of Class in America* (Princeton, NJ: Princeton University Press, 1998).
45. *Kinematograph Monthly Film Record* 12 (April 1913): 59–60.
46. *Bioscope* 18: 20 (March 1913): 880–881.

5

Trilby's Community of Sensation

Kaveh Askari

While early cinema scholars have shown longstanding interest in the technological and narrative aspects of film history, writing on cinema's pictorial history has been more scattered. Recent attention to the cross-medial connections in this period suggests a timely need for sustained consideration of cinema's relationship with the pictorial. This essay treats the abundance of visual material that followed the 1894 publication of George du Maurier's *Trilby* as a case study in this pictorial history.[1] The initial publication of the story – in which the mesmerist Svengali kidnaps Trilby, a young Latin Quarter artist's model, and forces her to become a singer under his musical and mesmeric influence – started a mania for material referencing the novel and its illustrations, including plays, paintings, dances, films, and items for more literal consumption such as Trilby sausages and ice cream in the shape of her foot.[2] The publicly circulated still and moving images of what was quickly termed Trilbymania raise a number of questions central to a discussion of the popular and projected image in this period. This study focuses on the technological acceleration of pictorialist intermediation during the turn of the twentieth century. It addresses the implications of this process for a conception of media aesthetics that places 1910s cinema in constellation with the media environment of the 1890s. In other words, how does the media environment of the earlier generation provide insight on pictorialist cinema in the 1910s? These arguments about cinema and media history will be used to frame a cultural analysis of the story's thematization of mesmerism.

A coherent intermedial aesthetic developed in the 1890s and flourished in the pictorialist cinema of the teens. It emerged out of the intersections between pictorialist practices rooted in the early nineteenth century and the production and distribution of new media at the turn of the twentieth century. Nineteenth-century pictorialism, although interpreted differently by historians of painting, theatre, and cinema, is characterized by a dynamic of exchange between each of these media and a sense of the ease of translatability from one medium into another.[3] *Tableaux vivants* replicated famous paintings, and theatre lobby paintings replicated the stage tableaux performed inside. In the theatre, character types evolved out of the interplay between pictorial representations of gestures and performers who con-

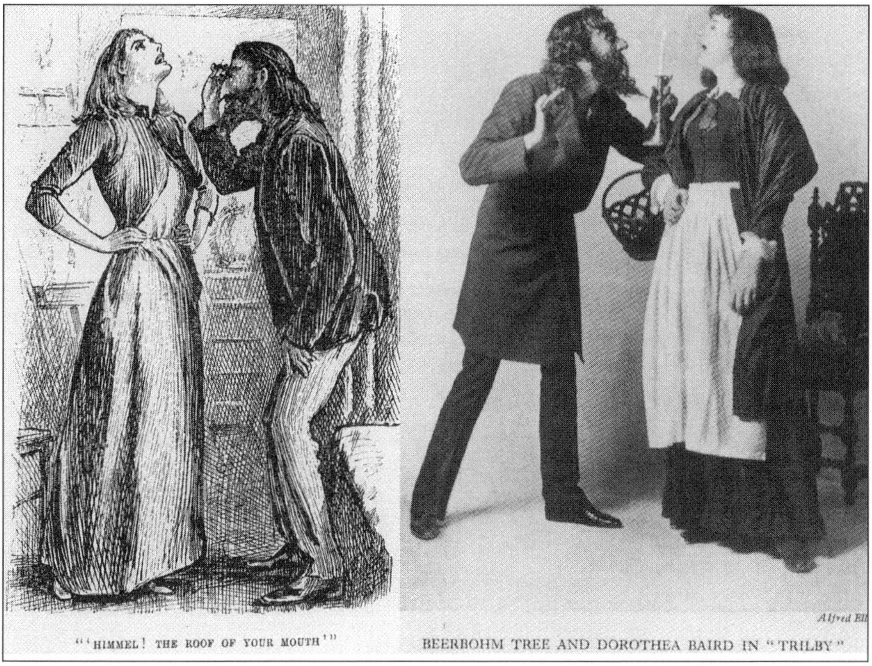

Fig. 1. DuMaurier's illustration (Harper, 1894) quoted in a publicity photograph for Tree's production. [Publicity photograph courtesy of the New York Public Library.]

ceived of their bodies in terms of such images. In this ubiquitous nineteenth century practice of citing a single theme across a variety of media, the pictorialist aesthetic became the means by which one medium could adopt the subject of another. Instead of discussing the changes that new technologies brought to this conception, I want to think about the way film and photography brought a new vitality to the translatability of pictures. Technical developments, such as the half-tone process, instantaneous photography, and film, initially used to supplement established pictorial practices, reframed these older aesthetic modes in the new media environment. Far from being expelled at the turn of the twentieth century as an archaic aesthetic mode, pictorialism engages aesthetic issues specific to modern mass media by virtue of its recontextualization. I will position this scene of interaction in the earlier generation in relation to pictorialism in 1910s cinema by way of Maurice Tourneur's adaptation of *Trilby* (1915). The broader historical narrative is reflected in the concrete relationship between the film and the Trilbymania of the 1890s.

The *Trilby* phenomenon has been taken up by cultural historians both because it is a watershed moment in the history of mass marketing and the best seller system, and for the way its themes of influence and control intersect with this history. My consideration of the Trilby phenomenon in relation to the history of cinema and related media focuses on the pictorial dimension of this remarkable case study. The cultural discourse of mesmerism popularized by *Trilby* depends on the heterogeneity of media used to propagate this discourse. Here, media history can serve as a corrective to cultural studies. The conspicuous juxtaposition of mesmeric influence

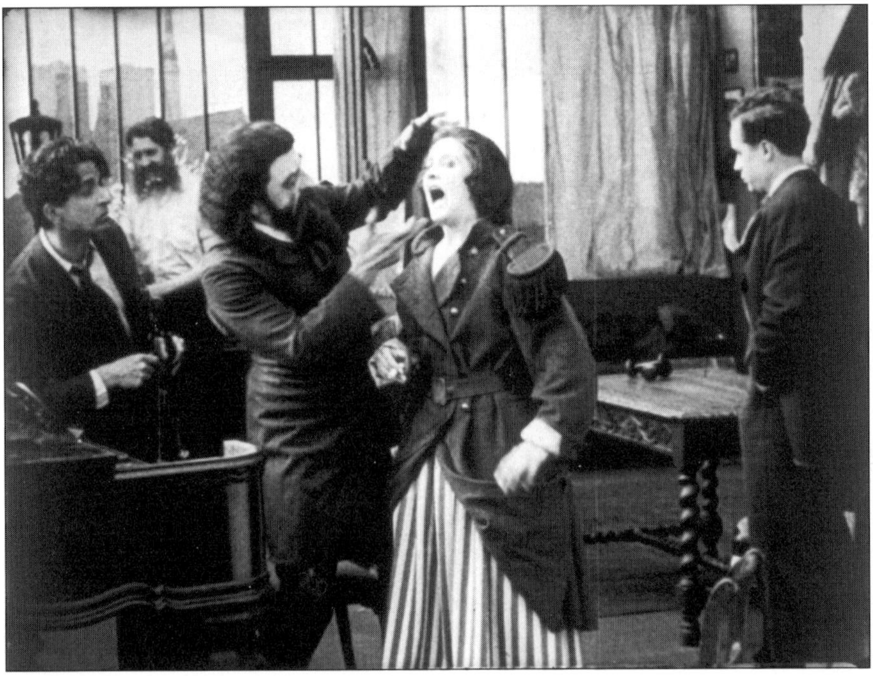

Fig. 2. Tourneur's version of the posture in Trilby *(Equitable-World, 1915). [Frame enlargement courtesy of the George Eastman House.]*

and pictorial transformation in the endless adaptations of *Trilby* cannot be understood apart from a broader history of intersecting media practices at the turn of the twentieth century.

Trilby exemplifies the integration of pictorial traditions with new media and mass visual culture by virtue of its origins in illustrated character types and its later permutations across media. The characters in Du Maurier's novel were derived from types he had developed over a twenty-year career as a satirical illustrator for *Punch*. The illustrations of Svengali, for example, are conglomerates of du Maurier's anti-Semitic caricatures and his recurring German pianist. As *Trilby* quickly became the most popular novel of the so-called golden age of novel illustration, it provoked an extensive debate about the relation between this popularity and du Maurier's profession as an illustrator. [4] In a review for *The Academy*, Frederick Wedmore rehearses some of these themes:

> When a finely capable draughtsman, and a draughtsman in vogue, happens to be, for the nonce, an author, then the result of his illustrations may be to bring home to folk easily, even more easily than his written chapters will do, the characters and scenes of the tale.[5]

At a time when the illustrated novel was commonplace, du Maurier's unique position as a draughtsman-turned-celebrated-author drew attention to the relation between text and image and its effect on the reading public. The critical attention to his illustrations was elaborated in the visual legacy of his characters and scenes.

One could say that the reception of *Trilby*, especially in North America, was a pictorial reception as much as a discursive one. Trilby's public presence took the form of a network of interrelated pictures. The illustrated journals printed stills from the plays as well as cartoons spoofing them. Several films were made from the story within a few years of its initial publication.[6] As its images and plot situations became part of the vernacular, the number of amateur and professional burlesques and adaptations increased exponentially. Gestures, poses, and styles of dress became famous through continual translation across visual media and extended into amateur fan culture, as evidenced by newspaper accounts of drawing room *tableau vivant* performances based on the illustrations.[7] Numerous copyright battles were fought over cartoons, photographs, and unofficial adaptations of the story. Popular journals often seemed ambivalent or even confused about the dividing line between good publicity and copyright infringement. '"Trilby' representations have broken out in all sorts of strange places,' begins one article about the phenomenon,

> At the Eden Musée, New York, Miss Ganthony has been restrained from impersonating du Maurier's heroine; and at 'The Greatest Show on Earth', Miss Marie Meers, who has not been restrained, appears nightly in costume, riding bareback (not barefoot) around the tan-bark to the snapping of ringmaster Svengali's whip.[8]

Given the confused state of the legal situation surrounding the story, it is unclear whether this article is reporting on the regulation of the adaptations or offering them free publicity. Legal rights became increasingly difficult to defend in proportion to the unprecedented volume and variety of pictorial references.[9] The same translatability that lent itself so well to mass distribution of the novel rendered these ubiquitous images difficult to control.

Theatrical adaptations were the major force in popularizing the story, but these in turn drew heavily from the tradition of *tableau vivant* performances adapted from the novel. Such performances occasionally made it out of the drawing rooms, as was the case with painter Eric Pape's production of *Scenes and Songs from 'Trilby'*. On 9 February 1895, three months before the first New York production of Paul Potter's play, Pape threw this benefit performance for the New York Kindergarten Association; it was comprised of twelve tableaux accompanied by twelve songs.[10] Pape played Svengali's sidekick, Gecko, and cast his wife as the title character. Each scene appears to reproduce an illustration from the novel, as the titles in the programme match du Maurier's captions. The musical accompaniment was derived primarily from songs sung by Trilby throughout the novel. Each tableau follows the general chronology of the novel with the exception of the last, 'It was Trilby,' which was similarly singled out as the frontispiece for the original Harper's edition. The performance not only realized each of the dozen illustrations from the novel, but also took sequencing cues from the book's layout.[11]

By the end of 1895, Paul Potter's melodrama *Trilby* had become successful on both sides of the Atlantic. The two most famous character actors to play Svengali were Herbert Beerbohm Tree in London and Wilton Lackaye in New York. Most of the

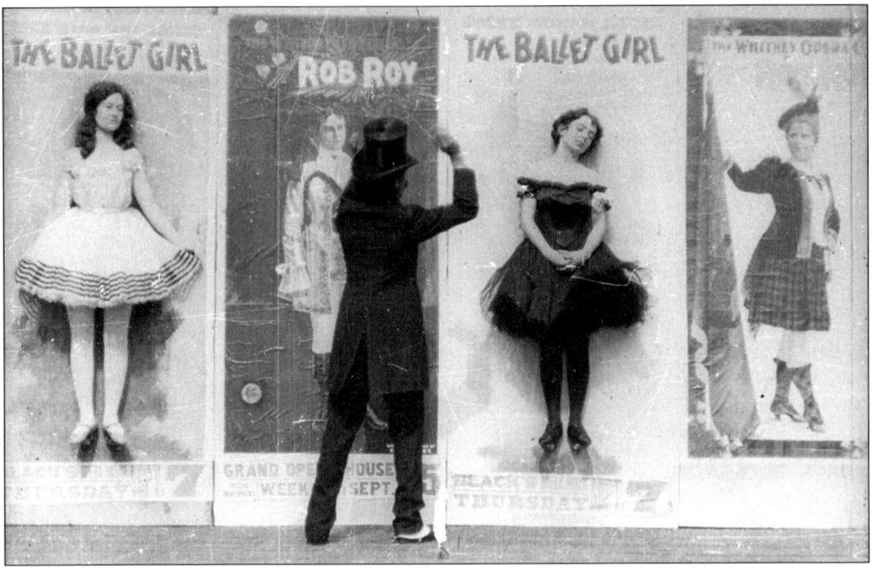

Fig. 3. The Poster Girls and the Hypnotist *(Biograph, 1899). [Courtesy of the Netherlands Film Museum.]*

film adaptations follow Potter's version of the story. Visually, however, *Trilby*'s stage and screen avatars must be understood in relation to the uncommonly broad range of pictorial quotations and adaptations. In many scenes in the stage productions, and in most of the publicity photographs, actors were arranged to correspond to the more familiar illustrations (Fig. 1). Audiences were thus acquainted with these scenes not only as pictures from the book, but also from photographs and live performances of living pictures. In a review of Tree's 1895 London production, Clement Scott contrasted the American enthusiasm for the play with a less optimistic take on the artistic merits of explicitly borrowing from other media. He criticizes Tree for casting actors based on their physical resemblance to the illustrations rather than for their talent:

> Anyone could be Trilby or Little Billee who could make up after a du Maurier picture. It is a mere question of posing. They are only artists models.'[12]

But reviewers were more enthusiastic about this borrowing in parodies of the play. A review of the most popular London parody, *A Model Trilby, or a Day or Two after du Maurier*, pokes fun at the influence of the illustrations:

> Mr. Rob Harwood is a fine Svengali, hardly to be distinguished from the original at some times ... As to Miss Kate Culter [Trilby], she is wonderfully like the pictures, albeit smaller in stature – because, as she explains, 'the part has been cut down'.[13]

Pictorial puns like Culter's, which can be found throughout the many burlesques of the story, show how keenly aware performers were of the way their characters emerged from this brief but promiscuous pictorial history.[14] The rapid creation of these pictorial characters on such a large, public scale was due to the ability of the illustrated press to accelerate older processes of pictorial translation.

Just as Trilbymania exemplifies how modern visual media reframed the aesthetic stakes of pictorialist translatability in the 1890s, Maurice Tourneur's version of *Trilby* (Equitable 1915) works as a parallel instance from the following generation. It allows one to extend the questions of this case study into the pictorialist cinema of the 1910s. Tourneur was publicly recognized as one of cinema's main heirs to the fine arts pictorial tradition. Articles in trade and fan journals often mention his early work as a novel illustrator, as an assistant to Auguste Rodin and Pierre Puvis de Chavannes, and as a stage manager before he began making films for Éclair in 1912.[15] It was this type of publicity that helped mark his combination of European and American styles of filmmaking as sophisticated and cosmopolitan and that gave legitimacy to Tourneur's systematic use of pictorialist devices such as arched framing, precision layered staging, and the framing of action with strong foregrounds. Through these devices, visual themes are developed across the director's films, building on each other through repetition and variation. His production of *Trilby* marks his first systematic use of these devices as well as his first adaptation of a major illustrated novel. Throughout the next decade, Tourneur would become known for these signature pictorial devices and for his illustrated novel adaptations.

When Tourneur adapted Potter's play, the story was already receiving interest in excess of the annual revivals. *Trilby* (1915) draws heavily from the culture of citation surrounding the publication of the novel. Tourneur's film, more than simply including elements of the popular iconography associated with the story, pointedly thematizes *Trilby*'s cross-medial genealogy. The relation to graphic illustration, to changing modes of address, and to performance practices such as the *tableau vivant* is explicit. Several of the intertitles are verbatim quotations not from the text of the novel but from captions of the illustrations. This quotation of captions suggests the film's affinity both with the graphic illustration in the book and with the many live recreations of these scenes also using the captions as titles. Several of the famous poses are also referenced, but not as single shot quotations. They are worked in dynamically in long scenes staged in depth. The pose in which Billie, Svengali, and the Laird lock arms is replicated with a brief pause in a longer scene motivated by different events than those in the story's illustration 'Tit for Tat'.[16] The same is true of the pose, 'Himmel! The Roof of Your Mouth,' in which Svengali conducts a physiognomic evaluation of Trilby's potential as a singer (Fig. 2).[17] These explicit citations, in addition to the broader sense of Tourneur's pictorial style, give a sense that he understood contemporary cinema as the hub of a network of pictorial media rather than as an isolated and contained medium.[18]

Like other pictoralist films of the teens, Tourneur's film suggests an aesthetic identity of 1910s cinema based in the voluminous record of interchanges between media. If, in the preceding period of film history, the cinematograph's use in existing media practices (*tableaux vivants*, magic lantern performances, and vaudeville acts) precluded the emergence of cinema as a singular social, cultural, and aesthetic apparatus, the cohesive aesthetic identity of many 1910s films drew precisely from these divergent roots.[19] Pictorialist directors did not reject these disparate uses of an adaptable device; on the contrary, this adaptability crystallized the aesthetic identity of pictorialist cinema in the 1910s. It was cinema not in spite of but by way of its intermediality. Tourneur's *Trilby* provides a film-specific example of the phenomenon evident in earlier *Trilby* phenomena, whereby pictorialism's intermedial dimension or ease of translation comes to facilitate the circulation of pictures by new technologies. This increased circulation of pictorialist motifs renders the mass media in which they are translated conspicuous. The remainder of this paper will address, through an analysis of visual examples from the1890s and 1910s, how the staging of mesmeric influence registers this conspicuous nature of modern pictorialism.

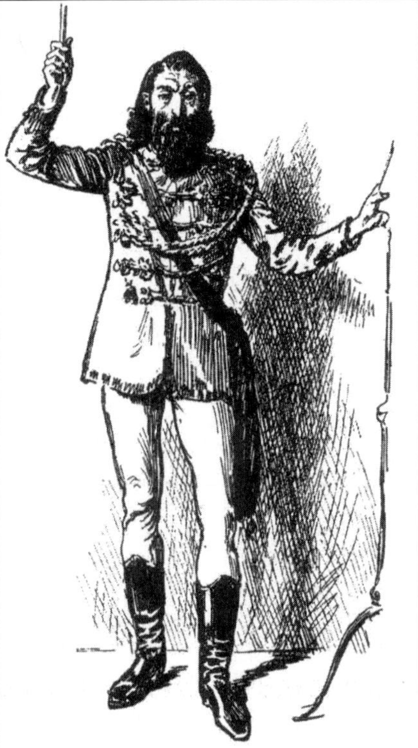

"OUT OF THE MYSTERIOUS EAST"

Fig. 4. DuMaurier's illustration of the mesmerizing photograph in Trilby *(Harper, 1894).*

With the popularity of *Trilby* came a renewed attention to the mesmerism practiced in the 1850s, before its energies were channeled into the spiritualist movement and clinical hypnotism.[20] Unlike later practitioners, Mesmerists believed in the existence of an intangible fluid, similar to ether or Galvanic fluid, which was able to pass between bodies and allow people to affect or influence each other's health, mental state, and behavior. The idea of such an interpersonal fluid and its promise of collective identity had helped ground political radicalism since the early years of the French Revolution. Mesmerism's anti-establishment vitalism enabled what Robert Darnton calls:

> The curious combination of scientific and political extremism that went into the making of several revolutionaries.[21]

A more irreverent writer might describe Franz Mesmer as the Wilhelm Reich of revolutionary France. His popular scientific theory of transpersonal influence was engaged from the start in a symbiotic relationship with more conventional modes of social and political persuasion. In later popular-scientific entertainments, mesmerist and subject would demonstrate this influence through the performance of a kind of sensory telepathy – a communication of feeling between bodies known as the 'community of sensation'.[22] If never fully provable as a science, Mesmerism was proven entertainment, and by the end of the nineteenth century it had fully migrated to the realm of popular spectacle. The combination of mesmeric influence and sensational fiction became commonplace in this period, with *Trilby* receiving the widest attention.[23] Both critics in the 1890s and contemporary scholars have offered similar readings of this combination in the various versions of *Trilby*. Playwright Augustus Thomas worried that the audience's thrill after each act of Potter's play was in excess of the play's merits. He suggested that this:

> Surplus of thrill was due to a relation between the mystic suggestion in the play and a keen and timely appetite in the public mind for all such suggestions consonant with a rapidly growing experience.[24]

Recent writing on the Trilby phenomenon has aligned this 'keen and timely appetite' with a broader historical narrative of changing modes of consumption, interpreting both the proliferation of Trilby-related goods and the entrancing character of modern sensational narratives within this framework.[25] This basic historical narrative is correct, but it overlooks how the Trilby phenomenon figures the sphere of influence between people as a sphere of influence between people and pictures. A media historical and aesthetic analysis of *Trilby*'s visual reception reveals how traditional pictorialist practices were combined with new media tricks to suggest a type of mesmeric influence specific to the media environment of the period.

The most striking consistency across the burlesques, brief citations, and full adaptations is the way they combine mesmeric absorption and influence with the production of a picture or its translation from one medium to another. In a significant number of performances Trilby and others freeze into pictures under mesmeric influence, while pictures in turn come to life. In a burlesque of the story called *Thrilby*, performed at the Garrick Theatre in New York in 1895, the mesmerist 'Spaghetti' uses his influence to freeze the characters into a series of *tableaux*.[26] In the 1897 vaudeville sketch 'Fun in an Artist's Studio,' a disguised Svengali uses his power to transform the artworks in the studio. He points at a canvas to make it change into different paintings and then mesmerizes a statue of Trilby. The statue emerges from the pose and does the Trilby dance popularized by *A Model Trilby*.[27] A visual record of this barefoot dance can be seen in the film, *Ella Lola a la Trilby* (Edison 1898). The most visually concise example from the period of Trilbymania is *The Poster Girls and the Hypnotist* (Biograph 1899). In a variation of a trick common in early cinema, a man makes mesmeric passes over a couple of posters, causing the women posing as billboard images to step off of the wall and walk away with him (Fig. 3).[28] In these examples, mesmerism becomes a catalyst for visual tricks involving translation from one medium into another. This emphasis on pictorial mediation is too obvious to set aside: more familiar arguments that mesmerism figured changing modes of consumption cannot be disentangled from parallel developments in media history. Typical historical arguments have linked the theme of influence and the novel to the changes in consumption signaled by its popularity. But in the examples I have discussed, mesmerism becomes a catalyst for visual tricks involving translation from one medium into another. Attention to these examples initiates a consideration of media history and pictorialism that further illuminates cultural readings of *Trilby*.

If mesmeric subjects become transfixed as pictures or animated from posters, the mesmerist's influence is also figured pictorially. A variety of media are used to this end. In the novel, Svengali – after his own death – continues to exert his final, fatal influence over Trilby by way of a photographic likeness.[29] The caption accompanying du Maurier's illustration of the photograph reads 'out of the mysterious east' (Fig. 4). The modifications of this scene continually foreground the trope of the mesmerizing portrait, either for comic or dramatic emphasis. In *Thrilby*, as Spaghetti dies, he holds up a photograph of himself to the heroine in a parody of his

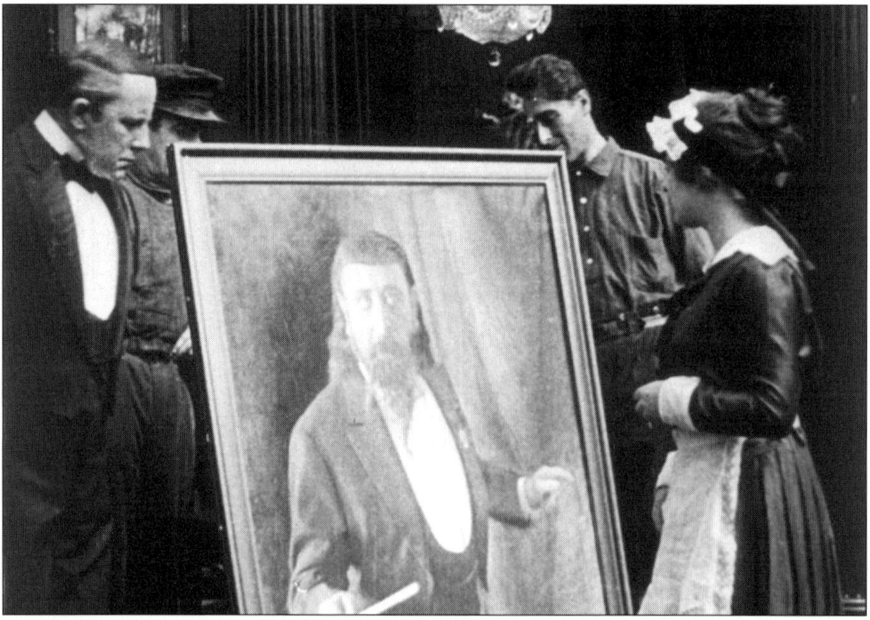

Fig. 5. The first appearance of Svengali's portrait. Frame enlargement from Trilby *(Equitable-World, 1915). [Courtesy of the George Eastman House.]*

ability to mesmerize her with a picture.[30] In Potter's stage version, the mesmerizing photograph became a painted portrait of the villain. Herbert Beerbohm Tree's London production of the play also gave special emphasis to the mesmerizing portrait. A reviewer for *The Critic* describes the final scene, in which 'the old spell is once more exerted by the disclosure of a terribly realistic portrait of Svengali (Mr Tree is, in fact, framed for it as a living picture)'.[31] In a reversal of the poster girls example, the mesmerist exerts his influence as a living picture. The use of the *tableau vivant*, more sensational on the stage than a painting, contributes to the 'terribly realistic' quality of the portrait. It solicits attention more directly and therefore emphatically conveys the theme of the painting's influence to the audience. Svengali could potentially emerge from the picture frame after his death, an anxiety more obviously manifest in the illustrated song 'That Hypnotizing Man' (Scott and Van Altena 1911). In an effect slide from this set Svengali is shown emerging from the mirror on Trilby's dressing table threatening to take hold of her.[32]

Tourneur extends this connection between mesmerism and pictorialism by using standard elements of pictorialist filmmaking style, such as vignetted shots and staging in front of multiple mirrors, to suggest mesmeric influence. The scenes following Svengali's abduction of Trilby are distinguished from the other scenes of the film by their arched vignettes. It is possible to read this emphasis on two-dimensional composition, common in Tourneur's films, as a temporal marker. While positioned in the narrative present of the film, the scenes were told in flashback in the novel. The way they are included in the film, however, suggests a stronger link to mesmeric influence, as they are preceded by an intertitle that reads, 'His thoughts were her thoughts, his wishes were her wishes, and thus, as in a dream, they journeyed into unknown lands.' The arched framings are placed in the context of Trilby's dreamlike journey in a mesmeric trance, and they are intercut with simultaneous scenes involving the other artists not under mesmeric control (where the vignettes are not used). The arches emphasize the pictorial composition of the scenes to set them apart from the scenes that do not take place in this temporally elliptical period of Trilby's trance-induced rise to fame. When the arches disappear after Trilby becomes famous, Tourneur uses precision staging in front of mirrors – a technique made possible by the single position of the camera lens – to show Svengali mesmerizing Trilby before her stage performance. He makes passes over her while she sits in front of a three-sided dressing mirror, and his reflection is multiplied by each of the panes surrounding Trilby. While this staging technique is common in films of the time, its association with mesmerism caused one reviewer, after praising Svengali's triple reflection, to imagine (unless a radically different version of this scene has been lost) a similar reflection in the final scene:

> Entering [Trilby's room], they find her dead, the reflection of a life-sized portrait of Svengali staring at them with baleful eyes out from the mirror before which Trilby had been standing.[33]

The association of precision staging with mesmeric influence, which stood out to this reviewer, is a cinematic parallel to the similar juxtapositions occurring during the Trilby boom of the 1890s.

In addition to the use of pictorialist style to suggest mesmeric influence, the citational character of Tourneur's film is used for similar purposes. The clearest examples of this are the dynamic references to Svengali's portrait. Beginning with the first shot, Tourneur frames the film with a reference to the mesmerizing portrait. The introductory vignette of Wilton Lackaye as Svengali is preceded by an intertitle that quotes the caption from the mesmerizing photograph 'out of the mysterious east,' drawn frontally by du Maurier and without its frame. This common filmic device introduces Lackaye in his famous role, but the quotation of the caption also calls attention to the relation between Lackaye's glance at the camera and Svengali's glance in the photograph.

When the portrait first appears in the middle of the film, it is accompanied by a shift in address. Servants bring the painting into the centre of the frame, place it on the floor, and discuss where to put it – all while Svengali's likeness stares into the camera (Fig. 5). This same painted stare would have been widely recognizable as the one that kills the heroine at the end of the story (Fig. 6). Tourneur gives the portrait its own brief scene in order to foreshadow its later deadly influence. This scene repeats the more direct address from the first shot of the film, only this time by way of a picture within the pictorially composed scene. The shift in address here, like Tree's *tableau vivant*, merges mesmeric influence with the pointed display of a picture. By presenting the portrait in this manner, Tourneur makes a medium-reflexive gesture similar to a newspaper advertisement for an earlier New York production of the play. The advertisement shows a caricature of the infamous portrait with the caption:

> Don't look at this too long, folks, unless you want to be hypnotized and made famous and sing 'Sweet Alice Ben Bolt' at the Paris Opera, because these mesmeric eyes belong to Svengali – Wilton Lackaye – in 'Trilby'.[34]

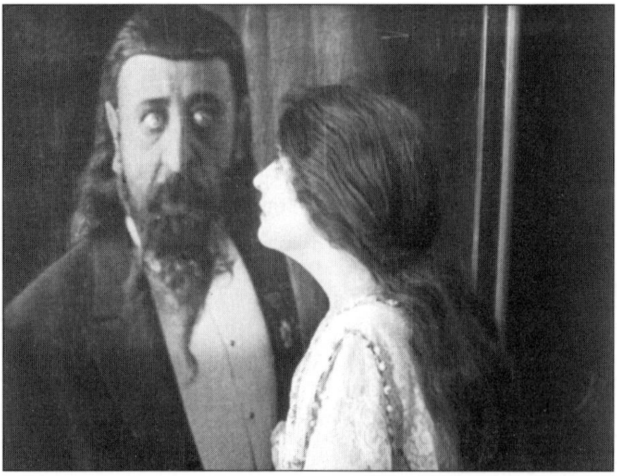

Fig. 6. Trilby is mesmerized by Svengali's portrait. Frame enlargement from Trilby *(Equitable-World, 1915). [Courtesy of the George Eastman House.]*

These parallel examples suggest a sphere of influence between people and pictures, but they more specifically describe a sphere of influence between the spectator and pictures on the page and the screen.

The broader parallel between Tourneur's pictorialist film style in the teens and the media environment of the 1890s is replicated in his staging of the community of sensation. In each of these examples I have discussed, the sensational effects, comic tricks, stylistic flourishes, and reflexive gestures adopt mesmeric influence as a catalyst. These pictorial fictions extend the collective sphere of influence described by Franz Mesmer and his followers to the pictures and gestures that are replicated across media. They show how questions of media history and aesthetics are essential to any association between the cultural metaphor of mesmerism in *Trilby* and changing modes of consumption. Mesmerism, an archaic theory of collective influence, is revitalized as a figure for intermediality at a time when pictorialism is reanimated by modern mass media. Even as we approach cinema's centrality to twentieth-century media aesthetics in terms of its association with modernity, we must not let the legacy and transformation of pictorialism be overshadowed by attention to mechanized representation and montage. We must also not let the preoccupation with the narrative movement in the 1910s obscure borrowings from other pictorial media practices so prevalent in this period. As the *Trilby* phenomenon demonstrates, the proliferation of new media and media experiments at the turn of the twentieth century gave the pictorialist tradition a new vitality. Pictorialist cinema reveals itself by reflecting this earlier constellation in a radically different period in film history.

Notes

1. The *Harper's Monthly* edition appeared from January to August 1894. The book was released by Harper and Brothers in September of that year, and a revised version appeared the following year.
2. See *Trilbyana: The Rise and Progress of a Popular Novel*, (New York: Critic Co., 1895): 26. The following description of the ice cream is from an undated clipping in the Billy Rose Theater collection of the New York Public Library: 'The congealed sweetness is packed into the molds, which are surrounded by broken ice until the hour of service, when a dainty foot, a model of a foot, the very apotheosis of a foot is turned onto the plate in all its virginal whiteness and plump seductiveness'.
3. For art-historical accounts of pictorialism see: Martin Meisel, *Realizations : Narrative, Pictorial, and Theatrical Arts in Nineteenth-Century England* (Princeton, N.J.: Princeton University Press, 1983); Anne Hollander, *Moving Pictures*, 1st ed. (New York: Knopf, 1989); Svetlana Alpers, *The Art of Describing : Dutch Art in the Seventeenth Century* (Chicago: University of Chicago Press,

1983); Michael Fried, *Absorption and Theatricality : Painting and Beholder in the Age of Diderot* (Berkeley: University of California Press, 1980). For discussions of pictorialism in the relation between theatre and cinema see: A. Nicholas Vardac, *Stage to Screen: Theatrical Method from Garrick to Griffith* (North Stratford: Ayer Company Publishers, 1949) and Ben Brewster and Lea Jacobs, *Theatre to Cinema : Stage Pictorialism and the Early Feature Film* (New York: Oxford University Press, 1997).

4. Roughly from the turn of the century through the mid-1910s. See Emily Jenkins, 'The Reading Public and the Illustrated Novel, 1890–1914', Dissertation, Columbia University, 1998.
5. Frederick Wedmore, '"Trilby" at the Haymarket', *The Academy* 48 (July/December 1895): 392–393.
6. Three Edison burlesques of the story were made in 1895: 'Trilby Hypnotic Scene', 'Trilby Death Scene', and 'Trilby Quartette'. The description for 'Trilby Death Scene' states that, 'The dramatis personae of this act are made up in exact imitation of the illustrations given in Du Maurier's book'. In Charles Musser, *Edison Motion Pictures, 1890–1900 : An Annotated Filmography* (Gemona, Italy: Le Giornate del Cinema Muto; Smithsonian Institution Press, 1997). In November 1896 Biograph made a kiss film, 'Trilby and Little Billee' following the popularity of the play as well as the popularity of 'The May Irwin Kiss' made earlier that year. See Kemp R. Niver and Bebe Bergsten, *Biograph Bulletins, 1896–1908* (Los Angeles: Locare Research Group, 1971):12–19.
7. An undated clipping from the Billy Rose Theater Collection contains a photograph of a woman in the 'Wistful and Sweet' pose from the novel with the caption, 'Society girl posing as Trilby on a pedestal'. See also *Trilbyana*: 19.
8. Reprinted in *Trilbyana*: 21.
9. A cartoon from a clipping file at The Billy Rose Theater Collection shows A. M. Palmer, producer of Potter's *Trilby*, defending his Trilby on a platform against a line of imitation Trilbys of every shape and size. On one of their aprons is written, 'Try Trilby Flour'. On legal issues see also Emily Jenkins, 'Trilby: Fads, Photographers, and "over-Perfect Feet"', *Book History* 1.1 (1998): 241–244.
10. Programme from The Billy Rose Theater Collection.
11. On the relevance of the *tableau vivant* for pictorialist aesthetics see Martin Meisel's writing on 'realization', Meisel, *Realizations : Narrative, Pictorial, and Theatrical Arts in Nineteenth-Century England*: 29–37.
12. Clement Scott, *The Illustrated London News* (9 November 1895): 573. Thanks to Jon Burrows for bringing this review to my attention.
13. 'Theatres and Music Halls', *The Ludgate* 1 (January 1896): 336–337. This joke seems to have been common. It can also be found in William Muskerry, *Thillby: A Shocker in One Scene and Several Spasms* (London: Samuel French, 1896): 1–5. See also "Trilby' on the Stage', *The Critic* 24 (9 November 1895): 306. 'The characters drawn by the author in pen and pencil are embodied on the stage with striking success.'
14. This is not to suggest that certain stock gestures that became associated with the characters did not come from the personal acting styles of the of the more famous actors. For a detailed discussion of Herbert Beerbohm Tree's own additions to the Svengali character see, Jon Burrows, 'His Every Movement "Tells": Gesture, Character Acting and Sir Herbert Beerbohm Tree in *Trilby*', *L'uomo Visible: L'attore Dalle Origini De Cinema Alle Soqlie Del Cinema Moderno*, ed. Laura Vichi (Udine: Forum, 2002): 121–126.
15. 'Tourneur began life – the important part of life, that is – studying Art and spelling it with a capital A, in the Latin Quarter of Paris.' Dorothy Nutting, 'Monsieur Tourneur: Otherwise Accurately Called "the Poet of the Screen"', *Photoplay* (July 1918): 55–56, 119. Nutting goes on to describe his work with famous artists, his textile designs, and his book illustrations as contributing to his film style. See also 'Tourneur of Paris and Fort Lee: His Methods and His Artistic History', *Photoplay* 9.2 (January 1916): 139.
16. This arrangement was also used as a publicity still for Tree's stage production and in the film that was made from this production *Trilby* (London, 1914).
17. Page 73 of the original Harper edition.
18. Tourneur makes a polemical argument for this dependence on other media in a response to a conservative article by Charles E. Whitaker entitled, 'Movies Destroy Art'. 'Isn't the history of the

acting drama and the printed word that inspires it a voluminous record of interchanges? Didn't the great romancer take largely from Montaigne? Doesn't Montaigne freely confess his own appropriations from multiple sources?' Maurice Tourneur, 'Movies Create Art', *Harper's Weekly* (1916): 459.

19. See Andre Gaudreault, 'The Diversity of Cinematographic Connections in the Intermedial Context of the Turn of the 20th Century', *Visual Delights: Essays on the Popular and Projected Image in the 19th Century*, ed. Simon Popple and Vanessa Toulmin (Trowbridge: Flicks Books, 2000): 8–15. See also Tom Gunning, '"Animated Pictures": Tales of Cinema's Forgotten Future, after 100 Years of Films', *Reinventing Film Studies*, ed. Christine Gledhill and Linda Williams (London: Arnold, 2000).

20. Sections of James Braid's *Observations of Trance* (1850) were reprinted. Doctors would discuss the validity of the mesmerism in *Trilby*. DuMaurier's old friend published an account of their Paris days with a detailed section on their experiments with mesmerism. Felix Moscheles, *In Bohemia with Du Maurier Microform : The First of a Series of Reminiscences*, T.F. Unwin, London, 1896.

21. Robert Darnton, *Mesmerism and the End of the Enlightenment in France* (Cambridge, Mass.: Harvard University Press, 1968): 110–111.

22. See Alan Gauld, *A History of Hypnotism* (Cambridge ; New York: Cambridge University Press, 1992): 103, 148, 153, 235

23. The adaptations gave stronger emphasis to the sensational elements of the story than the novel. Mesmerism and the erotic sensationalism surrounding Trilby's bare feet and her posing in the 'altogether' took priority over du Maurier's comedy of manners. It has long been argued that these elements of modern sensational genres such as these are deeply related to other institutions of modernity such as the railroad. Interestingly in this case, the draw of *Trilby* affected railroad magnate Henry B. Plant so much that he decided to name a town in Florida, 'after the heroine of a story which has lately deeply moved me'. Horace Howard Furness, 'The Town of Trilby', *The Critic*: 767 (31 October 1896). Publicity for this town was accompanied by pictures captioned, 'The river near which Trilby lives', and Svengali Square, Trilby, Florida. Remsen Crawford, 'Trilby Lives in Florida', *Leslie's Weekly* (20 May 1897). Scott Black, the current mayor of Trilby Florida, told me that one of the explanations for the name in town lore is that Plant was in love with an actress who had played Trilby on the stage. While as Mr Black admits, the story is probably apocryphal, it stands as myth of origin with a familiar nineteenth-century plot.

24. Augustus Thomas, 'Something New in Plays', *The Sunday World* (12 May 1895).

25. '[I]t was as though the very reception of the book and the play manifested the hypnotic problem described in its plot – readers and viewers falling prey to the same captivation, disorientation and irrationality conveyed on the page', in Daniel Pick, *Svengali's Web : The Alien Enchanter in Modern Culture* (New Haven, CT: Yale University Press, 2000): 22. For a discussion of this effect of captivation in the sensation fiction genre, see Alison Winter, *Mesmerized : Powers of Mind in Victorian Britain* (Chicago: University of Chicago Press, 1998). For a discussion of *Trilby* in relation to consumer culture and the history of the illustrated novel see, Jenkins, 'Trilby: Fads, Photographers, and "over-Perfect Feet"'.

26. Joseph W. Herbert, *Thrilby*, play, New York.

27. Carelton S. King, 'Fun in an Artist's Studio: Musical Comedy Sketch', Vaudeville Sketch, Rare Books and Special Collections Division, Library of Congress, Washington D.C.

28. According to Daniel Pick in *Svengali's Web*, this film was also known as 'Svengali and the Posters'.

29. This association of imaging technologies with occult forces is not an isolated occurrence in du Maurier's novels. In *Peter Ibbetson*, he provides a remarkable analogy between the out-of-body travels of his characters and visual amusements such as the panorama and the camera obscura. George du Maurier, *Peter Ibbetson* (New York,: Harper & Brothers, 1891):118.

30. Herbert, *Thrilby*: 28.

31. '"Trilby" on the Stage': 307.

32. Scott & Van Altena, 'That Hypnotizing Man', 1911, slide 1911, sequence #10: Marnan collection, Minneapolis.

33. Charles Condon, 'Trilby', *Motography* 14.13 (25 September 1915): 639.

34. Undated clipping from a Scrapbook in the Billy Rose Theater Collection.

6

Dead Babies: Representations of Infant Mortality Before the First World War

Ine van Dooren and Amy Sargeant

Introduction

In spite of Oscar Wilde's notorious quip regarding the death of Little Nell in Charles Dickens' 1841 novel *The Old Curiosity Shop*, that 'one must have a heart of stone' to read it without laughing, the following essay will endeavour to treat both the author of the epigram and its subject with even-handed (albeit provisional) seriousness.[1] Wilde is, of course, directing his criticism as much to the style of Dickens' delivery as to the pathetic or bathetic content of the scene and Wilde, we know, was deeply attached to his own children, producing for them the delightfully fanciful tales collected in *The Happy Prince* (1888) and *A House of Pomegranates* (1891).[2] Populated as these are by matchgirls and beggars (the cold, the poor, the weak and the hungry), and dealing as they frequently do with love, understanding and compassion, they might themselves be thought to constitute 'Dead Babies' in precisely the contemporary idiomatic sense invoked by Martin Amis' eponymous novel.[3] Wilde's theoretical position represents a trend in literary criticism against emotional vulgarity which *may* have a wider currency: *The Bioscope* reviewer of Hepworth's 1914 adaptation notes that Nell is a 'singularly improbable child' and that some may 'find the film a trifle sickly sweet ... with [the novel's] Victorian sentimentality and somewhat mawkish emotionalism "ill-suited to the present virile age of emancipation and enterprise".'[4]

But, nevertheless, pathos as subject or as dramatic force (in an individual work or as an affective element within a programme of works) has proved persistently appealing to popular audiences.[5] Clarendon's 1907 *The Soldier's Wedding* (a companion piece to *The Sailor's Wedding*) advertsised itself as 'Romantic, Exciting, Pathetic and Humorous'. Sometimes this may be accounted for in direct adaptations – for instance, Dickens' own powerful rendition on stage of the deaths of

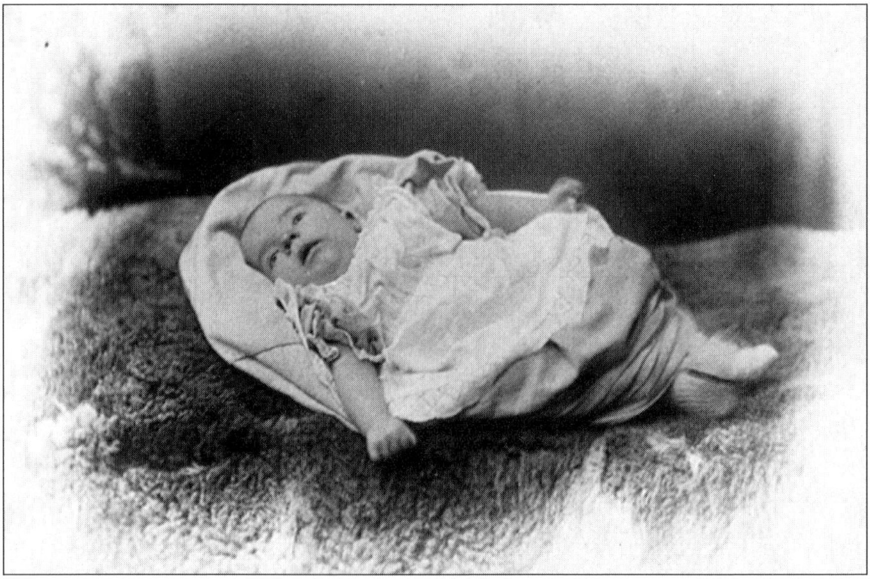

Fig. 1. Cabinet Card (image of dead baby taken from a Victorian cabinet card). [Simon Popple Collection, n.d.]

Little Nell and Paul Dombey, Frederick Fox Cooper's play *Master Humphrey's Clock* (named after the periodical in which Nell first appeared), Charlie Chaplin's imitation of Bransby Williams as grandfather Trent, various lantern tableaux condensing the stories to their most memorable episodes and various film versions (including that of Essanay which boldly deviates from the original by allowing Nell to live).[6] More significantly, it seems, dead children survive in a range of media and are variously affectively employed to aesthetic and didactic purpose.

A poem lovelier than a tree

For Edgar Allan Poe, as is well known, 'a poem lovelier than a tree' was the body of a dead young woman. For Poe, the image of Anna Lee is erotically charged (the drowned woman, her body unmarked by pain, disease or decay, as if merely sleeping, is passively available to him). There is also a sense in which, by dying in water, the figure is returned to her natural element.[7] Symbolically, disposal by burial places the body in a cycle of death and re-birth but the elemental relationship between the body and nature is doubled when that body is deemed closer to nature already – in other words, a body which has not been cultivated and conditioned into adulthood. Dickens has Nell laid out in a ruined chapel with flowers strewn across her pillow (the mise-en-scène dutifully followed by Hepworth) while Marie Corelli has little Jessamine, the country verger's daughter, wreathed by blossoms in her little coffin.[8] A popular ballad by George R. Sims, with an accompanying life-model lantern slide series produced in Holmfirth in the 1890s, has anther poor Nell venturing out in the snow in pursuit of a rose to satisfy her brother's last wish:

> In the summer you remember how the mission took us out
> To a great green lovely meadow, where we played and ran about,

> And the van that took us halted by a sweet bright patch of land,
> Where the fine red blossoms grew, dear, half as big as mother's hand.[9]

The organic affinity between the child and nature had been evoked also in plaster casts and carvings of limbs fringed with foliage, represented in still life [*nature morte*], as in those of the royal children at Osborne (1843), and in many photographs of children on their death-bed sometimes, as in the case of Lizzie Carpenter, impossibly forever embalmed and preserved in a miniature floral bower. Corelli and J.M. Barrie perpetuate the Romantic cult of the child as a being separate from the adult world. In *The Mighty Atom* (1896) and *Boy* (1900), the wreckage of children's lives is blamed on an over-zealous, positivist and atheist education. In J. M. Barrie's unrelentingly whimsical *The Little White Bird* (1902) it is said that at the age of eight (or thereabouts), when girls put up their hair and boys get addressed by their surnames, 'children fly away from the Gardens and never come back, When next you meet them they are ladies and gentlemen holding up their umbrellas to hail a hansom';[10] Peter (who, could he but get the hang of it, thinks life 'an awfully big adventure') and the lost boys (those who fell out of their prams when nanny was not looking) inhabit a Never Never land in which they neither grow up nor can return to the nursery, while the artist's daughter in *Dear Brutus* (1922) never grows up because she was never actually born.[11] The ageing of the child-woman in *Marie Rose* is arrested, yet she despairs at the loss of her own child when he continues to grow to manhood. However cloyingly sentimental Wilde may have thought such imagery in print, its lineage was as firmly rooted in pictures and, we would suggest, the popular imagination. In other words, just as we can refer Corelli's Jessamine to Wordsworth and Coleridge, Williamson's 1902 film *The Little Match-Seller* and The Sheffield Photographic Company's 1906 film *Lost in the Snow* can be referred to peasant girls depicted by Gainsborough and Constable or to similar figures which appear in the decorative arts.[12]

The picturesque citing of children in physical nature is sometimes transformed into a metaphysical association of the child with the supernatural: 'house swallows', says Barrie, 'are the spirits of little children who have died. They always build in the eaves of houses where they have lived when they were humans ... Peter loves them best of all the birds'.[13] In Mrs Henry Wood's *East Lynne* (like *The Old Curiosity Shop*, known from a much performed stage play and Harrison's 1902 episodic adaptation on film, as well as the 1861 source novel), little Willie reaches out to the angels who have come to greet him just before he collapses in his mother's arms. In Hans Christian Anderson's *The Little Match Girl* the child is carried off to heaven by her dead grandmother, the only person who had ever been kind to her, and in Williamson's adaptation an angel descends to gather up the child's spirit (Fig. 2). R.W. Paul's 1902 scenic illustration of a well-known song, *The Poor Orphan's Last Prayer*, follows a similar scenario. In this tradition of transfiguration, the death of Penelope Boothby, daughter of the famously suède Brooke Boothby, seems to be particularly indicative. In life she was painted by Reynolds, in death immortalised in Fuseli's *Apotheosis* and Thomas Banks' creamy marble monument in Ashbourne.[14] Penelope (who died, age six, in 1791), is shown sleeping on her side, her dress nonchalantly slipped from her shoulders, the fine folds of the muslin clinging to her legs and ruffling across her ankles. The event was significant less for the rarity of such a death (such deaths were common) but rather for the expression

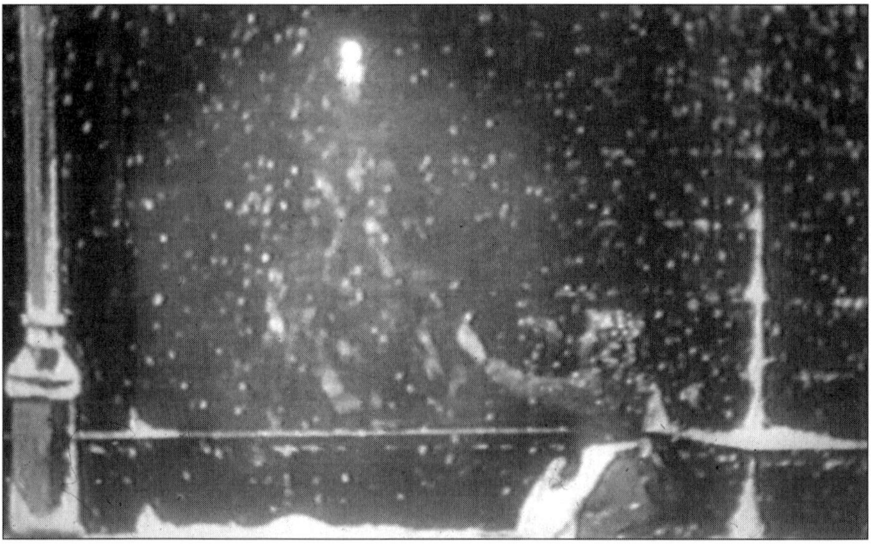

Fig. 2. Seasonal fare conjuring up a vision of a Chrsitmas tree in The Little Matchseller *(Williamson, 1902).*

of sentiment which it occasioned. Queen Charlotte is said to have broken into tears when she saw the statue exhibited: Penelope was, reads the monument's inscription 'in form and intellect the most exquisite/the unfortunate parents ventured their all/on this frail bark and the wreck was total'. The popular memory of Penelope proved persistent. In 1879, a girl attended a ball given by the *Graphic*, impersonating the Reynolds portrait. She was duly painted in this role by John Millais and the colour reproduction sold 600,000 copies.[15]

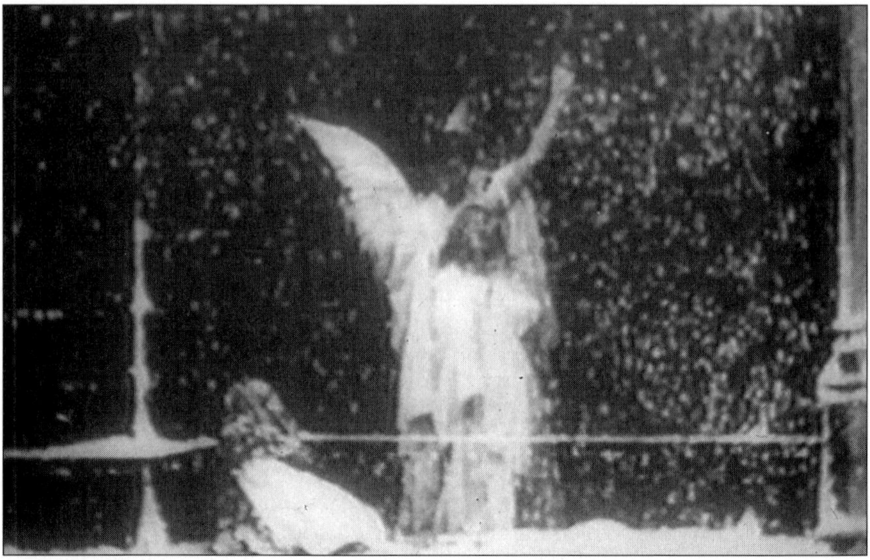

Fig. 2a. Death and apotheosis: Scene from The Little Matchseller *(Williamson, 1902).*

What use is a baby?

Life model lantern slides depicting pathetic subjects employ a narrative structured by clear contrasts and absolute opposites: Good and Bad; Temperance and Intemperance; Sin and Redemption. Often a transformation is effected from one state to another in the course of the story. Many of the early films advertised as 'pathetic' concern recurrent cross-genre plots featuring coincidence, retribution and reconciliation and a familiar cast of estranged lovers, poachers and gamekeepers, rich and poor, cops and robbers and intrepid family pets. Indeed, sometimes the interpretation of the scenario *as* pathetic would seem to call upon the recognition of a character (for instance, Warwick Trading Co.'s 1900 *The Death of Poor Joe*, in which a child crossing-sweeper dies in the snow, takes its name from a famous photograph posed by Oscar Rejlander after an episode in Dickens' *Bleak House*);[16] or of a story or its accompanying music (for instance, Paul's *The Poor Orphan's Last Prayer*, Harrison's 1902 *Little Jim* or Urban's 1907 *His Daughter's Voice*).[17] In her novel *Mary Barton* (1848), Mrs Gaskell describes the air to which The Oldham Weaver is sung as 'a kind of droning recitative, depending much on expression and feeling':

> To read it, it may, perhaps, seem humorous; but it is that humour
> Which is near akin to pathos, and to those who have seen such distress
> It describes it is a powerfully pathetic song.[18]

Lecturers accompanied slides with suitably forceful and emotional readings from popular stories, ballads, poems, hymns and plays. Programmes for Welsh-Pearson's 1921 *The Old Curiosity Shop* (like its Hepworth precursor, directed by the stage actor Thomas Bentley) suggested that Bourgault-Ducoudray's *Internment of Ophelia* (1877) be played alongside Nell's demise.

Sometimes an 'appropriate' response to a pathetic subject is cued by a work's seasonal setting or performance. In the lantern story *Christmas in Paradise*, Tommy, the ragged boy, lies dying yet 'brightly exclaiming, I'm comin'! What a contrast between the last Christmas wee Tommy spent in the Paradise below and the first he spent in the Paradise above!'[19] In Barrie's wartime play *A Kiss for Cinderella*, the cockney waif lies in a white street, silent in snow, succumbs to pneumonia and is taken to hospital by a policeman.[20] Hepworth's *Tempered with Mercy*, featuring a policeman who urges sympathy on a hard-hearted baker who seeks to prosecute a thieving child, was a Christmas release in 1909;[21] Clarendon's *The Water Babies, or the Little Chimney Sweep* (an adaptation of Charles Kingsley's 1863 children's novel) was released for Christmas 1907; Hepworth's *The Old Curiosity Shop* was announced in December 1913 with Cricks' and Martin's *The Motherless Waif* (featuring a drunkard father and another kindly policeman) was released in December 1909 while *A Child's Prayer* (in which a poor child's letter to Santa is blown up the chimney and down into the rich house next door) and Hepworth's *Little Meg and the Wonderful Lamp* (in which a rich couple save an orphan who has stolen a pantomime lantern were both released in December 1906.[22] Williamson's *The Little Match Seller* topically features a Christmas tree. These films are presented to the audience as exemplary exhortations to charity during the Christian season of goodwill and prompt resolve with the advent of the New Year: as Dickens' Tiny Tim (who did *not* die) observes, after Cratchett has pledged himself to total abstinence, 'Gawd bless us, Every One'.

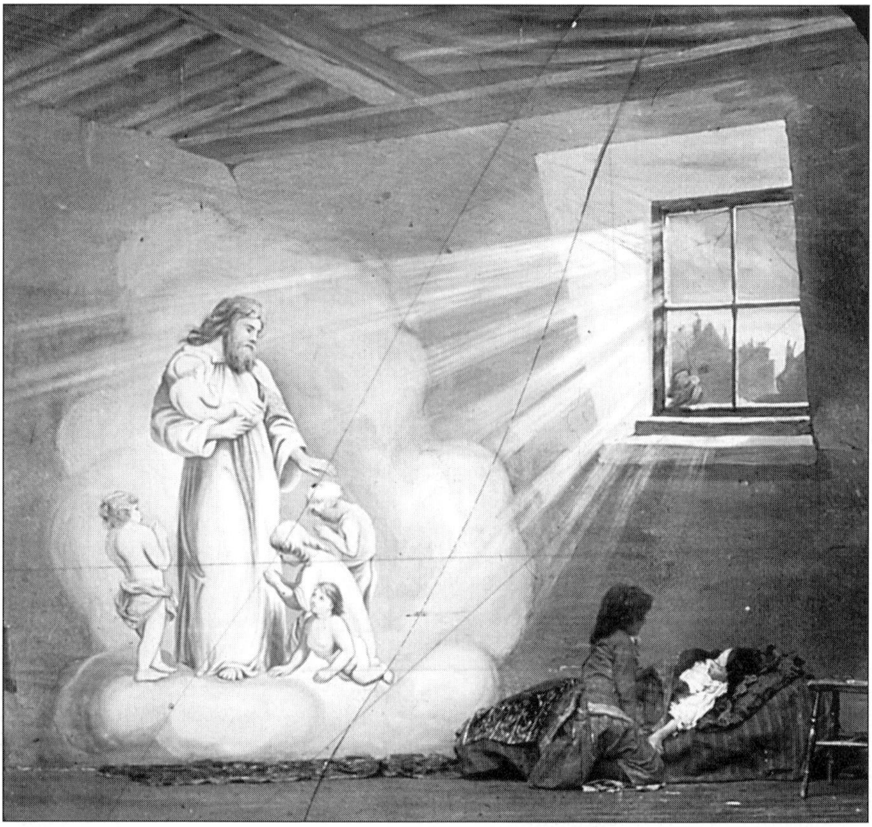

Fig. 3. Scene from Billy's Rose by George R. Sims (1847–1922), slide number 3. The ballad was reprinted and used in different ways by lantern slide producers. York & Son, a 10 slide series, who supplied the verse from the 'Dagonet reciter'.

The death of a child is often depicted as an exemplary, good death, relieved of the physical decay, moral dilemmas and emotional sorrow which is the burden of a full life's span.[23] It may even be seen as a welcome respite, with Jesus and the angels (as in Sims' *Billy's Rose*) beckoning to a comfortably domestic heaven beyond the grave. (Fig. 3) For the dying children it is a relief, a wish come true, a glorious reward, eternal happiness free from all care. In the words of a slide series:

> Let my sins be all forgiven;
> Bless the friends, I love so well;
> Take when I die in heaven;
> Happy there with thee to dwell.[24]

Children, wise beyond their years (like Penelope Boothby, Nell and Willie, Dickens' solemn Paul Dombey and Corelli's earnest Lionel Valliscourt) may be reconciled to the consequences of a fatal illness before their elders are ready for their loss (as in *East Lynne* and *Mary Barton*), precociously contradicting all protestations of resistance. Indeed, it was the function of many evangelical tracts to prepare children for an imminent departure (Figs. 4 and 5). In the lantern story *City Sparrows*, a

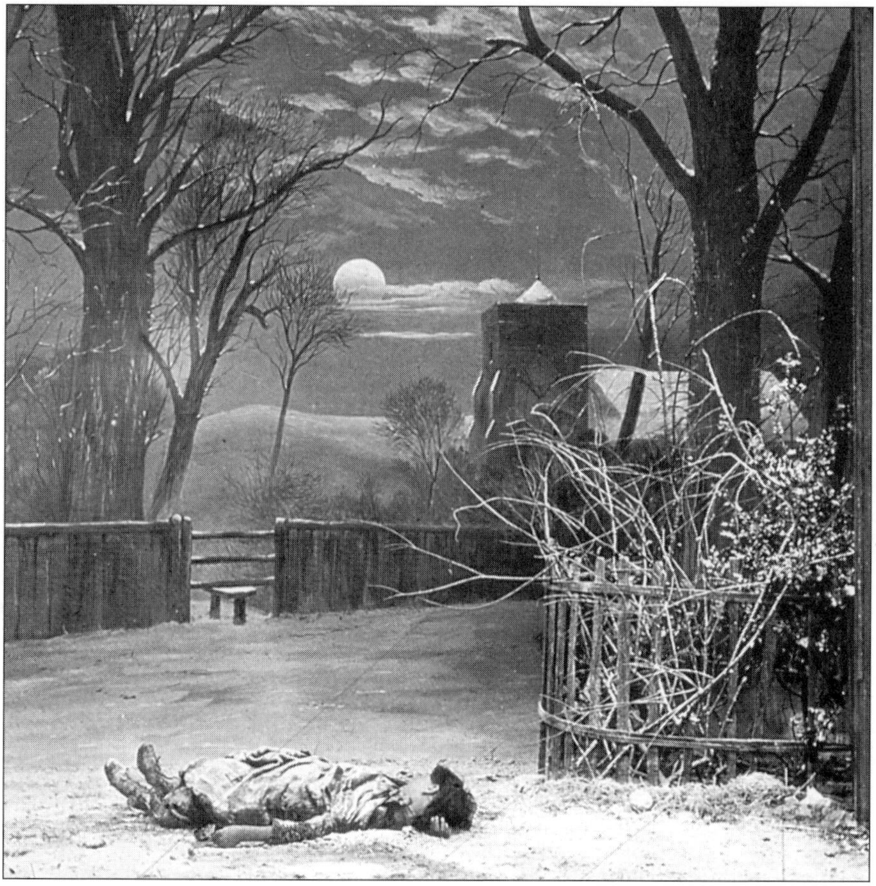

Fig. 4. Scene from Billy's Rose by George R. Sims (1847–1922), slide number 9. The ballad was reprinted and used in different ways by lantern slide producers. York & Son, a 10 slide series, who supplied the verse from the 'Dagonet reciter'.

feverish boy expresses himself already on the opening page: 'Oh, I wish I was dead, I wish I was dead!' and in *Left Alone*, the crippled boy Peter says to Sally: 'I get very weary of living, Sally! I think how peaceful and quiet I shall be in the churchyard with the daisies growing over my grave'.[25] In *Mary Barton*, a veritable catalogue of dead babbies and other clemming folk, Old Alice (simple, uncomplaining Alice) returns to childhood before she dies. 'Yo're mourning for me', she says to Mary, 'no need. I'm as happy as a child, whom the Lord is hushabying to my long sleep':

> Alice spoke and sang during her waking moments like the child she deemed herself but so happy with the dearly loved ones around her, with the scent of the heather and the song of wild birds hovering about her in her imagination … pure and good, true although so humble a Christian, nearing her desired heaven.[26]

However, there is nothing arbitrary about the positioning of a 'good' death in the

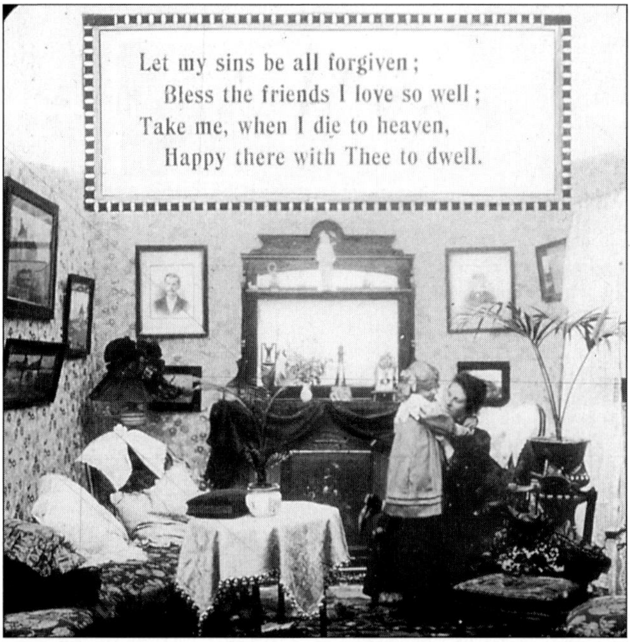

Fig. 5. Illustration from a Hymn slide. Many of these types of slides were produced for presentations in church meetings, Service of Songs, Sunday School etc. (The Hymn slide - see footnote 24.)

course of the novel; Alice survives for just long enough to know Jem cleared of murder and reunited with Mary; Willie in *East Lynne* dies once the dastardly Levinson has been convicted of murder in place of one wrongly accused. In the 1910 British and Colonial film *Two Little Shoes*, a man is driven to crime to provide food for his wife and child, but the infant nevertheless dies and the father is sent to prison with only a shoe by which to remember her. On release, he breaks into a house and finds the pair to the shoe and is thus re-united with his wife.[27] In Williamson's *Orphans* (1907), a boy is led into crime by bad company and burgles the house of his sister's benefactress; he recognises a locket belonging to their mother and 'with God's help' and the sister's good example he determines to reform. Cricks' and Sharp's *A Woman's Sacrifice* (1906) affords a reconciliation of a father and mother over 'the little peacemaker's' sick-bed whereas in Hepworth's 1907 *A Lovers' Quarrel*, a boy is despatched to return a lady's engagement ring to her fiancé, is run over by a motor car but re-unites the couple in hospital before dying. In other words, some sense or purpose results from these accidental or troublesome circumstances. In *The Motherless Waif* the death of the little match-girl brings about the drunkard's reform: 'in deep remorse, the father, with hands raised to Heaven, swears never again to touch the cursed bottle and ... dreams that his beloved wife comes and takes the child with outstretched wings up into the starry firmament';[28] in Hepworth's 1912 *The Passing of the Old Four Wheeler* a dying daughter persuades a cabby to return a lost £5 note.

In most of these pathetic stories, the death of the child, natural or unnatural, is qualified by narrative or moral purpose. Against these, it seems, we need to place the more ghastly and senseless deaths, with their gruesomely awful deformations of flesh, of, for instance, Tess' child, Fanny Robbins and her new-born baby and

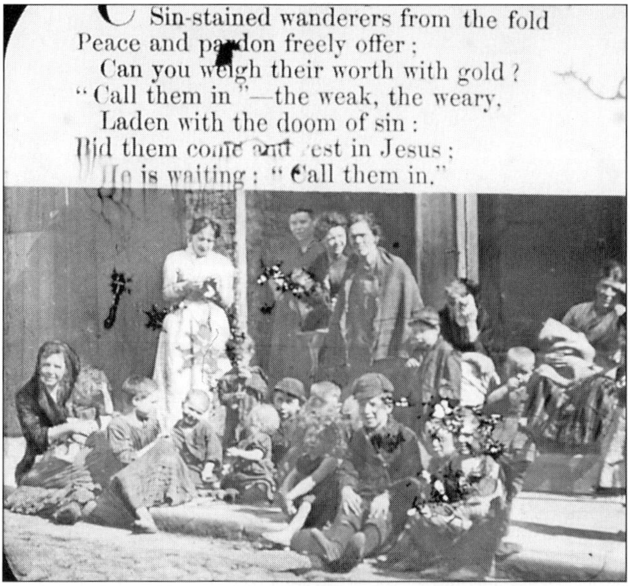

Fig. 6. Another unknown Hymn Slide.

of the children of Arabella, Sue and Jude in, respectively, Thomas Hardy's *Tess of the d'Urbevilles* (1891), *Far From the Madding Crowd* (1874) and *Jude the Obscure* (1895). Indeed, Marie Corelli (one of Hardy's most vociferous critics) appears to have written *The Mighty Atom* in response to the stark hopelessness of his 'Done because we are too menny', producing her own morose child suicide in return.[29] The lantern series *The White Slaves of London* explains the exploitation and ordeals of home match-box makers:

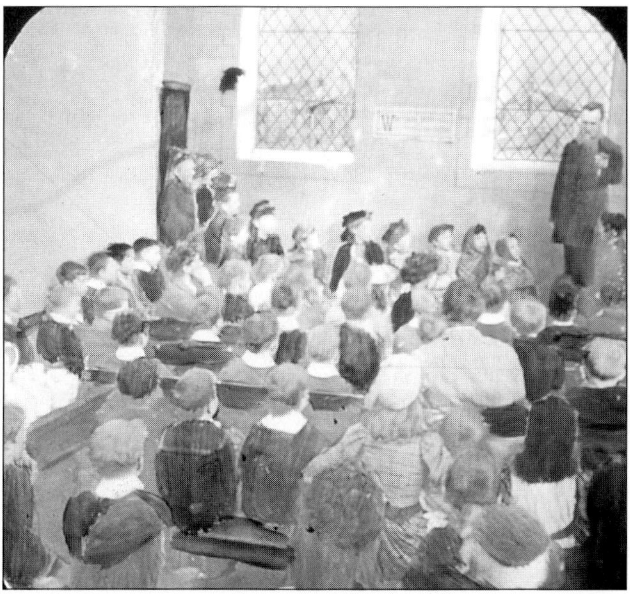

Fig. 7. The way to Heaven - Slide no. 32. Service of song. Composer: James Tipton (Publisher: Bayley & Ferguson, London and Glasgow, n. d Associated slide set by: Bamforth, 38 slides This slide set was number 464 in Riley Brothers' hire stock.

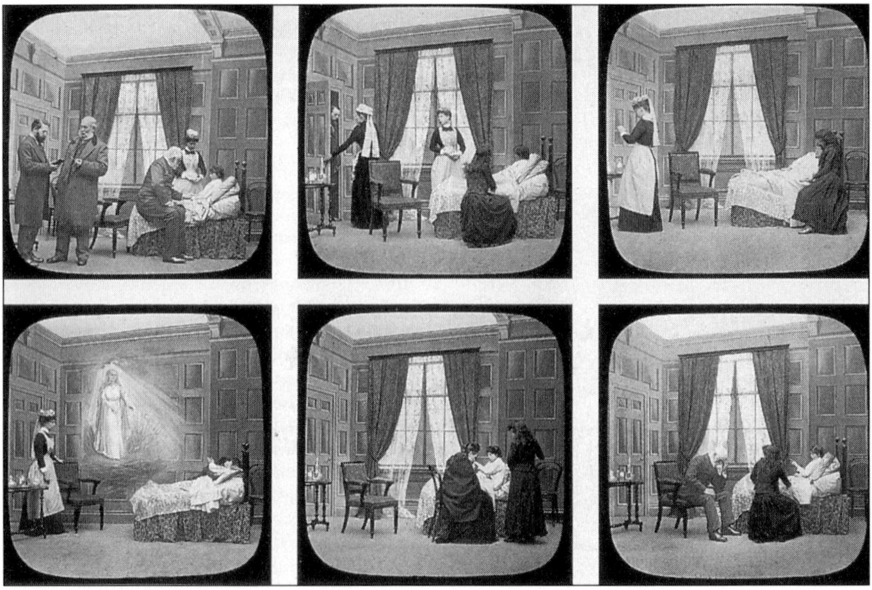

Fig. 8. Paul Dombey's death from Dombey and Son. *The six slide lantern set was made in 1893 or earlier by the firm York & Son.*

> At last, with an hysterical scream, the desperate little sister throws her work down: 'I can bear it no more! I will bear it no more! This hard pitiless life is killing me. I want air, I want life, I want food. Oh,God! Why did you make me and put me in a world to suffer like this! What have I done! What have I done![30]

Waifs and toffs

In pathos subjects, the poor or disadvantaged are frequently seen to benefit from the intervention of the better-off, but charity, philanthropy and compassion are by no means the preserve of the rich. In Walturdaw's *Jessica's First Prayer* (named after Hesba Stretton's bestseller, published by the Religious Tract Society in 1882), a stall-holder adopts a waif after testing her honesty and in Clarendon's 1909 *Hard Times* (again, a title invoking Dickens), a tale of equally 'deserving' poverty, a doctor pays for a broken window when an unemployed man steals bread for his starving child and helps them both.[31] Hepworth's *One Good Turn Deserves Another* has the little girl of a well-to-do family inviting a hungry boy into her home and giving him the contents of her money box; when the girl is subsequently kidnapped, the boy, Joe, returns her safely to her mother.[32] Walturdaw's 1911 *A Child's Charity* has a rich little Nellie giving a pearl necklace to a starving woman and child, who promptly pawns it, is unfairly accused of theft but in the nick of time is cleared by Nellie's testimony.[33] Both Hepworth's *Tempered with Mercy* and Gaumont's *The Two Orphans* portray sibling loyalty. In the former, one sister works as a flower-girl to support the other; in the latter, a girl disguises herself in her brother's clothes in order to gain work as an errand boy. Yet another tender-hearted policeman

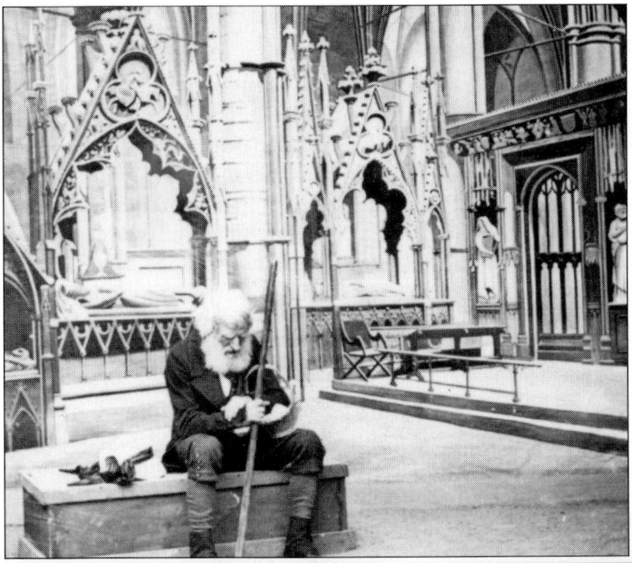

Fig. 9 (above) and Fig. 10 (below). The Old Curiosity Shop, *written by Charles Dickens in 1841 and adapted for the Magic Lantern in 1881 by York & Son who produced a set of 24 slides. (Slides 22 and 24.)*

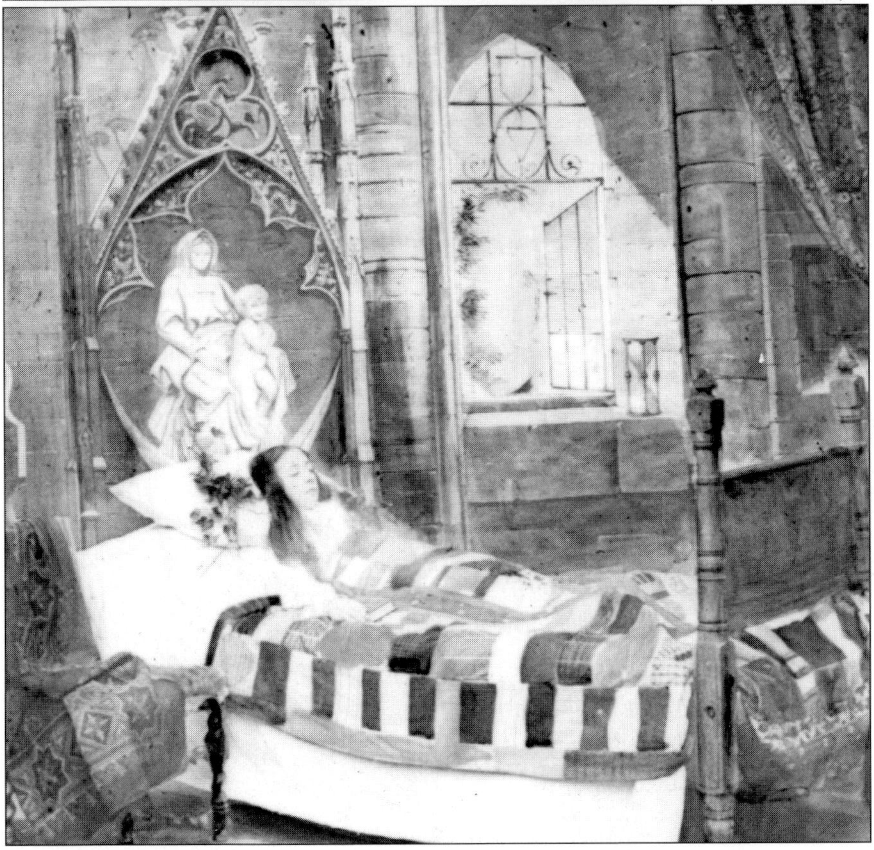

intervenes sadly too late for the brother, but Elsie thrives and remains devoted to him, even in death. Adopted in an act of Christian kindness, she is finally unrecognisable as a puny weak child of the slums and is seen placing flowers on a neat little grave.[34]

Alongside the depiction of charity, parental and filial devotion and sacrifice, we need to consider the numerous accounts which describe a situation in which many died in infancy needlessly, 'unnaturally' even, in the sense that their deaths were preventable. Deaths amongst toffs (the descendants of Penelope) were not unknown – the melancholic-looking Oliver is hired by Mrs Sowerby in Dickens' *Oliver Twist* as a suitable mute attendant at the cortèges of the children of the well-to-do – but the poor are alarmingly disproportionately represented.[35] Friedrich Engels' *The Condition of the Working Class in England* (first published in Germany in 1845) is acquainted with the Manchester of Gaskell's *Mary Barton* (set against the depression of 1839–1841 and the rise of Chartism) and corroborates her sad register of deaths. Disparities in infant mortality rates between households of different incomes and in different areas of the country were recorded throughout the century. In 1902, Jack London draws statistical evidence from Rowntree and Booth, but relies, like Dickens before him, on his own observation of 'starvation, disease, stunted development and moral degradation' in the heart of the 'greatest, wealthiest and most powerful empire the world has ever seen':[36]

> In such conditions, the outlook for children is hopeless. They die like flies, and those that survive, survive because they possess excessive vitality and a capacity of adaptation to the degradation with which they are surrounded.[37]

According to London, fifty five percent of East End children die before they are five years old.[38] Robert Tressall's 1914 *The Ragged Trousered Philanthropists* suggests that the 'Domestic Tragedy' delineated by Hardy was not the unique product of the author's vivid imagination and asserts that drink is not, in spite of the Church's proselytising, the root of all evil and nor is Christian charity an adequate solution to the evils he describes.[39] This is a conclusion with which Wilde, as a Socialist, might well concur.

Acknowledgements: Information for this article taken from the Magic Lantern Society Slide Readings Library, compiled by Richard Crangle. Courtesy for use of slides from Peter Gillies (Billy's Rose), the Netherlands Filmmuseum (Paul Dombey's Death), David Henry (The Old Curiosity Shop), Lewis Collection at the South East Film & Video Archive (a.k.a. Screen Archive South East) at the University of Brighton (Hymn slides and The Way to Heaven).

Notes

1. Alvin Redman (ed), *Wit and Humor of Oscar Wilde* (New York: Dover, 1959): 84.
2. See Oscar Wilde, 'The Happy Prince', 'The Young King' and 'The Birthday of the Infanta' in *The Happy Prince and Other Stories* (Harmondsworth: Puffin, 1994). Wilde also inherits some of the folkloric and fairy elements catalogued by Lady Wilde: see Katharine Briggs, *A Book of Fairies* (Harmondsworth: Penguin, 1997): 49.
3. Martin Amis, *Dead Babies* [1975] (Harmondsworth: Penguin, 2000): 56 and 137.
4. *The Bioscope* 15 January 1914: 217; see also 25 December 1913 using the death of Nell as one of two scenes advertising the film" release and BFI Special Materials, James Anderson Collection Box 22. Jenny Dennett, 'Sentimentality, sex and sadism: the 1935 version of Dickens' *The Old Curiosity Shop*' in Robert Giddings and Erica Sheen (eds), *The Classic Novel: from page to screen* (Manchester: Manchester University Press, 2000): 54–70 discusses intellectual hostility to senti-

mental literature; see also [with thanks to Tony Fletcher!] A.O.J. Cockshut, 'Children's Death in Dickens: a Chapter in the History of Taste' in Gillian Avery and Kimberley Reynolds (eds) *Representations of Childhood Death* (London: Macmillan, 2000): 133–153.

5. Neil la Bute's *The State of Things* [2001] and Lee Hall's *Spoonface Steinberg* seem appropriate current citations here; also John Sweeney 'How Saddam "staged" fake baby funerals', *The Observer* 23 June 2002: 22 and the Trupti Patel case covered by Jo Revill and Gaby Hinsliff, 'Call for an end to cot death court anguish', *The Observer* 15 June 2003: 8.
6. On the writing and extraordinary affect of Nell on her first audience see John Forster, *The Life of Dickens* I (London: Chapman and Hall, 1872): 177–193 and, Elizabeth M. Brennan (ed), *The Old Curiosity Shop* (Oxford: Clarendon, 1997): 556–559; 630; for the affect on Dickens himself [with thanks to Mick Eaton!] see Peter Ackroyd, *Dickens* (London: Sinclair-Stevenson, 1990): 318; for the affect of the early death of Paul Dombey on readers, see Hye-Joon Yoon, *Physiognomy of Capital in Charles Dickens* (San Francisco: International Scholars Publications, 1998): 154. Britannia's 1912 *The Old Curiosity Shop* was released to mark Dickens' centenary.
7. In Poe's 1849 *Annabel Lee* the mourning is intensified when the object of love dies in youth; see also his 'The Philosophy of Composition' [1846] in *Essays and Reviews* (New York: Literary Classics of the United States, 1984), and re 'For Annie' Gaston Bachelard, *L'Eau et les rêves* [1942] (Paris: Librairie Livre de Poche, 2003): 80–81, 98, 108 and Elisabeth Bronfen, *Over Her Dead Body* (Manchester: Manchester University Press, 1992): 59–75; see also Hélène Pinet, 'L'eau, la femme, la mort: le mythe de l'Inconnue de la Seine' in *Le Dernier Portrait* (Paris: Réunion des Musées Nationaux, 2002): 175–190.
8. Marie Corelli, *The Mighty Atom* [1896] (London: Methuen, 1937): 195–196; see also Bertha Vyver *Memoirs of Marie Corelli* (London: Alston Rivers, 1930): 56 and 141and Redman: 80, re Wilde being asked by a prison warder at Reading if Marie Corelli was a great writer: 'Now, don't think I've anything against her *moral* character, but from the way she writes *she ought to be in here*'. See also Val Williams and Greg Hobson (eds), *The Dead (*Bradford: National Museum of Photography, Film & Television, 1995), and Audrey Linkman, *The Victorians* (London: Tauris Parke, 1993): 121–122.
9. George R. Sims, 'Billy's Rose' (published c. 1880s). The ballad was reprinted and used in different ways by lantern slide producers. The pictures referred to by the authors came from York & Son, a 10 slide series, who supplied the verse from the 'Dagonet reciter'. Another slide series was made by Bamforth from Holmfirth, possibly a 24 slide series using the verse from 'A Garland of Fair Flowers'. See also Olive Cook, *Movement in Two Dimensions* [1963], Stephen Herbert, A History of Pre-Cinema III (London: Routledge, 2000): 103–106.
10. J. M. Barrie, *The Little White Bird* (London: Hodder and Stoughton, 1902): 268
11. J. M. Barrie, directions concluding *Peter Pan*: 'If he could get the hang of the thing his cry might become'. To live would be an awfully big adventure! 'but he can never quite get the hang of it, and so no one is as gay as he'; girls, Barrie tells us in *Peter and Wendy*, are too sensible to fall out of their prams.
12. We are thinking especially of Gainsborough's 1782 painting after Murillo, *Girl gathering Faggots in a Wood* (Manchester City Art Gallery) and an 1880 Crown Derby vase (Derby City Art Gallery) showing a usual cloaked girl in the snow, gathering winter fu-el, though the frost was cru-el; see also James Christen Steward, *The New Child: British Art and the Origins of Modern Childhood* (Berkeley: University Art Museum, 1995): 25.
13. Barrie, *The Little White Bird*: 224.
14. The plaster model for the statue is now in the Soane Museum, London, the statue itself in Derbyshire. Brooke Boothby was painted by Joseph Wright reading a text by Rousseau (his friend and protégé).
15. M. H. Spielmann, *Millais and his Works* (London: Blackwood and Sons, 1898): 139–140 and Carol Mavor, *Pleasures Taken* (London: I.B. Tauris, 1996): 14.
16. Charles Dickens, *Bleak House* [1852–3] (Oxford: Oxford University Press, 1978): 649: 'Dead, your Majesty. Dead, my lords and gentlemen. Dead, men and women, born with Heavenly compassion in your hearts. And dying thus around us every day'. See also Raphael Samuel, *Theatres of Memory* (London: Verso, 1994): 319.
17. Rachael Low *The History of British Cinema* I (London: Routledge, 1997): 95–96.
18. Mrs Gaskell, *Mary Barton* [1848] (London:Oxford University Press, 1911): 39; see also Dave

Russell, *Popular Music in England 1840–1914* (Manchester: Manchester University Press, 1997): 65–66.

19. The Lantern reading for 'Christmas in Paradise' was written by John Colwell (Temperance Series Publication – Wesleyan Conference Office). Bamforth produced a 26 lantern slide series to accompany the reading.

20. J.M. Barrie's *A Kiss for Cinderella* (in performance at Wyndham's Theatre in 1916) was acknowledged by Chaplin as the source for the pathos sequence in *The Kid* (1921).

21. *The Bioscope* (6 January 1910): 49.

22. *The Bioscope* (16 December 1909): 53.

23. On the notion of the good death, see Mary Bradbury, *Representations of Death* (London: Routledge, 1999): 143.

24. Verse from a Hymn slide. Many of these type of slides were produced for presentations in church meetings, Service of Songs, Sunday School etc.

25. City Sparrows, a Service of Song reading arranged and compiled by E. Fordham, weekes & Co by permission of the Religious Tract Society to accompany a York & Son lantern set (18 slides) from 1896.

26. Gaskell: 182.

27. *The Bioscope* (24 November 1910): 61.

28. *The Bioscope* (16 December 1909): 53; Hepworth catalogue 1907.

29. See Harold Orel intro. to Thomas Hardy, *The Dynasts* (London: Macmillan, 1978): ix for notoriously hostile reviews; Thomas Hardy, *Jude the Obscure* [1894–95] (London: Macmillan, 1974): 356 and Vyver: 168 re Corelli's attack on 'Pagan' London.

30. A Horner's Lantern reading, based on a story by Fannie Eden, with 24 slides by Pexton.

31. For this 'remarkable Victorian survival' see Jonathan Rose, *The Intellectual Life of the British Working Classes* (New Haven: Yale University Press, 2001): 245 and 386 and Thomas Burke, *Son of London* (London: Herbert Jenkins, 1946): 22. See also Alexander Welsh, 'Charity', *The City of Dickens* (Oxford: Clarendon, 1971): 86–100.

32. *The Bioscope* (1 July 1909): 44. Several lantern sets were produced to accompany *Jessica's First Prayer*. 1884 York & Son's slide series followed the illustrations of the book closely. Bamforth and at least five other producers also made a series to illustrate this popular story.

33. *The Bioscope* (30 March 1911): 42.

34. *The Bioscope* (6 January 1910): 49.

35. Charles Dickens, *Oliver Twist* [1837–39] (Harmondsworth: Penguin, 1980): 78–79; for a description of a child's funeral see also Randal Keynes, *Annie's Box* (London: Fourth Estate, 2002): 181–182 (one of three deaths in Charles Darwin's family); see also Bradbury: 82.

36. Friedrich Engels, *The Condition of the Working Class in England*, tr. W.O. Henderson and W.H. Chaloner (Stanford: Stanford University Press, 1968): 122.

37. For Dickens' observations on dead babies looking like pigs' trotters see John Cary, *The Violent Effigy* (London: Faber and Faber, 1991): 131; as he notes, in Dickens' writing babies are not just dead but pickled, preserved and bottled; see also Henry Mayhew, *London Labour and the London Poor* [1861], Gerorge Sims, *How the Poor Live* [1883], Walter Besant, *Children of Gibeon* [1886], Arthur Morrison, *Tales of Mean Streets* [1894], Charles Booth, *Life and Labour of the People in London* [1889], William Booth, *Darkest England* [1890].and Benjamin Seebohm Rowntree, *Poverty: A Study of Town Life* [1901] (New York: Howard Fertig, 1971): 242; and Jack London, *The People of the Abyss* [1903] (Upper Saddle River: Literature House, 1970): 78.

38. London: 303; see also Ford Madox Brown, *The Soul of London* (London: Alston Rivers, 1905): 145, regarding an anonymous tablet 'In memory of Elizabeth, Dear Child', setting 'us thinking of all sorts of dead children, dear in their day, and now how utterly unremembered, as wavelets are forgotten!'

39. Robert Tressall, *The Ragged Trousered Philanthropists* [1914] (London: Grant Richards, 1918): 50.

7

The Neo-Institutionalisation of Cinema as a New Medium

André Gaudreault and Philippe Marion[1]

Not so long ago, the rumor of cinema's imminent demise gripped the field of media studies. But how many times has the spectre of cinema's death come to haunt discussion of this 'seventh art'? Let us note that the cinema, for the most part a narrative art, already contains within it, in a sense, the anguish of the end. In early cinema, this anguish of the end manifested itself in the fear that the film magazine, which in those days had a severely limited capacity, would run empty before the end of the event being filmed. This, essentially, was a technological problem. In classical cinema, we might say that the anguish of the end was, at the very least, doubled. On the one hand, there was the anguish of the end of the story that the film had to tell, an anguish that was resolved by resorting to the simple solution of the famous happy end. One the other hand, there was the anguish of the end of the budget, of its exhaustion, its limits.

For the past thirty years or so, however, it has been the anguish of the end of cinema itself that has been on people's minds. And in a sense, this anguish returns us to the anguish of early cinema, because like early cinema it is an anguish directly linked to technology. It is true that today, with each passing day, films are no longer made the way they used to be. The apparatus is changing constantly, and filming techniques are becoming 'virtual'. The cinema, like all media moreover, is in the process of dematerialising (the material it is made of is no longer as easily grasped as it once was). Before, editing was a matter of pulsion and pulsations, a question of rhythm. Now it is a question of algorithm. Beats have been replaced by equations. But does this signify, for all that, the death of cinema?

Film stock itself is fated to perish. Soon they'll be showing films in movie houses by remote satellite feed. Does this disappearance or death of the film stock mean, however, the death of cinema, the death of the medium? If it did, we would, on the one hand, be reducing a medium to one of its constituent technologies or materials, and on the other, be ignoring the way every medium's identity develops over time and is inscribed in a historical context. Certainly film prints, some day, will no longer circulate. But signs will continue to circulate, and this is the important thing.

We are now entering, moreover, an era in which signs circulate in a completely unbridled manner, particularly through the Internet, and media convergence is something that we will absolutely have to take into consideration in the near future. And so the disappearance of film stock, and its replacement by different ways of preserving the 'trace' of cinema, has more to do, in our view, with a movement towards atomisation, with parcelling off, with scattering. And even if this movement has always been a feature, more or less, of the development of every medium, it seems to be accelerated in the present context. Contemporary media thus reveal a marked tendency towards parcelling off, towards intermedial scattering. This, as we shall see, is not necessarily incompatible with the preservation of a unique media identity.

For a dynamic definition of media

Put in black-and-white terms, the question of a medium's death betrays a fixed and monolithic conception of media. Now, a medium can only define itself by acquiring an active presence in the media environment in which it is found. This presence, however, is subject in turn to the way in which the medium is analysed and its constituent components categorized. A medium can thus be understood as a temporarily stabilised federation of various parameters whose tendency towards transmedial circulation is more *intermedial* than *medial*. Above all, it is the process of institutionalisation that contributes to this temporary crystallisation – or rather, to this evolutionary crystallisation – of the *composite* materials which constitute a medium. These composite aspects, which can burst forth or be dispersed according to the way the winds of intermediality are blowing, are thus organised, or federated, by the directionality of the institutionalising forces – by the cluster of determining factors.

These considerations bring us to the crucial question of cinema's birth, and more generally to that of the birth of any medium. More than one hundred years ago now, the cinema imposed both a model of 'communication' based on the image and an iconic culture which was destined to dominate the century. At the same time, it introduced a new conception of the performinge arts, simultaneously breaking with and developing out of the different kinds of popular entertainment that preceded it. The cinema can thus ultimately be located at the place where technology, industry, art, the performing arts, popular entertainment, and education meet. The cinema therefore poses the crucial question of how a technological invention comes into its own. The future of such an invention is never fixed in advance, as the example of the Internet today attests. In this sense, the study of cinema is essential to an understanding of contemporary media.

In order to buttress our concept of a medium as a *fragile and institutionalised homeostasis*, we will follow two different paths, suggested by the example of cinema:

1. The first path will lead us to develop, briefly, the necessarily composite quality of media and to demonstrate the extent to which a medium is, in fact, nothing more than an organised federation of parameters: parameters which develop according to their own logic, both upstream and downstream from that singular equilibrium which constitutes a medium. These parameters of a medium play a role in its constitution. In order to demonstrate this, we will

examine one or another of those constituent parts which, although they form part of a unique medium, also exist quite easily outside of that medium – when they themselves, these constituent parts, are not full-fledged media in their own right, as the expression 'multimedia', for example, attests.

2. The second path is more historical, and is linked to the model of the double birth of cinema that we proposed a few years ago now.[2] This model is characterised by a refusal to consider the medium a static, fixed entity, as having a finite, closed, and definitive essence. The genealogy of cinema thus supports our idea, as we shall see, of a federating prism which, guided by the process of institutionalisation, unifies such diverse parameters as apparatus, film stock, technology, forms of representation, semiotic materials, and even genres and cultural series.

The first path: constituent, but non exclusive, components of the cinema

In order to obtain a good understanding of how a medium such as the cinema functions, we need to think of it like a prism, as a cluster of convergent elements in which various parameters are interwoven. Most often, these parameters do not pertain exclusively to the sole medium in question. On the contrary, they often exist in a system of intermedial relations. This prism constitutes precisely what we describe as 'mediativity',[3] or that thing which configures, in a singular manner, various parameters as they circulate in the space of intermediality.

To understand the differential singularity of a medium is, then, to attempt to grasp its mediativity. This mediativity assembles all of the parameters which define the expressive and communicative potential that a medium has developed. More systematically, mediativity can be understood according to the way various significant aspects are combined; such as, for the external parameters, the conditions in which a medium is circulated and distributed; or again, the ways in which the public 'consumes' the medium. In this way photography, at first, was seen as a substitute for the sort of portrait fashionable among the better classes.

At the other extreme, on an internal level, a medium's mediativity is gauged, of course, in terms of the expressive semiotic materials that the medium brings into play. For a long time now a distinction has been made between the cognitive and affective mechanisms associated with 'digital' and 'analog' media. In the same way, there has often been a distinction made between 'iconic' and 'textual' media. There have even been attempts to evaluate the complex practical effects of audio-textual-visual media. And we haven't even mentioned the various ways the imagination is put into play by different expressive systems found within the same category of representation such as *monstration* for example. There is a world of difference between a hand-drawn caricature of a media personality and a publicity photo of that same individual, even if they date from the same period. The nature of the medium's material base and the technological apparatus associated with it also guide the practical meaning of a medium's mediativity. Think of technological innovations such as the Barco system, which makes it possible to give televised images a new, 'projected' quality, thus making it possible to transform how the message is received and even to alter its meaning. Once again, we should emphasise here that these clusters of meaning opened by mediativity only take shape to the extent that they combine and interact.

Let's return to the cinema and consider it from the perspective of one of the parameters that constitute its *mediativity*, alongside what we call in French the *projections lumineuses*, illluminated images, considering this parameter in terms of its intermedial 'polyvalency'. By choosing the parameter 'illuminated images', we do not obtain the same array of media configurations that we do when we select the parameter 'animated pictures', for example. Thus Émile Reynaud's *Théâtre optique*, which could in no way be considered to belong to the medium we know as 'cinema', nevertheless corresponds to each of the parameters 'illuminated images' and 'moving pictures', and to the ways these are configured. Indeed, the category 'illuminated images' suggests both the material base of the medium and its technological apparatus. Generally speaking, it includes equally well within its purview such things as the magic lantern, the *pantomimes lumineuses*, the kinetoscope, and the *cinématographe*.

A relatively similar observation could be made if we were to privilege, in today's media universe, the parameter we might call the '*universal illuminated domestic screen*', the central access point to all sorts of images and data that we can, nowadays, already imagine. Indeed such a parameter 'cuts through' numerous and varied media and genres, such as television, video games, DVD, the Internet, multimedia, etc.

By privileging the category we call in French 'vues animées' ('moving pictures'), which can be substituted for the problematic expression 'early cinema', it becomes possible to include Raynauld and his illuminated pantomimes in the same cultural series as the *cinématographe*. All of a sudden the 'medium' of moving pictures is able, synchronically, to designate an entire historical, transmedial, or transtechnological constellation. So too the French term 'machines à vues', used to designate a variety of devices and apparatuses, allows for a similar kind of inclusion. In a sense, it seems more respectful to use the expression 'moving pictures' to describe early cinema, given the intermediality of the various multimedia manifestations popular at the time, because it does not distinguish among the mass of technologies used to project moving images. We might note, however, that this expression, 'vues animées', and all the possible corresponding terms in English ('animated pictures', 'moving pictures' or 'moving images', etc.) excludes the magic lantern, at least in principle. And yet we know that a significant proportion of magic lantern slides allowed for some form or another of moving pictures. The use of the expression 'projections lumineuses' to designate this series may make it possible however to identify a significant genre, a more inclusive genre, which would group together the magic lantern, Reynaud, and so-called 'early cinema'. Strangely enough this category would exclude, however, Edison's Kinetoscope, as well as the Mutoscope, since they do not involve any projection at all.

Perhaps in the end is it just as abusive to speak of turn-of-the-century moving pictures as 'cinema' as it would be to describe the Bayeux Tapestry as belonging to the graphic novel or comic strip (the series that is known in French as the *bande dessinée*).

The second path: genealogy as a dynamic method for understanding a media 'prism'

So-called early cinema is, then, a 'bric à brac' or hodge podge of otherness; to become 'cinema', and find a possible identity, it had to pass through a period of alterity, when the *cinématographe* was considered, both implicitly and explicitly, as a mere means of reproduction, a means of reproducing some spectacle occurring in front of it, at a time when the 'art' was in front of the camera (theatre, magic, circus acts, etc.), not 'in' it. At the time, the *cinématographe* was an apparatus that operated within the realm of these other media before it had the chance to develop by itself, by its own means, by trying to define a specificity of its own.

One might wonder whether, as a prototype, the cinema is the ideal choice for demonstrating the idea that a medium's genesis is slow and problematic. Indeed, the history of the cinema is well documented and the chronology of its birth would appear to be easily established. Moreover, cinema's arrival within the constellation of media can obscure the fact that its technology represented a *rupture* and was clearly distinguished from the neighbouring technology of its day. The *technology* of cinema was, in fact, the result not of a steady progression but rather of a brusque *qualitative* leap. The kinetoscope's and *cinématographe*'s arrival in the world of media constituted an event whose proportions were nothing less than that of an epistemological break. We have only to compare these apparatuses to chronophotography to illustrate this. In chronophotography, the series of photographs remains a concrete and measurable phenomenon: the chronophotograph recorded onto a light-sensitive plate 12 separate images, say, of a man running. Afterwards, one can observe these same 12 images on the plate: nothing has been lost, but nothing has been created. Of course, the chronophotograph has its own slightly magical side: it makes it possible to see things, to see details that are invisible to the naked eye. But it did not create a truly new phenomenon. It is of course more complex than photography alone, but this complexity is the result of an additive process; on the representational level, the leap it introduces is merely *quantitative*, calling to mind the expression 'what you see is what you get'.

In the case of the kinetoscope and *cinématographe*, things were different, because the apparatus made it possible to reach the threshold of another level, to introduce a truly new representational paradigm. This is how one can think of the arrival of the new technology in the media environment as a rupture. But why is this so? Simply because, by using *still* images, the kinetoscope and the *cinématographe* create *movement*; because, by combining numerous single images, they create a radically new object. They do so by fusing these images – the same kind of single images that were used in chronophotography – and *voiding their singularity*. 'What you see', initially, on the strip of film – numerous fixed and discontinuous photograms – 'is *NOT* what you get', finally, on the screen – a *unique and animated continuous image*. The nature of the image has changed. *The invention of the cinematographic process thus results in a 'subsuming' of the singular into the multiple*. A subsuming which, by definition, causes the thing being subsumed to disappear into the thing doing the subsuming.

We thus pass, in the case of the first birth of the cinema, its birth as a technology, to a radically new form of 'presentification' of the image from one day to the next.

This new form is directly linked to a technological process whose historical foundation is relatively confined in time: that of the invention. This is the source of the temptation that has been present throughout the history of the medium to view cinema as having a single and unequivocal birth date. In our view, the case of cinema is thus also exemplary in the mistaken interpretation of its appearance as a novelty (which was, it is true, fascinating for its technological procedure of *capturing* and *reconstituting* reality in all its spatial and temporal dimensions). But it is a mistake to confuse this procedure with a full-fledged identity, that of the fixed and definitive category of cinema, a point of view illustrated by expressions such as 'the birth of the seventh art'.

We would like to suggest, rather, that the cinema's singularity as a medium is instead the result of a slow process of maturation, despite its historically demonstrable irruption as technology. Ultimately, to view the birth of a medium as synonymous with the invention of a technology can only be, and not only in the case of the cinema, a 'Grande Illusion'. That this is true can be seen in the fact that despite the 'attraction' of the new apparatus, despite its status as a technological novelty, the medium was nevertheless used back then to do the same old things. It was used as a new way of continuing to do what had 'always' been done, to perpetuate stage shows and itinerant entertainments, or as a new way of presenting already well-established entertainment 'genres': magic and fairy shows, farce, plays, and other kinds of public performances. Here we could note, in passing, another transverse parameter which participated in the evolutionary prism of the medium 'cinema'. But this parameter, which itself shifts intermedially among various media, is no longer tied simply to questions of the mechanics of the device or the technology of the apparatus. It has more to do with a *qualitative* dimension inherent in the content and the relational (practical) means of representation: that of genres and cultural series.

We might note, finally, that it wasn't until cinema's practitioners arrived at a reflexive understanding of the medium and until the cinema achieved a certain degree of institutionalisation that the medium became autonomous. It is in this way that the cinema, as a medium, could be said to have been born twice (see note 2). The *first birth* is when a new technology is used to extend earlier practices, to which it was at first subservient. The *second birth* is when it sets out on a path that enables the resources it has developed to acquire an institutional legitimacy that acknowledges their specificity. This is the moment when *the prism is set into play*.

Our perspective has led us to think that instead of talking about the birth of a medium, or more specifically its second birth, we should instead be talking about its *constitution*. Surely a medium's second birth can not be categorised as a discrete and momentary event which can be assigned a date and identified as occurring at a precise instant. This would only be possible if we were to reduce the medium merely to the technological advance that made it possible.

Furthermore, we should consider this path a gradated process, specifically a gradated process of three moments. We have identified these moments by three terms from the same semantic field, but to which we have assigned a co-efficient that is specific to each. These terms are *apparition, emergence*, and, precisely, *constitution*. The history of early cinema leads us, successively, from the sudden *apparition* of a technological process, the apparatus, to the *emergence* of an initial culture, that of 'moving pictures', and finally to the *constitution* of an established media institution. On the level of production, the social agents associated with the apparition of the technological process are its numerous *inventors*, while those associated with the emergence of the initial culture are the camera *operators* (or *cinématographistes*, to use the French terminology of the day), and those associated with the constitution of the media institution are the first film *directors*.

After the recording device appeared and produced a kind of craze for novelty, film production *defined itself as a practice*, making it possible to pass to the next step, the emergence of 'moving pictures'. This is the first 'cinematic' culture, although it is still only tenuously institutionalised. This culture was of necessity intermedial and was characterised by an ongoing institutionalisation – by a hodge podge of neighbouring institutions which by definition were not 'cinematic'. It was by means of this unstable culture that the *cinématographe* began the process of becoming an *autonomous* medium of expression. This subsequently led to the cinema's constitution, to its *establishment as a unique medium*. This in turn allowed the cinema to pass into a second culture, its second birth. A culture, this time, that was truly 'media-centric'. Three stages thus order the cinema's institutional quest within the zone between these two bordering cultures. The first stage is the subordination to neighbouring institutions, followed by, as a second stage, a movement towards detachment and then, as the third stage, a period of insubordination, which was a necessary development for cinema's institutionalisation.

We might ask ourselves whether this double birth, given dynamic expression through these three phases, could constitute a model that might be generalised and applied to other media, or perhaps all media. To what extent have other major media, such as photography, graphic novels, radio, television, the Internet, etc., experienced a double birth themselves?

To add precision to our model of the three phases and the dual birth, we might call the first birth a medium's *integrating birth* and the second birth its *distinguishing birth*. At the moment of its appearance a new technology is still only a 'crypto-medium', because its singularity, as a medium, is not yet clearly apparent. This technology thus becomes engaged with the range of relatively legitimate types of existing media, practices and genres that form the context into which the technology is thrust. Then the new technology is adapted to the social and cultural uses associated – at a certain historical moment and by a certain society – with these other accepted cultural series. The need to render this technology autonomous, to take advantage of its possible media specificity, is not yet felt, or not yet felt to be relevant. The medium's new possibilities thus remain at a stage of complementarity, dependence or continuity vis-à-vis older and better established generic and media practices. At least from the point of view of content alone, while the new technology itself perpetuates fascination with the *novelty*.

By inheriting an apparatus that stands at the intersection of various pre-existing intermedial combinations, the 'crypto-medium' becomes a 'proto-medium'. But at this stage it still remains a simple auxiliary to existing genres. Its auxiliary task is to facilitate access to these genres by improving their performance and by affording them wider dissemination. At this stage the proto-medium reveals hardly any self-awareness as a medium, none of the self-awareness of a full-fledged and stable medium. An air of indecisiveness surrounds it, a hesitation in the way it quotes the various identities it seems to cloak itself in simultaneously.

After mimetically relaying its surrounding genres, a medium then unfolds along the path of its singularity. This is the emergent phase. The *possibility of autonomy* is connected to the evolution and potential of the medium. Its second birth, or constitution, will appear when its quest for identity and autonomy coincides with institutional recognition and a decisive improvement in the economic resources devoted to its production. Logically enough, in taking on an identity the medium loses its initial intermediality – that spontaneous intermediality which characterised the period of its first birth. However, although it has lost this initial intermediality, it has acquired another, one compatible with this assertion of its identity. This is the intermediality that is always present in it but which it negotiates in its own fashion, in interaction with its own potential. This goes hand in hand with the displacement of fascination and the technology's turn towards the sort of content made possible by the new medium. This latter intermediality, which we could call a subjugated intermediality, could be compared to the intertextuality found in any process of cultural production. Such a *negotiated intermediality* is of particular importance in the contemporary media landscape, marked as it is by flux, contamination, interconnectedness, and global 'webs'.

The genesis of a medium's neo-institutionalisation, like that of the cinema in the teens, should be understood as the product of the intersection of the various paradigms that govern the medium in its early years. Only the metaphor of the 'prism', which functions to blend the colours of the spectrum into white, can account for the institutionalisation of a medium like the cinema. In the cinema this prism, which the authors of this paper have described as the medium's 'second birth', takes the spectrum of rainbow colours and renders them as a single 'organic' and directed light. Each paradigm (such as the technological paradigm of 'illuminated images') exists prior to its concentration in the prism and, after its concentration by the process of institutionalisation, can just as easily persist, possibly in another form.

We thus describe the 'medium' as a 'pregnant moment' in which different 'colours', or paradigms, meet and are transformed through the mediation (the summons, the contingency, the attraction) of a prism. Each of these paradigms is capable of 'resigning', of becoming diluted in the medium; alternately, or simultaneously, they may strike out on a different path. In short, the medium is a prism which manages, at a given point in time, to concentrate (to render syntagmatic? to brand?) various paradigms that existed before the invention of the 'diluting' prism and which are still capable of existing outside of it. Unless the centripetal force of the medium prevents it from doing so, which appears to be the case of cinema after 1910.

'A prism which manages, at a given point in time ...', we remarked. If we were to adopt the terminology of old Saussure, a medium is a *temporary synchrony*, or perhaps a *synchronic illusion*, in the implacable and decisive development of the diachrony. And it is the diachrony, without a doubt, that makes and unmakes the collusion of media. To continue to recall ideas from the olden days, we might just as easily invoke Marshall McLuhan's intuition that each medium carries within it the medium that will follow it and supersede it. We believe that the 'diachronic succession of media' that McLuhan proposed should today be measured, above all, by the yardstick of synchrony. Our contemporary media are characterised by a centrifugal tendency. They possess a propensity to scatter their constituent parameters. It is therefore necessary to reformulate McLuhan's idea and to suggest rather that every medium carries within it the media with which it is contemporary.

Translated by Timothy Barnard

Notes

1. André Gaudreault's share of this article was written under the aegis of GRAFICS (Groupe de recherche sur l'avènement et la formation des institutions cinématographique et scénique) at the Université de Montréal. GRAFICS receives funds from the Social Sciences and Humanities Research Council of Canada (SSHRC) and the Fonds québécois de recherche sur la société et la culture, and is a part of CRI (Centre de recherche sur l'intermédialité/Centre for Research on Intermediality). Philippe Marion's share of the article was written under the aegis of the Observatoire du récit médiatique (ORM) at the Université catholique de Louvain, Belgium. Parts of this article reproduce elements of a previous article by the present authors, already published in French in 2000 (see note 2), forthcoming in 2005 in English, at the same time as theses ideas are considered in a new light here.
2. André Gaudreault et Philippe Marion, 'Un média naît toujours deux fois ...', *Sociétés & Représentations*. Paris, Publications de la Sorbonne, no 9, 2000, pp. 21–36. To be published in English in the journal *Early Popular Visual Culture*, Vol. 3, No. 1 (2005).
3. See Philippe Marion, 'Narratologie médiatique et médiagénie des récits', in *Recherches en communication*, no. 7 (1997): 78–79.

8

The May Irwin Kiss: Performance and the Beginnings of Cinema

Charles Musser

> After the chamber had been cleared, they allowed each sense to be gratified: the eyes, which are the entrance way of love, and which carry messages to the heart, take satisfaction in the glance, for they rejoice in all they see; after the message of the eyes comes the far surpassing sweetness of kisses inviting love; both of them make trial of this sweetness, and let their hearts quaff so freely that hardly can they leave off. Thus, kissing was their first sport.
> (Chrétien de Troyes, *Eric and Enide*)

> Mei-Li: Is that the kiss that makes you light up inside?
> Ta: No. Compared to the kisses you see in the movies, this is only half done.
> Mei-Li: Half done? Well done, please.
> *Flower Drum Song* (1961)

This essay is concerned with some of the ways in which the cinema impacted on turn-of-the century American culture. It focuses on *The May Irwin Kiss* (April 1896), the first screen kiss and one of the first Edison films to be made for the new era of cinema (of projected motion pictures). In previous work I have considered other aspects of cinema's disruption and transformation of American culture, particularly as it affected various types of performance that were illegal or semi-legal in late nineteenth century America. If prizefighting, enactments of the Passion play, and children performing on the stage were forbidden, showing films of such subjects was not. The underage Ewer Sisters were not allowed to dance on the Broadway stage, but they could dance before Edison's kinetograph and the results shown in a kinetoscope parlour on Broadway near Herald Square. Films not only circumvented but quickly undermined many of these long-established prohibitions. By 1899 boxing matches – including prominent championship bouts – were being conducted on a legal basis in New York. In 1902, a Passion play was shown on Broadway. Such activities would have been unimaginable a decade earlier.

Closely related to the changed cultural status of certain types of performance, film brought commercial popular culture into areas of American life where they had heretofore been off limits. Here again cinematic representations involving the absence of presence easily circumvented long-standing prohibitions. Thus many religious groups (most notably Baptists and Methodists) prohibited their members from attending theatrical amusements but showed films of these forbidden performances (including *The May Irwin Kiss*) in their churches as a way to appeal to their membership! From their earliest appearances, motion pictures simply upended the cultural status quo.[1]

My concern has been that the significance of these phenomena, though important, can become exaggerated. There must be many other ways that cinema affected the cultural realm – particularly theatrical or performance culture – at this very early stage. It is not just that the cinema wormed its way into virtually every form of popular culture – the fairground, the magic lantern, vaudeville, the beer garden. It must have altered them, destabilized them, and done so in unexpected ways. In this respect *The May Irwin Kiss* offers some notably differences from films of fights and passion plays. For example, its antecedent was a very successful musical comedy running on Broadway. So here it would seem that the cinema was not energized by its ability to circumvent legal or de facto prohibitions. *The May Irwin Kiss* was also a very popular film – undoubtedly the most discussed Edison film of 1896 and one of the most successful films of the novelty era. Certainly its very popularity should make the film an interesting case for further study. Perhaps its pleasures and its importance were for reasons that we have not yet adequately understood. In fact, I will argue that to better grasp the way this film functioned during cinema's first year of successful commercial operation, we must ultimately reassess the prevailing historiographic paradigms within which contemporary film, media and cultural scholarship have tended to function.

The Widow Jones on tour

The May Irwin Kiss was a short, filmed extract from the musical comedy *The Widow Jones*, which had its debut on 19 August 1895, in Brockton, Massachusetts. After playing small cities and towns in Massachusetts (Lynn, Lowell and so forth), the May Irwin Company staged its Boston debut on 2 September and, after a two-week run, opened at the Bijou Theatre in New York City on 16 September. Eight weeks later, May Irwin and her company moved to the Harlem Opera House for one week (11–16 November), then played a week in Philadelphia (18–23 November) and another in Washington, D.C. (18–23 November). After a return appearance in Boston for another two weeks (2–14 December), the company embarked on a cross-country tour, which took them to San Francisco (23 December 1895 – 4 January 1896), Los Angeles (10–11 January 1896), Denver (20–24 January), and Chicago (9–22 February). The musical first appeared in the era of 'pre-cinema': that is, it was part of theatrical life before this included commercially viable, projected motion pictures on the screen.[2]

The Widow Jones had a rather absurd, light-hearted plot:

> The story is based on the experiences of an heiress whose life is made miserable by a set of suitors, who are set down as presumable fortune hunters. To escape them she takes flight to a village in Maine, and there passes herself

> off as the widow of a man who was supposed to have been drowned in that vicinity the year before.
>
> Consequently his seventeen-year-old daughter and an avalanche of unpaid bills are saddled upon the widow. Matters grow complicated when the supposed dead man appears upon the scene, and shows a decided tendency to make things lively. Among other annoying features of his sudden resurrection is the fact that one of his numerous wives has collected [an] insurance policy on his life.
>
> The predicaments in which the pseudo-widow is thus placed affords no end of humorous complications, but everything is straightened out and satisfactorily explained before the final curtain.[3]

When *The May Irwin Kiss* was made, we might assume that the filmmakers chose one of the musical's better-known moments to shoot. If this assumption seems logical, then the reader (like myself) might be surprised to learn that the now famous kissing scene was never mentioned in advertisements or promotional notices during the performance's first months. Nor did it receive much attention in reviews. *The New York Herald* characterized John C. Rice as 'a veritable virtuoso in the art of osculation' but never actually commented on the kissing scene itself.[4] The emphasis was on song and witty lines well-delivered. According to an advertisement in the *San Francisco Chronicle*, it boasted:

> New Comedy! New Songs! New Dances! New Specialties! Hear May Irwin sing 'The New Bully' and 'I Want Yer, Ma Honey.' They will create a vocal epidemic.[5]

May Irwin's personality and her singing, particularly her Negro or 'Coon' songs, were selling the show. John J. McNally's 'witty' script was alternately praised or dismissed as a valuable contribution. Unfortunately only Act Two of the book is readily available. Here is a brief sample of the dialogue, involving Beatrice Byke (May Irwin) who is posing as the widow of Jones and Felicity Jones (Ada Lewis), the 17-year-old daughter of 'Jones,' whom Beatrice Byke has inherited (so to speak) and is trying to educate:[6]

> *Felicity*
> Well, you know, dear, my one thought was to please you so I read your book called the Unnecessary Man and I have been living up to your ideas.
> (Business)
>
> *Beatrice*
> Well, I am glad you tried to please me, Felicity. But you know I might not have been exactly happy when I selected that word 'Unnecessary'. Man has his uses.
> (Business)
> (Gin Fizz)
>
> *Felicity*
> Thank you. Ah, me! This reminds me so much of school. I was sure I would do you credit.
>
> *Beatrice*
> Well, you do. One year at Vassar and you have learned all this.

Felicity
I say, dear, talking of credit – I still owe a bill or two.
Beatrice
Felicity, you don't mean to tell me you take after your father?
Felicity
There never was anything to take, after him.[7]

Unfortunately Act Three with its now famous kissing scene is not currently available. So what about the kiss?

The first newspaper mention of the soon-to-be-famous *Widow Jones* kiss that I have located appears in a rather long review from *The World-Herald* of Omaha, Nebraska, in early February 1896. After much praise of Miss Irwin, the reviewer noted that the other actors were talented: 'Then there is John C. Rice who knows how. If you don't believe this just watch him kiss the widow'.[8] Obviously, there are many reviews I have not seen, so this observation is subject to future qualification or revision. Nonetheless, the delayed nature of this attention to the kiss seems worth pondering. Why did reviewers – and perhaps your average theatregoer – not talk about this moment until some five months after the play was first produced?

Nethersole's *Carmen*

If theatrical columns and trade journals are to be believed, the history of the kiss in theatrical entertainment entered a new phase not with *The Widow Jones* but with Olga Nethersole's salacious performance in a dramatic version of *Carmen*, written by Henry Hamilton. Miss Nethersole's long and passionate kissing in *Carmen*, which had its New York City debut on Tuesday, 24 December 1895, created a stir and generated extensive critical comment in ways that was obviously not true for *The Widow Jones*. A reviewer for the *New York Dramatic Mirror* wrote:

> In view of the number and duration of the kisses she bestows it is not hard to understand why the three men who impersonate the parts of her lovers have clean shaven upper lips. An ordinary moustache subject to such treatment would soon be reduced to a shapeless hirsute mass. It is no exaggeration to assert that if Miss Nethersole were to reduce the duration of her kisses one-half, the performance would be over considerably more than a half hour before midnight.
>
> Notwithstanding all this, however, it must be admitted that she is at her best in her love-making scenes ...[9]

Nethersole's performance was much discussed and by week's end, the *Herald* noted that:

> Miss Nethersole's kisses have made a good deal of talk in town, and you may or may not, according to the sort of person you are, regard their fervor, duration and audible unctuousness necessary to the artistic depiction of Carmen's character. Most persons, I believe, will regard this part of the personation as much overdone, inasmuch as one irresistibly forgets the fiction in speculation as to whether Mr. Leicester (not Don Jose) does not feel embarrassed in being the recipient of such extraordinary greetings in public. The recollection of these few moments of too passionate osculation hangs rather heavily over the balance of the performance.[10]

Nethersole's kisses seemed so ardent, so heartfelt, so 'real' that they created a certain amount of discomfort. One thing was certain: as one critic put it, Nethersole had created 'an osculatory hit.'[11]

Carmen clearly put the kiss on the critical map so far as theatregoers were concerned. Now this may have meant that any stage kiss was given more scrutiny than in the past. That is, it may be that *Carmen* led critics to take more notice of that smooch between May Irwin and John C. Rice. Or, given the fact that Irwin and her company of comedians were always adding new specialties to *The Widow Jones* to keep it fresh and up-to-date, the actors may have elaborated on or even added the kiss – building it into a memorable moment. Or some mix of these possibilities. Certainly a direct link between the Rice-Irwin Kiss from *The Widow Jones* and Nethersole's kiss in *Carmen* was made on at least one occasion. When films were shown between acts of a play in Indianapolis, a critic noted that 'The first [picture] was the 'May Irwin Kiss' a burlesque on the famous Nethersole kiss in 'Carmen'. It was received with roars of laughter and is certainly very lifelike.'[12]

In many respects, it made sense to think of *The Widow Jones* kiss as a spoof of the Nethersole kiss. Nethersole kissed and kissed and kissed. In contrast, as one commentator noted:

> The widow isn't much of a hand at kissing. In fact, the characters about her are not of the kissable kind. So when in the last act the widow and Billie come to the widow's only kiss in the play, it stands out as prominently as a hill on a prairie.[13]

Certainly, they were not your usual romantic couple but rather – shall we say – middle aged. John C. Rice not only had graying hair, he was losing what he had. Irwin also plays a rather stout widow with a daughter in college and little use for men – or so she once claimed. She spends much of the play trying to get away from them. And when the widow and her suitor finally kiss, they admit to being somewhat out of practice – if the report in the *New York World* is accurate. According to the *World*:

> the Widow Jones told Billie Bilkes [sic] that the room between their lips admitted no argument. Bilkes [sic] thought he was out of practice, but could accomplish something in the osculatory line. Then he twisted his mustache out of the way and the Widow held up a pair of tempting lips.

Unlike the actors playing Carmen's suitors, Rice had a mustache; while the much practiced Carmen was seeking out kisses, Widow Jones had been avoiding them from her many suitors. Thus we have a good old-fashioned American kiss, one that spoke to the 'filthiness of imported English and French stage shows'[14] – not with sanctimonious outrage of easily offended critics, but with a distinctly American brand of ribald humor. Bilke may claim to be **rusty**, but the man who was performing this kiss – John C. Rice – enjoyed nightly practice.

Putting *The May Irwin Kiss* on the screen

The Widow Jones returned to the Bijou Theatre in New York City on 16 March, where it continued to be greeted with unabashed enthusiasm. The musical had turned May Irwin into a major star (just as *Carmen* had turned Nethersole into a major star), and it was soon approaching its 200th performance, This was an important milestone worthy of press comment and special commemorative trinkets. The occasion was to occur on Tuesday, 21 April – just two days before the premiere of 'Edison's Vitascope' at Koster & Bial's Music Hall in New York City. *The New York World*, one of the major New York City newspapers then engaged in a circulation war, effectively linked these two events. The newspaper arranged for Irwin and Rice to travel to Edison's Black Maria studio in Orange, New Jersey, where their kiss was 'kinetographed' by William Heise. *The World* then published an article on the film and its making, accompanied by a large number of frame enlargements reproduced (via line drawings) in its Sunday edition immediately following these two milestones. Part of its headline read: 'WIDOW JONES'S KISS FORTY-TWO FEET LONG'.[15] If Nethersole's kisses went on and on – and Irwin's kiss was mocking it, then the *World* played with this notion of excessive duration in its presentation of the Irwin kiss to its readership.

With the stage kiss provoking controversy in the theatre and the press, the *New York World* analysed and dissected one of the better known examples. In the case of a kinetographic kiss, 'Six hundred different phases of a kiss leave little to the imagination.' And how good at analysing a stage kiss are critics anyway? 'The first section was devoted to what apparently was a kiss, but was really only the preparation for one. These pictures show very distinctly how easily a person watching a couple might think they kissed when they didn't. The real kiss is a revelation.' Moreover, 'When a young woman insists on sending her betrothed kisses by mail, she may simply tear one by one yard of them from a kinetoscope strip, and the recipient will know what he gets'.[16] Like Nethersole in *Carmen*, the *World* article would seemingly never stop.

Newspaper coverage was obviously seen as good promotion for all sides, but there seems to have been some hesitation about showing the film itself. We should recall that newspapers and journals such as *Harper's Weekly* had published articles accompanied by frame enlargements of films (e.g. *Fred Ott's Sneeze*) that were never shown commercially.[17] Readers would not have expected to see the film on the screen: nothing in the article itself actually suggests that the film was screened or was intended to be screened. Certainly *The May Irwin Kiss* was not shown at the Vitascope's debut at Koster & Bial's Music Hall, nor in the weeks immediately after the article appeared in the *New York World*. It was apparently not screened until Monday, 11 May, the final week of the 1895–96 theatrical season for *The Widow Jones,* which closed on 16 May. This is admittedly somewhat speculative since little attention was paid to the specific titles of films shown at Koster & Bial's Music Hall after opening night. Nonetheless, in reviewing the theatre's program for that week, the *New York Dramatic Mirror* reported that 'The kissing scene from The Widow Jones was shown on the Vitascope along with the other pictures'.[18]

For one week at least, New York theatregoers had the novel opportunity of being able to see May Irwin and John C. Rice perform their kiss in two different theatrical venues and in two different modes. New Yorkers could see their live performance in one venue (as part of the complete musical) or their 'life-like,' indexically disembodied performance in another. As this unprecedented conjunction emphasizes, the arrival of projected motion pictures and *The May Irwin Kiss* heralded a fundamental change in the subjective experience for theatregoers, one that, when extrapolated to the larger culture, has been characterized as closely connected to the onset of modernity.[19] The use of a closer view compensated for the actors' absence, giving live performance and film different but perhaps approximately equal degrees of immediacy. That theatregoers could see May Irwin and John C. Rice at Koster & Bial's while the actors themselves were performing at the Bijou meant that theatregoers could experience a vertiginous disorientation and pleasure in the back and forth.

The decision not to show *The May Irwin Kiss* until 11 May is an intriguing one. A print could easily have been made available so why did Raff & Gammon not screen the film sooner? May Irwin and her management were probably not eager to give New Yorkers the choice between seeing her kiss on the screen or on the stage. The film might be good promotion, but would it benefit them financially? In truth they would be competing against themselves and might lose customers who chose to see them at Koster & Bial's rather than the Bijou. Perhaps they imagined that *The May Irwin Kiss* would appear during the summer months and function as a mirror of memory, reminding theatregoers of Irwin's talents. It would encourage them either to fondly recall her performance during the recently concluded season or regret having missed it – and anticipate her forthcoming appearance with the new theatrical season.

Irwin and her management recognized that this new form of virtual performance had both pitfalls and opportunities. For the first time theatrical audiences saw performances that were indexically disembodied: they watched actors perform even though the actors were not present. As André Bazin would say, motion pictures could embalm time, allowing for spatial as well as temporal dislocations. Irwin could find herself competing with her own image; or her virtual performance shown in one venue could compete with an identical performance shown in another venue. This is a twist that Chuck Jones would savor and extend half a century later in his animated cartoon *Duck Amuck* (1954) as Daffy battles his own image (which in the case of animation has an ontologically identical status). Motion pictures permitted not just one, but an endless multiplicity of identical performances. Copies of this fifteen-second film could present a taste of Irwin & Rice performing to the entire nation while she spent her summer months relaxing first in Europe and then at her summer home in Thousand Islands, New York.[20]

The May Irwin Company concluded its theatrical season on Saturday, 16 May. Two days later, on 18 May, entrepreneurs began to show the Vitascope in theatres outside New York City, opening first at Keith's New Theatre in Boston. *The Widow Jones* had a special relationship to Boston since its author, John McNally had been the dramatic editor for the *Boston Herald* and remained based in Boston. It was not entirely surprising then that *The May Irwin Kiss* was not only on the opening night program, it was featured prominently in newspaper advertisements:

> **THE PICTURE OF A KISS**
> Being a perfect reproduction of that long dawn-out and evidently enjoyable osculation indulged in by John C. Rice and May Irwin in John J. McNally's farce comedy, 'The Widow Jones,' including Rice's famous wink at the audience, admittedly one of the funniest episodes contained in any play.[21]

Although the entire Vitascope program 'caused a sensation', the *Boston Globe* noted that it was 'the kissing match between May Irwin and John C. Rice that caused the

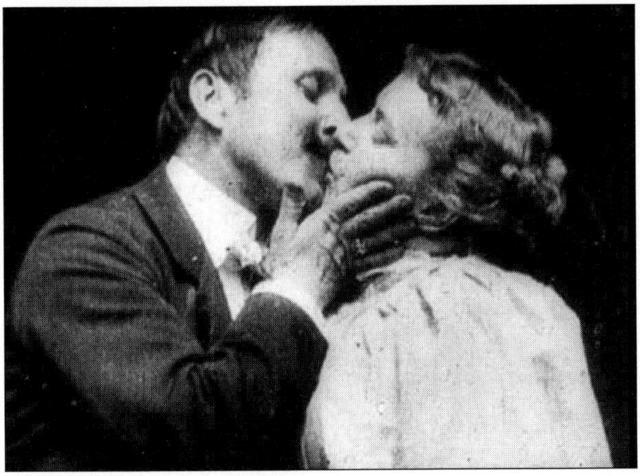

Fig. 1. The Kiss.

audience to shout with laughter and applaud as if mad'.[22] As a critic for the *Boston Herald* elaborated:

> The vitascope is going to be the greatest drawing card of the season, and will pack Boston's handsome playhouse from pit to dome at every performance so long as they choose to keep it running. Its possibilities are unlimited. Starting out with a series of pictures that are interesting, instructive and beautiful, they can add to them every week, aye, every day, if need be.
>
> Just think what it means. The scenes shown are local, full of life and action, simply lacking in vocalization, so far as the figures are concerned. The first indication that the public had been aroused to the importance of this invention was made manifest at the matinee yesterday, when standing room only was reported on the floor and in the gallery at Keith's. The same report was made of the evening attendance. To describe the enthusiasm aroused would be impossible. Worthy professors and scientific men vied with grocery clerks in the warmth of their applause; my lady in her box was, perhaps, a little more enthusiastic even than Brigit in the gallery. There was no hitch of any consequence in the first day's exhibitions, and as a result the big crowds poured forth to relate to their friends the wonderous thing which they had witnessed, and Mr. Albee moved about the lobby with his face wreathed in smiles. It denoted that he had struck a winning streak for the summer.
>
> Of the 10 pictures included in yesterday's programmes, it would be difficult to say which will leave the most lasting impression, but there is no shadow of a doubt as to which created the most laughter. That kissing scene in the 'Widow Jones,' taken part in by May Irwin and John C. Rice, was reproduced on the screen, and the very evident delight of the actor and the undisguised pleasure of the actress were absolutely 'too funny' for anything.[23]

At any rate the large audiences thought so, and many of them laughed until they almost cried. Keith advertisements continued to promote the film in subsequent weeks, and *The May Irwin Kiss* probably remained on the bill throughout the Vitascope's twelve-week run (18 May – 7 August). At least during the tenth week, it was announced that 'The only "original" picture that still maintains a place in the vitascope program is the Rice-Irwin kiss, and it bids fair to continue to the end of the chapter'.[24]

When people went to a vaudeville show and saw the Vitascope, they did not just see Irwin and Rice work their way into a single kiss. Because the vitascope showed film loops, they saw them kiss again and again and again. According to the *Los Angeles Times*,

> Their smiles and glances and expressive gestures and the final joyous, over-powering, luscious osculation was repeated again and again, while the audience fairly shrieked and howled approval.[25]

Considering the movie-going experience primarily from a phenomenological or theoretical perspective, we might say that the repetition of the kiss within the theatre echoed, duplicated and so multiplied the repetition of this disembodied performance in different theatres. A more narrow textual analysis of *The May Irwin Kiss* would suggest that its repetitive kissing structure parallels the constant kissing done by Nethersole in *Carmen*. The film spoofs her excessive kissing through its mechanical means. Again this is an American kiss with American technology.

Chasing an image with a will of its own

As spring turned to summer in 1896, the Vitascope opened in various cities across the United States: Philadelphia on 25 May, New Haven on 28 May, Providence on 4 June, San Francisco on 8 June, Baltimore on 15 June, Brooklyn on 22 June, New Orleans on 28 June, Wilkes-Barre, Pa. on 29 June, Detroit and Cleveland on 1 July, Chicago and Los Angeles on 5 July, Milwaukee and Kansas City on 26 July, and Denver on 16 August. Almost without exception *The May Irwin Kiss* was the favored film on the bill and proved very popular. Soon it was being shown in cities never visited by *The Widow Jones*. Even as Rice and Irwin were enjoying a summer's respite from their grueling schedule, they remained an omnipresent phenomenon in the theatre. Not just their image (photographs, engravings) but their performance – their disembodied but virtual selves – had achieved an independent existence. Although they were drawing huge crowds into the theatres and were receiving significant newspaper attention, this required no effort on their part. Effortless utopia perhaps, but at the same time, they lacked any control over their performance. Nor did financial benefits accrue to them personally.

The film's relationship to *The Widow Jones* was not severed but it became much more distended. The film no longer functioned simply as a brief simulacrum, a nostalgic reminder of the stage phenomenon and a promo for Irwin's next theatrical tour. The film generated laughter and pleasure on its own terms. In this respect, the repetitive nature of the Vitascope kiss was significant. Repetition of the film via looping gave the kiss a new context – another kiss that was absolutely identical. (As Henri Bergson would remind readers a few years later, repetition was a key element of comedy.[26]) The Vitascope kiss came to stand not simply or primarily in relationship to May Irwin's stage smooch but in relationship to the whole controversy surrounding the stage kiss – lampooning the controversy with its endless and apparently effortless repetition. If the Irwin and her managers were unhappy with these unanticipated consequences, there were compensatory values. They must have recognized that *The May Irwin Kiss* provided them with commercial opportunities that were difficult to ignore. Or, considered from another perspective, even if they could not control the image itself, they could create the illusion of control by using the film's success to their own ends. They thus found themselves having to chase their own image – their virtual selves.

Forever joined together in the world on the screen, Rice and Irwin were not chained together in real life. As the 1896–97 theatrical season approached, their responses to the opportunities and dilemmas of the film differed substantially. This was perhaps inevitable given two inter-related decision that had been made as the 1895–96 theatrical season drew to a close. First, theatrical columns had announced that May Irwin would begin the 1896–97 season with a new musical comedy.[27] Second, it was announced that 'Mr. Charles Dickson will take Mr. John C. Rice's place in Miss May Irwin's company next season. Mr. Rice will join Mr. William Hoey in the revival of 'A Parlor Match'.[28] Sally Cohen, Rice's wife, left Irwin's company as well. Rice's departure was not particularly unusual in that these actors often sought out new combinations from one year to the next. Nonetheless, the implication seems to have been that Rice was too often sharing the spotlight with Irwin. Now that she was an established star, his supporting presence was unnecessary. Moreover, Rice appeared rather old: he was losing his hair. More youthful and debonair than Rice, Dickson would allow Irwin to escape the middle-age epitaph. Because Dickson was a light rather than a farce comedian, he would also keep her more clearly at the center of the comedy.[29]

Despite his departure from the *Widow Jones* company, John C. Rice wholeheartedly embraced and exploited the famed screen smooch as the new 1896–97 theatrical season commenced. Despite advancing age, Rice suddenly found himself to be the most famous male kisser in America; he would not waste this fleeting opportunity by participating in a revival of *A Parlor Match* (if such was ever seriously contemplated). Rather Rice and Sally Cohen started their own vaudeville routine, which made the vitascope kiss a central ingredient. The duo began a series of one-week engagements on Monday, 17 August, at Boston's Grand Opera House, which began its new theatrical season on that day. The Grand Opera House was then presenting a series of dramatic works by its repertory company, supplemented by vaudeville. According to the *Boston Journal*:

> In the vaudeville portion of the program, perhaps the greatest interest was taken in the appearance of John C. Rice and Sally Cohen. It is scarcely necessary to say that they pleased the large audiences. Mr. Rice is an extremely versatile comedian and kept the audience convulsed with his fund of witty sayings, his odd grimaces and, more than all else, his remarkable agility in dancing. Sally Cohen proved a delightful adjunct to the popular star, and the sketch as voted most pleasing.[30]

By this time, the Vitascope had departed Keith's Theatre in Boston, replaced by the Lumière Cinématgraphe. *The May Irwin Kiss* remained a strong memory, and the *Boston Journal*, which disapproved of the kissing fad, gave few details about the sketch's contents.

Rice and Cohen went on to tour the top vaudeville houses along the East Coast; many of these same theatres had featured *The May Irwin Kiss* earlier in the summer. The couple helped to open the new theatrical season at Keith's Bijou in Philadelphia on Monday, 24 August 1896, given billing second only to the Lumière Cinématographe.[31] The following week their act was the headline attraction at Proctor's Pleasure Palace in New York City (31 August – 5 September) and advertised in the following terms:

> The quaint comedian and best dancer on the stage, formerly of Monroe and Rice, and more recently identified with the success of 'The Widow Jones': the hero of the famous 'May Irwin Kiss,' assisted by the dainty singing comedienne of farce-comedy repute in a new and wholly original act.[32]

According to the *New York Clipper*, 'they became great favorites, their clever work winning great applause'.[33] Much of their vaudeville sketch, entitled 'The School of Acting', involved Rice demonstrating his kissing technique to his pupil (Sally Cohen), playing off his hit role in *The Widow Jones* as well as *The May Irwin Kiss*.[34]

The following two weeks, Rice & Cohen were at Keith's Opera House in Providence, Rhode Island (7–12 September) and then at Keith's Union Square Theatre in New York (14–19 September). In Providence,

> John C. Rice and Sally Cohen have a bright sketch, the success of which is dependent on witty dialogue and good acting, not on a song, a dance and a few local hits. The lesson on kissing, with Mr. Rice as the instructor and Miss Cohen as the pupil, was enjoyed by everyone in the theater.[35]

This was also the week of The Rhode Island State Fair, where the Vitascope was being shown – presumably with *The May Irwin* Kiss. At Keith's Union Square,

> John C. Rice and Sally Cohen were the only performers who had their names printed in heavy faced type here last week. It is needless to say they made a hit. Their sketch is bright and amusing, abounding in witty lines and up-to-date gags. Of course, there is a good deal about osculation in it, as, since his exploitation of the Vitascope, Mr. Rice has a reputation to sustain in this line of business. They wind up with a very graceful dance during which Mr. Rice turns several handsprings in very nimble fashion.[36]

Rice & Cohen's appearance at Keith's Union Square also coincided with the reappearance of the Vitascope, which reopened in F.F. Proctor's two Manhattan vaudeville houses on 14 September – the top offering in both theatres. At Proctor's 23rd Street Theatre, according to the *Dramatic Mirror*, 'The new views met with instant favor, as the audiences were familiar with the scenes they represented'.[37] For this opening week, *Inventor Edison Sketched by World Artist* (aka *Blackton Drawing Edison*) received most of the praise and took the place of *The May Irwin Kiss* as the hit film. Why wasn't *The May Irwin Kiss* shown? Perhaps Raff & Gammon, who held the exhibition rights to New York, chose to show their newest films. Or perhaps Proctor's objected to showing a film that would promote Rice & Cohen when they were performing in a rival vaudeville house. That is, he may have preferred to wait until Rice & Cohen returned to New York to play in one of his theatres.

Rice and Cohen completed the Keith circuit, which then consisted of four theatres, by traveling next to Keith's New Theatre in Boston (21–26 September). As a *Boston Globe* reviewer noted, 'John C. Rice of 'Widow Jones' fame and Sally Cohen took part in a farce comedy that wound up with a kissing scene that discounted the famous vitascope episode'.[38] Keith's manager did not give Rice & Cohen the same prominence they had enjoyed in New York, perhaps because they were performing their skit in Boston for the second time. Nonetheless, Irwin and *The Widow Jones* had just concluded another two-week run at the Boston Museum the previous week. Rice's kissing demonstrations, as we shall see, certainly remained timely and perhaps even pointed. Rice and Cohen were placed in the third position – after the Lumière Cinématographe and J.K. Emmett, Jr., a legitimate actor who was making his first appearance on the vaudeville stage, but ahead of Lillian Burkhart in a comedy sketch 'Two Can Play at that Game.' Even so, *The Globe's* advance announcement pointedly ignored Rice and favored Burkhart:

> Lillian Burkhart, wife of May Irwin's leading man, Charles A. Dickson, and a very bright and talented young woman, is to appear in the comedy sketch, 'Two Can Play at that Game,' supported by Adolf Jackson, formerly with William Crane, and George W. Leonard, both competent actors. The piece is a very strong one, and when Mr. and Mrs. Dickson presented it earlier in the summer at Keith's it was a great success.[39]

The *Boston Herald* advance announcement was similarly silent when it came to Rice and Cohen. Nonetheless, the duo proved popular. In a brief acknowledgment that was buried in the middle of the review's fourth paragraph, *The Boston Herald* critic wrote, 'Of course, John C. Rice and Sally Cohen received a warm welcome, and their share in the entertainment was of the usual high class that has made them such favorites with theatregoers'.[40]

Rice & Cohen returned to New York to play Proctor's 23rd Street Theatre for the week of 28 September – 3 October. According to a review in the *New York Clipper*,

> This cozy house continues on the wave of popularity, good attendance being the rule during the day and evening. The programme presented 28 September for week, contained many popular favorites and was awarded a favorable verdict on the opening day. Edison's vitascope was continued a leading headline and was still high in popular favor. ... John C. Rice and Sally Cohen were pleasing entertainers.[41]

During the week that Rice & Cohen were at the 23rd Street venue, newspaper advertisements indicate that *The May Irwin Kiss* was shown at both Proctor's 23rd Street Theatre and Proctor's Pleasure Palace.[42] The film also remained in Proctor's Manhattan venues during the following week as well.[43] Theatregoers could see Rice kiss May Irwin on the screen as a reminder of his past performances and then witness him explaining how it was done as he kissed his wife Sally Cohen live and in person on the vaudeville stage. Physically present and performing in the present tense, this aging actor could explain how with proper practice even he had been able to become America's favorite Don Juan, the cinema's first heartthrob.

The Dickson-Irwin Kiss

By July Irwin's management had postponed the introduction of John J. McNally's new musical *Courted Into Court* in order to exploit the enthusiasm for *The Widow Jones* that was generated by *The May Irwin Kiss*. Irwin reopened the musical comedy in Trenton, New Jersey, on 2 September 1896, and after a few tune ups, resumed her serious tour with a three-week stay in Boston, opening 7 September at the Boston Museum. Although this was the show's third stay in Boston, *The Widow*

Jones did a booming business. This was the first chance to see her after *The May Irwin Kiss* was screened and, reversing the normal box office trend, she completed one of the most successful weeks in the history of the Boston Museum. 'Instead of showing a decrease in public favor, it has disclosed an even stronger drawing capacity than ever.'[44] There were new songs and specialties and a handful of new actors. Dickson was given the same billing as all the other cast members – whereas advertisements in the previous season had consistently indicated that Irwin was 'supported by John C. Rice.' Now the musical featured 'The *Only* **MAY IRWIN** and Her BIG COMPANY of Comedians'.[45] As the *Boston Globe* reviewer noted, 'There are some changes in the cast. Mr. Charles Dickson plays the role of Billy Bilke in a quieter manner than did his predecessor. He was very satisfactory.'[46] Perhaps, but he was no John C. Rice – and this proved to be a serious problem.

Let us consider the *Boston Herald* review, which presumably reflected the interests of its former dramatic editor, John J. McNally. It hailed the farce musical as a classic:

> The 'Widow Jones' wears well. This is the third engagement of the company in this city, yet the bright points of the text, the comical situations, the laughable incidents and the funny accidents and episodes created as much merriment yesterday as they did when the piece was first presented here. It is a clean, wholesome, bright and thoroughly amusing play, and no other musical comedy presented here in a decade has so entertained and satisfied our audiences.[47]

Miss Irwin was also praised at considerable length for her comic talents:

> Miss Irwin is a great popular favorite. She appeals to all classes and is as great a favorite with women as with men. She is vivacious, magnetic and artistic. Her personality is pleasing, and her power over an audience is remarkable. She attracts, holds the attention and fascinates. She has a keen sense of humor which few actresses possess; she has the remarkable gift of being able to do the same thing and speak the same lines night after night with all the appearance and effect of spontaneity, and she has the skill to judge her audience with such accuracy that she seldom misses hitting the right note for effect. She seemingly takes her audience into her confidence and each one in the house feels that she has been acting for his especial interest.[48]

Finally, in praising the 'best company ever put together in this country for the presentation of a work of this character,' the reviewer endorsed the change in cast – with much enthusiasm.

> Mr. Dickson, who has frequently been seen here as a star at the head of his own companies, this season replaces Mr. John C. Rice, and he won a decided success yesterday. He dresses the character of the successful lover of the widow with great taste, and plays it with a lightness of touch and skill which make it stand forth prominently. Miss Hattie Williams, another new comer to the cast, plays Marcia well; Mis Etta Gilroy, who now plays the character impersonated last season by Sally Cohen, is a very pretty and vivacious little actress, and Miss Clara Palmer's handsome face and graceful dancing add materially to the strength of the company.[49]

Dickson may have been a delight, but he was not the man famed for kissing the widow in *The May Irwin Kiss*. Given that the success of the film had much to do with the box office patronage of the musical comedy, this **absence of commentary on the kiss** can only be considered an awkward one – a structuring absence that called for superlatives in other areas. The long and enthusiastic kudos for the musical, its star, and the entire cast was covering over the fact that audience would not see an embodied performance of the famed osculation, which they had seen many times on the screen.

The Dickson-Irwin kiss went unmentioned in most Boston newspapers, but there was at least one notable exception. Because the *Boston Journal* was enthusiastic about the change in actors and action, it analysed the new stage kiss in considerable detail:

> Mr. Charles Dickson, who succeeds Mr. John C. Rice in the part of Billy Bilke, has to compete not only with Mr. Rice's undoubted hit in the part last season, but with that dreadful vitascope picture called the May Irwin kiss, in which Mr. Rice appeared as the osculator.
>
> Mr. Dickson plays this part rather more rationally and less extravagantly than his predecessor, and with no diminution of its effect.
>
> It is gratifying to find that the kiss episode has been largely bequeathed to the vitascope, from which it may be inferred that Miss Irwin has seen the picture.[50]

This would suggest that the kiss was downplayed, perhaps because efforts to duplicate its effect with Irwin's new osculatory partner were doomed. For those critics who opposed excessive kissing, this was to the good. For fans of *The May Irwin Kiss*, the opposing reaction – that of disappointment – was the likely response.

Irwin and Rice – reconciled and reunited

Although neither Rice nor Irwin had control over their disembodied kiss, they were both making use of the film's tremendous popularity. And yet despite the slights each directed at the other, there was a problem that Irwin and Rice shared. While Rice was kissing Sally Cohen (his wife!) and May Irwin was kissing Lillian Burkhart's husband, neither one was kissing the person s/he had kissed in *The May Irwin Kiss*. The film had created a strong desire among theatregoers to see Irwin and Rice osculate live and on stage. This desire was being thwarted, and it was ultimately to no one's advantage. That is, the film had fostered a yearning for the original cast, and that original cast was not intact. Something had to be done.

As it turned out Rice & Cohen did not complete a full week of vaudeville at Proctor's 23rd Street Theatre. Rice and Irwin's management finally reached an agreement, and the two kissing stars were reunited. Although the details are unknown, we can certainly speculate as to the terms. Rice and Cohen returned to Irwin's company with improved pay and certain guarantees as to billing and long-term employment. Unlike Dickson, Rice was once again given special notice in newspaper advertisements for *The Widow Jones*. And when May Irwin introduced the new musical farce *Courted Into Court* in December 1896, Rice played her charming but difficult husband. The following year, May Irwin's sister, Flo Irwin, toured with *The Widow Jones* and Rice teamed up with Marie Dressler and toured with *Courted into Court,* while May Irwin launched a new farce comedy, *The Swell Miss Fitzwell*, by H.A. Du Souchet.[51] As a result of this pragmatic reconciliation, when May Irwin played New Haven on Saturday, 3 October, the big news was that

'John C. Rice has rejoined the company and will be seen in his old role'.[52] Ditto Sally Cohen.

The Irwin-Rice reunion was greeted with widespread approval. Their first full week as a reunited duo was at the Walnut Theatre in Philadelphia for 5–10 October. As the Philadelphia correspondent for the *Dramatic Mirror* reported, 'The Widow Jones ... as usual is attracting applause and large patronage. John C. Rice is again in his old place, introducing many new specialties'.[53] According to the *Philadelphia Public Ledger*,

> John C. Rice, a favorite in Philadelphia, catches Miss Irwin's humor perfectly and matches her acting with his own in a most harmonious manner. Both have a fund of dry humor, which bubbles up spontaneously, is never forced and always catches the audience.[54]

A proper order or correspondence between virtual and actual performance had been restored. And what happened to Charles Dickson? He was in Philadelphia that same week, performing with his wife, Lillian Burkhardt, at Keith's Bijou in 'Two Can Play at That Game'.[55]

The ramifications of this renewed symmetry between film and play were evident in Pittsburgh, later that fall. The Vitascope came to Pittsburgh rather late compared to most other U.S. cities, opening at the Bijou Theatre on 7 September. Although *The Widow Jones* had not yet appeared in Pittsburgh, *The May Irwin Kiss* was nonetheless the featured film – still advertised as 'THE PICTURE OF A KISS, Being a perfect reproduction of that evidently enjoyable osculation indulged in by John C. Rice and May Irwin'.[56] It remained on the bill throughout the Vitascope's four-week stay, and easily received more press attention than any of the other films. One fact was unknown to most local audience members at the time: although the film represented a moment from *The Widow Jones*, the presumed correspondence between screen and stage performance no longer existed. This breakdown loomed as a serious problem for the musical's management. With the re-engagement of Rice, however, there was a renewed symmetry even before the end of the film's Pittsburgh run. Here again, the relationship between signifier and signified was demonstrably unstable.

The Widow Jones finally reached Pittsburgh on 16 November, a month after the Vitascope's departure, and was performed at the same Bijou Theatre. In contrast to the situation in Boston, New York, New Haven and Philadelphia, this was the first opportunity for Pittsburgh theatregoers to see the musical comedy and so many had seen the film before they saw the stage musical. For these patrons, the sequential experience of musical and film was inverted. Moreover, in contrast to the publicity and promotion of the musical in Boston two months before, newspaper advertisements for *The Widow Jones* now told prospective patrons to come 'See the Great May Irwin Kiss!' Irwin's kiss was given equal billing with her songs.[57] And of course, the kiss received much attention from theatre patrons and critics, including a reviewer for the *Pittsburg Press* who remarked,

> It is a long-drawn-out affair and looks as though one were biting the end off the other's tongue. It will undoubtedly become famous around Pittsburg among lovesick swains.[58]

Irwin had indeed seen *The May Irwin Kiss*, and with her old osculatory partner knew how to fully exploit it.

Irwin's company had been chasing the motion picture, and was finally able to reassert some semblance of control. Spectators could see the kiss as a re-embodied performance involving both actors. Potential discordance had been replaced by harmony between virtual and real performances. (The correspondence, however, may not have been perfect: the stage version of the kiss seems to have become just a little more salacious than the filmic standard!) As we have seen, Irwin's management expended substantial energy to ensure that this would occur. Appearances to the contrary, the commercial logic dictated by *The May Irwin Kiss* was so powerful that Irwin's management had little choice. Rice and Irwin were victims (in some respects 'happy victims') of their own image, their virtualized (i.e. kinetographed) performance.

Reflections

I am still thinking through the impact and implications of *The May Irwin Kiss* for theatrical culture. There are some obvious and fairly narrow aspects to be noted. According to Robert Grau, the introduction of projected motion pictures made vaudeville a highly profitable form of theatrical entertainment and was largely responsible for its rapid expansion.[59] *The May Irwin Kiss* was not only a financial boon for exhibitors and theatrical venues showing the film, it also provided box office benefits to the musical comedy from which it was taken. Certainly the film helped to boost the careers of Irwin and Rice. Although films in the peep-hole kinetoscope era had fostered the public's interest in certain performers, projected motion pictures greatly magnified this effect. Once the Edison film *Inventor Edison* (August 1896) was shown in various vaudeville houses, its star – lightning sketch artist J. Stuart Blackton – immediately moved up into big time vaudeville.

Since *The May Irwin Kiss* was one of the most popular films in the United States during cinema's novelty year, it must be considered an extreme example of cinema's initial cultural impact. Yet it was by no means atypical. Vaudeville stars Vernona Jarbeau and Cissy Fitzgerald both performed for Edison's camera in the spring of 1896. Both the actresses and their disembodied performances appeared in vaudeville houses over the course of 1896. Trick bicycle rider Lee Richardson performed on stage and then before Edison's camera. Eugen Sandow appeared before the Biograph cameras and then used the Biograph exhibition service as part of his touring vaudeville program in the fall of 1896. The back and forth between actual and virtual performances was a crucial dimension of the cinema's novelty year. It was one way for spectators to make phenomenological sense of this new form of representation, and find pleasure in the experience as well. People understood projected motion pictures to be another aspect of theatrical entertainment. The theatre-film hybrids were logical because both virtual and live performances were seen as part of the same vital theatrical culture of this period. Indeed, as Terry Ramsaye remarked,

> The year 1897 saw an ingenious effort to find a place for the motion picture in the technique of the stage by its inclusion in a drama.
>
> The play was *The Good Mister Best,* written by John J. McNally, the George

> M. Cohan of the 1890s. The major interest of the piece revolved about a bit of business by which the master of the household could press a button and see revealed on the wall what was taking place in any room of the establishment. He saw plenty. The revelation on the wall was a motion picture.[60]

On one level, this combination of media was syncretic, on another it was a 'natural' integration of theatrical forms.

Despite my hopes to the contrary, it does seem that May Irwin's screen kiss shares something with fight films and Passion plays. As Olga Nethersole's *Carmen* demonstrated, kissing on the stage was still capable of creating unease in critics and spectators – particularly if the kiss was too realistic. Certainly *The May Irwin Kiss* also had its detractors – as the *Boston Journal* article cited above suggests. But its comic success vanguished all opposition. By presenting a very realistic kiss in close up, over and over again, *The May Irwin Kiss* made future representations of kisses in the theatre rather ordinary. It would seem to have been a minor instance in the overall breaking down of cultural prohibitions.

The May Irwin Kiss had a significant if localized impact. It changed the way that people looked at the musical comedy. It disrupted the smooth functioning of the Irwin company as Rice had to be recalled from the vaudeville stage, suggesting the potential power that cinematic images could have over live performance. It also demonstrates that film cannot be fully appreciated apart from its full theatrical context. The repetitive looping of the kiss became a way to spoof the Nethersole kiss (and stage kissing in general), extending whatever burlesque was intended in the musical comedy itself. The film then is not just a significant intervention in film history, it has an essential relevance for the history of the stage. And in fact, it shows how these histories of stage and screen, of embodied and virtual performance, can only be separated at a certain loss. To situate this film within a history of intermediality – of the interaction among media is, I think, insufficient. Both the film and the play must be analysed within a unified history of theatrical culture broadly defined. The legitimate stage, vaudeville, and the cinema were (and are) all forms of theatrical culture (various genres of theatrical practice) and had much in common: performers, intertexts, advertising, critics, audiences and most importantly the theatrical venue.

This process of exploring the cultural moment surrounding *The May Irwin Kiss* occurs at a time when we are situating film within many different kinds of historiographic frameworks: those of cinema, of motion pictures, of moving images, of the screen, of theatrical experience, of visual culture, of performance culture, of media, of intermediality, of popular culture, of culture itself. *The May Irwin Kiss* has a place in all of them. And so, while we may argue for and pragmatically make use of one or another of these historical paradigms, we will need to think about these different kinds of histories and what their implications are for us as we move forward. Film Studies and individual film scholars have provided histories of cinema – in one or more volumes, often divided along national lines. But we have not begun to approach coherent, sustained and in depth histories within many of these more ambitious frameworks. It is a daunting task and one that very few of us are as yet prepared to undertake. Before some of these more ambitious cultural histories become feasible, it may be necessary to explore cultural activities on an intermediate level. Situating the cinema and *The May Irwin Kiss* within the history of theatrical culture – as I have just begun to do here – is a small step in trying to understand how the motion pictures had a profound impact on American life and culture from the very outset. The theatre world played a crucial role in the psychic and cultural life of the United States. After the Vitascope's Koster & Bial's debut, the cinema participated in this cultural realm in wide-ranging ways. This is not to suggest that theatrical culture was the only area where the cinema had such an impact. Quite the reverse. Photography, the lantern world, and what Tom Gunning has called cultural optics are just some of these other areas.[61] The cinema did much more than present a new media, a new form of amusement: it operated within and so disrupted and transformed any number of existing cultural practices of which the theatre was exemplary but by no means unique. In fact, one might argue that the total effect of cinema's disruptive impact on these many different realms was one of the compelling reasons for motion pictures to be seen as a new form, a new practice, a new art.

Notes

1. Many thanks to Vanessa Toulmin and Simon Popple for their support as I first presented this paper at the Visual Delights Conference in Sheffield, England in July 2002. Charles Musser, *The Emergence of Cinema: The American Screen to* 1907 (New York: Scribners, 1990), 193–218; Edison *Motion Pictures, 1890–1900: An Annotated Filmography* (Washington, D. C. and Friuli, Italy: Smithsonian Institution Press and Le Giornate del Cinema Muto, 1997): 37, 112–113; 'Passions and the Passion Play: Theater, Film and Religion, 1880–1900', *Film History*, 5:4 (1993): 419–456; Musser with Carol Nelson, *High-Class Moving Pictures: Lyman H. Howe and the Forgotten Era of Traveling Exhibition, 1880–1920* (Princeton: Princeton University Press, 1991): 72.
2. There are many examples of projected motion pictures being shown in the United States in 1895, notably with the Eidoloscope and the Phantoscope. Nonetheless, the cinema did not become commercially successful and so a significant cultural force until the Vitascope's debut on 23 April, 1896. Within the American cultural context, this date seems to be a particularly crucial one.
3. 'At the Theatres', *New York Dramatic Mirror* (21 September 1895): 16.
4. 'May Irwin as the Widow', *New York Herald* (17 September 1895): 7.
5. Advertisement, *San Francisco Chronicle* (22 December 1895): 12.
6. For a review of the play spelling out the relationships between the different characters, see 'At the Theatres', *New York Dramatic Mirror* (21 September 1895): 16.
7. Excerpt from Act Two of *The Widow Jones*, page 58 of play script, Billy Rose Theater Collection, New York Public Library.
8. 'Amusements', *Omaha World-Herald* (3 February 1896): 5.
9. 'At the Theatres', *New York Dramatic Mirror* (4 January 1896): 14.
10. *New York Herald* (29 December 1895): 4D.
11. 'At Other Houses', *New York Dramatic Mirror* (11 January 1896): 14. When playing in Brooklyn, 'She did not carry the kissing effects to the limits reached in New York, but she was sufficiently realistic to suit her Brooklyn admirers.' 'Brooklyn Theatres', *New York Dramatic Mirror* (22 February 1896): 16.
12. 'Sinbad's Success at English's', *Indianapolis Journal* (15 September 1896).
13. Mrs. McGuirk, 'The Anatomy of a Kiss', *New York World* (26 April 1896): 21.
14. 'Notes', *The Chap-Book* vol. 5 [15 July 1896], 5:239–240, quoted in Terry Ramsaye, *A Million and One Nights: A History of the Motion Picture* 2 vols. (New York: Simon and Schuster, 1926) 1:260.
15. McGuirk, *New York World* (26 April 1896): 21.
16. McGuirk, *New York World* (26 April 1896): 21.
17. See Barnet Phillips, *Harper's Weekly* (24 March 1894): 280; and 'Wizard Edison's Kinetograph', *New York World* (18 March 1894): 21.

18. 'Last Week's Bills', *New York Dramatic Mirror* (23 May 1896): 19.
19. See Leo Charney and Vanessa R. Schwartz, eds., *Cinema and the Invention of Modern Life* (Berkeley: University of California Press, 1995); Ben Singer, *Melodrama and Modernity: Early Sensational Cinema and Its Contexts* (New York: Columbia University, 2001): 17–37.
20. 'Foyer and Green Room Gossip', *Boston Globe* (17 May 1896): 18.
21. Advertisement, *Boston Globe* (17 May 1896): 19. Various scholars have pointed to advertisements to suggest that showmen were promoting the novelty of cinema on the basis of specific technology and that the actual subject matter was not important. (See Gunning, 'The Cinema of Attractions' in Adam Barker and Thomas Elsaesser, *Early Cinema: Space Frame Narrative* (London: BFI, 1990), 58. Advertisements by Keith, Proctor and other showmen in this period suggest that this was not the case.
22. 'Keith's New Theater', *Boston Globe* (19 May 1896): 8.
23. 'Keith's New Theatre', *Boston Herald* (19 May 1896): 9.
24. 'Keith's New Theater', *Boston Globe* (19 July 1896):18.
25. *Los Angeles Times* (7 July 1896): 6.
26. An application of Bergson's comedic theory to *The May Irwin* Kiss would produce many correspondences. For example, he remarks that 'We laugh ever time a person gives us the impression of being a thing.' Henri Bergson, 'Laughter' in Wylie Sypher, ed., *Comedy* (Baltimore: Johns Hopkins University Press, 1956), 97. The projection of life-like images on the Vitascope, with its repetitions and loops, did precisely this.
27. 'Theatrical Bits', *New York Herald* (10 May 1896), 6F.
28. 'Theatrical Bits', *New York Herald* (3 May 1896): 5E.
29. When Irwin and Dickson played at the Boston Museum, one critic remarked, 'That she is the mainspring of the vast amount of fun in 'The Widow Jones' there is no gainsaying. 'Boston Museum', *Boston Journal* (15 September 1896): 7.
30. 'Another Opens', *Boston Journal* (18 August 1896): 4.
31. Advertisement, *Philadelphia Record*, (23 August 1896):11.
32. Advertisement, *New York World* (30 August 1896): 14. The other half of Monroe and Rice was George W. Monroe.
33. 'Proctor's Pleasure Palace', *New York Clipper* (5 September 1896): 424.
34. For the title of Rice & Cohen's vaudeville skit, see advertisement, *New York World* (13 September 1896):14.
35. 'Keith's Opera House', *Providence Journal* (8 September 1896): 8.
36. 'Keith's Union Square', *New York Dramatic Mirror* (26 September 1896): 17.
37. 'Proctor's', *New York Dramatic Mirror* (26 September 1896): 17.
38. 'Keith's New Theater', *Boston Daily Globe* (22 September 1896): 2.
39. 'Keith's New Theater', *Boston Sunday Globe* (20 September 1896): 8.
40. 'Keith's New Theater', *Boston Herald* (22 September 1896): 12.
41. 'Proctor's Theater', *New York Clipper* (3 October 1896), 8.
42. Advertisement, *New York World* (27 September 1896): 18; According to one afternoon newspaper, 'Edison's Vitascope still continues to astonish and delight the throngs at Proctor's. The views this week are the May Irwin Kiss, Street scene Herald Square ...' 'Proctor's Pleasure Palace', *New York Mail and Express* (29 September 1896): 7.
43. 'Proctor's Pleasure Palace', *New York Mail & Express* (10 October 1896): 14.
44. 'The Widow Jones', *Boston Sunday Globe* (13 September 1896): 18.
45. Advertisement, *Boston Sunday Herald* (6 September 1896): 11.
46. 'Welcome to May Irwin', *Boston Daily Globe* (8 September 1896):12.
47. 'At the Playhouses', *Boston Herald* (8 September 1896): 7.
48. Ibid.
49. Ibid.
50. 'Plays and Players', *Boston Journal* (8 September 1896): 7.

51. 'At the Tremont', *Boston Herald* (3 October 1897):10.
52. *New Haven Evening Register* (2 October 1896): 4.
53. 'Philadelphia', *New York Dramatic Mirror* (10 October 1896): 10.
54. 'The Walnut–'The Widow Jones'', *Philadelphia Public Ledger* (6 October 1896): 17.
55. 'Advertisement, *Philadelphia Press* (4 October 1896): 9.
56. Advertisement, *Pittsburgh Press* (6 September 1896): 16.
57. Advertisements, *Pittsburgh Post* (15 November 1896):16.
58. 'Theatrical', *Pittsburgh Press* (17 November 1896): 7.
59. Robert Grau, *The Business Man in the Amusement World* (New York: Broadway Publishing, 1910): 108–110. See also Robert Grau, *Theater of Science* (New York: Broadway Publishing, 1914): 7–10.
60. Ramsaye, *A Million and One Nights*, 378.
61. Tom Gunning, 'Phantasmagoria: Cinema, Magic and Cultural Optics', delivered at the Communities of Sense: Re-Thinking Aesthetics in Practice Conference (Columbia University, New York City), 19 April 2003.

9

'What The Vicar Saw' or 'The Kiss in The Park'

David R. Williams

Preface

The issue of censorship and propriety in relation to cinematograph was first reported in any detail in the 31 March 1899 edition of *The British Journal of Photography*, with a description of a breach of contract case brought by F. and W. Dodsworth against The Reverend B.S. Spencer, the Curate of St Paul's Church Gateshead, for non-payment due to the stopping of the film show for exhibiting immoral material. This early case has only been referred to by historians since 1899 on two occasions. Firstly 1967 in *Film Censors and the Law*, where there is a brief description of what the author describes as the first discoverable reference to a court case regarding the propriety of cinematograph films.[1] The original account was first brought to my attention when it was reprinted in *The Kingdom of Shadows: A Companion to Early Cinema* in 1996.[2] Although both later accounts draw attention to the particular importance of the occurrence as an observed first, the full proceedings of the case as reported by *The British Journal of Photography* seemed incomplete. My enquiries concerning the existence of the court records in Newcastle and in the Public Records Office were thwarted by the fact that these records had been destroyed during the 1939–45 War. Contemporary reports in the local newspapers contained further material but the accounts varied in their detail and in their lengths of testimony.[3] In addition no references to the case in any of the Diocesan papers or ecclesiastical newspapers of the period, could be found at Durham Cathedral Library. Presented with these overlapping and disordered testimonies, I have sought to attempt a reconstruction of the court proceedings with other researched details of the film programme itself. Therefore, the following historical narrative has been reconstructed using a number of newspaper reports in Gateshead and Newcastle Newspapers on 22–23 March 1899, and from the description in the 31 March edition of *The British Journal of Photography*. In order to preserve the narrative and to facilitate the presentation of the arguments of each of the participants, I have dispensed with end notes attributing particular reports to the particular newspapers or magazines referred to above. Some references to trade journals are included within the text and comment.

* * *

The weather on Saturday 11 February 1899 was dreadful. Two boats on their way from Sunderland to Newcastle had got into difficulties, but inside the Parish Hall of St. Paul's Church, Askew Road, Gateshead the tables were set for the Parish Tea. The local brass band had been engaged to play before and during the actual tea itself. It was only the second Parish tea for the new curate, the Reverend Bertram Stone Spencer, and, no doubt, he was in an impressive mood by choosing to have a Cinematograph show included in the entertainment. Out of the storm, John Bolton and Thomas Sutherland arrived with the Cinematograph equipment. The hall had no curtains to darken the room, but the cloudy sky and the late evening winter light would assist the limited illumination of the portable lamp house. Whilst Thomas Sutherland erected two stands and stretched a sheet between them, John Bolton attempted to set up his projector in the centre of the hall. There were no specific fire regulations in Gateshead to prevent this, but the tea had not quite finished and John Bolton could not commence illuminating his limelight until the tables had been cleared. By the time, this had happened the performance was already fifteen minutes late in starting. The arrangement of the seats was not ideal but no more delays would be accepted and the show commenced.

John Bolton had been able to join a number of short films together to make up two reels. He showed these with an interval for the reel change. Whilst the second reel was being shown, the film entitled 'Courtship' began to click through the projector. In a park there were three benches. As a young lady sat on one of them a man stealthily crept up behind her and kissed her. At this point, the shadow of hand appeared on the screen, and a voice demanded that the entertainment be stopped.

There are several versions of what happened next. The explanations took place in the Newcastle County Court on 22 March 1899. His Honour Judge Francis John Greenwell was presiding in a breach of contract case between F. and W. Dodsworth, Booksellers of 17, Collingwood Street Newcastle upon Tyne and The Reverend B. S. Spencer of 10 Tyneside Terrace, Bensham, Gateshead. The Dodsworth Brothers had brought the action against the curate of St. Paul's Church for non-payment of £1. 16s, the agreed fee for a cinematograph entertainment in the Parish Hall of the Church.

Mr. D.E. Stanford for the plaintiff said that the usual charge for his client's shows was £2. 2s but the lower amount had been accepted because it was to be paid from Parish funds.

On arrival at the hall, the defendants' man was asked by the vicar if the pictures were in order and fit to be shown. The operator said that one of the pictures showed a man painting one side of a fence with black tar whilst his wife was on the other side painting it with white wash. The film ended with them whitewashing and tarring each other. To laughter from the court, he said the man had said this was a 'dirty picture'.

The Judge remarked that only half of the picture was dirty. 'No' said Mr. Stanford clearly not seeing the funny side, 'Both halves'. The Judge continued to assist the hilarity by saying that the whitewashing could not be dirty.

Mr. Stanford said that towards the close of the exhibition some pictures were shown which appeared to have created a terrible sensation in Gateshead. Again there was laughter in court. Mr Standford continued;

> One picture represented a fisherman upon a rock, and three or four boys dressed properly in ordinary bathing costume who were anxious to bathe. The boys succeeded in throwing the fisherman in the water. Then there was depicted a scene in a garden or park. There were three seats and on the middle one sat a young lady. A man came up slyly behind her and kissed her. That was the picture objected to as unfit to be shown to an audience.

To further court laughter, the judge said, 'It is an indecent assault? ...'

The actual films being shown can only be vaguely identified. The black and white opponents theme was popular on the halls and in early films. R.W. Paul's *Quarrelsome Neighbours* of 1897 had two men fighting over a fence with what is described as soot and whitewash. One witness in Newcastle actually describes the film as showing two men. Since some of the early knock-about films did use men dressed as women, the description might have been accurate and the film could have been Paul's. George Albert Smith's *The Miller and The Sweep*, also made in 1897, survives to show us how this kind of single-shot gag was handled. The fisherman film could be Haydon and Urry's *The Impromptu Bath*. The kissing scene can be more certainly identified as another Haydon and Urry film, *On the Benches in the Park*, since it was also advertised under the name *Courtship*. Both these 75ft films were included in a Haydon and Urry advertisement in *The Era* of 1 April 1899.

Mr. Stanford then read to the court a letter to the plaintiffs dated 16 February and written by the curate, the Reverend Spencer. The writer said that he was sorry to have to report more than unfavourably on the entertainment. It had been the cause of serious complaint. The first complaint was that the machine was not ready to commence at the appointed time, and that the first part of the entertainment lasted only twenty minutes instead of thirty. Secondly, the sheet had been placed so low that bonnets and hats appeared on it. The pictures also were very indistinct. There was one picture, the writer continued that disgusted most of the audience. He thought it was the bathing scene but he did not recognise it at the time as it was so indistinct. Court laughter greeted this remark. Some parishioners had mentioned it afterwards and were surprised that the picture was not stopped.

The second part of the programme was stopped because of a picture called *Courtship*. The vicar told the operator to withdraw it. But the man refused and commenced to pack up his machine. The vicar at the outset had said 'We are very particular and not only do we not want anything indecent but nothing low or vulgar'. The picture called *Courtship* had done a lot of injury on the parish, concluded the writer. Allowing himself a modicum of sarcasm and to further hilarity from the court, Mr. Stanford suggested that parishioners who had been so injured might find it impossible to get redeemed. The Plaintiffs replied on the same day saying that they were perfectly astounded at the letter and expressed the opinion that it was a mere outburst of spleen, there being no reason to complain of the pictures that were being shown. These had been satisfactorily shown to scholars

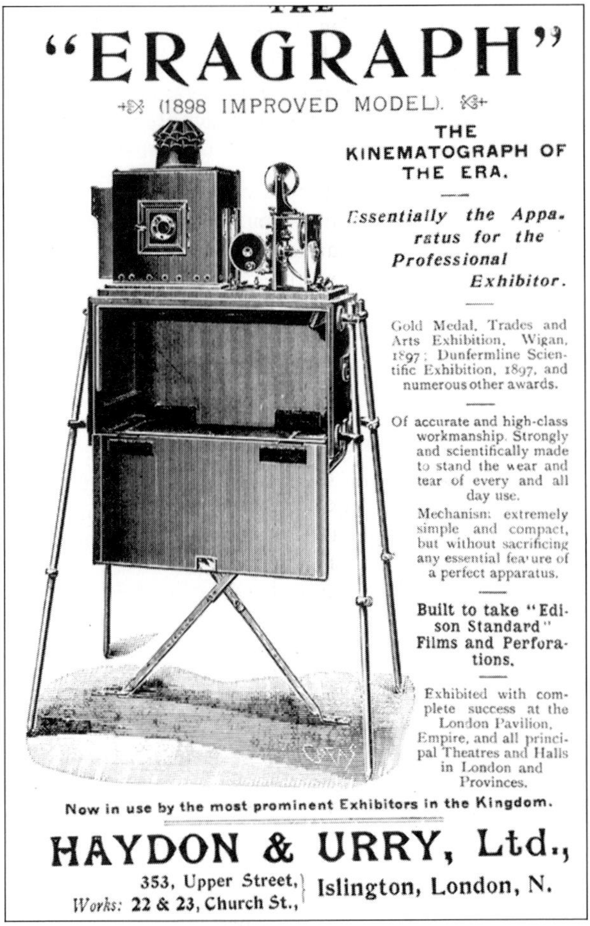

Fig. 1. The Haydon and Urry Eragraph. Possibly the projector used at St. Paul's Church Gateshead in February 1899.

and spectators in other places. At Longhurst, the same pictures had been shown and the Reverend Proctor had expressed great delight and said that his people were pleased. (Longhurst was a pit village near Morpeth, Northumberland. In 1871 the mine owner was a Reverend Ed Robson). Mr. Hick for the defendant interrupted at this point and said that they did not wish to suggest that the pictures had not pleased the parishioners at St. Paul's. The case rested entirely upon a question of breach of contract. They objected to one of the pictures, and it could have been taken out and the entertainment proceeded with. Mr Stanford, obviously attempting to exploit the judge's unfamiliarity with the operation of film projectors, said that the action of the vicar in placing his hand over the glass of the machine was a dangerous one. It was liable to cause a serious explosion.

John Bolton, the operator was then called. He said that the reason the performance was late in starting was because there were some forms in the way, which could not be removed until after the tea was finished. Mr Slack, the vicar, had objected to the kissing picture and compelled him to take it out. He placed his hands on the machine and as a result he had to switch off the gas to the light. The vicar had then said, 'I want no more of this' Bolton took this to mean that he didn't want any more pictures.

When cross examined by Mr. Hick, Bolton said that he did not refuse to exhibit more when the picture was stopped, and he not turn to the audience and say he could see no harm in the picture. What he did say to the audience was that he was extremely sorry that the vicar should have stopped the picture. He did not hear the vicar say that he had to go on with the entertainment leaving out the kissing picture.

He was not swearing at the machine as had been suggested. He was excited when the picture was stopped and not until then.

To more laughter from the court, he said he did not need to swear at the machine because it was one of the very latest. Mr. Hick said, to more laughter, that he was puzzled how the latest machine could show things so indistinctly that some people could not see them.

The witness said when he was packing up the vicar told him that he would not be paid. He did not refuse to carry on in a fit of temper. After the stoppage, it would have taken 10 to 15 minutes to get the machine working again. But the band struck up The National Anthem, and he assumed this meant it was the end. No actual indication of the type of projection machine was given but since at least two of the films mentioned were from the Haydon and Urry catalogue, I am inclined to think that the machine might have been one of theirs too. The newness of the machine is mentioned and the Haydon and Urry slightly improved new model had just appeared.[4] John Bolton's testimony would indicate that he was using a limelight lantern activated by gas cylinders. If the limelight had been allowed to cool, it would certainly have taken upwards of ten minutes to get it up to full illumination again. I have seen descriptions by operators of this era saying that twenty minutes was a fair time to get a good illumination going from limelight.

After he had finished his questioning of Mr. Bolton, Mr.Hick continued with his case. He said that the vicar was perfectly justified in asking for the kissing picture to be taken out. The vicar objected to kissing. To even greater laughter from the court, Judge Greenwell asked if this meant that kissing was less well-known in Gateshead, or was it that it was so well known that they wanted to stop it. Attempting to bring the hilarity to an end, Mr. Hick said that showing this sort of picture at a parish hall was one thing, and showing it at a music hall was another. Seemingly wishing to let the comic badinage continue, the Judge observed that since the kissing picture was called *Courtship*, it did not seem to him to be indecent. 'If the girl were a stranger to the man then it would be very indecent'. Mr. Hick said that the distinction could not be ascertained from the picture. 'But', repeated the Judge, 'if it is called Courtship, where is the indecency?'.

At this point, one is reminded of the anecdote attributed to Cecil Hepworth in which a showman was able to show one of Annabelle's Kinetoscope cavortings under the disguising title of 'Salome Dancing before Herod', In the absence of any clear plot detail the title determines the content. Seeing that he was getting nowhere with his prepared line of enquiry, Mr. Hick said that it was not an actual question of whether the picture was indecent or not. The question was whether the Vicar wanted such a picture to be shown. Apparently now moving in favour of the plaintiff, the Judge said that he was astonished to find that the vicar was such an unreasonable man. 'Here is a machine that cannot be started when stopped, without difficulty, and you ask me to say that he ought to have it stopped as he chose. He ought to have asked for details.' 'My instructions are', said Mr. Hick, 'that the Vicar did ask for them but that he did not get them.' Mr. Stanford interrupted with 'That is not the fact'.

When the Vicar, the Reverend T. Slack was called to give evidence, he said he had warned the operator that if anything improper was shown he would stop it. He

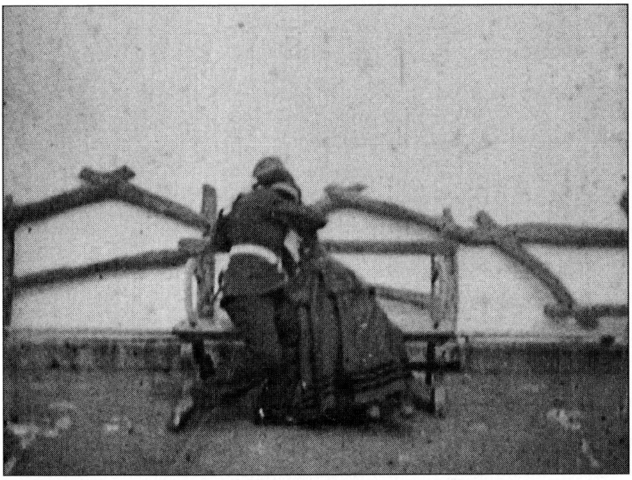

Fig. 2. The Soldier's Courtship. A 'kissing' film made by R.W.Paul in 1896.

repeated the statement of what John Bolton, the operator, had said about the nature of the whitewashing picture, and told the court that he had warned him what would happen if the pictures were not acceptable. He said that he made particular mention of 'kissing matches'. The subject of courtship and male/female embrace was also extensively exploited in popular paintings, engravings and picture postcards.[5] Clearly the vicar had come across, or had reported to him other examples of 'kissing films'. Numbers of these had appeared in trade catalogues and trade advertisements at this time and some may already have been shown in local cinematograph entertainments. One of R.W. Paul's first films *The Soldier's Courtship* (1896) featured incidents of kissing on a park bench.

When the kissing picture appeared on the screen, the vicar continued, he told the man to take it out and go onto the next. He said that the man turned to the audience and made a speech. According to the vicar, he said 'Our worthy vicar objects to this picture. I suppose he does not agree with kissing'. The vicar then told him that if he did not go on with the entertainment he would not be paid. To further court laughter the vicar said 'The picture was a most violent windmill affair with their arms in a most elaborate and grotesque style'. 'It was utterly low', he concluded.

The curate, the Reverend B.S. Spencer then gave evidence. He said that he was present at the entertainment but could not see the pictures clearly from where he was. He heard the man make a speech about the 'worthy vicar' objecting to the picture and saying that he would not go on with the entertainment in any circumstances.

John Bolton's assistant operator Thomas Sutherland was also called to the stand. He said that he heard the vicar ask for another picture to be shown. He agreed with John Bolton that it would have taken fifteen minutes to put the machine right after the stoppage. In his final statement, Mr. Stanford said the plaintiff could not have been in breach of his contract since it was the vicar who had terminated the performance. The Judge had seen the picture and it seemed that he did not find it objectionable.

Mr. Stanford was quite wrong in this assumption, however, for in his assessment of the case, the Judge found in favour of the defendant. His remarks were very significant in the light of many later judgements across the country. Legal status and public morality were intertwined. He said that he found the picture to be entirely vulgar. He had no doubt that part of the audience would have enjoyed it extremely, but that was 'no reason why those who were trying to raise them should not have the right to object'. This curious statement must mean those, i.e. vicars and church people, who were attempting to better the morals of the people had the right to object to immorality as they saw it. He thought the vicar was within his rights in putting his hand in front of the lens and stopping the pictures. He could come to no other conclusion that the contract was not completed. 'It is monstrous', he maintained, 'that gentlemen such as the vicar should have no power in their hands in such circumstances, but needed to leave it up to the discretion of others as to what they were going to exhibit'.

Though the circumstances of the action itself, and the reporting of it, seemed to be, as *The British Journal of Photography* put it 'An Amusing Case', the Gateshead Guardian saw a more serious concern with its headline 'Corrupting The Morals of Gateshead. A Singular Court Action.' A further subheading declared 'What a Cinematograph Can Do'. Although the first line of the report talked of 'a rather novel action', there is little reason to believe that this and the other headlines were only suggestive of an amusing irony. The Gateshead reporter concluded his report with a paraphrase of the judgement. 'People who provide entertainment should not be placed at the mercy of exhibitors in the selection of the pictures shown'. In the early years of the new century, this was a growing concern both inside and outside the practices of the film industry.

Final thoughts

Why was anyone prepared to go to court for a £1.16s debt, and who were these Dodsworth Brothers? There is no answer given. However, it does raise a question as to whether other historians have researched these private-function cinematograph exhibitors. The cinematograph was displayed in a variety of non standard private venues and further examination is needed of *The British Journal of Photography* and the *Optical and Magic Lantern* weekly, in order to ascertain if this practice is widelymentioned during the years before the introduction of the 1909 Cinematograph Act.

Notes

1. Neville March Hunnings, *Film Censors and the Law* (???????, 1967): 39 (London: Allen & Unwin, 1967).
2. Colin Harding and Simon Popple, *In the Kingdom of the Shadows: A Companion to Early Cinema* (London: Cygnus Arts: 1996): 73–74.
3. See *Gateshead Guardian* (22 and 23 March 1899) and the *Newcastle Daily Chronicle* (23 March 1899) for details of the local reporting of the case.
4. John Barnes, *Pioneers of the British Film* (London: Bishopsgate Press,1983): 94–95.
5. For further examples of 'Kissing Films' see Charles Musser's article in this volume on the impact of the May Irwin Kiss, Charles Musser, 'May Irwin's Kiss: Performance and the Beginnings of Cinema' in *More Visual Delights: Performance and Reception* (London: John Libbey, 2005): 96.

10

Viewing Deadly Targets for Feminine Identity: Alar, the Human Arrow

Peta Tait

Picturing Alar

> [T]he lady is actually shot from a monstrous cross-bow, and traverses some 30 f[ee]t of hot vitiated atmosphere before striking the target. [...] The distance is short, the regulation net is used and the target, on being touched, retires as gently and as gracefully as the 'Arrow' herself does shortly afterwards. [...] powerful springs have more to do with this aerial flight – than the strings of the bow.[1]

In this death-defying aerial stunt, the human arrow, Alar, was projected into the air through a paper bull's eye target and caught by her older sister. This risky action was performed by British teenager, Pansy Murphy (Frances Elizabeth Mary Murphy),[2] who was with The Flying Zedoras, international stars with Barnum and Bailey's (BB) Greatest Show on Earth, by 1896. The contribution of the aerial catcher, Adele (Adelaide Murphy), also made the act important, as female catchers are rare even today. The act was almost certainly invented and patented by Adele's husband, Tony Zedora. Pansy began classes in singing, dancing and acting at twelve, and by fifteen she had joined her sister in aerial performance.[3] She subsequently had a twenty-year stage career as a versatile music hall entertainer.[4]

The human arrow trick – further details of the Zedoras' performance are given towards the end of this article – facilitates a discussion of how an aerial performer's body can be 'conceptualized and articulated within different cultural discourses'.[5] How is an aerial body extracted from written and/or visual discourses? The discursive evidence from visual records is of primary importance to an investigation of acrobatic performances. As Samuel Raphael asks, 'How often has the visual been the original prompt for an historical inquiry?'[6] Yet he maintains that pictures remain neglected as historical sources, and argues that even photographs represent 'theatricality' rather than transparent evidence of reality.[7] 'We have little patience

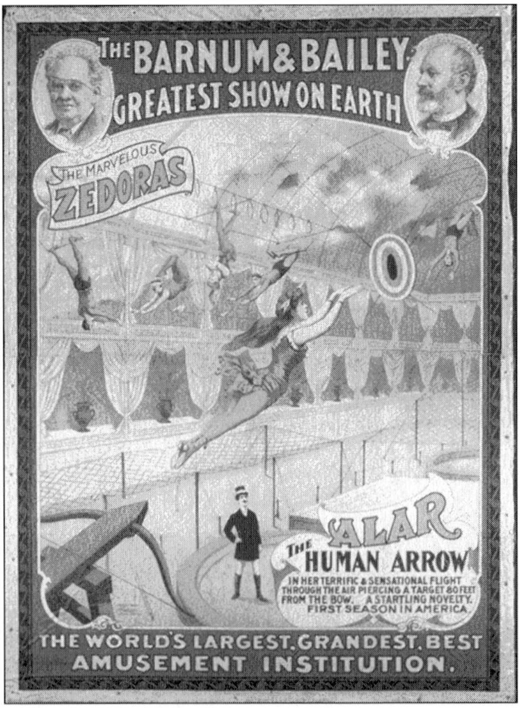

Fig. 1. Barnum and Bailey's Greatest Show on Earth Poster, featuring The Marvellous Zedoras 'Alar the Human Arrow' 1896. [Courtesy of Special Collection, Milner Library, Illinois State University, and Steve Gossard.]

with pictures which keep their secrets'.[8] In the example of Alar, the poster drawings place the body mid-air while the photographs locate it standing or perched ready to begin. They deliver a question: how was the performer traversing the space in between? The body's motion in the trick, its performance, remains invisible in the visual record; performance history keeps its secret.

The arrow trick was probably the climax to the Zedoras' act and can be reconstructed because the visual material is supported by a number of written descriptions in the publicity, reviews, and nineteenth-century circus hyperbole. The latter also offers a useful clarification of cultural images surrounding this aerial trick. The problem of researching the composition of the body's motion in this aerial performance predates the preservation of the movement of aerial bodies on film – aerial performances remain notoriously difficult to film. The action and movement of the Zedoras and other nineteenth-century aerialists must be notated from incomplete multiple sources. While the visual legacy informs the desire to see and see more, it presents either artistic impressions or momentarily inactive bodies; moving bodies as blind spots in the scopophilia of performance. These are bodies in action that fragment and disappear within their representation. As Peggy Phelan writes: 'The enactment of invocation and disappearance undertaken by performance and theatre is precisely the drama of corporeality itself'.[9]

Like the action of the arrow trick, the membership of the Flying Zedoras, Pansy's later groups, and the details of her long working life are hard to verify even with photographic evidence. The composition of Pansy's acts can be pieced together speculatively from visual material, the studio photographs and publicity posters. A photograph taken in 1894 when Pansy was fifteen corroborates the poster; the three-member Flying Zedoras (Pansy, Adele and Tony) are suspended on wires in a theatre. Pansy stands above the stage area at the back, on a structure that looks like a large ironing board tilted upwards – the bow. Adele is sitting mid-air on apparatus out over the audience in the auditorium, and Tony is sitting on other mid-air apparatus. It is possible that both were catchers for Alar at different points in the act.

A studio photograph taken in 1895 shows Pansy advertising her performance persona. Alar is a fifteen-year-old with a mass of loose curly hair dressed in an acrobat's smocked top and bloomers, and soft shoes, and in a standard pose with her left foot behind and her right foot turned out, her hands behind her head with her elbows out. Her 1896 studio photograph makes an arrow in her hair visible, with a neck frill and a sash across her hips. By 1897 Pansy and her sister Adele were photographed in New York with the standard smocked, bloomer suit cut higher on the thigh, wearing bows, and with flowers in their hair.[10]

Although the images in photographs and drawings are invaluable, their 'theatricality' is static. A photograph captured an aerialist off-stage, in repose rather than in motion. A sequence of drawings was used generally to represent the body's progression through the act. Even the poster drawing which shows Alar in the air, with her arms outstretched like a prototype of superwoman, references rather than captures the body's trajectory. Ironically then, the active body in this aerial act must be found in descriptive words rather than pictorial records. This raises questions about the extent to which audience perception of a performer's bodily identity was influenced by the words that surrounded the act, the circus hyperbole, as much as the actual viewing of the act. In her own words, Pansy remembers:

> I am 88 and from the age of 16 was shot from a giant bow. I was billed as Alar, The Human Arrow in music halls and circuses and in many countries. I know the Sensation of being shot, I have never been shot from a cannon but there have been about 3 that I remember. Well it is so quick that you hardly realize it. I was shot from a bow and caught by my sister hanging by her ankles in mid-air.[11]

Pansy continues her letter with a comment about her pity for ill-treated circus animals.

The human arrow act was very controversial, not only because it was dangerous but also because the 'Arrow' body was that of a young female. John Munro writes that:

> In 1895 a sixteen-year-old girl was shot through a target from a bow, and caught by another girl hanging in mid-air by her feet, a stunt which prompted questions in the House of Commons concerning the young lady's safety. Parliament was reassured, however, by the President and Managing Director of the Aquarium, who announced that every possible precaution had been taken.[12]

But was the British House of Commons reassured, as Munro claims? It does not seem to be the case. The public campaign to ban juvenile performers actually gained more support, and two years later the minimum age was raised from fourteen to sixteen for males and eighteen for women under *The Dangerous Performances Act 1897*.[13] This horrified reaction, by some members of the public, to an act in which a young woman's body is used to crash through a target may have been heightened by the publicity. The reaction suggests the social impact of Pansy's gender and youth, which were deliberately promoted as part of the act. In the poster publicity, the performing body is coded as feminine by long, flowing hair. Alar is described as graceful, beautiful and delicate. The difficulty of the trick and its implied violence as a circus attraction were accentuated because it was executed by a young female performer. The trick's promotion depended on implicit social beliefs that a female body is weaker in physique and therefore more vulnerable than the male body. It is likely, however, that Pansy's smallness and lightness gave her an advantage over male counterparts in this type of stunt, as it does with the execution of some flying tricks in trapeze acts.

As I argue elsewhere, aerial acts are performances of liveness carried out by, and watched by, bodies as phenomena that are lived social entities.[14] They happen in the present. An understanding of the impact of an act from aerial history as visual spectacle together with its music, depends on what is filtered through written accounts by eyewitnesses. Granted, words can be pictorial.[15] The effect of liveness, however, was and is achieved by performing bodies that engage spectators bodily. The reception of Alar's body in the aerial motion was dependent on visual perception in tandem with the responses of a phenomenological, sensory body of a spectator. The sight, sound and what Maurice Merleau-Ponty terms the 'corporeal schema' of movement[16] from the watching body, influenced by habitual cultural beliefs and inherent limitations in seeing, are translated into words describing the action. In this retrospective retranslation of physicality through written languages and static images, active aerial bodies go missing.

Caught in the act

The Flying Zedoras had four seasons with America's BB Circus, the last one on tour back in London. Publicity drawings of the act on a poster show a male performer walking upside down with his feet in a line of rings, the human arrow act, a blindfold dive to a female catcher, possibly some kind of fall from the trapeze bar to a net which had become fairly common in aerial acts, and a female performer doing an iron jaw, or dental act. Pansy almost certainly did an iron jaw act during her career. (In the iron jaw act the performer clenches a leather mouth guard in his or her teeth and suspends him or herself from a bar or, hanging upside down from his or her knees, suspends another performer below.) If most of these tricks were an established part of the aerial repertoire in the late nineteenth century, the arrow stunt gave this act uniqueness. Even so, the sprung projection of aerial performers into space and the use of a target were well-established strategies, and it was the bow and arrow apparatus framing the arrow trick that was new, as were several techniques for movement. In an interview, Mr [Tony] Zedora explains that the Human Arrow took time and money to invent. Speaking of their group as having five members, he explains that:

> We may certainly claim to have introduced our style of diving, the passing leaps side by side, the Human Arrow and the general mounting of the aerial act.[17]

This apparatus had been legally patented in England, the continent and in the USA.

The centrality of female performers on this new apparatus gave such acts additional appeal as a popular attraction. Thus, the gender identity of female aerialists was promoted to heighten the impact of the act. It is worth noting that circus publicity of the time linked extreme risk-taking to ideas of social change in female behavior. The circus made use of the phrase 'the new woman' in its posters and publicity.[18] Aside from its opportunism, this practice of cultural quotation in its promotion suggests that the circus was deliberately making connections between these extreme displays of female physicality and muscular prowess and the social campaigns to achieve greater suffrage rights and freedoms for women. The political effect of spectators identifying with gender subversion within popular theatrical performance may be longstanding.[19] Female circus performers repeatedly defied traditional beliefs about the physical limitations of female bodies. They were the muscular equals of their male counterparts and it seems likely that these physical achievements, which were very popular, had significance for 'the new woman' outside circus. The performance showed that fearlessness and courage were not exclusively attributes of the male body. Even if the publicity surrounding Alar's act emphasised her embodiment of feminine difference, her vulnerability and beauty, to enhance its marketable appeal, the gender codes of aerial bodies became interchangeable for the duration of the performance.

Admittedly, circus appropriated any new fashion and aesthetic for its sensationalist value. Circus plied a trade in cultural extreme and excess. Alar and the new women were billed in a programme that included images of exotic orientalism ranging from Indian dancers and jugglers to fakirs. These were bodies pushed to extremes. The 1897 BB season included contortionist, Francis Era, known for his animal imitations. To some extent then, aerialists were viewed as the embodiment of exceptional cultural others because circus set out to present extraordinary bodies. But because Alar was depicted as young and feminine in an act that defied all notions of weakness and dependency, she challenged the perception of what it meant.

Alar's act was very dangerous. It appears that there was at least one accident and probably more. A caption to an unidentified newspaper drawing proclaims:

> 'Stunned the Human Arrow', String was pulled too soon and Alar was knocked senseless on her loft perch at Madison Square Garden, New York City.

The drawing shows men on a rope ladder, Alar laying on the platform and behind her the cross bow hanging by ropes. As well, the 1897 BB route book entry for Wednesday, 11 August, Owosso Michigan: 'Pansy Zedora attempts the arrow act again today, but meets with another accident'.[20]

Joseph Roach explains that definitions of performance 'commonly assume that performance offers a substitute for something else that preexists it. Performance, in other words, stands in for an elusive entity that it is not but that it must vainly aspire both to embody and to replace.'[21] In Alar's act, the performer's body literally embodies and replaces an arrow as apparatus. But the accompanying idea of flight suggests how the performer stands in for more elusive entities in cultural fantasy. As Helen Stoddart explains 'By the mid-nineteenth century metaphors of flight became attached more exclusively to equilibrists and trapeze artists'.[22] But the performance encompassed much more than imitations of flying. It performs a cultural idea of physical risk. But the risks are performed and can be illusionary as the accident reports reveal. Falling out of the air was less likely than apparatus failure. Crucially then, in imitating flight, the live aerial body performs danger. The pre-existing idea in Alar's embodied substitution is a dead body, both literally because she performed the risk of dying and, as I will argue below, metaphorically in alluding to dead cultures.

The 1896 publicity for Madison Square Garden boasts: 'Unapproachable and most brave performances on patent aerial gymnastic apparatus by the celebrated originators'.[23] A BB handbill for the first show in 1896 describes Alar's act as the 'The Crowning Miracle of Physical and Mechanical Sensation'. There is a comparison with a cannon ball's flight and it continues:

> Beautiful ALAR. The Only Human Arrow. Shot Headlong from a Monster Crossbow across the Great Arena in Full Open View without intent or possibility of the slightest deception. A lithe, winsome, living weapon, governed by such Heroic Nerve and Skill and aimed with such precision that ALAR pierces a distant target and is caught in mid-air by a lady suspended from a trapeze. That the phenomenal character of this feat may be appreciated, it should be understood that the Catapult is an engine resembling a massive crossbow, used by the ancient Greeks and Romans for throwing huge stone, arrows, spears, etc., and its terrific propulsive force would alone rend an ordinary mortal piecemeal. As an Exact Reproduction of this Gigantic and Formidable Crossbow of Ancient Times, the one used by Alar is of itself a great curiosity, but when upon its massive and mighty string the dainty feet of the Bravest of all Living Artists take the place of insensate wood and stone, and her delicate form responds, with scathless speed, grace and accuracy, to a force they can scarcely withstand, the result must be enthusiastically and unanimously proclaimed The Martial Miracle of Aerial Motion.[24]

Audiences were familiar with human projectile cannon acts, which dated from 1877. Farini's Zazel and George Loyal were described as humans fired from cannons in acts in which the apparatus also starred.[25] The human body was substituted for the cannon ball. The target in Alar's trick was functional and, together with the bow and arrow, symbolised older and less lethal machinery. Perhaps the female presence also enhanced the suggestion of games and playful competition. Balsamo writes that:

> Gender, like the body, [...] is at once related to physiological sexual characteristics of the human body (the natural order of the body) and to the cultural context within which the body 'makes sense'.[26]

The body in the arrow act was depicted as feminine, which made cultural sense as a passive presence and at the same time made the completion of the trick seem all the more extraordinary. The absence of cannon fire made Alar like a dart, something thrown as much as fired. The coding of the body's naturalness was prefigured in descriptions of its physical vulnerability. Publicity descriptions emphasised how Alar might not withstand the force of propulsion. As Elizabeth Grosz explains, the female body is polarised as belonging to a category of nature.[27] The body's passivity in the action of propulsion through space coincided with its femininity, and thus signified nature and its inexplicable wonders. The consequences of impact for the actual body were unseen. The speed of the body's motion was the crucial element of the act and its suggestion of flight. The cannonball apparatus was emblematic of the triumph of technological progress in the industrial age and made the human body seem part of an invincible man-made machine. It demonstrated how machine inventions were destined to conquer nature and its limited bodies. These acts personified the new age. The speeding body suggested one able to compete with machines.

Alar's act, however, would seem to have generated a different discourse to that of cannon acts. The images in the advertisement cited above, convey how the act was designed to appeal to the late nineteenth century's fascination with flight, but configures it in ancient Greece and Rome, in bygone dead worlds. The idea of the human body as an object catapulted into the air was diverted from the mimicry of futuristic technology to an imaginative re-invention within a neo-classical aesthetic of seemingly timeless cultural space. As Raphael points out, notions of period are aesthetic concepts, and historical illustrations including neo-classical images became widely available in the nineteenth century.[28] Alar's act was presented in promotional descriptions in an aesthetic that framed Alar's social identity as other-worldly. The references to stone and wood in the publicity suggest how the human body stands in for an inanimate entity that might be a classical statue. If the social labels that were accorded to the performing body recognised it as not quite human, its action made it more than human. The act expanded on the earlier cultural association of aerialists with birds and their human hybrids, angels, in the 'miracle' of Alar's act. The imitation of flight became a performance of surpassing the material limits of humanness. The aesthetic in the act's publicity alluded to the spaces inhabited by mythic gods and goddesses watching over life and death below. If the act specified deadness in weapons, places and potential dangers, this was offset by a cultural imaginary of an everlasting golden past and its legends. The performing body would move beyond becoming a dead entity. As Alar's flesh substituted for an inanimate arrow piercing the target, an inert entity, the action of the living body acquired a supernatural aura.

The descriptors for the performing body in this trick evoked flight as divine wingless action, as they camouflaged its mechanistic propulsion. The act triumphed because the feminine identity of the performer and the motif of flight had pre-existing ideas culturally conjoined in insubstantiality.[29] The arrow act set up a liminal space in which a natural body's action was surpassed in a performance of supernaturalness.

Epilogue: tracking the Flying Zedoras and after Alar

A group called The Flying Zedoras existed by 1893 and consisted of one man and at least two or three women. In a photograph of the group it is unclear if Pansy was already a group member, but it is likely that Adele was an original member of the group.[30] Pansy's name appears in a photograph of the group taken in 1894. The Zedoras were working at Tudor's Circus, Cambridge, and regional England in 1895 and London's Royal Aquarium.[31] At the beginning of 1896 the group was working with Poole's Myriorama in Bristol after a successful season in Hamburg in which they received a tribute of gold medals.[32] Booked by BB's manager to open at Madison Square Garden 1 April 1896, The Flying Zedoras consisted of Adele and Pansy and Tony.[33] By the time The Flying Zedoras reached England in 1897 for the season at the Olympia, they had become 'The Five Unapproachable Zedoras' The publicity advertises 'A Quintette of Champion Aerialists in most wonderful feats'[34] The act went on to work in Europe where the halls and theatres were able to accommodate it more easily.[35] For the Christmas season in 1900, the group was again working with Poole's Myriorama and had grown to six members.[36] The 'Flying Zedoras created quite a sensation' and held audience spellbound with 'marvellous mid-air' feats.[37] An interview with Mr Zedora in his Colston Hall dressing room reports:

> Yes, we are perhaps quite as well known on the continent as in England, indeed we have just returned from a tour in France, to join Mr Poole, travelling from Lyons.[38]

It would appear that the group with four members may have had a three month season with Cirque Rancy and one with Cirque Plège.[39] They would appear to have been with Poole's in Bristol through into January 1901,[40] and again in Sheffield in 1902.[41] Very sadly, the reason for the change of the group's name and its break-up is probably the death of Adele. Pansy's hand-written notebook of bookings between 1901 and 1903 records 'Adele died', July 1902. John Turner writes that she was 32 when she died on 30 July 1902.[42] Pansy survived the dangerous human arrow act, and performed much less risky but still spectacular aerial tricks with later groups. By 21 November 1904 Pansy was in a group of two women and a man, probably The Uniques.[43] They were working at Alhambra, The National Theatre of Varieties, in an 'Original Gymnastic Ladder Potpourri' by 17 July 1905. Nonetheless there are additional photos of the Zedoras dated around 1906–07.

Although Pansy married Horace Osborne in 1904, it is unclear when the Mars Trio, the Mars Military Sensation Gymnastic Potpourri Act, first started. It placed an advertisement in *The Performer Annual*, 25 December 1909.[44] The trio promoted themselves as military gymnasts on their publicity labels. They described their act at the Royal Hippodrome as:

> A sensational climax is reached when one of male gymnasts mounts a high horizontal bar and with body perfect rigid, describes a series of revolutions, his feet presumably being locked to the turning bar, though the connect is invisible to the auditorium.

They were working in Kirkcaldy, Clydebank, Edinburgh in 1909 on tour. A list of venues for the group has forty-three towns. In 1910 the Mars Trio publicity lists thirty-eight towns. The Mars Trio's Military Gymnast poster depicts their costumes and impressions of their tricks. In one photograph where they are standing saluting, the two men wear striped pants, uniforms with short jackets and little box hats tied under the chin. Pansy is wearing a dress with frills, tights, a little box hat caught under chin, and a short version of the men's jackets. The poster has diagrams of how the group whirl around with one male performer turning three hundred and sixty degrees on a fixed bar. Another image shows an upright Pansy with a plait, in a dental act but called 'teeth spinning'. The last image is of a 'poster' on a wall with the trio looking at it with backs to the viewer. A contract for the Hippodrome Theatre of Varieties, Belfast, reveals that the Mars Trio did two performances every evening for one week, commencing 2 November 1910, and were paid eighteen pounds but would not do more than twelve night performances if required. They were also contracted not to appear within ten miles for fifteen months prior and two weeks, after except where the population was over 70,000. A review for their performance at the Royal Hippodrome, Eastbourne, possibly towards end of 1910, calls them:

> A Sensational Gymnastic Feat [...] Now days patrons of 'the halls' are accustomed to tall business in the gymnastic line. Evidently, however, the last

> word in physical exercises is far from being said, for several of the feats of the Mars Trio (lady and two gentlemen) are alike novel and daring. They are, moreover, performed with such agility and finish that, despite the seemingly dangerous nature of one or two of them, the audience never betrays any apprehensiveness as to the artist's success. A sensational climax is reached when one of the male gymnasts mounts a high horizontal bar and, with body perfectly rigid, describes a series of revolutions, his feet presumably being locked to the turning bar, though the connection is invisible from the auditorium. This tour de force does not fail to bring down the house.

In a 7 October 1912 advertisement, Horace Leighton and Pansy Lindford, now called Leighton & Lindford, are presenting an entirely new trapeze, teeth and dancing act at the Crown Crockfield.[45] This act continues into the next year on 22 February 1913 and Empire Palace, and 14 July 1913 working at the Transfield's Palace Pier circus, probably Brighton. They are billed as 'original gymnasts' with shows daily at three and eight, handwritten on a bill. A programme for Leighton & Lindford, at The Palace Winchester, has them at number seven on 5–7 September (no year), in their 'Modern trapeze and Teeth Performance'. There are posters for Leighton & Lindford in 1913 at the Picture Theatre. It is clear that the duo 'Present Original Teeth, and Dancing Act A Genuine Novelty' in both picture theatres and on variety stages.

A further name change in their promotional material says:

> Ritz and Ritz Present a Versatile Comedy Act. A Clever and Graceful Exposition of the Art of Gymnastics, introducing Dancing and Teeth Spinning, Funny and Refined Fixed on any stage. English Performers.

The timing of the transition to Ritz and Ritz is unclear but they performed at the Cornford Exchange, Sleaford, 18–20 March (no year), at the Calton Cinema theatre, Monday 13 April (no year), Dover Court 14–16 May (no year). However, the duo were definitely using the name Ritz and Ritz, and listed on a programme as a 'Comedy Act and Gymnastics', by 23–25 March 1914 at The Oxford Hippodrome, with one evening show and a Saturday matinee. On another programme, 22–24 April (no year), The Palace Lymington they are number seven out of eight acts. 'Comedy Act, Gymnastics, introducing Dancing and Teeth spinning'. A newspaper cutting from 8 January 1914 describes Ritz and Ritz as a novelty and very highly appreciated:

> The lady performer in her acrobatic performances and step dances being much admired, and her exhibition of teeth holding and swinging is excellent. The gentleman partner does his share and is very amusing in his clownish tricks, etc., keeping his audience in roars of laughter.

This would appear to be for the Taft Wells Cinema where the pictures also are excellent and the star picture is *The Snare of Fate*. They are still working as Ritz and Ritz in 1915, judging by a receipt for printing brochures.[46] There is an image of Horace with the painted face of a clown in striped top and baggy pants with 'sold' on the front. Pansy is wearing white sailor boy's shorts and top, black stockings, and a big bow in her hair. Two photographs show Pansy, hanging from a trapeze by a hook and leather teeth hold, arms folded, and shoes with big bows.

Clearly Pansy's work continued to present images of physical strength and daring in conjunction with touches of feminine display long after her performances as Alar ended. Her capacity to become Alar should remain linked to her training as a performer, and her long career as an aerial artist.

Unless otherwise stated, the photographs, posters, drawings, programmes, advertisements, notebook, contracts, receipts, reviews, and personal documents discussed in this article are held at the 'Pansy Chinery' Collection, Theatre Museum Study Room Archive Storage, Blythe House, London.

Notes

1. *The Strand Magazine* X (1896): 470.
2. According to Pansy's baptism certificate, she was born '8 Martii 1879 nata et die 12 Matui', named Frances Elizabeth Mary Murphy, and her parents were Joseph and Cecila Murphy, of Liverpool. Pansy Murphy's sister was Adelaide Murphy. Pansy became Pansy Osborne by her first marriage to Horace Stanley Osborne, 9 June 1904, at the Parish Church of All Saints, Ipswich. He was 26 and a performer, although he lists hosier as his profession, and the son of a farmer. She was 25 and does not list her own career and lists her father as a tailor. Pansy's second marriage was to Hugh Chinery, 31 March 1945, at St Nicolas Old Meeting House, Ipswich. He was 71 and listed his profession as carpenter, and she was 66, a tailor, and both were widowed. Hugh Chinery died 24 December 1957 and Pansy Chinery died 6 May 1969 aged 90 resident at 6 Trent Rd Ipswich, although her home had been 10 Cramwell Cres, Lindburgh Road. Pansy's will left the residue, 340 pounds, 13 pence and 5 p, to Rosalie Muriel May Chinery, and 50 pounds to four other Chinerys', Reginal Charles, Cynthia Evelyn, Blanche Edith and Kathleen Agnes.
3. A Letter from S. Menzies of 70 Oxford St, Liverpool, 15 May 1891, quotes '10/6 every ten weeks paid in advance. If two are sent together the terms are reduced to 7/6 each. One hour weekly lessons on musical instruments included banjo and piano.'
4. A poster for the Merchant Seaman's Orphan Asylum Snaresbrook, on board *SS Maritoba*. Commander Capt R Griffith. 23 October 1897. 'The Sailor's Orphan is England's Charge' 3. Dance Miss Pansy Zedora. Pansy featured as a dancer for fundraising appearances even during the period of her greatest international fame as an aerialist around 1897.
5. Anne Balsamo, *Technologies of the Gendered Body* (Durham: Duke University Press, 1997): 3.
6. Samuel Raphael, *Theatres of Memory*. Vol. 1 (London: Verso, 1994): 29.
7. Ibid 39.
8. Ibid 328.
9. Peggy Phelan, *Mourning Sex* (London: Routledge, 1997): 4.
10. By 7 August 1899 Pansy has returned to Ipswich and was photographed in a black dress. In 1906 an older Pansy was photographed wearing her hair up, a frilled neckline and in 1907, she posed dressed as an oriental woman lounging on cushions. She can also be seen posing in what seems to be a tennis costume although not necessarily to publicise her act.
11. Pansy Chinery, Letter, 30 July (circa 1967 based on her age cited in the letter, a reply to a published letter), unpublished.
12. John M Munro, *The Royal Aquarium: Failure of A Victorian Compromise* (Beirut, Lebanon: American University of Beirut, 1971): 21. *The Times* (London), 22 October 1895, 5. 'What may be described as a novelty in acrobatic performances is being added to at the Aquarium, Westminister. A girl about 16 years of age is being shot from a huge bow at one side of the building and, passing through a target in the centre, is caught by another girl hanging by the feet in mid-air at a distance of 50 feet. This exhibition … is wholly new to London.'
13. A.A. Strong, *Dramatic and Musical Law* (London: The Era Publishing Office, 1898): 97. Also see *The Music Hall Act*, 1752 (ibid 93). *The Children's Dangerous Performances Act*, 1879, did not permit 'any person who shall cause any child under the age of fourteen years to take part in any public exhibition or performance whereby, in the opinion of a court of summary jurisdiction, the life or limb of such child shall be endangered' (ibid 95).
14. Peta Tait, 'Fleshed, Muscular Phenomenologies: Across Sexed and Queer Circus Bodies'. In Peta

Tait, (ed). *Body Show/s: Australian Viewings of Live Performance* (Amsterdam: Rodopi 2000): 60–80.

15. Raphael 36.
16. Maurice Merleau-Ponty, *The Phenomenology of Perception* (London: Routledge, 1996): 142.
17. F.F. 'Poole's Twentieth Century Novelty. A Chat with Mr Zedora'. *The Bristol Magpie* (24 January 1901): 14.
18. Barnum and Bailey Handbill (undated) with the information about Alar also reads: 'The New Woman is also a picturesque and novel exhibition, for not one, but many charming maidens this season are seen in the rings at one time. There are Lady Clowns, Lady Ringmasters, Lady Object Holders, Lady Equestrians, Menagerie Performers ...'
19. Paula R. Backscheider, *Spectacular Politics: Theatrical Power and Mass Culture in Early Modern England* (Baltimore and London: The Johns Hopkins University Press, 1993): 129.
20. Route book for the Barnum & Bailey Tour of 1897, 96 (Milner Library Special Collection, Illinois State University). In comparison, 7 June, Indianapolis, Indiana, the entry describes clear weather and plenty of business, and notes: 'Twice to-day our canvas tested to its capacity, and the show leaves a lasting impression. Zedoras' aerial work highly commended, the flight of Alar being particularly admired.' (Route book of Barnum & Bailey Tour of 1897, 81, Milner Library Special Collection, Illinois State University).
21. Joseph Roach, *Cities of the Dead* (New York: Columbia University Press, 1996): 3.
22. Helen Stoddart, *Rings of Desire* (Manchester: Manchester University Press, 2000): 169.
23. Barnum and Bailey Greatest Show on Earth, The Campaign of 1896. The first appearance of The Flying Zedoras in the USA. It also included 'Messrs Melville and Cleotas'. 'Opened with the Hippdrome Races, elephants. Display No. 2. Consisted of East Indian Natives and Exhibition of Living Natives. Display No. 11.' 'Three Magnificent and Thrilling Double Aerial Acts'. An accompanying act, The Arrigossi Sisters worked 'in full evening costume, with long skirts executing a series of amazing acts' on the swinging trapeze (New York Public Library, Performing Arts Collection).
24. Patsy Chinery Collection, Theatre Museum Archive, Blythe House, London.
25. Farini's Zazel was a 'beautiful lady' 'Farini's latest great invention. ... To conclude with her Wonderful Headforemost Dive, a distance of 97 feet 6 inches, and afterwards Fired from the Cannon, a distance of 70 feet'. (Royal Aquarium Programme, 15 October 1877, John Johnson Collection, Bodelian Library, Oxford). Ella Zuila and George Loyal. 'The only lady who accomplishes the daring feat of riding a bicycle on the high wire; also of turning a complete somersault in mid-air from hand to hand, assisted by Mr. George Loyal, the Human Cannon Ball and Living Projectile, in his incomparable and original performance of being shot from a cannon loaded with powder a distance of 50 feet diagonally and catching a trapeze'. *The New York Clipper* (26 July 1879):143.
26. Balsamo 9.
27. Elizabeth Grosz, *Volatile Bodies*. Sydney: Allen and Unwin, 1994.
28. Raphael 21, 31.
29. Bram Dijkstra, *Idols of Perversity: Fantasies of Feminine Evil in Fin-de-Siècle Culture* (New York: Oxford University Press, 1986): 87–89.
30. John Turner, *Victorian Arena. Vol. One* (Liverpool: Lingdales Press, 1995): 140. The origins of members of the group are unknown at this time. In a 1901 interview Mr Zedora reported working with Barnum and Bailey in 1891 (F.F., 14). In 1891 the European troupe, the Flying Cleos, appeared in the USA with Barnum and Bailey Circus (Route book of Barnum and Bailey, 1891, Milner Library Special Collection, Illinois State University). The troupe consisted of John, George, Laura and Adele but it is recorded in the circus' Route Book that by 17 August 1891, Cleo (possibly John) and wife were both unable to work because Mrs Cleo is sick. She stays in Detroit for medical treatment. In 1897 the names John and George appear in the Barnum and Bailey programme with the Flying Zedoras in the USA. These names could be in lieu of Tony Zedora (Route Book, Barnum and Bailey 1897, 42. Milner Library Special Collection, Illinois State University). There is a 1887 photograph of Pansy's brother-in-law taken in a Copenhagen studio wearing satin shorts, tights, top with v-necked decoration, and soft shoes, and a 1891 photograph of Adele Zedora in Iowa with a man in civilian clothing.

31. *The Era* (6 July 1895): 22.
32. *The Era* (4 January 1896): 30.
33. Barnum and Bailey Souvenir Annual, 1896. The Flying Zedoras on double trapeze were either listed as act No. 10 or 11, Ring 2. 'The famous Zedoras, in most wonderful performances, concluding with the flight of Alar, the human arrow.' The 1896 route book has an entry for the 10 April, Saturday, aerials Zedoras, popular and for 9 June Indianapolis, flight of Alar 'particularly admired'. (Barnum and Bailey 1896, 62, 67, Milner Library Special Collection, Illinois State University) In 1897 Adele and Pansy Zedora and Tony Zedora were act No. 10 (Route book Barnum and Bailey 1897, 62. Milner Library Special Collection, Illinois State University).
34. Barnum and Bailey programme, first edition, 1897, Greatest Show on Earth at Olympia. No. 15. Same information in fourth edition. Still listed in sixth edition but billed next to other aerial groups, The Silbons and The Siegrists.
35. F.F. 14.
36. First ad for show at New Colston Hall, Bristol, starting 24 December 1900 with a short season. On Christmas day there were two performances starting at seven thirty and matinees on Tuesday, Wednesday and Saturday. Poole's Myriorama included scenes from The Boer War, The Chinese Crisis, Joseph Poole's Vaudeville Organization, and 'The Marvellous Flying Zedoras, Six in number (3 ladies and 3 gents). The most Original Flying act in the World.' *The Bristol Magpie*, (20 December 1900): 17. The advertisement for Zedoras for 27 December 1900 reads at 'enormous expense'. A 1901 review of Poole's Myriorama does not mention The Flying Zedoras in its three-hour programme. *East Anglian Daily Times* (10 September 1901), Poole's were advertising in 3 September 1901 at Ipswich but no mention of the Zedoras.
37. *The Bristol Mercury* (27 December 1900): 3.
38. F.F., 14.
39. There is a programme reference to La Troupe Zedoras at Cirque Plège, and they performed at Newcastle.
40. *The Era* (5 January 1901): 30.
41. *The Era* (4 January 1902): 34.
42. Turner, loc. cited: 141.
43. The Zedoras had studio photographs taken in 1906 and 1907 in Brixton, the area where performers often lived when working in London. The Uniques as a group of four wearing embroidered costumes were performing their 'Gymnastic Potpourri Ladder Act' in 1905. The act consisted of all four balancing off two ladders, and then one group member, probably Tony, holding two ladders (possibly perched midway up a ladder) with the other performers hanging by the knees, doing back bends off the held ladders or doing a vertical balance. The group also performed a four-high pyramid, and a trapeze suspension with dental act possibly done by Pansy. The names of the group members is not evident but included Lauri. There is a photograph taken in 1897 in New York in which a four-to-five-year-old child Laurie is photographed possibly with Adele. There is also a photograph of a Lauri Bailey, dated 2 February 1918. The other woman might have been called Laura and there is reference to Leo 1903.
44. By 1909 Pansy was in a group called the Mars Trio with Horace and her brother Leo, doing variety shows. After 1910 Pansy and Horace became a duo with Mars & Mars, then called Leighton & Lindford by 1913, and Ritz and Ritz by 1914 so that her stage name is Pansy Ritz in 1917. In 1914 Pansy was definitely doing a dental act as well as dancing.
45. From Monday to Friday doors opened at six thirty and two shows on Saturday when doors opened at six forty five and eight fifty and entry cost three, four or six pence. 'The Hall thoroughly Disinfected, Up-to-date, Warm and Comfortable.' Further receipts for Leighton & Lindford; 24 December 1912 (paid to Harry Leaton's Agency) for eleven shillings twelve pence; 16 November 1912 for ten percent commission; paid to Sydney Thomas, 7 December 1912, fourteen shillings.
46. According to the Wright & Company receipt letter, this was printed on 12 May 1915, for a cost twelve shillings and sixpence.

11

Early Political Films in Britain

Alan Burton

> A contemporary says Mr Gladstone had one thing to be thankful for. 'He died before the kinematograph added a terror to the life of public men'[1]

The emergence of a political cinema in Britain has largely been seen as an interwar development. The establishment of the Conservative and Unionist Film Association in 1925 and the Federation of Workers' Film Societies in 1929 being the watershed events that mark the appropriation of cinema by the two dominant political groupings. Only a few isolated cases of films being put to political use before the 1920s have been acknowledged, such as the cinematograph show hosted by the Independent Labour Party at Southwark in 1908.[2] In such cases, moving pictures were present to draw crowds for the speakers, and were likely to be conventional films for amusement rather than political persuasion. Historians of political film in Britain have approached the practice of political cinema at the level of Party, and this has confirmed the Party political appropriation of the cinema to be an interwar affair. In this respect, the issuance by the Labour Party of the circular *Labour Cinema Propaganda* in 1920, although its immediate consequence was fruitless, is seen of particular relevance, and historians have charted in detail the coming to film work of the Conservatives and various Labour groups in the later 1920s.[3]

Writers on modern political propaganda have explained the rapid developments in mass persuasion of the 1920s and 1930s in terms of the tremendous advances in propaganda during the Great War, the resultant extensions to the franchise in 1918 and 1928, and the concomitant appreciation of a mass democracy consisting of a potentially volatile electorate.[4] This has deflected attention away from significant developments in the first years of the twentieth century, a period that witnessed some interesting local experiments in political film. For example, F. Geo. Pyne, the Organising Secretary and Registration Agent for the North-West Devon Unionist Association, claimed to have been active with film since the turn of the century. He reported in 1905 that:

> For the past 5 years I have used the cinematograph (Walturdaw Bioscope)

> in connection with my political meetings in different parts of the country, and have proved it of great value, not only in the way of entertainment, but also for imparting instruction on political questions of the day. I am thoroughly convinced that there is a wide opening for the cinematograph in the political world[5]

In 1905, Pyne was acting on behalf of Mr W.E. Horne, the Unionist candidate for Barnstaple, Devon. It was reported that he was 'fighting for the constituency on the most up-to-date lines',[6] and the films screened related to the two leading political issues of the day, immigration and tariff reform. In 1905, the Conservative and Unionist Government had passed the Aliens Act, a popular measure designed to stem the flow of Jews from Eastern Europe. It is possible that a film screened by Pyne was *The Aliens' Invasion*, the first of a series of political films that had been produced for Hepworth by Lewin Fitzhamon.[7] A contemporary account reported:

> These pictures are thrown on a screen and illustrate the speeches of the candidate, the result being that the Unionist meetings have attracted an extraordinary amount of interest in the constituency.

With the aid of film, Horne sought:

> [T]o convince the Devonshire electors of the effects of the Liberal policy [through] showing them a series of cinematograph pictures which depict in the most convincing way the evils of unchecked alien immigration into England.[8]

A brief glimpse of the approach to the issue is given in a further trade paper report:

> The contrast between the films of aliens arriving in East London and English workmen leaving Liverpool to seek work overseas needed few words to enforce their truths. The pictures have attracted big crowds to the meetings.[9]

To pronounce on the subject of tariff reform, Pyne seemingly drew on a film produced by G.A. Smith in 1904,[10] *John Bull's Fireside* (aka *John Bull's Hearth*). Without naming the film, a trade paper described it in the following terms:

> The picture of John Bull's fireside is very instructive. John is ousted … by Frenchman and German, Russian and American, who enter singly, and, seeing the words 'Free Trade' over the mantelpiece, seat themselves comfortably round John's fire, leaving him standing room only. While in this position a Colonial arrives, and with the help of John, turns out the foreigners … and proclaims the victory of 'Fair Trade' over 'Free Trade'.[11]

Happily, Smith's film survives, enabling a positive identification of the title used by Pyne. The film (185 ft) is a single-shot, with a static camera fronting on to a fireplace-hearth above which is placed a sign declaring 'Free Trade'. It is theatrically staged, placing the characters with their backs to the camera. The foreign representatives enter through a doorway screen right. The Colonial, in contrast to Bull a fine figure of rugged manhood and attired to suggest an Antipodean origin, shows the Briton (and the camera) a drawing of the unmistakably be-monacled arch-imperialist Joseph Chamberlain. He then rudely disperses the other nationals and replaces the 'Free Trade' sign with a 'Fair Trade' alternative. The film ends with the Colonial and Bull contentedly seated by the roaring fire, with the foreigners floored and wildly gesticulating. The contemporary account of the film is interesting on two points: its surprising failure to report the 'presence' of the politician Chamber-

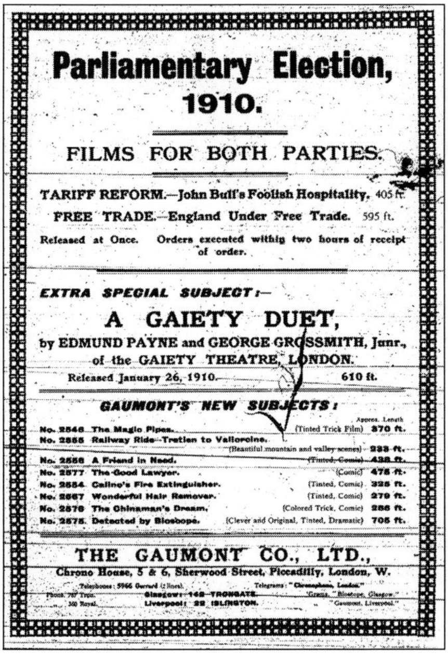

Fig. 1. The Bioscope, *13 January 1910.*

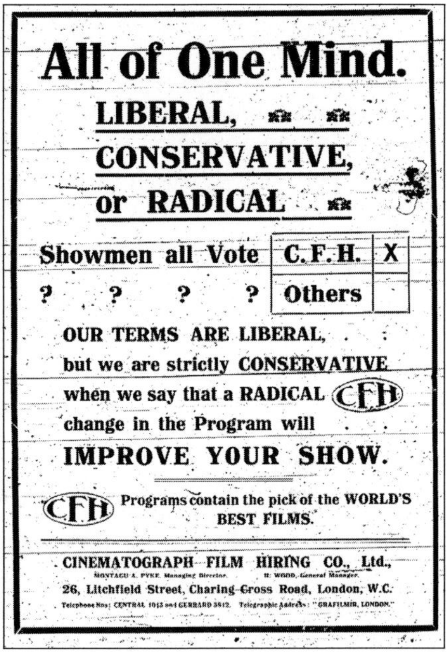

Fig. 2. The Bioscope, *15 December 1910.*

lain as a validation of its protectionist message; and its misrepresentation of the narrative suggesting a joint action on behalf of Bull and the Colonial to put the foreigner in his place. The man from the Empire acts singularly, and, as we shall see with a later film, the configuration of masculinity and gender is not without significance in the matter of imperial relations and trade.[12]

A significant new initiative in political film appeared in the latter part of 1905, when the formation of the Pictorial Politics Association was announced. This came from the fertile mind of Lewin Fitzhamon and was part of his responsibilities for Cecil Hepworth at Walton on Thames. As already suggested, Fitzhamon could well have been a source of suitable films for Pyne, and sensing a business opportunity sought to develop a new market for film sales.[13] The timing of the new venture was no doubt predicated on the forthcoming General Election in January 1906, a moment of political turmoil and polarity centring on the tariff question. The scheme was considered a boon for Parliamentary candidates of 'limited oratorical attainments':

> By subscribing to that firm a prospective M.P. will be relieved of the necessity of addressing meetings of his constituents, an advantage that may be mutually appreciated. Instead he will merely observe from the platform, 'We will now have the next picture – "Fair Trade versus Free Trade"'.

The film, 'an animated Fiscal story in several scenes', is anticipated for viewers in some detail:

> John Bull will be observed in slumberous attitude dominated by the bad fairy of Free Trade. But there enters the good fairy of Fair Trade, who conjures up a telegraph boy. From the messenger John Bull receives a telegram which

> reads, 'Handed in at Empire's Standpoint. To John Bull, Queer-street, W. The Unemployed problem must be solved. – Britannia'. The Fair Trade fairy then manufactures a vision for John Bull's edification – the bare interior of a cottage and a starving family. This is followed by a baker's shop and the symbolic big and little loaves, Finally, the fairy of Fair Trade – whose personal charms are infinitely superior to those of her rival – vanquishes the fairy of Free Trade, and all is well with John Bull.[14]

The Conservative rhetoric is maintained in a further film addressing the immigration issue, wherein a 'capital object-lesson is realistically taught' with the depiction of:

> ... scenes in the life of an alien, commencing with his embarkation at Bremen and ending with his ousting of an Englishman from work.[15]

Two further titles were listed, *Wake Up, John Bull* and *Back to the Land*, while several more films were in preparation, and all were to be narrative in form.

Evidence is sketchy regarding the success of the initiative, however, a handful of reports indicate that the Primrose League drew on the services of the Association, such as at the political 'revival meeting held at Wargrave late in 1905:

> The feature of the meeting was 1,500 feet of cinematograph pictures shown by Mr. Lewin Fitzhamon. Starving men and women were depicted stretching out their hands to the 'large loaf', for which they have no money to pay. A second series entitled 'The Unemployed question Must be Solved', shows strikingly the results of the present lack of employment in England.[16]

A demonstration of political films was made to the committee of the Primrose League in the winter of 1905–06. The exhibitor was not identified in the report, but it was most likely Fitzhamon, given his recent participation at Wargrave and the subjects of the films described. The exhibition was described in the following terms:

> In most cases the photographs were from acted scenes expressly made to depict the producer's particular opinions on subjects of current political interest; but some of the views were of actual occurrences or conditions, as in the case of those having a bearing upon the alien question. The fiscal controversy came in for a considerable share of attention; and if the views expressed by the cartoons were of a wholly one-sided character, that is only to be expected from a scheme formed expressly for party purposes.[17]

A slightly extended version of this report also appeared in a popular journal, where it was added that:

> Presumably the pictures will be seen over many a platform, in preparation for the coming contest, and they should at least serve to adorn the tale and point what moral there be, even if they do not actually convince in themselves. In a circular issued by the proprietors of the venture, the cinematograph is described as a new weapon in the hands of the propagandist. 'Weapon' is distinctly good.[18]

The only surviving film from Fitzhamon's Pictorial Politics Association is *International Exchange* (1905). This two-shot film (296 ft) commences with a long, wide-angle shot of a theatrical stage set. Five doorways are marked America,

Germany, Great Britain, Russia and France, and the corresponding characters, identifiable in national costumes, parade the set. Britain's door is open, signifying a free trade policy, but the others are firmly closed and marked 'tariff'. John Bull strides the stage with a basket of goods and to enter a competitor's door (market) he has to pay a toll. This is represented visually through the action of Bull passing over a large 'disc' from among a number that are visibly strapped around his waist. The precise meaning of this business would most likely have needed explanation by a lecturer (or political representative), as it is quite unclear through image alone. Meanwhile, foreigners enter Britain at will. Eventually, Bull runs out of 'discs' and is subsequently refused admission to foreign markets. Learning his lesson, John Bull closes his door and like the others it is marked up 'tariff'. The other nationals gather on the stage in surprise and anger, but are only admitted into the British market upon presentation of a 'disc'. Two females enter the stage, representing Canada and India. They are surprised to find the British market protected by tariffs, but are gratified when they receive 'imperial preference' and are allowed to enter freely.

The second shot, a little closer in framing, is in the form of a tableau. It is an election and Britannia presides over a pair of ballot boxes marked 'Fair Trade' and 'Free Trade'. The 'Fair Trade' box is attended by an Angel who shows Bull a loaf of bread and watches over two paupers who are pleading for assistance. By contrast, a mean Witch attends the 'Free Trade' box. In conclusion, John Bull patriotically asserts his support for Protection and votes for Fair Trade.

The film presents the same political viewpoint as the earlier *John Bull's Hearth*, that Protection best serves the national interest. The two films, though, configure the relationship between the Mother country and the Colonies somewhat differently. As we saw in *John Bull's Hearth*, the Colonial figure was ruggedly masculine and aggressively assertive, qualities effectively bringing the quiescent John Bull to the position of Tariff Reform. In the later film, the symbols of Empire are feminised and require Bull's 'Protection' to bring about an equitable arrangement of 'Fair Trade', yet being provided with the advantage of 'imperial preference' to facilitate trade throughout the Empire. In their support for Protection, the films are in accordance with the views of the Tariff Reform League, which had been formed in 1903 specifically to produce and distribute tariff reform propaganda.[19] The League utilised a variety of visual materials in its campaign, including lantern-slides and postcard-sized reproductions of political cartoons. The figure of John Bull was a common presence in the imagery.[20]

The moving picture trade came alive, for the first time, to the prospects for business of the political film around the election of 1906. Taking stock of opportunities, one commentator opined:

> The filmmaker who looked sufficiently ahead during the bright days, and who can now produce suitable subjects for election purposes, should reap a rich harvest. In many instances politicians have experienced the greatest difficulty in getting electors to their meetings. Dry speeches from more or less able orators are not the class of entertainment the present working man desires after the days' (sic) task, but give him living pictures, or even common place slides, and he takes his political medicine with occasional spoonfuls of jam, and, what is more, the truths depicted on the screen have more effect

> than much of the platform twaddle. The firm who can get quickly to work and produce suitable slides and films, and who can supply operator and apparatus, and can offer an effective program, can command big money, and, we trust, it will not be said that the trade was too apathetic to 'go' for an opportunity which, in many minds, has 'been a long time a-coming'.[21]

A later report confirmed the optimistic outlook and judged the lantern and moving picture to have made a splendid showing at the election. It also provides an interesting overview of the different uses to which the visual technologies were put:

> At the time of writing, the country is recovering from the excitement attendant on what will probably prove to be the most momentous election of modern national history. Our old friend, the optical lantern, and its first cousin, the kinematograph, have impartially helped either side. Hundreds of thousands have been able to obtain early news of election results, and, in the intervals of waiting, have been politically educated with slide and film. Each party has made strenuous efforts to get the first knowledge, and the waiting crowds have heartily appreciated the splendid results of this rivalry.
>
> Very numerous too, have been the political meetings assisted. The would-be M.P., who is 'unaccustomed to public speaking', must bless the day in which optical projection was first put to political uses. The animated fiscal story has told its tale, and Fair Trade and Free Trade have each had their innings, and triumphed respectively according to the company they were in. Political cartoons from the comic and daily papers have been circulated as lantern slides in thousands, and even the most turbulent spirits have postponed their interruptions until the show was over.[22]

The election of 1906 was a landmark moment for the origin of political film in Britain. It established precedent and moving picture propaganda would be a constant presence at all future political contests. Both lantern-slides and films were employed at the London County Council Elections of 1907, which quickly followed on the heels of the General Election. One writer was critical of the moving picture propaganda that he witnessed, believing it to be used in a very 'unenterprising manner'. In contrast to the earlier writer cited below, he also thought that there was limited opportunity for the film trade from political bodies as 'The amount of business to be done in this direction is so small that it would not be worth while for a manufacturer to cultivate it'.[23]

The pessimistic view did not hold, and informed views expressed in the *The Bioscope* during the lead in to the following election in 1910, reckoned that 'The moving picture will be a very big factor in the next General Election' and 'Moving pictures will play an important part in the coming General election, and the power of the bioscope as an educational factor, so far as the voters are concerned, will make itself felt'.[24] The elections of 1910 witnessed some significant innovations in the area of political cinema and a broader engagement by film companies with political film as they sought to extend trade. For example, the firm of Messrs. Power and Pryor, situated on Denmark St., London and operators of the Acton Picture Palace, were contracted by the *Daily Mail* on behalf of the Budget Protest League 'to supply bioscope exhibitions at most of the great centres of this country'.[25] The ever-active Walter Payne was charged with the organisation of the undertaking, confirming him as the country's first professional political film propagandist. Each evening event lasted from 7.00pm to 10.30 pm and consisted of a mixed performance of films ('political or otherwise'), lantern slides and music presented by a Pathephone player. Specific mention is only made of some 'Tariff Reform' films supplied by Hepworth, and presumably, or including, the fiscal films of 1905/6. In addition, 'over 80,000 slides were made specially for this huge contract'.[26]

Meanwhile, Hepworth continued to innovate in the field, bringing the novelty of sound to its political film work through the presentation of political speeches:

> Such speakers as Mr. F.E. Smith, K.C., and Mr. Bonar Law, who are in great request, are through the aid of the moving picture, coupled with the Vivaphone, able to address as many meetings on one night as there are demands made upon them. The Hepworth Company have manufactured at their studios, Walton-on-Thames, films showing these two members of Parliament speaking, and records of the speeches, which absolutely synchronise with the pictures have been prepared. The expressions and gestures of the two politicians are most faithfully reproduced in the films, which prove that in this, as in all other fields where the moving picture has entered, it is a force to be reckoned with.[27]

Novelty was a quality of *The Dissolving Government* released by Kineto for both the January and December elections. This was a trick film stressed as 'non-political, but mirth provoking', in which, 'Portraits of the leading members on either side of the House, gradually emerge from a molten stream, take shape, and as mysteriously and weirdly disappear'.[28] The film was calculated 'to act as an incentive to good humour during the election'.[29] The constitutional procedures provided companies with the opportunity for producing topical comedies, usually featuring one of their popular comic characters. Cricks and Martin chipped in with *Scroggins Puts Up for Blankshire*, 'a rollicking topical election film', available around the January turnout; while Hepworth put out *Tilly at the Election* in time for the December poll.[30] Such films were not restricted to the political platform and could readily play conventional picture houses. This was clearly a consideration behind the Gaumont Company's programme of political films that appeared early in 1910. Unlike the Fitzhamon films, the aim was one of political balance, an approach commended as good for trade:

> Both sides of the tariff Reform controversy are presented, and we think it would be a good 'draw' for any showman to boom both of these. It would create further interest in his show without hurting the feelings of any of his patrons who were party politicians. We can assure him that in securing these two films he has an attraction that is decidedly interesting at the present time, and the films are well produced in every respect and in thoroughly good taste.[31]

Not wishing to limit business in any way, the films were also touted as eminently suitable for 'Parliamentary candidates, election agents, and leagues and societies of both schools of thought'. The report continues with a detailed description of the two films and *Tariff Reform* bears striking similarity with Smith's earlier *John Bull's Hearth*. Once again, Bull's hospitality to the foreigner, this time played around a dinner table, is abused and he only reasserts mastery in his own house with the help of a Colonial. The tale concludes with a strong plea for Imperial Preference, spiced with some xenophobic slogans:

> Having done this piece of work the Colonial tells John Bull to again take the head of his own table, which he does, and they swear that they can and will work together. The film finishes with mottoes such as: 'Preferential treatment through-out our Empire, and Britain for the British', 'Free Trade spells R-U-I-N', and 'Free Trade means England for the Foreigner'.

The opposite political view was expressed in *Free Trade*. This promotes the widely accepted 'cheap food' benefit of the laissez-faire ideal and the achievement of social reform under the Liberals:

> It opens with a butcher's shop, in which is displayed clean and fresh meat, which the workman can buy cheaply. We follow him to his home, where a happy wife lays the table in readiness for his arrival. He brings home toys for his child, beer for himself, and plenty of wages, which he hands over to his wife. He has a poster on the wall, depicting Old-age pensions, and crowns Mr. Lloyd George with a halo of flowers … Finally, we are shown some old people going to the Post Office to draw their Old-age pensions, which the recipients fondly show when they receive the hard cash.[32]

In summary, a number of conclusions can be made in regard of political propaganda and cinema in the early period in Britain. Firstly, those political films before the Great War did not emanate from within the party political machinery. Rather that the pioneers were to be found at the local level and a consequence of local initiative, as in the case of F. George Pyne in Devon. Historians of political cinema in Britain have missed that significant point through an over-attention to formal political parties and the strategic operations of the National HQ. Such a research emphasis on Party has missed a further crucial aspect to political film in the early period, the role of the cinema industry. As we have seen, members of the trade sensed new business with political subjects, especially around election times. On the initiative of well-placed filmmakers in the industry (Fitzhamon at Hepworth is exemplary here for the election of 1906), political films were made speculatively and sold to party agents and groups who could use them in their campaigning. Gaumont developed an alternative approach for the election of 1910 with its politically balanced package of films, which could be sold on the basis of their topicality to the broader market of showmen and picture houses. By the time of the latter election, at least four firms were actively involved in the business of political films, Hepworth, Gaumont, Kineto and Cricks and Martin, and articulating political subjects through topicals, comedies, experimental sound productions and straight-forward propaganda films.

While Gaumont approached the opportunity objectively with a carefully balanced programme of political films, Hepworth seemingly betrayed its own political bias with the distribution of outrightly protectionist narratives and a series of Vi-vaphone productions that featured Conservative-Unionist politicians. Considering some circumstantial evidence, the industry in this period was to a degree protec-tionist-minded, a consequence of the increasing dominance of foreign firms in the home market. In response, the trade established a Cinematograph Defence League in 1910, largely to mobilise against the proposals for censorship that ultimately became concretised in the British Board of Film Censors (1913), but highly revealing in the nomenclature. Certainly, many of the political films of the period portray a pronounced xenophobia, whether dealing with immigration, fiscal policy (both fair trade and free trade variants) and in the wider dramatic portrayals of political undesirables, notably the iconic bomb-wielding European anarchist.

In one important sense, the experiences of the 1906 and 1910 elections did connect significantly with the practise of party political propaganda in the post-Great War period. The disastrous showing for the Conservatives in 1906 and 1910 led to significant re-organisation for the Conservative and Unionist Party and 'the first signs of the new broom that would sweep the Party and prepare it for the organisational demands of the twentieth century.' Timothy Hollins senses here the move towards modernisation that would eventually lead to that Party political approach to propaganda film that has been the focus of scholarship to date. As he argues:

> The 1911 re-organisation was of great significance for the structure, working, and organisational efficiency of the Conservative Party ... and it provided the organisational basis for a new approach to party propaganda.[33]

The parties, in a national, operational sense, did come to political cinema in the 1920s. However, the origins of political film in Britain are located in the experiments and initiatives practiced around the General Elections of 1906 and 1910, momentous political times for modern Britain when the seeds were planted for the modern and sophisticated use of visual propaganda based on powerful moving image technology.

Notes

1. *Kinematograph and Lantern Weekly* (4 July 1907): 115.
2. Cited in Hogenkamp, B., *Deadly Parallels. Film and the Left in Britain 1929–39* (London: Lawrence and Wishart, 1986): 17.
3. Hollins, T.J., 'The Conservative Party and Film Propaganda between the Wars', *English Historical Review*, 96, 379 (1981): 359–369; Hogenkamp op.cit; Jones, S.G., *The British Labour Movement and Film*, 1918–1939 (London: Routledge and Kegan Paul, 1987). A recent exception to this tendency has occurred with regard to the Co-operative Movement, see, Burton, A., 'The emergence of an alternative film culture: film and the British Consumer Co-operative Movement before 1920', *Film History*, 8(4) 1996: 446–457.
4. Taylor, P.M., *British Propaganda in the Twentieth Century. Selling Democracy* (Edinburgh: EUP, 1999); Hollins, T.J., *The Presentation of Politics: The Place of Party Publicity, Broadcasting and Film in British Politics, 1918–1939*, unpublished PhD Thesis, University of Leeds, 1981.
5. *The Optical Lantern and Cinematograph Journal* (1905): 104.
6. 'Aliens on the Cinematograph', *Primrose League Gazette* (May 1905): 17, reproduced in Bottomore, S., 'A Selection of Documents to Accompany the 1995 Pordenone Non-fiction Screenings', photocopy compilation available to delegates.
7. Hepworth, C., *Came the Dawn. Memories of a Film Pioneer* (London: Phoenix, 1951): 69. It is claimed here that the film was the first in a series, but this could well be a mis-remembrance.
8. 'Aliens on the Cinematograph', op. cit.
9. 'Pictures to Win Votes', *The Optical Lantern and Cinematograph Journal* (May 1905): 167.
10. It is interesting to speculate on the appearance of the film at this time, see endnote 17.
11. *The Optical Lantern and Cinematographic Journal* (March 1905): 98. It also editorialises here, that, 'The objection to such pictures as this by political opponents, is the best recommendation for their continuance'.

12. Gifford lists a second political from Smith at this time, *The Free Trade Bench* (50ft).

13. Gifford lists an earlier title for January 1905, *The Voter's Guide*, which may well have been a speculative effort that led Fitzhamon on to a programmatic approach.

14. In one crucial sense, the tariff issue centred on the cost of living. This was symbolically played through the contrast of the 'Big Loaf' (cheap food) and the 'Little Loaf' (dearer food). Free traders maintained significant working-class support by invoking the spectre of high food prices, and the Free Food League (formed 1903) was predicated on this very principle.

15. 'Picture Politics. Cinematograph Speeches for the General Election', *The Optical Lantern and Cinematograph Journal* (December 1905): 47.

16. 'Cinematograph in Politics', *The Optical Lantern and Cinematograph Journal* (December 1905): 41. The Primrose League had been formed in 1883 in memory of Lord Beaconsfield (Disraeli), and served to promote the Conservative cause 'out of doors'.

17. *The Optical Lantern and Cinematograph Journal* (January 1906): 49.

18. 'The Cinematograph in Politics', *Chamber's Journal* (25 November 1905), reproduced in Harding, C. and Popple, S., *In the Kingdom of Shadows. A Companion to Early Cinema* (London: Cygnus Arts, 1996): 38.

19. The Tariff Reform League enjoyed support from wealthy industrialists and drew on considerable financial resources. It issued millions of pamphlets in the run up to the Election of 1906 and established nearly 300 constituency branches. Rempel, R.A., *Unionists Divided. Arthur Balfour, Joseph Chamberlain and the Unionist Free Traders* (Newton Abbot: David and Charles, 1972): 45–46.

20. Turner, Barry, *Free Trade and Protection* (London: Longman, 1971): 76.

21. *The Optical Lantern and Cinematograph Journal* (January 1906): 50.

22. 'The Election', *The Optical Lantern and Cinematograph Journal* (March 1906): 91. For the use of the lantern to announce election results, see, 'The Lantern', *The Optical Lantern and Cinematograph Journal* (February 1906): 78; and for a humorous example of the misapplication of the technology to electioneering, see, ibid: 67–68. The election of 1906 was a landslide victory for the Liberals and the ethos of free trade, bringing to an end a considerable period of Conservative ascendancy.

23. W.H.B., 'The Kinematograph a Political Power', *The Kinematograph and Lantern Weekly* (July 1907): 162–163. For proposals to use the lantern at the L.C.C. election, see, 'Lantern Propaganda', *The Optical Lantern and Kinematograph Journal* (December 1906): 53.

24. 'The Bioscope and the Election', *The Bioscope* (30 December 1909): 5; 'Pictures and the Election', *The Bioscope* (13 January 1910): 4. There were two elections in 1910, January and December, both won by the Liberals.

25. 'The Bioscope and the Election', op. cit.

26. 'A Large And Succesful Undertaking', *The Bioscope* (13 January 1910): 59. The Liberal's 'People's Budget' of 1909 was the centrepiece to a constitutional crisis developing between the Liberal Party and the House of Lords (dominated by Conservatives). The Budget Protest League was financed by bankers like the Rothchilds and publicised by the Harmworth Press, Aikin, KWW, *The Last Years of Liberal England 1900–1914* (London: Collins, 1972): 63.

27. 'Pictures and the Election', op.cit. Smith was an ally of Chamberlain in the ranks of the Unionist Tariff Reformers; Balfour was the leader of the Conservative and Unionist Party throughout the period, but was forced to resign in November 1911 following three successive election defeats.

28. 'Dissolving the Government', *The Bioscope* (8 December 1910): 37. The title is a pun on the dissolution of the Liberal Administration in 1909 over the constitutional crisis with the upper House, and the reason for a general Election in 1910.

29. *The Bioscope* (24 November 1910): 37.

30. The plot of the Cricks and Martin film is presented in *The Bioscope* (6 January 1910): 47.

31. 'Election Films', *The Bioscope* (13 January 1910): 11.

32. 'Gaumont's Election Films', *The Bioscope* (13 January 1910): 61.

33. Hollins, T.J., *The Presentation of Politics*, op. cit.: 25.

12

Punch and the Lantern Slide Industry

Helen Walasek

Punch magazine was first published on 17 July 1841. At first a satirical magazine that targeted the hypocrisy of the political and social elites, over the course of the nineteenth century it became a widely-known and influential national (and indeed, international) institution and a fully-functioning part of the British establishment. By the early years of the twentieth century two of its editors, Francis Burnand and Owen Seaman, had been knighted, as were two of its principal cartoonists – John Tenniel and Bernard Partridge. It was *Punch*'s full-page political cartoons and smaller social pictures (as they were known at *Punch*) that were perhaps the primary source of the magazine's renown, and from the first *Punch* was good at marketing new uses for its pictorial material as a tool to increase circulation, as well as being an additional source of income.

In 1906 Herbert Heather, the astute and energetic Secretary of Bradbury and Agnew, *Punch*'s proprietors, began a large promotional campaign to capture new subscribers to the magazine. All the techniques of modern marketing were used including targeted mailshots and the sale of compilation volumes and mounted art proofs of *Punch* cartoons and pictures. The move into lantern slide lectures, as we shall see, was to be another element in Heather's marketing strategy. During World War I Heather saw other possibilities for the use of lanternslides. Through examining the letter books, bound volumes and collection of ephemera in the *Punch* Archives it is possible to trace *Punch*'s involvement in the lanternslide industry.

At least one lantern slide lecture had been produced with *Punch*'s co-operation six years earlier in 1900. Titled *An Evening with Punch*, with a script by Arthur Croxton, it was produced for hire or purchase by Eyre and Spottiswoode. Herbert Heather mentions in 1906 '... two or three lectures on similar lines were in use some three or four years since'.[1] One of these other lectures may have been *Popular Humourists of the Day*, which consisted largely of Punch cartoons, also produced by Eyre and Spottiswoode. In any case, neither lecture was advertised or promoted by Punch.

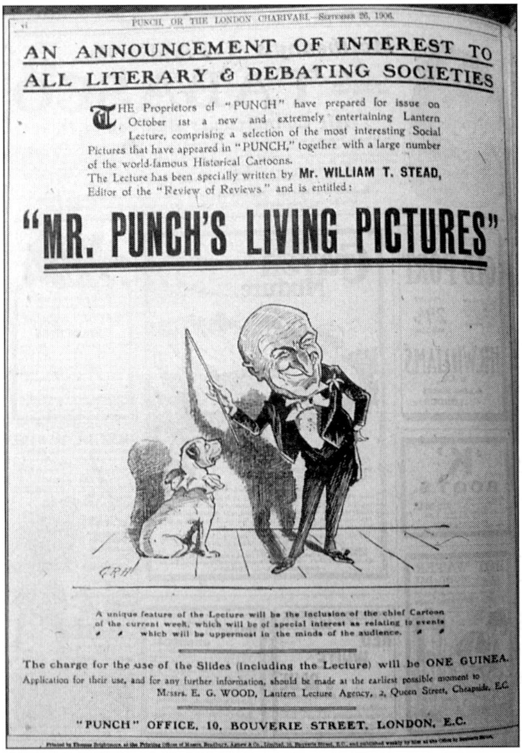

Fig. 1. Advertisement from Punch, *26 September 1906 for Punch's first lantern lecture, Mr Punch's Living Pictures.*
[All photographs copyright Helen Walasek.]

They had appeared, however, before the period of Herbert Heather's managership. Heather joined Bradbury, Agnew & Co in 1895, becoming its Secretary in 1903.[2] His business acumen brought about a revival in *Punch*'s fortunes through his use of modern marketing techniques and by the establishment of an innovative advertising department.

The impetus for introducing a new lantern slide lecture based on *Punch* cartoons and pictures seems to have come from a combination of demand from the public and approaches from the trade. In May 1906 Heather received an approach from E.G. Wood's Lantern Lecture agency.[3] However, later in the year he wrote to Edgar Rolfe, a solicitor who was booking the new lecture, 'Your letter to us of 3rd April ... may possibly have influenced us in deciding to issue this lecture ...'.[4] From the first Heather saw the lecture (and its successors) as a vehicle for increasing Punch's circulation and mentions this specifically in a number of letters. In December 1906 he wrote to a prospective agent in Capetown: 'Our object in placing this lecture on the market has been to advertise "Punch". Would it be possible in South Africa to arrange that at each lecture a distribution could be made of leaflets or some similar advertising material in respect of Punch?'[5]

On 29 May Heather wrote to E.G. Wood saying that *Punch* was considering the proposed lecture. He enquired how many words the lecture should be and requested copies of similar lectures.[6] The next day he wrote to E H Stout at *Review of Reviews*, with whom *Punch* had a number of business dealings, asking his advice on the lecture. E.G. Wood, he wrote, '... is the biggest man in this particular line; he advertizes that he has a selection of over two hundred thousand slides'.[7]

On 9 August Heather informed E.G. Wood that Bradbury and Agnew had decided to proceed with the lecture and outlined the terms of their agreement:

> It is understood that you will give a specially favourable position in your catalogue for this lecture, and that a charge of £1.1.0 will be made for the use of the slides; that you will prepare at your cost sufficient slides to meet the demand, and will render an account to us at the end of each month

> showing the receipts and paying us for each use of the slides a Royalty of 10/6.
>
> We will have the lecture written and printed and will undertake to advertise it in 'Punch' and 'Review of Reviews'.
>
> This arrangement to last for one year from this date.
>
> It is hoped that it will be possible to considerably extend this scheme in the season of 1907–08.[8]

We learn from further correspondence that *Punch*'s royalty was split with *Review of Reviews* whose editor, William T. Stead, wrote the lecture.[9]

Mr. Punch's Living Pictures was launched with a full-page ad in *Punch* on 16 September 1906. At the same time, *Punch* carried out a special circularising of lecturers on E.G. Wood's mailing list. *Punch* bore two-thirds of the cost for this and E.G. Wood one-third – '... the result will justify the expenditure', Heather assured them.[10] The advertisement read: 'An announcement of interest to all Literary & Debating Societies. The Proprietors of "Punch" have in preparation for issue early in October a new and extremely entertaining lantern lecture comprising a selection of the most interesting social pictures that have appeared in "Punch", together with a large number of the world-famous Historical Cartoons.'[11]

Like many of the later lectures, the slides began with a selection rehearsing the well-known mythology of the magazine and its personification, Mr Punch. Subjects included the early covers of *Punch*, the editors of *Punch*, Linley Sambourne's celebrated cartoon *The Mahogany Tree*, depicting *Punch* staff seated round the famous *Punch* Table, and even a slide of the *Punch* dining room. They moved onto social pictures such as Charles Keene's *Zoology* and George du Maurier's *A Disenchantment* as well as works by contemporary artists such as Phil May's *The Latest from Dottyville* and Leonard Raven-Hill's *Evident*. The third section of the programme showed such famous cartoons as Tenniel's *New Crowns for Old Ones* of 1876 showing Disraeli in the guise of an oriental pedlar offering Queen Victoria a new crown as Empress of India and John Leech's *General Février Turned Traitor* of March 1855 depicting Czar Nicholas on his deathbed, the news of the defeat of Russian forces in February clutched in his hand while a skeletal General Février, enveloped in a snowstorm, touches him with an icy finger.

Later ads point out a special feature of the lecture: '... the inclusion of the Chief Cartoon of the current week, which will be of special interest as relating to events which will be uppermost in the minds of the audience'.[12] This feature, however, did not appear to last long. By November the advertisements were carrying endorsements from satisfied customers: 'We never had an Entertainment so much appreciated', 'We found it from beginning to end interesting to the audience' and 'The Entertainment was splendid'.[13]

The first, free, programmes, produced and initially distributed by *Punch*, included a coupon entitling members of the audience to a mounted Art Proof of a *Punch* cartoon worth five shillings, free of charge except for postage. With this offer Heather hoped that he could, as he wrote, '... after securing their names, induce them to become subscribers to Punch'.[14] Heather was anxious that the programmes with the free proof offer went only to those attending the lectures, and that they were not to be given to children.[15] He further requested that any unused copies

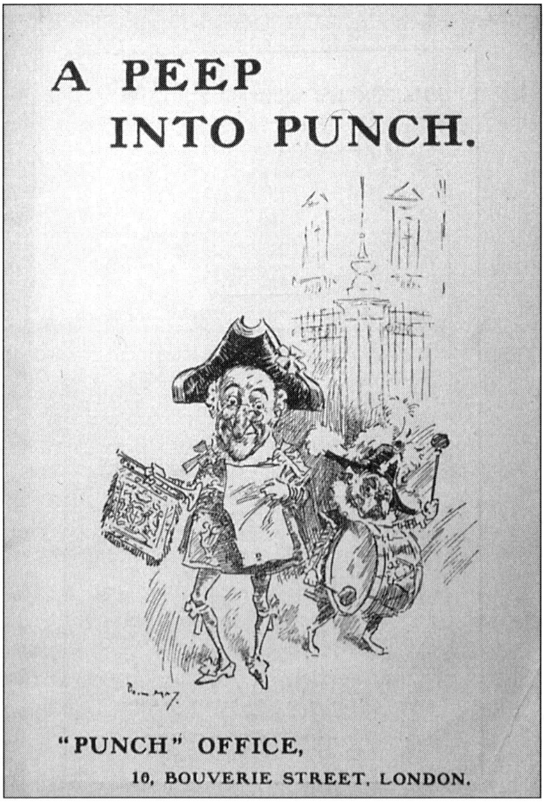

Fig. 2. Lantern lectures booklet for A Peep into Punch *written by A.A. Milne from the series first introduced in 1907.*

were to be returned to him.[16] Twelve different Art Proofs were included in the offer, among them such classics as Tenniel's *The British Lion's Vengeance on the Bengal Tiger* (which was also in the lecture).[17] On 6 October Heather wrote to the Rev Goodhart 'We should feel indebted to you if you would be good enough to have an announcement made to the audience pointing out to them our offer to send these Art Souvenirs free, full details of which will be found in the fourth page of the programme'.[18]

From an internal letter dated 17 October 1906[19] we learn of Heather's marketing plans and techniques, including his usual practice of monitoring results by keeping a careful record of customer responses. Each request for an Art Proof was recorded and, along with every Art Proof posted, a pamphlet promoting the compilation volumes *Cartoons from Punch* and a catalogue of the other Art Proofs available were enclosed. Non-subscribers also received an order form for *Punch*. The names and addresses of those receiving the Art Proofs were typed in at the head of the form letter in ink matching the body of the letter. Heather had also prepared a 'follower letter' to be sent to those who did not respond to the letter accompanying the proof. All the names and addresses of those ordering the proofs were to be kept to be made available to *Review of Reviews*. In another internal letter dated 5 November 1906 Heather gives a list of all the lectures held during October at which programmes were distributed and writes: 'I want to have separately for each lecture the results: the number of applications for Art Proofs at 6d and 3/-; the number of sets of "Cartoons" and sets of "Pictures" sold; the number of Art Proofs at 5/-, 7/6, etc, etc. I think there have been no new subscribers to "Punch" resulting from the Lantern Lectures?'[20]

Requests were coming in from clients for posters to advertise the lectures.[21] By 13 October two sizes of posters were being offered to those booking the lecture. Printed in black and red with a space at top and bottom for local matter, they cost 1d each for the window bills (with a minimum order of 2/6) and 2d each for the large posters (with a minimum order of 5/).[22] Heather offered to print lecturers' own matter on the posters for an extra 2/6 for each size.[23]

By November Heather was writing to an appreciative Rev Watson: '... the success of the present series has led us to contemplate the issue of another ...'.[24] He also began seeking agents for the lecture abroad in South Africa and Canada.[25] He had already shipped a set of slides and twelve copies of the lecture to *Punch*'s agents in Australia. 'It should be useful for advertising purposes ...' he wrote.[26] This promotion of the lantern lecture series overseas in English-speaking countries, including the United States, was to continue over the years as new lectures were introduced.

In June 1907 preparation began in earnest for the expansion of the lecture series and the coming season. On the 4th Heather wrote to A.A. Milne, later to be famous as the author of *Winnie the Pooh*, but then Assistant Editor of *Punch*, enquiring on the progress of the lantern lecture Milne had been asked to write.[27] On the same day he wrote to Eyre and Spottiswoode making arrangements for them to return the slides and scripts of *An Evening with Punch* – and also requesting them to withdraw from the market their lecture, *Popular Humourists of the Day* as it consisted largely of *Punch* drawings.[28] Another letter went to E.G. Wood seeking their views on the proposed expansion of the series.[29]

In the following days he wrote to the publisher George Newnes requesting to use the title of their book *A Peep into 'Punch'* for the new lantern lecture. He did not imagine they would object, however, as they had used the illustrations for book 'entirely gratuitously'.[30] He wrote again to E.G. Wood asking them to recommend a suitable writer for a lecture on English history of the Victorian era, as well as asking them to destroy all programmes which included the free Art Proof offer: it was not to be continued in the new season.[31]

In early July Heather wrote to Laurence Bradbury outlining the coming lantern lecture series: 'I have arranged for the inclusion in our Lecture programme this year of an Historical Lecture on the Victorian Era, which is intended to be sufficiently educational to appeal to schools, and sufficiently interesting for general audiences. It is being written by the Rev. Barrass, Vicar of St. Laurence Jewry, City.' There were to be four lectures in all – last year's, a new one by Mr Milne (*A Peep into Punch*), the revival of *An Evening with Punch* and the new historical lecture.[32]

On 12 August Heather wrote to E.G. Wood formalising their agreement for the coming season. This year Wood's were receiving only a 25 per cent commission on bookings rather than the 50 per cent of the previous year. *Punch* would again provide (and print) the lectures and readings, but the old stock of *An Evening with Punch* was to be made to last the season.[33]

Heather was also corresponding with the Rev Stephen Barrass about the historical lecture. 'I should be glad', he wrote, 'if your lecture could come up to, say, the end of 1905, closing with the accession to power of the present government. I am afraid people may think that a lecture terminating with the death of Victoria might be stale'. He adds 'you would, of course, as a true historian, see that the lecture was perfectly impartial as to the parties, or we shall get into hot water with our friends'.[34]

But Heather was to have trouble with the scripts for the two new lectures. By 6

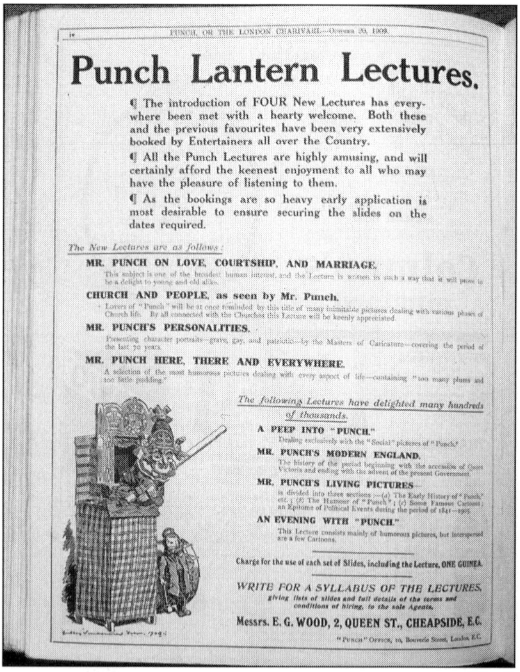

Fig. 3. Advertisement from Punch, *29 September 1909, introducing a new series of lectures.*

September, with the beginning of the lecture season rapidly approaching, he had still not received the text of the historical lecture from Rev Barrass. After some no doubt frantic writing and the to-ing and fro-ing of proofs, Heather finally received the passed proof from Barrass on 23 September. He wrote testily to the Reverend: 'I am sorry to say that we have been caused a very great deal of trouble in editing the lecture, as a very considerable part of it was left by you merely in the form of notes which could not possibly be read in that form by the lecturer'. He closes 'I fear that this result must be due to the pressure we have been compelled to put on you to obtain the lecture'.[35]

He later complained to E.G. Wood 'I am sorry to say that we are having considerable trouble with both "Punch's Modern History" and "A Peep into 'Punch' ". We have had to make a very large number of alterations in R. Barrass's lecture since he handed it over complete, and there has been difficulty in making "A Peep into 'Punch'" make sufficient matter.'[36]

Once again, circulars were sent to the 4,300 names in E.G. Wood's address book and on 28 August the first advertisement appeared in *Punch* for the new season. It announced: 'The Entertainment which was issued last season "Mr. Punch's Living Pictures" and the older lecture "An Evening with 'Punch'" have met with such considerable success as to encourage the hope that the wider choice which is now presented will be welcomed by those who have the arrangement of programmes of Literary and Debating &c societies for the forthcoming season.'

A Peep into 'Punch' had been specially written, it declared, in response to a demand for an entertainment dealing exclusively with the social pictures of *Punch*, while the slides in *Mr. Punch's Modern England* were 'peculiarly interesting in that they show just how the great events of the past seventy years presented themselves to the eyes of the nation at the moment of their happening'. *Mr Punch's Living Pictures* had, it said, achieved a 'phenomenal success', delighting 'hundreds of audiences throughout the country', while *An Evening with 'Punch'* provided 'continuous laughter and merriment'.

In 1909 a further four lectures were added to the programme: *Mr. Punch on Love, Courtship and Marriage* with a script written by Frederick Sherlock, the editor of *Church Monthly*; *Church and People as seen by Mr. Punch* by A Clifton Kelway, editor of *Goodwill*; *Mr. Punch's Personalities* by Robert Morgan and *Mr. Punch – Here, There and Everywhere* by Gerald Maberly. With his three years of experience in producing lantern lectures Heather was now more active in making suggestions about structuring the programmes and suggesting alternative cartoons if a particular illustration was repeated in different scripts. The general theme of the lectures appears to have been chosen by Heather, no doubt in consultation with the editor of *Punch*. And while the choice of illustrations rested with the authors of the scripts, they all appeared to have met with Heather at *Punch* for a preliminary discussion when the direction each lecture was to take was no doubt discussed. To make their selection the authors were sent various compilation volumes of *Punch* cartoons such as *Cartoons from Punch* and titles from *The Punch Library of Humour*. This year, Heather informed them, the scripts were to be mimeographed rather than printed.[37]

Once again, all the original drafts were too short by 2–3,000 words and were returned to the authors, but there seemed to be less of a problem than with the 1907 texts. The main difficulty now was with the titles, for as Heather wrote to Clifton Kelway, 'It is essential to secure a title which shall look attractive for as you know, the lecture itself has not a chance, unless the title attracts us in the first place'.[38] The title of the clerical lecture seemed a particularly knotty problem and the title was changed from one advertisement to another. Clifton Kelway's first venture, *Mr Punch and the Parsons* was deemed by Heather to be not 'altogether respectful' nor '... to possess the necessary attraction from the point of view of the possible users of the lecture'.[39] By mid-September Heather was more pressing. 'I hope you may have hit on a good title' he wrote to Clifton Kelway, 'we advertised the lecture in "Punch" a week or two since as "Mr. Punch's Excursions into Theology". Messrs Wood suggest "Mr. Punch's Critical Theology" or "Ecclesiastical Jottings in a Jester's Note-Book". Neither of these titles are ideal.'[40] Clifton Kelway seems to have suggested as further title *Mr Punch in Clerical Circles* before the final title, *Church and People as seen by Mr Punch*, was chosen.[41]

The new series was launched with a half-page teaser advertisement in *Punch* on 8 September 1909. The titles of both the clerical and the personalities lectures had changed by the time the first full-page ad and cover banner appeared in the 22 September issue. The ad announced:

> All those who have enjoyed the pleasure of listening to these highly entertaining lectures, and those who have in hand the preparation of syllabuses for the ensuing lecture season, will be glad to learn that Four Entirely New Lectures are in preparation and will ready October 1.[42]

The new programme was heavily advertised in *Punch*. Heather asked E H Stout for a page in November's *Review of Reviews* while Frederick Sherlock offered to place a notice in *Church Monthly*.[43] By 20 October the ads read 'The introduction of four new lectures has everywhere been met with a hearty welcome. Both these and previous favourites have been very extensively booked by Entertainers all over the country.'

The brochure for the expanded programme again emphasises the importance of the *Punch* Cartoon which has '... epitomised the chief idea, situation or affair of the moment ...' and '...truthfully represents the feeling, the sound common-sense,

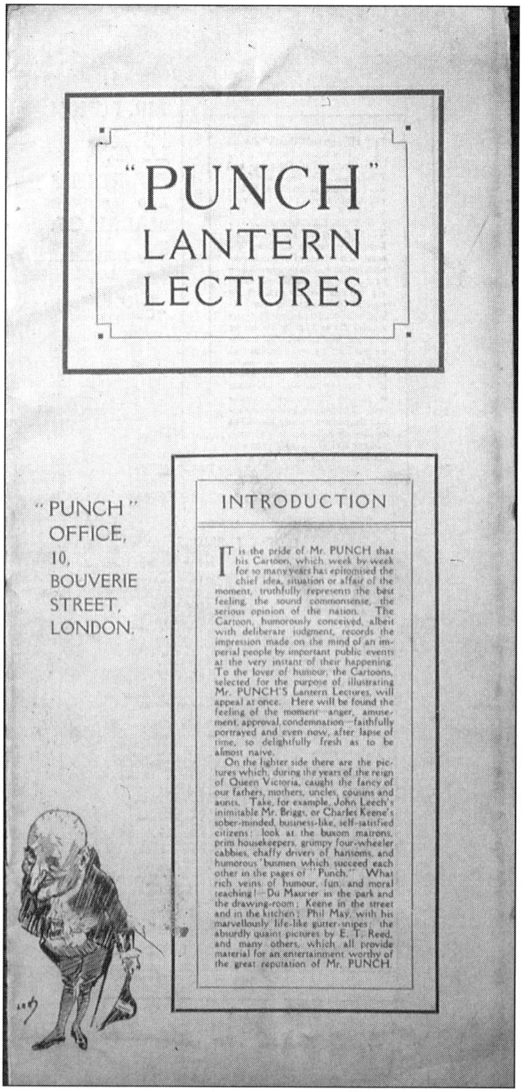
"PUNCH" LANTERN LECTURES

"PUNCH" OFFICE, 10, BOUVERIE STREET, LONDON.

INTRODUCTION

IT is the pride of Mr. PUNCH that his Cartoon, which week by week for so many years has epitomised the chief idea, situation or affair of the moment, truthfully represents the best feeling, the sound commonsense, the serious opinion of the nation. The Cartoon, humorously conceived, albeit with deliberate judgment, records the impression made on the mind of an imperial people by important public events at the very instant of their happening. To the lover of humour, the Cartoons, selected for the purpose of illustrating Mr. PUNCH'S Lantern Lectures, will appeal at once. Here will be found the feeling of the moment—anger, amusement, approval, condemnation—faithfully portrayed and even now, after lapse of time, so delightfully fresh as to be almost naïve.

On the lighter side there are the pictures which, during the years of the reign of Queen Victoria, caught the fancy of our fathers, mothers, uncles, cousins and aunts. Take, for example, John Leech's inimitable Mr. Briggs, or Charles Keene's sober-minded, business-like, self-satisfied citizens: look at the buxom matrons, prim housekeepers, grumpy four-wheeler cabbies, chaffy drivers of hansoms, and humorous 'busmen which succeed each other in the pages of "Punch." What rich veins of humour, fun, and moral teaching!—Du Maurier in the park and the drawing-room; Keene in the street and in the kitchen; Phil May, with his marvellously life-like gutter-snipes; the absurdly quaint pictures by E. T. Reed, and many others, which all provide material for an entertainment worthy of the great reputation of Mr. PUNCH.

Fig. 4. Brochure for 'Punch' Lantern Lectures, *c. 1910.*

the serious opinions of the nation'. 'The Cartoon' it goes on, 'records the impression made on the mind of an imperial people by important public events at the very moment of its happening …', and later states confidently 'No better commentary on these events could possibly be found than that which is furnished by the "Punch" Cartoons – some of which, indeed, themselves have not been without influence on the making of history'. Punch's unique and unrivalled position is promoted as 'the most notable of the humorous journals of the world', able 'to command the services of all the best talent that England has produced for a couple of generations'. It was their pictures that 'have made Punch famous throughout the world'. *Mr Punch on Love, Courtship and Marriage* included cartoons of two of *Punch*'s most famous couples, George du Maurier's Edwin and Angelina and Douglas Jerrold's Mr and Mrs Caudle. 'Mr. Punch' the brochure declared, 'ventures further than do most novelists – he shows *how* "happily ever after" the wedded couples live'. *Mr Punch, Here There and Everywhere* was a mixed bag of 'the best Punch had to offer'. 'Too many plums and too little pudding' was the catch phrase used by the lecture's author, Gerald Maberly, in a letter to Herbert Heather and subsequently used in the brochure and advertisements.[44]

As he had insisted on impartiality towards the parties in the political cartoons used in *Mr Punch's Modern England*, Heather once again took care to appeal to the broadest audience in the advertising copy for *Church and People*. He wrote to Clifton Kelway 'You will see from the Punch adv't that we have tried to convey the impression that the jokes are not all connected with the Established Church'.[45] The brochure text emphasized this further: 'In view of the place occupied by the

Churches in the life of the nation' it began, 'it is natural that the artists of "Punch" should have depicted largely the humorous aspects of their relation to the people. One thinks at once of many highly amusing illustrations in which ministers of all denominations, elders, deacons, church-goers, district visitors, and Sunday School children figure.'[46] In a slightly less ecumenical manner the text continued 'In a more serious vein "Punch" has dealt with the relations between Church and State. Lord John Russell asserted that the famous "Punch" cartoon "No Popery" did more to displace his Government from office than all the efforts of his opponents.'

The copy for *Personalities of Punch* continued to restate the political influence and importance of the *Punch* cartoon. It began 'Lord Goschen took an exalted view of "Punch's" prestige when he declared that he had attained to the highest ambitions which a Statesman can reach – namely, to have a cartoon in "Punch" all to himself'. It continues '"Punch" is justly celebrated for his caricatures – many of which are doubtless masterpieces. No one who examines critically a collection of them can be blind to the talent, often times genius, which is displayed.' The lecture intends to show 'a series of character portraits – grave, gay, and patriotic – covering the political, literary, and art history of the past 70 years'. The subjects ranged from the obvious – Queen Victoria, Wellington, Tennyson, Garibaldi, Bismarck and Disraeli – to the less well-known today such as Stafford Northcote and Lord Goschen. There were contemporary figures such as Winston Churchill, Teddy Roosevelt and Lloyd George. As Heather had advised Robert Morgan, these recent figures were 'possibly more interesting to prospective audiences'.[47]

The lectures continued to be advertised in *Punch* until the year of its 70th anniversary in 1911, when a half price offer was made for the coming season in order to bring the lectures '… within reach of those to whom the price has hitherto been a bar, and so still further popularize the Famous Lectures'.[48] No further advertisements for the lantern lecture series appear in *Punch*.

At some point between 1909 and 1914 a collection of miscellaneous slides of *Punch* cartoons and illustrations was added to the lecture series. Slides in the Miscellaneous Section could be hired at 3/- a dozen for a single evening's use. The brochure suggested 'A sufficient number can be ordered to provide a whole evening's entertainment, or a few may be had to supplement the regular Lectures. For instance, some users of Set Nos. I, III and V, which consist of humorous pictures only, like to add a few Cartoons, whilst users of the Cartoon Lectures IV, V and VII like to add some purely humorous subjects.' There were eleven slides relating to *Punch* and its history, 97 'Humorous and Satirical' pictures and 29 Cartoons in the selection. After the death of Edward VII in 1910 a seventh lecture was introduced. Intended to be a continuation of *Mr. Punch's Modern England*, it was titled *Mr. Punch on the Life and Times of King Edward VII*, and ended with the accession of George V.

After the outbreak of war in August 1914 *Punch* became an enthusiastic propagandiser on behalf of the war effort. On 30 September Heather agreed that E.G. Wood could add a selection of war cartoons to the Miscellaneous Series: 'We think these would be extremely popular just now' he wrote.[49] On 9 October he wrote again regarding the promotion of the war-related slides. He enclosed two small advertising leaflets in which the new slide series was mentioned. The first leaflet *Punch* would insert in packs of postcards of *Punch* war cartoons that were being produced

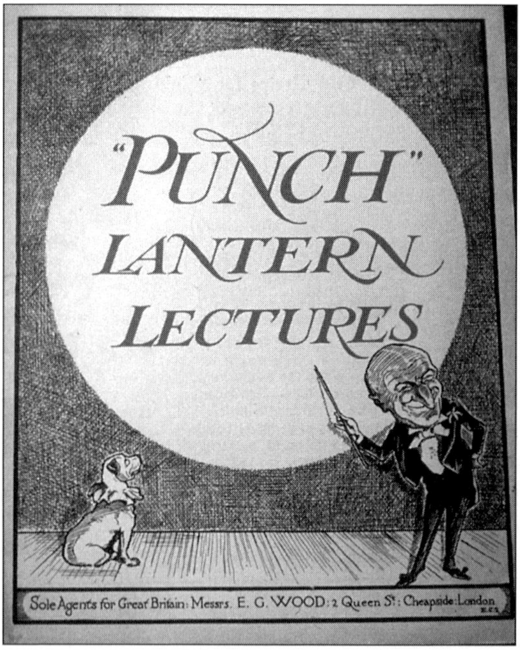

Fig. 5. Brochure for 'Punch' Lantern Lectures, *c. 1919.*

by Jarrold, while the second, which promoted both the postcards and the slides, was being enclosed in all applications for renewal of subscriptions – not less than 8,000 were expected to go out between then and Christmas. Regarding this second leaflet Heather wrote '... would you be willing to enclose these in all correspondence from your office for the rest of the year? This should provide reciprocation in respect of the lantern slide advertisement inserted in the packets of postcards'.[50] E.G. Wood agreed to take 2,500 as an initial supply of the leaflets.[51]

Heather went on that there was to be a full-page advertisement in the next issue of *Punch* – which would have an extended sale – along the same lines as the second leaflet. The ad, which appeared on 14 October read, below the main text about the postcards : 'Lantern Slides. A large number of slides have been prepared from "Punch" Cartoons, illustrating the attitude of Germany towards the Powers during the past 50 years.' Applications were to be made to E.G. Wood.

In mid-October Heather wrote to a number of slide manufacturers, including E.B. Fry Ltd, Underwood & Underwood, H.L. Toms, J.H. Stewart Ltd, H.S. Richardson, Chatham Pexton, Newton & Co, Trythall's Ltd and E.G. Wood, asking for quotes for the production of slides of six *Punch* illustrations. He asked them to quote for '50 slides of each, 10 slides of each, and per 100 up to 750 slides of each subject. There would be a regular weekly order for the number required. Also please quote us for 500 and 1,000 two-colour slides of the cover design of "Punch".'[52] However, 5 days later he wrote to all those who replied that *Punch* regretted they would be 'unable to utilize your service, as we have decided not to proceed with the scheme we had in contemplation'.[53] The scheme appears to have been a suggestion by J.E. Park of the Kensington Picture Theatre to reproduce as slides (no doubt for presentation at cinemas) cartoons from *The New Rake's Progress*, a supplement that had appeared in *Punch* on 16 September illustrating Kaiser Wilhelm's career through *Punch* cartoons from 1888 to 1914.[54] In the event Heather decided not to proceed with the scheme, though he gives no reason for the decision.

But Heather was already in the middle of planning an extraordinary undertaking – a massive campaign to boost enlistment in the Army waged through lantern slides, posters and handbills. It is clear from the outset that the idea of showing lantern slides at cinemas across the country was the initial impetus for the campaign. As he wrote later in the year to a supporter of the campaign 'One of the most effective ways of getting publicity is by the means of Lantern Slides. For a cost of about £25 a subject may be brought to the notice in Cinemas, etc. of approximately five million people per week.'[55]

Heather had been approached in mid-September by the manufacturers Trythall's Ltd about the production of lantern slides. Although he was unsure how this stood with regard to *Punch*'s sole agency agreement with E.G. Wood, he nevertheless invited them to a meeting[56] where he came to an arrangement with them, as can be seen in later correspondence, regarding the production lantern slides for the recruiting campaign. On 22 September he wrote to E.H. Parks 'We have in mind the possibility of arranging for the exhibition of "Punch" slides at the various Music Halls, Cinemas, etc.'[57] and on the 30th he wrote to E.G. Wood: 'As we explained to you a few weeks earlier, we are proposing to do something in the way of distributing lantern slides to cinemas, &c., through some of the big distributing agencies, and in fact have already done something of this kind'.[58] He continued 'We wish it to be understood that there is to be no restriction upon our liberty of action in this respect'.

On 28 October Heather wrote to the Reverend A.H. Dykes of the Holy Trinity Vicarage in Leeds giving him permission to reproduce as a lantern slide Raven-Hill's cartoon of 21 October, *The Greater Game*, an attack on the Football Association for continuing with a full Cup Competition when the services of its athletes were required by the country for the 'greater game of war'. Rev Dykes proposed to exhibit the cartoon at picture theatres in Leeds. Heather informed him that *Punch* was hoping to have the cartoon widely shown at cinemas throughout the country – they had in fact already distributed slides of an earlier recruiting cartoon to 1,000 cinemas and had passed out 60,000 posters and 500,000 handbills at their own cost. This cartoon was undoubtedly *To Arms*, Raven-Hill's cartoon of 2 September showing Mr Punch as a hectoring recruiting sergeant. 'We are inviting a few people who are interested in the subject' Heather wrote 'to contribute towards the cost and think it is possible that you would like to also'.[59]

In another letter dated 27 October Heather wrote to S. Taprell Holland giving more information on *Punch*'s campaign:

> We propose to print a number of handbills and posters and to insert a small notice in the next issue of Punch offering to send supplies of these to anyone who would like to distribute them. We also propose to have the Cartoon reproduced as a lantern slide, and have it sent to a considerable number of Cinemas throughout the country for exhibition on the screen. The cost of doing this would be 5d for each Cinema, and, if the funds were forthcoming, some 4,000 cinemas in all could be sent to, nearly all of these would show the Cartoon upon the screen a considerable number of times, thus obtaining a large amount of valuable publicity.

He continued:

> We ourselves do not see our way to bearing the cost of this. We have recently, in connection with an earlier Recruiting Cartoon, distributed at our own cost 1,000 such slides, and have also produced and distributed some 50,000

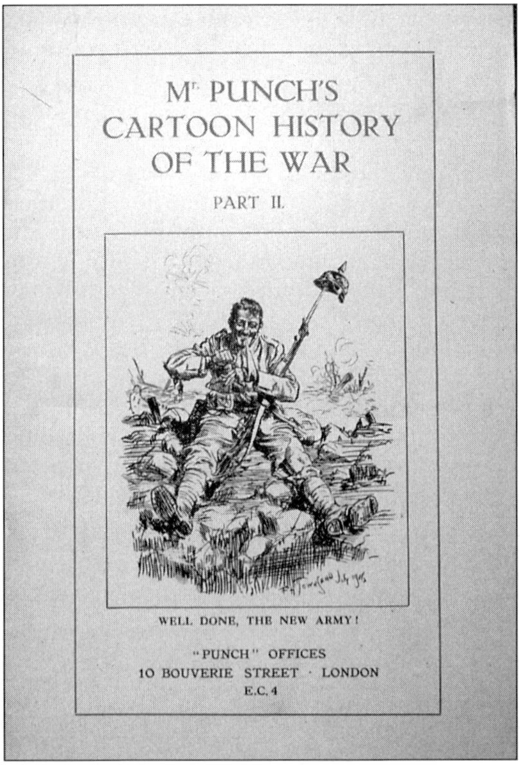

Fig. 6. Lantern lecture text booklet for Mr Punch's Cartoon History of the War, *Part II.*

posters and 500,000 leaflets of the Cartoon. Some 120 of our employees have enlisted, largely at our instigation, and the allowances which our Firm are making to their dependents amount to approximately £2,000 per annum. In many other ways also expenses have been incurred by us – so that we feel a difficulty in contributing to the present scheme, admirable though we believe it to be.[60]

Still, he hoped that his correspondent's offer of £10 towards costs still held – another subscriber had offered £50 for the distribution of leaflets which would enable them to cover a good bit of the ground contemplated.

Heather wrote to Trythall's on 30 October asking them to produce slides of *The Greater Game* and dispatch them to 2,000 cinemas. The slides were to be made as before – the full page just as it appeared in the magazine – Heather was always concerned that the cartoons were branded as coming from *Punch*. He wanted them sent to 2,000 different cinemas from the 1,000 the earlier cartoon had been sent to. He continued 'I am hopeful that in the course of a few days I may be able to send you a further order for another 3,000 to contemplate the whole of your list'. The slides were to be sent at the earliest possible moment and, he concluded, 'I should also be glad if you could oblige with a copy of the letter which you will send out with the slides, so that I can form some opinions to the proportion which are likely to be shown'.[61]

The small notice Heather had referred to in his letter of 27 October to S. Taprell Holland appeared in the 4 November issue, on the same page as Owen Seaman's poem *To a False Patriot*, which was also to figure in the campaign. The ad read:

> 'The Greater Game'
>
> This cartoon, which deals with professional football and the war, and appeared in the issue of *Punch* for October 21, has now been reprinted in the form of Posters and Handbills. These will gladly be sent free of charge, for the purpose of distribution or exhibition, to anyone interested in recruiting among football players at the enormous crowds that attend League Matches.

> Applications, stating the number required should be addressed to The Secretary, *Punch* Offices, 10, Bouverie Street, E.C., who will gratefully acknowledge any contributions towards the expense involved.
>
> 'The Greater Game' is also being reproduced in the form of a Lantern Slide for exhibition at Cinemas, etc.

The Greater Game, depicting working-class men at leisure, cigarette in hand, watching other working-class men playing football – rather than enlisting in the army – seemed to excite in *Punch*'s middle class readers the most interest of all its recruiting cartoons.

On 12 November Heather wrote again to Trythall's asking them to make two dozen slides of *A Glorious Example* which had appeared in the 11 November issue; the cartoon, this time drawn by Bernard Partridge, depicted a soldier of the Territorial Army challenging an 'Able-bodied Civilian' to join up. Trythall's, in addition, were to make and despatch 500 further slides of *The Greater Game*, delivering one dozen to him as well as a dozen of *To Arms*. These he sent out in sets of three, along with posters and handbills, to contributors to what was now called the *Pro Patria Fund*, as well as to others who had expressed an interest in the enlistment campaign.

A full-page ad in *Punch* on 18 November announced the institution of the fund. Under a quote from Lord Kitchener: 'I shall want more men, and still more' and titled *'Punch' and the War*, it outlined the campaign as well as listing the contributors so far. Posters and handbills of the three cartoons *To Arms*, *The Greater Game* and *A Glorious Example* along with two poems by *Punch*'s editor, Owen Seaman, *To the Shirker and To a False Patriot*, and lantern slides of the cartoons were offered for distribution free of charge. 'Nothing' it said 'appeals more strongly to the imagination than a striking Cartoon or a telling Poem, and the more widely these are disseminated among those whom it is desired to influence, the greater, undoubtedly, will be the result secured'. Readers of *Punch* could help their country by distributing handbills or exhibiting posters or by contributing to the fund to help defray costs. The Cartoons had also been produced as Lantern Slides and 3,500 Lantern Slides had been made and exhibited, it was estimated, to audiences numbering upwards of 25 million people. In another full-page ad on 2 December the number of slides produced had risen to 3,600 and the audience estimated as upwards of 30 million.

On 16 November Heather had written to Captain J.W. Dowden of Edinburgh, the principal contributor to the *Pro Patria Fund* with his donation of £50, reporting on the distribution of *The Greater Game* (for which he had originally given the donation). The manufacture and distribution of 2,500 slides had cost £52.1.6. Two thousand slides had been despatched a fortnight ago and their Cinematograph agents estimated that they were being shown to two million people daily; a further 500 slides were to be despatched that night.

Heather wrote on 8 December to Dr A. Green of Norwich who had sent a donation to the fund and had who had enquired regarding the showing of lantern slides of the cartoons, that they had been sent to some 3,500 cinemas. He continued, however, 'We should have sent them to considerably more but for the fact that funds have not been forthcoming to justify our doing so. Although the cost is not great for each Cinema theatre, it amounts to something considerable when dealing with thousands.'[62]

The last advertisement for the *Pro Patria Fund* ran in the issue of 30 December 1914; the fund was to be wound up on the 31st. A total of £426.3.5 had been donated (including £105 by the proprietors of *Punch*) and the expenses incurred were £429.19.8. 125,000 posters and 900,000 handbills had been distributed and no less than 3,716 Lantern Slides had been made and exhibited to audiences all over the country totalling 'many millions'. The posters and the handbills were still available, but now there was to be a charge for them.

At the end of 1916 a new prospectus for the lectures was published, no doubt to include the new lecture that was being prepared: *Mr. Punch's Cartoon History of the War*,[63] the first of what was to become a total of five lectures on the war. Heather wrote to E G Wood that they need only prepare about a dozen extra slides for the lecture, apart from those already in the War Section. He also requested that they include a slide of the *Punch* cover (in colour) inscribed 'The Famous Cover of "Punch" drawn by Richard Doyle, Uncle of Sir Arthur Conan Doyle' and a picture of the *Punch* Table showing the staff and proprietors seated around it at the time of *Punch*'s jubilee in 1891.

Unfortunately this series of letter books ends in November 1918 so we cannot trace the post war history of *Punch*'s involvement with the lantern slide industry or when it ended. However, we do know from a surviving brochure that after the war an expanded programme of lectures was launched, twelve in all. *Mr. Punch's Living Pictures* and *An Evening with 'Punch'* were no longer in the brochure. The seven other pre-war lectures remained while four new lectures focusing on the recently-ended war were added to the first of 1916. As the brochure points out, it was the 'greatest event of our times'. 'Mr. Punch's prestige had been enormously enhanced by the Titanic struggle' it went on. 'In the darkest hours *Punch* never ceased to maintain an attitude of cheerful confidence'. He encouraged men in the trenches, lightened the burden of the wounded and did '... yeoman service to the nation and the Allied cause'.[64]

Mr Punch's Cartoon History of the War came as three separate lectures. The brochure stressed that '... no collection of Cartoons on the war can compare with these comprised in these lectures'. It featured such cartoons as *Unconquerable*, *Gallipoli and After?* and *America to the Front*. A further two lectures came under the title *Mr. Punch's Humour of the Great War*. The brochure admits 'At the beginning of the Great War Mr. Punch thought that there could be no place for humour in a world of horror and mourning; but Tommy's gay courage – that blend of light-heartedness and perpetual sense of the ridiculous amidst all his hardships, convinced Mr. Punch that it was not only his privilege but his duty to continue ministering mirth'.

It is difficult to discover figures in *Punch*'s records to determine the level of success of the lantern lectures. There are few references with exact figures of bookings or levels of income in the letter books. There is an internal letter dated 5 November 1906, soon after the first lecture was introduced, monitoring the response to the free Art Proof offer, that lists all the bookings for *Mr Punch's Living Pictures* at which programmes were distributed for the previous month. There were 20 in all, although of course there were lectures at which no programmes were distributed – for instance those shown to school-children.[65]

A few years later on 17 July 1909 Heather wrote to E.H. Stout at *Review of Reviews* sending him an account of the royalties due to him with regard to *Mr Punch's Living Pictures* for the past year. He remarks that 'bookings of the Lantern Lecture have dropped to nearly zero'.[66] On 3 December 1909 however, Heather wrote to Frederick Sherlock, author of the script for the newly-introduced lecture *Mr Punch on Love, Courtship and Marriage* that E.G. Wood 'have obtained 41 bookings of your lecture up-to-date, this includes your own bookings – so that you will see that you are by far the most profitable customer'.[67] One year later on 3 December 1910 in another letter to Sherlock he wrote 'The "Punch" Lectures are going satisfactorily, but they are naturally adversely affected at the present moment, when everybody is thinking more or less exclusively of the election'.[68]

Apart from these few references there is nothing more regarding the financial success of the lectures. Nor are we able to discover whether the lectures achieved Heather's aim in introducing them – to increase the number of subscribers to *Punch*. However, we must assume that the lectures were both a financial and marketing success – enough for both *Punch* and E.G. Wood to think it worthwhile to expand the series after the end of World War I at a time when the market for lantern slide lectures were generally declining in the face of the expansion of the cinema. This post WWI series seems to have been the last of *Punch*'s activities in the lantern lecture industry, which, while it lasted, appears to have achieved – at least according to *Punch*'s advertising – a 'phenomenal success'.

Notes

1. AF11/949.
2. I am grateful to Professor Peter Mellini for the information on Herbert Heather's career.
3. AF11/97.
4. AF11/949.
5. AF12/361 and similar letters AF11/102, AF11/942, AF13/701.
6. AF11/97.
7. AF11/102.
8. AF11/387.
9. AF12/151.
10. AF11/507.
11. 19 September 1906.
12. 26 September 1906.
13. 14 November 1906, 10 December 1906, 13 February 1906.
14. AF11/942.
15. AF11/594.
16. AF11/651.
17. AF12/780.
18. AF11/651.
19. BB02/206.
20. BB02/209.
21. AF11/681.
22. AF11/738.

23. AF12/118.
24. AF11/732.
25. AF12/361, AF12/366.
26. AF11/942.
27. AF13/257.
28. AF13/259.
29. AF13/260.
30. AF13/306.
31. AF13/360.
32. AF13/20-07-07.
33. AF13/764.
34. AF13/768.
35. AF13/25-09-07.
36. AF13/993.
37. BF05/187.
38. BF05/186.
39. BF05/233.
40. BF05/186.
41. BF05/233.
42. *Punch*, 22nd September 1909, iv.
43. BF05/545 and 675.
44. BF05/187.
45. BF05/233.
46. *Punch Lantern Lectures* brochure, c. 1909.
47. BF05/67.
48. *Punch*, 13 September 1911.
49. BF20/559.
50. BF20/645.
51. BF20/497.
52. BF20/675.
53. BF20/713.
54. BF20/650 and BF20/719.
55. BF21/561.
56. BF20/464.
57. BF20/497.
58. BF20/559.
59. BF20/875.
60. BF20/876. A set of posters from the campaign can be found in the Imperial War Museum.
61. BF20/906.
62. BF21/720.
63. BF28/812.
64. *Punch Lantern Lectures* Brochure, c. 1919.
65. BB02/209.
66. BF04/797.
67. BF05/923.
68. BF06/190.

13

Skylights Onto Infinity: The World in a Stereoscope

William Merrin

In a well-known attack in his review of the salon of 1859 upon the public's taste for photography, Charles Baudelaire excoriated his own 'loathsome society' which 'rushed, like Narcissus, to contemplate its trivial image on the metallic plate'.[1] Less well known is his attack immediately following this upon the public passion for the latest photographic effect: 'It was not long before thousands of pairs of greedy eyes were glued to the peepholes of the stereoscope, as though they were the skylights of the infinite'.[2] Following its success at the Great Exhibition of 1851, thanks in part to Queen Victoria's interest and David Brewster's gift to her of a Duboscq-made viewer, the stereoscope quickly became a popular entertainment. It sold a quarter of a million viewers in England and France within three months,[3] and, through peaks and troughs of interest and competition from new crazes and media, survived well into the 20th century. By then, through its popularity, commercial success and longevity, it had established its place as probably the dominant photographic form of the 19th century and one of the most important visual media of the period becoming, Earle says, 'nearly as pervasive in its time as electronic media is today'.[4] Baudelaire's antipathy, to its popular success at least, was well founded.

Baudelaire's venom, however, was not simply aimed at photography's popularity, but, more particularly, at its effect upon artistic appreciation and expression, reflecting his concern at the transformed sensibilities of a public who believed art to be merely 'the exact reproduction of nature' and whom forsook 'the divine art of painting' for this new, idolatrous form of sun worship. A hostility towards the profane pleasure of the masses, therefore, animates his attack on the stereoscope, as he describes the public as gazing into its depths as if it gave access to the divine; as if *infinity* itself could be seen in its skylights. It is this image of a public with its eyes pressed to the stereoscope, greedily devouring its infinite sights, that I want to consider here, for I believe Baudelaire's metaphor gives us a way to understand the stereoscope's place, role and meaning within the society that so avidly produced and consumed its views.[5]

To begin, in opposition to Baudelaire, I first want to dissociate the stereoscope from photography; an act that might seem strange given that its popular, commercial success would have been unthinkable without its mass-reproducible, photographic stereographs. However, it is important to remember that the stereoscope predates photography, its origins lying in the scientific investigation of binocular vision with Charles Wheatstone first presenting a reflecting stereoscope using hand-drawn geometrical figures in 1838, describing work dating back to 1832. Moreover, although photography provided the most effective means of producing stereo images, it was neither necessary for the defining stereoscopic effect nor capable of alone producing it in requiring either a free-viewing subject, or, more commonly, the use of a stereoscope for its manifestation. These points justify seeing the stereoscope, therefore, as a separate technological form: one aiming at the simulation of three dimensional experience through a technical ensemble uniting the stereoscope and its viewer, producing the visual illusion of 'solid' ('stereo') space and its depth of field through the simultaneous presentation of two, separate images in a binocular, immersive form. Such a conception of the medium allows a greater historical contextualisation of the stereoscope within the wider history of western media and the technical project of representational verisimilitude allowing us to better understand its lineage and role. In particular it allows us to move beyond its identification with photography to recognise its affinities with earlier media forms and methods.

The Renaissance discovery and development of 'perspective', first demonstrated by Brunelleschi in 1425, can be seen as one of the most important of these precursors of the stereoscope. It attempted to represent a three dimensional object on a two dimensional plane, creating the illusion of solidity by its presentation of the correct relationships of height, breadth and depth of an object, or between objects, in the visual frame, with all lines of sight converging upon the single point of an ideal, external observer. This is *perspectiva* – 'seeing through' a frame as if it were a 'window' onto a 'slice of reality'.[6] Breaking from medieval symbolic and tactile representation and experience,[7] and even from our 'psychophysiological' perceptual experience,[8] human vision could now imitate the single, omniscient gaze of the divine to survey its harmonious, physical and moral ordering of the world of creation; a world conceived for the first time as uniform, continuous, and *infinite*. Even if the window available for humanity was bounded, with divine infinity being beyond their sight, they could at least partake in it, assured that the world diverged from this single, originary point beyond all frames and that all material things had their apportioned and proportioned place within this empirical spatiality. With perspective, therefore, human double vision was abstracted and mapped onto the single point of the divine to share in its vision.

This perspectival tradition gave rise to one of the stereoscope's closest predecessors, the peepshow. Alberti, author of the treatise on perspective, *Della pittura*, is credited with the development in 1437 of 'perspective boxes' which accentuated the apparent solidity of painted views when seen through their viewing hole; a technique developed by Dutch artists in the 17th century who achieved their three dimensionality from internal mirrors, and eventually developed into the popular 'peepshow' boxes of the 18–19th centuries which employed height or depth to create a solidity from either a flat image or a series of arranged views.[9] By creating the box view, however, the act of observation was changed from a detached *seeing-through* a window to a *pushing-against* a viewing hole that filled one's sight and immersed the viewer who, accordingly, passed through into the scene itself. Many later media retained and developed this immersive form, most notably the panorama and phantasmagoria which enveloped their audience, to present a multi-media, three dimensional virtual reality environment.[10] The stereoscope, therefore, can be better understood when placed within this wider lineage, owing its success to its combination of the immersive, three dimensional, scenic simulations of the peepshow and panorama which transported the viewer into the distant scene itself, with photography and photographic realism – its presentation of the sights of the world as they actually appeared. Prepared by the earlier media and by the revolution in print making from the 1820s and in popular illustrated newspapers from the 1830s, the stereoscope took advantage of a public eager to see –and to actually experience – the world. With this new instrument, that sight – and even that experience – was now possible.

'Seems madam! Nay, it is!'

Contemporary accounts repeatedly emphasise their own amazement at first viewing the stereoscope. The *Illustrated London News* declared in 1852 that those who had yet to see the effect, 'can form only a small idea of the amount of astonishment they have yet to experience',[11] and 56 years later, a 1908 catalogue for Sears, Roebuck and Co., could still declare that 'seen for the first time, the effect is almost startling, and if you have never looked through the scope at one of these pictures you have still before you one of the real pleasures of life'.[12] The stereoscope's success was the result of this rapturous, magical transformation of two, flat images and the virtual state produced in the viewer; a state never better described than by Oliver Wendell Holmes in 1861 as 'a dream-like exaltation of the faculties, a kind of clairvoyance, in which we seem to leave the body behind us and sail away into one strange scene after another like disembodied spirits'.[13] The stereoscope transcended its content as its subject was less important than the experience of its own effect; of that ephemeral moment of revelation and transportation when two images fused in a form that could not even be guessed from the flat card and whose wonderful sight could barely be remembered after viewing, thus driving its viewers back to the same scenes again and again to 'sail away' anew into their depths.

Commentators, almost without exception, shared this view of the experience of the sights offered, almost accepting the images as the reality itself. Thus the *Illustrated London News* wrote of the stereoscope's ability to transmit the 'exact image' of things,[14] *Notes and Queries* praised its effect in 1857 as equivalent to 'viewing the scenes themselves,[15] and *Photographic Mosaics* in 1870 added it to the telescope and microscope in showing us 'the true form and configuration of the distant world'.[16] Others saw more than an effective resemblance, with the London Stereoscopic Company's banner headline for an 1856 advert quoting *Hamlet* to declare the absolute reality of its views: 'Seems madam! Nay, it is!'[17] Many were ready to confirm this, with *Scientific American* declaring the same year that in the view of a city, 'the reality itself seems presented to the sight', and the *Art Journal* asserting in 1858 that, in Frith's views of the Holy Land, 'the actual is absolutely before us and we know it'.[18] As Holmes said, this was a 'divine gift', carrying us 'into the very presence of all that is most inspiring to the soul'.[19] For others the stereoscope even eclipsed reality with a hyperreality, with the *Illustrated London News* claiming of photographs of the Great Exhibition, 'no one has ever seen the interior of the exhibition from end to end with such clearness as it is seen in M. Claudet's pictures'.[20] The stereoscope, therefore, partook of photographic truth but also superseded it in the difficulties of tampering with the image, the addition of another dimension, and in the hyperrealism of its imagery such that, as one 1914 cartoon declared, reality itself 'is going to have to go some' to give us the same thrill as the stereoscope pictures.[21]

As we have seen in Holmes' testimony, the experience of the stereoscope was often likened by commentators to travel. Holmes himself provides the best description of this in his explanation of the possibilities of 'this enchanted door (of pasteboard)':[22]

> Oh infinite volumes of poems that I treasure in this small library of glass and pasteboard! I creep over the vast features of Rameses, on the face of his rock-hewn Nubian temple; I scale the huge mountain-crystal that calls itself the Pyramid of Cheops. I pace the length of the three Titanic stones of the walls of Baalbec, – mightiest masses of quarried rock that man has lifted into the air; and then I dive into some mass of foliage with my microscope, and trace the veinings of a leaf so delicately wrought in the painting not made with hands, that I can almost see its down and the green aphis that suck its juices. I look into the eyes of the caged tiger, and on the scaly train of the crocodile, stretched on the sands of the river that has mirrored a hundred dynasties. I stroll through Rhenish vineyards, I sit under Roman arches, I walk the streets of once buried cities, I look into the chasms of Alpine glaciers, and on the rush of wasteful cataracts. I pass, in a moment, from the banks of the Charles to the fords of the Jordan, and leave my outward frame in the armchair at my table, while in spirit I am looking down upon Jerusalem from the mount of Olives.[23]

Holmes' 'spirit' travel instantly crosses continents, and even human scale itself, to eliminate all spatial and temporal boundaries without any of the discomfort or danger of 19th century travel. His essay also includes a virtual stereoscopic tour of 'these pictured, nay real memories',[24] taking in New York, the United Kingdom, Europe, and the Near East in a few breathless and effusive pages. With the stereoscope we enter the image as 'the mind feels its way into the very depths of the pictures', Holmes says, feeling its way around objects whose solidity could even harm us: 'the scraggy branches of a tree in the foreground run out at us as if they would scratch our eyes out'.[25] This is no photographic sun painting, but, as he says, a sun *sculpture* – a solid and tactile experience – moving beyond the perspectival *standing back* with a stereoscopic *passing through* and transportation. Thus, for him, to look at the image of the chariot ruts at Pompeii, 'is the same thing as stooping down and looking at the pavement itself'.[26]

But if Holmes describes a journey out into the world, in the same passage he also describes bringing this world back to him: 'these sights, gathered from the Alps, temples, palaces, pyramids, are offered you for a trifle, to carry home with you, that

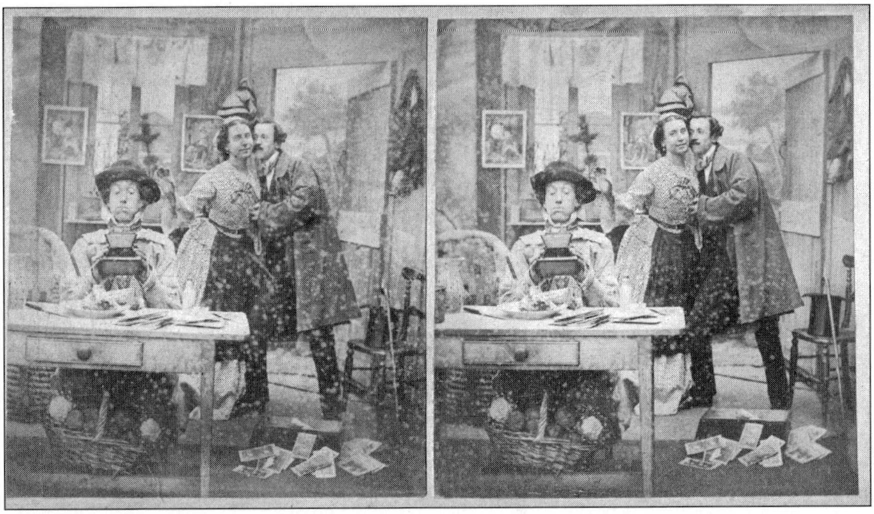

Fig. 1. Stereocard: 'An Optical Delusion. Things Seen and Things Not Seen' (No date, P&S 184). A popular image, showing a stereoscope salesman seducing the wife of a customer too engrossed in the stereoscope to notice. As viewers were themselves required to use a stereoscope to enjoy the joke an interesting reflexivity was introduced into the scene.

you may look at them at your leisure, by your fireside, with perpetual fair weather'.[27] As he says of a trip to Canterbury:

> These old Cathedrals are beyond all comparison what are best worth seeing, of man's handiwork in Europe. How great the delight to be able to bring them bodily, as it were, to our own firesides. A hundred thousand pilgrims a year used to visit Canterbury. Now Canterbury visits us.[28]

The explanation for this apparent contradiction in the direction of movement of viewer and view lies in contemporary changes in technology and mediation.

By mid-century, when the stereoscope came to prominence, improvements in press reporting, production and dissemination, in printed illustrations, and in new photographic processes, had all brought the world closer, whilst tours of the world were being offered in popular entertainments such as the new 'moving panoramas', and the emerging magic lantern industry, and international exhibitions and public museums developed representational systems allowing the experience of other places and cultures. For Marshall McLuhan, however, it was the electric telegraph that represented an epochal break in the history of media, in electrically extending humanity and abolishing temporal, spatial and affective boundaries to 'implode' the world into a 'global village'.[29] This implosive effect, however, can be seen to predate the telegraph as visual media such as the peepshow, panorama, and diorama, had, for a long time, contemporary reviewers believed, offered an immediate transportation into the unmediated reality, negating inconvenient travel in bringing the sites to the viewer, 'on the wings of the wind'.[30] The developments in visual media and mass communications through the mid-century only intensified this process and it is apposite that the part inventor of the telegraph, Charles Wheatstone should in the same period, also be responsible for the stereoscope which offered a more concrete experience and implosive transportation than the telegraph's coded signals. The dual direction of travel discovered in the stereoscope, therefore, was not contradictory but rather a defining experience of an implosive society and its collapse of spatial and temporal experience. Holmes even went so far as to proclaim a global village of empathetic, linked humanity would result from the stereoscope, lauding the stereograph as 'the card of introduction to make mankind acquaintances'.[31]

Most commentators were similarly optimistic, with *Household Words*' 1853 judgement of the stereoscope, as 'one of the most beautiful little discoveries that grace the science of the day', being typical.[32] Indeed, although new technologies usually produce a pathological reaction – of a physical or mental, medical or moral, or real or imagined, nature – the stereoscope seems to have elicited comparatively few such responses. One can be found in an 1860 cartoon in *Harper's New Monthly Magazine*, illustrating the consequences for a family of the father's purchase of a stereoscope. By the final panel the once-content and perfect family are unhappy, unkempt, and uncommunicative, with haggard eyes and ruined eyesight: even the family dog, seen in one panel peering into the Brewster stereoscope, is now boss-eyed.[33] Another familiar warning might be deduced from a popular series of views showing a stereo salesman seducing a customer's wife whilst the husband is engrossed in his views.[34] The moral theme of the passion for the image blinding us to the true reality is an ancient one, being central to Christian theology and receiving its paradigmatic philosophical expression in Plato's simile of the cave, but this idea is also common in illustrations of the media with many showing peepshow viewers having their pockets picked,[35] or Kaleidoscope viewers and camera operators missing the seduction of their partners.[36] The stereoscope card, however, literally adds an extra dimension to this, for the viewer who is invited to laugh at the stereoscopic image of the man so caught up in the stereoscope as to miss their wife's infidelity must surely feel a shudder at the thought of what might be taking place at that moment behind their own back. This particular stereograph series ends with the husband stamping on the stereoscope; a curious expression of comic hostility towards its own medium.

'A stereoscope for every home'

For the most part, however, the Victorians seem to have taken the stereoscope to their hearts and to their home. It was George Swann Nottage's London Stereoscopic Company which adopted as their famous advertising slogan, 'a stereoscope for every home',[37] and, given the numbers in which both viewers and cards sold, this was no wild boast. Indeed, the medium was so closely identified with the home as to become known, in both England and America, as 'the parlour stereoscope': as the *Art Journal* reported in 1856, 'the stereoscope is now seen in every drawing room; philosophers talk learnedly upon it, ladies are delighted with its magic representations, and children play with it'.[38] It is curious then that the question of its relationship to that domestic environment has not yet been considered. Many texts locate it within the parlour as a domestic entertainment but the significance of this seems to hold little interest.[39] However, it is only by considering the issue of its domestic use that we can begin to understand the medium and its specific role within Victorian society.

Despite Nottage's best hopes the stereoscope did not find a place in *every* home, as

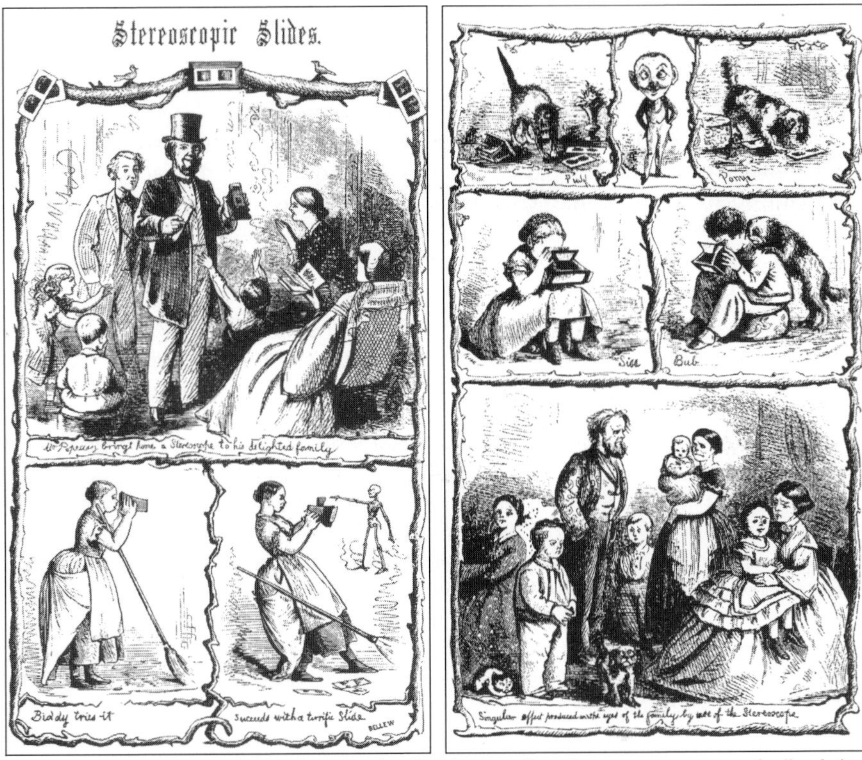

A cartoon from Harper's Monthly, *July 1860, showing the deleterious effects of a new stereoscope upon family relationships and upon both human and animal eyesight!*

financial and cultural considerations ensured that, for much of its life, it remained a middle class entertainment. Nor was the stereoscope for every part of the home – as the *parlour* stereoscope it was most closely identified with one particular space within the home, taking its place within a specific environment – that of the bourgeois interior, functioning not only as a medium of entertainment but as a key signifier of this private sphere. Evidence of this close relationship can be found in the viewers themselves. One highly decorated 1862 model is listed as having been given as a wedding present, providing strong evidence of its domestic associations given the bias of such gifts as the expression of the couple's relationship and future home-life.[40] Moreover, as many of the cabinet stereoscopes were high quality, expensive, ornately decorated, luxury models and items of furniture, they were clearly objects of great value, of display, and of 'conspicuous consumption'. As a social medium, shared with one's select guests, this quality was not merely, as Thorstein Veblen says, 'honorific' to oneself, but also served to display one's wealth, rank and 'respectability',[41] with the use of the stereoscope also implying, Becker argues, a claim to 'refinement' and 'culture'.[42] The home and its activities, formed, therefore, a spatial and temporal leisured sphere for the bourgeoisie where the social processes of competitive display found a class expression.

More constructed evidence of the stereoscope's position can also be found in the adverts for the viewers and their line drawings of their idealised clientele, reinforcing the image of the shared, familial or social, domestic nature of the medium and its user's wealth and status. Thus one 1856 London Stereoscopic Company advert shows a family group and guests around a table in a well apportioned dining room, all well dressed and affluent and enjoying a selection of views in table-top viewers, though their respectability is, if anything, over-signified by the inclusion of the chandelier above them.[43] Stereographs showing such family scenes are also known, not only confirming the familial associations but also raising the intriguing, regressive possibility of an evening's family entertainment watching a family's evening entertainment.[44]

Another important indicator of the stereoscope's domestic significance is their appearance in *cartes de visite* and cabinet photographs. Both Tagg and Lalvani have discussed the role of photographic portraiture for the Victorian middle classes as a symbolic act appropriating the aristocratic forms of the portrait and the visiting card to make their social ascent visible and to announce their status and identity.[45] As Lalvani argues, photography was used to communicate 'a particular discursive and ideological formation', operating as a 'disciplinary practice' for their own cultural regulation and reproduction.[46] Family photographs, therefore, had a particular role in promoting the importance of the private sphere but, due to technical limitations, this sphere had to be represented in the studio. The photographer had to simulate the bourgeois interior, showing his subjects either in the drawing room, 'the centre of bourgeois domesticity', or on a balcony off this space, both spaces 'that savour the hegemony and presence of a particular class', representing a space of bourgeois 'cultivated leisure'.[47] However, just as the bourgeois drawing room simulated the aristocratic salon, so the studio simulation, despite being poorer in presentation than a drawing room, was also grander in its aspiration to aristocratic décor. Significantly the stereoscope appears as a common prop for sitters within this simulated drawing room.[48] Its use is central to the semiotic hyperrealisation of the domestic interior within the public space of the studio, being primarily employed to signify – among its many cultural connotations of modernity, technological achievement and novelty, entertainment, leisure, culture, refinement, and education – the class position, home-life, and private sphere of the sitter.

As we have seen, however, one of the appeals of the stereoscope was its ability to bring the world back into this sphere, into one's own armchair: 'you need not cross the ocean' for such sights, Holmes says, as you can now carry them home with you, 'that you may look at them at your leisure, by your fireside'.[49] This arrival of the world at one's hearth appears to have been easily accepted, with few reservations of its reality. We can recognise, however, that commercial decisions concerning subject matter, the photographer's subjective framing and compositional decisions concerning the best stereoscopic arrangement and effect, and judgements concerning the topicality of scenes and events shown (often necessitating captions or explanations before their meaning is apparent) all produce a constructed experience of the real. The cards reflected cultural biases, assumptions, and interests, being produced simultaneously as spectacle, entertainment, information and education, and to be appropriated as a commodity in a collection of things and as an image by a particular class. As Holmes admits, this appropriation is important: 'you only have to give a paltry fee ... to own ... the best sights the world has to show'.[50] The aim of the medium, therefore, was not simply travel, but the capture and possession of the world as both commodity and image.

For Heidegger the modern world was 'the age of the world picture', of 'the world perceived and grasped as a picture' by the modern, representing subject: a process of 'the conquest of the world as picture, a specifically western position towards, mode of revealing, and control of, the world'.[51] In the 19th century developments in technologies of image making and mass reproduction, as well as in communications and transportation, with the western, bourgeois (capitalist, scientific-technical and imperial) world view, combined to produce a powerful series of representational systems for the world and for other societies and cultures. The stereoscope was a central medium in this process, as part of a wider transformation of the world into a thing to be viewed, and an image, exhibit or commodity for scopic pleasure, contemplation and control. Darrah's 1977 estimate of up to two million different European and possibly six million different American stereographs, each potentially produced in huge numbers, gives some indication of their prevalence.[52] As the most popular stereographs were scenic views of other places, cities and countries, and as it would not be until much later in the century, and even into the next, until amateur photography and the reproduction of photographs in newspapers or books became common, it was the stereoscope that provided the dominant photographic representation of the world, in a format, in particular, that could be easily owned and collected. This, therefore, was *the age of the world as stereograph*.

The stereoscope's importance lies, however, not simply in this transformation of the world into an image, but in its consumption in the comfort of the home, and in the drawing room, in particular. This room originated in the early 19th century, Schivelbusch argues, as 'a bourgeois imitation of the aristocratic salon', though was rarely used, except for family gatherings and celebrations, remaining the 'lifeless centre' of the bourgeois home until it 'gradually opened up to family life' from mid-century to evolve into that centre of familial and social life, the 'living room'.[53] The name, 'drawing room' is a shortened form of 'withdrawing room', denoting not simply a space of withdrawal after dinner but, Logan says, 'a private place removed from more public reception areas'.[54] It developed alongside the growing separation of private and public spheres as a space of class and familial withdrawal from the world to represent both an interior world and an interiorised perspective.

This bourgeois retreat can be briefly seen in two examples: upholstery and curtains. Schivelbusch attributes the origins of furniture upholstery to the railway's attempts to cushion middle class passengers from the buffeting of rail travel and thus from the industrial reality they had created. This cushioning soon reappeared in the bourgeois home to cushion the class not only from the industrial origins of their possessions.[55] but, implicitly, from the external industrial reality, to protect the bourgeoisie within a padded and overstuffed interior. For Schivelbusch, curtains performed a similar function, being introduced in the early 19th century as a thin covering for the top of the window, becoming a transparent muslin or gauze covering to diffuse hard, natural light and close the room to outside eyes without destroying one's enjoyment of this light.[56] With a growing separation of homogeneous light into 'inside' and 'outside' light; the association of outside, natural light and the public view; the increasing separation of public and private spheres and the growing antipathy of the private sphere towards the public, curtains became darker and thicker resulting, by the centuries end, in 'the oft-cited twilight atmosphere of the bourgeois interior'.[57] The drawing room came to incarnate a withdrawal from the view – and even from the light – of the world: as Schivelbusch says, 'the anxiety over which everything private, and especially the family, was shut off from a public that was felt to be more and more unpleasant, is reflected in attempts to prevent light from the street falling directly into rooms'.[58] In this interior, therefore, the bourgeoisie withdrew from the world.

For Walter Benjamin this bourgeois interior was one of the key cultural forms of the 19th century, representing a private form of the phantasmagoric arcades, panoramas and dioramas.[59] 'With an aversion to the open air' these were places with a thick, covering 'Uranian atmosphere':

> To live in these interiors was to have woven a dense fabric around oneself, to have secluded oneself within a spider's web, in whose toils world events hang loosely suspended like so many insect bodies sucked dry. From this cavern one does not like to stir.[60]

As 'a stimulus to intoxication and dream', this was a space of familial and class entertainments, of leisure and distraction, Benjamin says, as 'the private citizen who in his office took reality into account, required of the interior that it should support him in his illusions ... From this sprang the phantasmagorias of the interior'.'.[61] These were the phantasmagorias of the kaleidoscope, the thaumatrope, phenakistiscope, and praxinoscope, with their shifting, mesmeric images; of the 'toy' magic lanterns and their garish children's slides and fantastic scenes, and of the stereoscope, with its dream-like intoxication and rapturous transport. Benjamin's claim that the interior 'represented the universe for the private citizen' and that 'in it he assembled the distant in space and time', as if 'his drawing room was a box in the world theatre', perfectly describes the stereoscope's role and effect.[62]

But, Benjamin notes, 'the interior was not only the private citizen's universe, it was also his casing,[63] functioning as a limit to experience and as an enclosure:

> The nineteenth century, like no other century, was addicted to dwelling. It conceived the residence as a receptacle for the person, and it encased him with all his appurtenances so deeply in the dwelling's interior that one might be reminded of the inside of a compass case, where the instrument with all its accessories lies embedded in deep, usually violet folds of velvet. What didn't the nineteenth century invent some sort of casing for![64]

Despite its content, therefore – the sights of foreign lands and the marvels of both the natural and industrial world – and despite too its apparent transportation of the viewer, the stereoscope was part of the interior not the exterior world. Standing in the drawing room as an expensive, ornate encasing for the world, the stereoscope trapped the world in its box or cabinet allowing it to be viewed from without through its binocular eyeholes. Having cut themselves off from the exterior the bourgeoisie reversed this again, to capture and enclose the world within their interior and within its own interior, the stereoscopic viewer. Separated from the world, the bourgeoisie discovered it again by looking inwards, finding, in the closed cases of the stereoscope, a safe, captured, selected and entertaining world; one indexed and arranged in a series of instructional views for one's idle contemplation and collection. At no point did the outside intrude, with even the light used for viewing being artificial. And so, cushioned within the deep velvet folds of their drawing room the world was kept with a box within their box: the stereoscope's casing and encasement of the world reflecting the bourgeoisie's own encasement and project of encasing.

Celeste Olalquiaga develops this Benjaminian analysis of the interior as 'refuges from an increasingly pervasive public realm', seeing the Victorian middle class's passion for ferns, natural history collections and aquariums as a sampling of the outside world, 'bringing it back to the safety of an individual home where it was susceptible to domestic control'.[65] As Olalquiaga observes of these collections, with them the bourgeoisie could save and nostalgically preserve a world they themselves had transformed, often employing the same technologies to achieve this that were implicated in its destruction.[66] The stereoscope's dream-like transports followed and expressed a similar technological and class strategy; one aiming at spatial control in closing off the external world to bring it back in safe and processed forms, and at a temporal control in halting the dynamic processes of modernity to fix and preserve the world in an image that could be examined at leisure. The Victorian interior, Olalquiaga suggests, was like 'those attics or chests', closed off to the world, within which their objects gather the dust of time'; a place where 'things come to rest ... in the certainty of a safe haven, a place where they will be handled adoringly, allocated to a shrine where they can themselves look back at the world'.[67] This is a rarefied atmosphere for a reified world, though here the world as image looks out of its stereoscopic skylights not at the world, but only at another dusty chest.

The stereoscope, therefore, was a private and isolating medium, reserved for family, for guests, and, ultimately, for the individual viewer. It allowed a vicarious simulacral participation in the world, though one predicated precisely upon one's distance from it and double enclosure, both in the viewer and in the parlour, seeing the world only through their skylights. Despite claims of transportation it reinforced the closure of the class, covering and distancing as surely as the curtains and upholstery closed off and cushioned the interior from the hostile public, reflecting and reasserting the same separation of the private sphere. It offered a form of literal *tele-vision* – of sight at a distance, a role that would be copied by later domestic media. Thus, for Jean Baudrillard, contemporary television produces a similarly simulacral participation, giving 'the great thrill of lived reality', and of 'the fact of being there without being there', such that 'we live', he says, 'sheltered by signs in the denial of the real'.[68] With it we consume its sights in the comfort, distance and security of the sign, without any of the danger or discomfort actual experience might presuppose, enjoying a vicarious participation in a reality whose technological realisation only distances us from the real experience, for, 'the more closely the real is pursued ... the greater does the real absence from the world grow'.[69]

Contemporary electronic media, Baudrillard argues, increasingly exteriorise all private realms, exposing all functions and relationships to their real-time transmission, resulting, he says, in the 'transparency' and 'obscenity' of an instantly available and hyperrealised world.[70] Of all 19th century media the stereoscope did most to begin this process, with company photographers crossing every continent to render, in hyperrealistic, solid minute detail, every scene and sight of man and nature, materialising and industrially reproducing their stereoscopic simulacra; making the world instantly available with a pornographic hypervisibility that invited the viewer to pore over every detail and even enter into the representation and revel in the '*orgy of realism*' it offered.[71]

We return here to Baudelaire's image of the public greedily pushing against the eyeholes of the stereoscope as if they were skylights onto infinity. Here, the Victorian bourgeoisie moved beyond the Renaissance's single-point, two dimensional, framed, visual representation of the infinite, using the stereoscope's double-point perspective to technically simulate and capture that infinity, to trap it in its box and, with every view produced, to reduce its unmapped expanse, appropriating, cataloguing and collecting its available sights. Where the Renaissance had represented infinity, the stereoscope's perspective aimed to overcome it and to possess a natural world since rethought as the 'standing reserve' of industrialisation; as inert matter from which the divine had been banished, and as scientific and capitalist property. Thus the ocular control and appropriation offered by the stereoscope reflected that already asserted by science, technology and capitalism.

If, therefore, the Renaissance was the age of the discovery of space, both terrestrially and conceptually, the Victorian age was that of its elimination and control through its implosive communicational and representational technologies and through its capitalist and colonial systems. Thus, when the bourgeoisie peered into infinite space with their profane, ocular hunger they did so not in order to stand back and share in the single gaze of the divine and God's harmonious ordering of the world, but rather to push through, out into the world from the comfort of their own homes, to assert their own control, possession and ordering, and to survey a world instantly brought back to them for their pleasure, edification and self-satisfaction. The stereoscope's viewers, therefore, only passed through the perspectival window in the security of their own home, enjoying precisely the simulation of that passage. In effect, in the darkened and draped bourgeois interior, this perspectival window was finally shut and the open and infinite world was closed within the stereoscope's box, and when the bourgeoisie now looked into it they no longer saw a world ordered by God, but one ordered by their own hands. Baudelaire's public was right. Infinity was indeed available through the stereoscope's skylights.

Notes

1. Alan Trachtenberg (ed.), *Classic Essays on Photography* (New Haven, Conn: Leete's Island Books, 1980): 86–87.
2. Trachtenberg: 87.
3. B.E.C. Howarth-Loomes, *Victorian Photography. A Collector's Guide* (London: Ward Lock, 1974): 69.
4. Edward. W. Earle, *Points of View: The Stereograph in America. A Cultural History* (New York: Visual Studies Workshop, 1979): 9.
5. Given the popularity of the stereoscope through the 19th century its contemporary neglect is surprising. It is most commonly discussed within histories of photography but treated there as an ill-fated historical curio and branch off the main path of development. A specialist literature does exist but much of it is long out of print or hard to find. Another problem is the type of information available. The existing literature broadly covers four areas: the technical principles of stereoscopy and its history (see Arthur T. Gill, 'Early Stereoscopes', *The Photographic Journal*, No. 9 (1969): 546–559;606–614;641–651); the cataloguing of the cards produced, the photographers and companies responsible and their subject matter (see William C. Darrah, *Stereoviews. A History of Stereographs in America and Their Collection* (Gettysburg, Penna: Times and News Publishing

Co., 1964); William C. Darrah, *The World of Stereographs* (Nashville: Land Yacht Press, 1977), and John Waldsmith, *Stereoviews. An Illustrated History and Price Guide* (Iola, WI: Krause Publications, 1991)); the classification and manufacture of the stereo viewers (see Paul Wing, *Stereoscopes. The First One Hundred Years* (Nashua, New Hampshire: Transition Publishing, 1996)), and the contemporary practice of stereoscopy. Little has been written on the cultural history and significance of the stereoscope (only Edward W. Earle, *Points of View: The Stereograph in America. A Cultural History* (New York: Visual Studies Workshop, 1979), and Jonathan Crary, *Techniques of the Observer. On Vision and Modernity in the Nineteenth Century* (London: MIT Press, 1990) offer any discussion of this aspect) and it is the aim of this paper to expand upon this, in offering an interpretation of its cultural place and impact.

6. Erwin Panofsky, *Perspective as Symbolic Form* (New York: Zone Books, 1997): 60.
7. Samuel Y. Edgerton, *The Renaissance Rediscovery of Linear Perspective* (London: Harper and Row Publishers, 1976).
8. Panofsky: 66; 30–31.
9. Richard Balzer, *Peepshows. A Visual History* (New York: Harry N. Abrams Inc. Publishers, 1998): 18; 20; 21–43.
10. See William Merrin, '"Buckle Your seat-Belt Dorothy": 'Cause Cinema is Going Bye-Byes', Jackie Furby and Karen Randell (eds.) *Screen Method: Comparative Readings in Screen Studies* London: Wallflower Press, forthcoming 2003–04).
11. 'The Stereoscope', *Illustrated London News* (20 March 1852): 229.
12. Earle: 93.
13. Oliver Wendell Holmes, 'Sun Painting and Sun Sculpture', *Atlantic Monthly* (July, 1861): 14–15.
14. *Illustrated London News*: 229.
15. Earle: 30.
16. Earle: 44.
17. Howarth-Loomes: 74.
18. Earle: 28; 13.
19. 'Sun Painting and Sun Sculpture': 28.
20. 'The Stereoscope, Pseudoscope and Solid Daguerreotypes', *Illustrated London News* (24 January 1852): 78.
21. Heinz K. and Bridget A. Henisch, *Positive Pleasures. Early Photography and Humour* (Penn: The Pennsylvania State University Press, 1998): 142.
22. 'Sun Painting and Sun Sculpture': 24.
23. Oliver Wendell Holmes, 'The Stereoscope and the Stereograph', *Atlantic Monthly* (June, 1859): 745–746.
24. 'Sun painting and Sun Sculpture': 25.
25. 'The Stereoscope and the Stereograph': 744.
26. 'Sun Painting and Sun Sculpture': 27.
27. 'Sun painting and Sun Sculpture': 18.
28. 'Sun painting and Sun Sculpture': 23.
29. Marshall McLuhan, *Understanding Media* (London, MIT Press, 1994).
30. Stephen Oettermann, *The Panorama. History of a Mass Medium* (New York: Zone Books, 1997): 113; 170.
31. 'The Stereoscope and the Stereograph': 744.
32. 'The Stereoscope', *Household Words* (3 September 1853): 39.
33. Wing: 16–17.
34. Earle: 60–74.
35. Balzer: 68–71.
36. Timothy Druckrey (ed.) *Electronic Culture. Technology and Visual Representation* (Fairfield Inc. Canada: Quebecor Publishing, 1996): 300.
37. William Darrah, *The World of Stereographs*: 3.

38. Earle: 28.
39. Jenkins, for example, promises us 'a history of the parlour stereoscope' but other than noting its place in that room says nothing more of the relationship (Harold F. Jenkins, *Two Points of View: The History of the Parlour Stereoscope* (Uniontown, Penna: E. G. Warman Publishing Inc., 1973)), and nor does any other text I have discovered.
40. D.B. Thomas, *Cameras, Photographs and Accessories. A Science Museum Illustrated Booklet* (London: HMSO, 1966).
41. Thorstein Veblen, *The Theory of the Leisure Class* (London: Dover Publications, 1994): 46; 48.
42. Earle: 95.
43. Howarth-Loomes: 74.
44. Howarth-Loomes: 79.
45. John Tagg, *The Burden of Representation. Essays on Photographies and Histories* (London: Macmillan Press, 1988): 37; Suren Lalvani, *Photography, Vision and the Production of Modern Bodies* (New York: SUNY Press, 1996).
46. Lalvani: 59.
47. Lalvani: 68.
48. See Wing: 1; 4; 5; 7; 21; 25; 31; 63; 73; 87.
49. 'Sun Painting and Sun Sculpture': 23.
50. 'Sun Painting and Sun Sculpture': 27.
51. Martin Heidegger, *The Question Concerning technology and Other Essays* London: Harper and Row Publishers, 1977): 129; 134.
52. *The World of Stereographs*: 6. The stereograph's rarity today is probably due to their greater wear (being used and handled more than cased and loved family photographs), and to the likelihood of their being thrown away at the end of their useful life (as opposed to family photographs which would be retained as heirlooms).
53. Wolfgang Schivelbusch, *Disenchanted Night. The Industrialisation of Light in the Nineteenth Century* (London: University of California Press, 1996): 158.
54. Thad Logan, *The Victorian Parlour. A Cultural Study* (Cambridge: Cambridge University Press, 2001): 12.
55. Wolfgang Schivelbusch, *The Railway Journey* (Berkeley: University of California Press, 1986): 122–123.
56. *Disenchanted Night*: 169.
57. *Disenchanted Night*: 184. As Logan argues, even the bourgeois preference for oil lighting as opposed to gas lighting in the parlour represented a fear of public connection and 'a symbolic reaffirmation of privacy', *The Victorian Parlour. A Cultural Study*: 123–124.
58. *Disenchanted Night*: 184–185.
59. Walter Benjamin, *Charles Baudelaire* (London: Verso, 1997): 167–169.
60. Walter Benjamin, *The Arcades Project* (London; The Belknap Press of Harvard University Press, 1999): 216.
61. *Charles Baudelaire*: 167.
62. *Charles Baudelaire*: 167–168.
63. *Charles Baudelaire*: 169.
64. *The Arcades Project*: 220–221.
65. Celeste Olalquiaga, *The Artificial Kingdom* (London: Bloomsbury Publishing, 1999): 285.
66. Olalquiaga: 284.
67. Olalquiaga: 288.
68. Jean Baudrillard, *The Consumer Society* (London: Sage Publications, 1998): 34.
69. *The Consumer Society*: 122.
70. Jean Baudrillard, *The Ecstasy of Communication* (New York: Semiotext(e), 1988); *Fatal Strategies* (London: Pluto Press, 1990).
71. *Fatal Strategies*: 32.

14

Optical Recreations, Transparencies, and the Invention of the Screen

John Plunkett

It's a truism that we now live in the age of the screen. Elements of postmodernism and cyberculture celebrate a world of depthless surfaces, where our posthuman bodies function in a ceaseless reverie with the screen. Virtuality rules. Our thinking about the screen is nevertheless caught within a series of over-familiar tropes. These revolve around interrelated notions of interactivity and realism, either through our entering the world of the screen or the life within the screen bursting out of its frame. Yet it was only at the beginning the nineteenth century that the screen acquired its meaning in English as a bearer of visual images. The earliest usage recorded by the OED is in 1810, when the *New Family Receipt-bk* described the process of making Transparent Screens for the exhibition of the Phantasmagoria. There is at least one earlier usage from 1802, when a Scottish reviewer, William Nicolson, similarly described 'a thin cloth or screen' being let down during a phantasmagoria show in Edinburgh.[1] Why should this modern definition of the screen have emerged with the phantasmagoria? It did so because the optical recreations that developed between 1780 and 1830, especially transparencies, the diorama and phantasmagoria, shared one important trait: namely, their screen practice was central to their appeal.

This essay examines the function and the figuring of the screen in early nineteenth-century optical media. It argues that the screen played an important role in the development of different visual entertainments. The new-found significance of the screen is also reflected in its recurrence as a trope in poems, satirical prints and literature. It is well known that the period's fascination with optical artefacts led to them being used as figures for consciousness, perception, imagination, dreamwork. Nonetheless, the prominence of the screen as a trope-in-itself has been neglected. Its deployment is an index to the range of meanings attached to this most fiduciary of artefacts. Of these meanings, I particularly want to unpack the reasons why both its function and figuring fed into notions of virtual space.

From the microscope and magic lantern of the Renaissance, optical media have been linked with the opening up of previously unseen cognitive worlds. Whether projecting devils or magnifying dust-mites, they have provided access to new imaginative and material spaces. Significantly though, the revelatory potential of instruments like the microscope relied on the lens rather than the screen. Similarly, in descriptions of the camera obscura and magic lantern from the seventeenth and eighteenth century, the idea of the screen does not really figure. Images are invariably described as being projected onto a white sheet or caught on a thin piece of paper. This lack of agency contrasts with the optical recreations that emerged from the late eighteenth century onwards. The screens they employed, because of their specific properties, determined the concrete form they gave to horrors, fantasies and dreams. The screen became part of a new way of imagining the material world, and simultaneously provided a new way for the imagination to materialise itself. As Steve Connor has argued, the matter of the imagination, and the imagination of matter, exist in a reciprocal relationship.[2] This conjunction is one of the reasons why screen entertainment became connected to a questioning about the relationship between self and world.

A phenomenology of the screen has to encompass a number of paradoxes. The first of these is that, to a large degree, it is the function of the screen to have no active existence. That is to say, when watching the TV or looking at a computer, we hardly ever see the screen. Our attention is occupied by the picture that is, as we still say, on the screen rather than in it. The screen itself disappears beneath the image that is overlaid upon it. This fiduciary quality stems, in part, from its ambiguous tactility. On the one hand, it has to be a solid surface able to bear an image. Yet, equally, it has a transparency, even an invisibility, that points through and past itself. The screen thus embodies a constant tension between the concrete and the transparent, the present and absent. Its weird materiality also takes us back to traditional definitions of the screen, as that of a veil or a permeous membrane. As Steve Connor has argued, a screen is a boundary but it is always a porous one.[3] It both encloses and discloses. Like the rood-screen in a church, it demarcates a separate and autonomous space without ever blocking it off. A second problematic issue concerning the screen is its relation to the science of catoptrics and dioptrics, and, more generally, to the use of glass in optical artefacts. The operation of a screen often seems to lie somewhere between a mirror and a lens. It can have the reflective properties of the former and the transparency of the latter. Certainly, the screen used by the phantasmagoria and diorama sought to imitate the effect of glass, particularly its potential for simultaneous reflection and refraction. Isobel Armstrong, in her recent work on nineteenth-century glass, has argued that many optical toys provided a sensory experience without a sensory, tactile image.[4] The unsettling thrill of this experience is bound up with the liminal nature of the screen.

The role of the screen in optical recreations, and the tropes correspondingly used to conceptualise its function, owes much to the fashion for transparencies in the last two decades of the eighteenth century. Transparencies were one of the earliest forms of popular optical recreation and provided the basis for the development of subsequent screen media like the phantasmagoria, cosmorama and diorama. They were originally large scenes painted on glass that were backlit from behind to create a translucent effect. Transparencies became increasingly common across Europe from about 1780.[5] At the Exhibition Rooms over Exeter Change in 1780, De Loutherbourg exhibited his famous Eidophusikon. Yet it was merely top of a bill that included stained glass and transparent paintings by De Loutherbourg and P. Sandby, as well as numerous 'novel and striking effects in OPTICS'.[6] De Loutherbourg was also renowned for using transparencies during his work as a scene designer for Drury Lane.[7] The year following the Eidophusikon, Thomas Gainsborough constructed an exhibition box that showed one foot square transparencies painted on glass. Around the same time in Paris, Louis Carmontelle, a court artist, held public shows of transparencies. Carmontelle's shows were precursors of the exhibition of moving panoramas and dioramas in that they consisted of a scene 12–18m long that had been painted on thin, translucent paper.[8] It was mounted on rollers and displayed in a box around 50cm high; a candle at the back of the box provided the necessary back-projection.

Large glass transparencies were too expensive and laborious to make for them ever to have a widespread impact. Transparencies were more commonly created through scenes painted onto specially treated Irish linen, fine calico or cambric muslin. It is the preparation of the cloth to create a translucent surface that marks transparencies out as being, above all, a screen practice. Whereas improvements in the magic lantern were invariably concerned with the art of projection, transparencies gave the screen itself a new prominence. Cloth transparencies became a common form of public entertainment, and were one of the attractions of pleasure gardens such as Vauxhall and Cuper's.[9] Large versions also invariably formed part of national and local celebrations: the exhibition of transparencies was as much a ritual part of public occasions as the illumination of buildings. Many were produced for the jubilee of George III in 1809; similarly, the famous Temple of Concord, which was erected in St James's Park in 1814 to celebrate the signing of the peace treaty, had numerous allegorical transparencies.[10] In rather different circumstances, George Cruikshank painted a transparency in honour of Queen Caroline's acquittal after the parliamentary affair into her conduct.[11]

The popularity of transparencies was keyed into the Romantic obsession with the ability of light to dissolve and go beyond the material world. As Birgit Verwiebe has argued, with transparencies the viewer was no longer looking at painted light, they were actually experiencing light refracted through painted glass or translucent cloth.[12] The success of transparencies is widely known, nevertheless little work has been done on the specific ways they fed into subsequent optical recreations. Transparencies proliferated because numerous different methods were devised to replicate the effect of illuminated scenes painted on glass. The multiplicity of formats meant they were employed in a corresponding variety of public and domestic spaces. Transparencies were available in small and large-scale versions, and were both sold by printsellers and produced by amateurs within the home.

To create a cloth transparency, linen or muslin was strained on a wooden frame, sized, and then covered with melted wax mixed with turpentine. The wax and turpentine solution gave the painted scene a luminous appeal. One guide warned that if the cloth was not sufficiently prepared then 'the oil or varnish of the colour, instead of setting on the sized surface, will be absorbed by the muslin, and show dark stains or spots'.[13] Unlike stained glass, the transparent image was painted onto the reflective surface of the cloth rather than being an inherent part of it. Transparencies are thus closer to the flatness of the plasma screen than to the projected image of the cinema. Their translucency stemmed from the fact that light was refracted through the image as well as reflected off the lacquered surface. This combined impact of reflection and refraction created the ethereal depth of the transparency. Crucially, it also gave it the permeable quality characteristic of a screen aesthetic. Artists were highly conscious of the mixture of surface and depth, reflection and refraction, which was central to the appeal of the screen; its diaphanous quality was deliberately enhanced through a sophisticated selection of colours and their method of preparation. Colours that had the most transparent qualities were recommended, such as Prussian Blue, Burnt Sienna, Verdigris, and Ivory Black. Conversely though, the ground colours were mixed with mastic varnish or burnt linseed oil in order to add to the reflective effect of the screen. Their sophisticated mixture of reflection and refraction is key to the way that cloth transparencies sought to replicate the effect of glass, and, in so doing, created a new kind of artefact.

Transparent prints were one new visual genre that sought to replicate the effect of large glass and cloth transparencies. They first seem to have been published in 1799, when Edward Orme and Thomas Rowlandson executed separate series. On 1 January 1799, Orme released the first of the prints that, later the same year, would be published together as *Subjects for Transparencies*.[14] Orme held the title of printseller to King George III, and his London establishment was at the corner of George and Conduit Street. *Subjects for Transparencies* consisted of black and white engravings that could be coloured and turned into transparencies. The subjects, including 'The Tomb Of Juliet', 'The Witches in Macbeth', and 'A Cottage on Fire', are typical of the genre in that their appeal relied on striking contrasts of light and shade. 'The Witches in Macbeth', for example, shows the witches grouped in a cave around their cauldron. The effectiveness of the print stems from the way that fire from the cauldron lights up the cave and the face of the arriving Macbeth. Rowlandson's already coloured transparencies consist of a similar range of subjects; the principal feature of 'The Wedding', for example, is sunlight streaming through the stained glass of a dark gothic church.[15] Orme and Rowlandson's series mark the emergence of transparencies as a genre in the print market; their small-scale format exemplifies the way that a screen aesthetic proliferated.

Orme admitted that transparencies on silk, glass, and even paper, had been carried out for centuries. He nevertheless claimed to have been the first printseller to publish transparent prints.[16] Their invention reputedly took place in 1799, when, by accident, he dropped varnish for an oil painting onto the dark part of an engraving, *The Death of Chatterton*. Like transparencies produced on cloth, the varnish made the paper transparent and simultaneously created a lacquered surface. Orme subsequently turned prints into transparencies by repeating the principal areas of light and shadow on the recto of the painted scene. These areas were then lightly soaked with varnish in order to accentuate the light source and create a greater experience of depth. The combination of reflected and refracted light gave Orme's prints a fluid and luminous translucency. Light flowed through the picture, and the picture itself promised to dissolve into light. Scraping away small sections of the paper also enhanced its transparency. Coloured paper soaked in varnish and added to the back of the print could also be highly effective. In this process, areas of the top layer of the print, usually of the sun, moon, or firelight, were cut away to leave the coloured paper placed behind. When backlit, the sun and moon were thereby experienced in a much more luminous fashion. Such multi-layered transparencies provided the basis for the transparent scenes used by many nineteenth-century peepshows and cosmoramas.

Orme's discovery was part of a broad process of attempting to produce transparencies on a much larger scale. His prints were obviously executed much more readily than transparencies painted on glass. According to Orme, a much greater effect was able to be achieved on paper: 'a shadow that will take you a month to work and stipple upon glass, may be produced with twice the force upon paper in the space of twenty minutes'.[17] Orme produced as many as fifty subjects between 1800 and 1807, and Rudolf Ackermann published a similar range of prints designed for use as transparencies.[18] Orme's published prints included 'The Castle Spectre' (10s 6d), 'The Temple of the Sun, from Pizarro' (10s 6d), 'A Cottage on fire'(12s), and 'Large Mount Vesuvius and Companion' (3s 3d).[19] At these prices, transparencies were affordable by only a wealthy few. Their success nevertheless belongs to a familiar pattern of large-format screen entertainment being adapted for the domestic sphere in order to reach a larger market.

What was the function of the large number of transparencies that were made? Why did they have such an appeal? In addition to the relative ease with which they could be produced, transparencies were so successful because large numbers of them fulfilled a decorative function within the home. Paper and linen transparencies sought to mimic the aesthetic effect and symbolic capital of glass. In so doing, though, new possibilities opened up for their domestic use. Ackermann noted that, although glass was too expensive a material for many, 'by the introduction of this beautiful style of [transparent] painting, so deservedly admired by the fashionable world, we may obtain a substitute nearly equal, appropriate it to different uses, as well ornamental as useful, at a comparatively small expense'.[20] The amateur making of transparencies also acquired an equally fashionable status. Several instruction manuals were also published for those desirous of making their own transparencies. Rudolf Ackermann published his first guide in 1799, with improved editions in 1800, 1802, and 1804. Orme published his own *Instructions for Painting Transparencies* in 1807, in a parallel text French–English edition.

Orme's manual suggested that a transparent print of a fire, with a light behind it, could be placed in a room in order to give the impression of warmth. Ackermann similarly advertised transparencies that were intended for incorporation into fire screens.[21] Transparencies were so successful because their permeability meant they were ideal for being incorporated into the variety of screens that filled the domestic interior. The architectural function of the screen was being superseded by its visual decoration and entertainment value. For a brief period at the beginning of the nineteenth century, there was a fusion between the traditional screen and the type that would soon be associated with the plethora of optical recreations. This fusion embodies a fascinating taxonomic shift that suggests optical recreations assimilated long-standing notions of the screen. It became a surface intended to bear images but maintained its permeable quality and its decorative importance within the home.

The centrepiece of Orme's manual is a double-page engraving showing transparencies inserted into fire screens, draught screens, window blinds, lamp screens, and fans (see Fig. 1). There was no inherent difference between the screens associated with optical recreations and those associated with the domestic interior. Transpar-

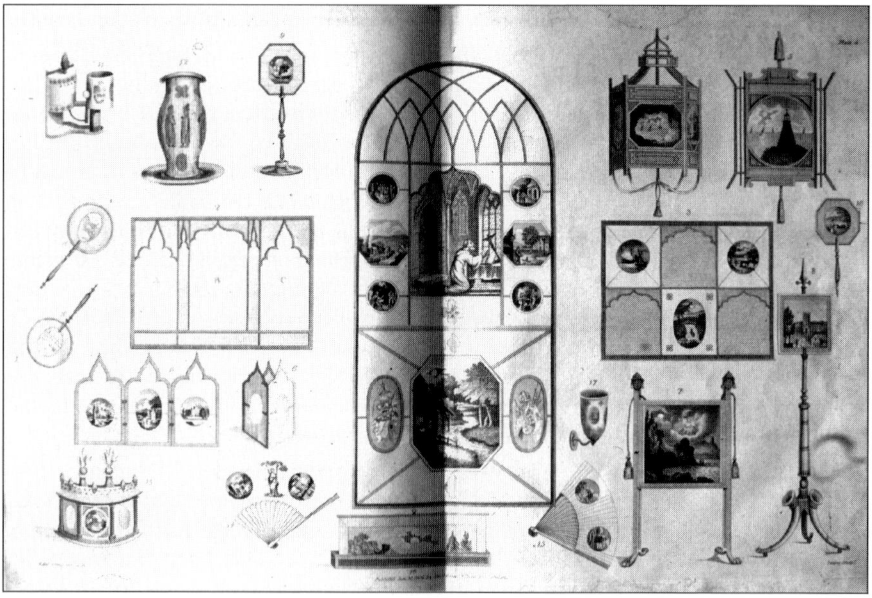

Fig. 1. Edward Orme, An Essay on Transparent Prints, and on Transparencies in general *(London: Edward Orme, 1806).*
[All images: Courtesy of the Bill Douglas Centre, University of Exeter.]

encies could be 'fitted up, for window-blinds, and upon glass for placing against the glass of windows, for springblinds, for lamps, for candle-shades, for hand-skreens, for fire-skreens, for temples, fans etc.'[22] Orme's examples include a hand held screen designed to protect the holder from candlelight; a chimney-piece ornamental screen; a transparent fan, and several different hanging lamps. Ackermann similarly advocated the appeal of transparencies within the home, declaring that 'nothing can be more beautifully decorative than illuminated painted lamps or lanthorns, either suspended in halls and staircases, or fixed on supper tables, the rich variety of light affording almost fanciful effect'.[23] The instruction manuals reveal the range of potential screens for decorating the genteel drawing room. These screens still have a practical function but they are also, if not entertainment, then certainly decorative images. Transparencies were artefacts that, like stereoscopes, television, and other subsequent domestic optical recreations, constituted a focal point within the home.

The fashion for transparencies was encouraged by the changing illumination of the domestic interior. One of Orme's examples was a white screen for an Argand lamp on which transparencies could be painted. The Argand lamp was patented in 1784 by Aimé Argand and gave several times more illumination than existing lamps. Argand lamps significantly increased the appeal of the magic lantern because of the brightness they gave to the projected image. Their installation in the home similarly encouraged the use of Orme's light-shade transparency because of the greater luminosity they gave to the painted scene. Chinese Box Lamps were especially suited for such transparencies. The glass would be treated with fluor acid in order that it could be painted like an etching. Their fashionable status was also aided by the Orientalist décor favoured by the Prince Regent. The Chinese Gallery of the Brighton Pavilion was filled with painted Chinese lamps and several vertical transparencies.[24]

The incorporation of transparencies into domestic screens did not stop them being heavily influenced by different optical recreations. Orme exploited the novelty of panoramas by suggesting that a transparent panorama could be incorporated into a drawing room fire-screen. The panoramas envisaged by Orme are more a set of prospects than a panorama in the true sense of the word. They nevertheless exemplify a convergence between transparencies, the panorama and the traditional screen. Domestic ornamentation combined with the latest vogue in public entertainment. Such hybrid experimentation exemplifies the way new optical recreations were created. One adventurous publisher went so far as to insert a transparency into a carriage-window. It reputedly looked beautiful from the inside, but from the outside it had 'too much the appearance of a moving picture shop'.[25] This moving image, although propelled by horses rather than mechanical projection, typifies the proliferation of transparencies. It also one of the first examples of the correspondence between a viewer's experience of screen movement and a passenger's experience of a moving landscape. This conjunction was subsequently embodied in numerous panoramic journeys right through to the Lumieres' famous film of a train arriving at La Ciotat station.

Unsurprisingly, the most effective transparencies employed subject matter that had striking contrasts of light and shade. Picturesque landscapes or gothic scenes were particularly appropriate. Subjects recommended by Orme include the interior of a cottage lit by fire-light; the reflection of moonlight off water; and light falling through gothic arches or a stained glass window. Ackermann similarly recommended gloomy gothic ruins and cathedral interiors. The best effect was also created by deepening the shadows and the colours in comparison with a standard watercolour. In contrast to the limited range of subjects, Orme's manual gave instructions for creating transparencies by a variety of methods. Fig. 2 shows transparencies added to a window containing six square panes of glass. To create a stained glass effect, Orme advised buying six new panes of glass of the same size. A paper transparency was attached to the second set of panes, which were then fitted against the glass already in place. This double-gazing process filled the room with coloured light. Plate glass could also be smeared with white putty to give it the appearance of ground glass; it was then painted upon with oil and varnish colours. The contrast of light and shade was accentuated by scraping the putty off the brightest lights so as to leave the glass clear. Isinglass size, a gelatinous semi-transparent substance, was also used for coating the surface of the glass prior to painting. All of the different methods for treating glass or cloth were concerned with creating a translucent surface that allowed light to pass through the material, but did not allow the viewer to see beyond the illuminated scene.

Another type of window transparency exemplifies the convergence between transparencies and other forms of domestic leisure in that it employed a technique akin to that used for making silhouettes. Five or six thin sheets of white paper were fastened together and the design marked out on the top sheet. Depending on the effect to be created, a different number of sheets were cut out using a silhouette-like technique. Thus, the foreground was delineated by cutting out its design from the

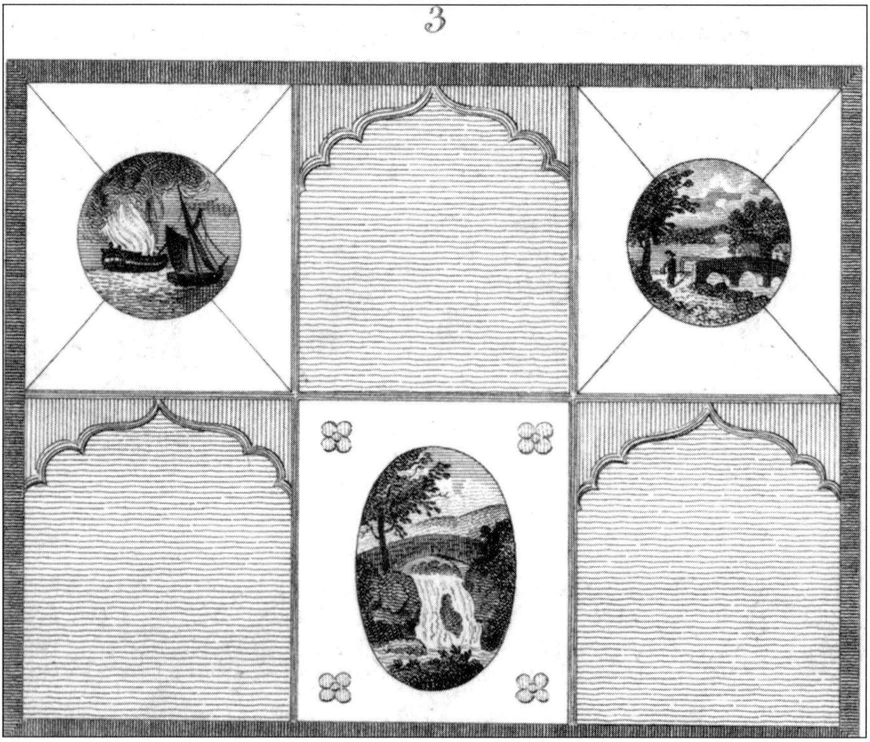

Fig. 1. Edward Orme, An Essay on Transparent Prints, and on Transparencies in general *(London: Edward Orme, 1806).*

top four sheets, while the hills and the background only had one sheet cut away. Cutting through all the sheets gave the impression of bright lights. Coloured paper could also be put over the back to enhance the effect. When the cut-out pictures were put between two sheets of glass and placed against a window, the whole had a translucent effect.

The demand for transparencies was such that their provision became part of the professional repertoire of drawing-masters and decorative painters. The ongoing overlap between home decoration and artistic creation is reflected by an 1825 trade card from Edinburgh, on which John Meldrum advertised himself as a 'transparent blind painter and teacher of drawing'.[26] Instructions for painting transparent blinds, which were particularly popular, also figure in Nathaniel Whittock's *Decorative Painters' and Glaziers' Guide* (1827). Like Ackermann and Orme, Whittock describes the preparation of the translucent screen as well as the colours and scenes that create the best impression. The best subjects were those that had 'one or two bold objects that can easily be executed and not too much foliage'.[27] Architecture was not a fit subject as there were too many dark masses, while moonlit subjects similarly excluded too much light. Whittock's manual included several illustrations of picturesque Alpine scenes suitable for transparent window blinds.

In contrast to the professional production of transparencies and transparent prints,

Orme and Ackermann's manuals were intended for those wishing to create their own transparencies. Much of the fashion for transparencies stemmed from the way their making was a leisure activity. It was a genteel pastime that was an extension of the popularity of amateur sketch and watercolour painting. Orme and Ackermann's print shops sold designs and all the necessary material, including paper already glazed on both sides.[28] Transparencies stand at the beginning of a long genealogy of homemade screen entertainment that includes panorama shows, toy theatres, peepshows, and magic lantern performances. Domestic optical recreations were often intended for the amusement of children, and transparencies were equally associated with the home in that their making was gendered as a refined feminine pursuit. Orme recommended the making of transparencies to 'my fair country-women, who have a taste for cutting out figures in paper, which many ladies perform in a very astonishing manner, to make experiments in this art, and endeavour to bring it to a greater degree of perfection'.[29] His method of creating transparencies through layers of cut-out paper seamlessly appropriates both the technique of silhouette cutting and its role as a domestic recreation. Ackermann, too, specifically referred to his female readers when providing the recipe for the varnish solution used to finish transparencies.[30]

In *Mansfield Park*, Jane Austen exemplifies the fashionable status of transparencies as a refined feminine activity. Fanny Price describes the secluded East Room at Mansfield Park, which is filled with the relics of past leisure activities:

> its greatest elegancies and ornaments were a faded footstool of Julia's work, too ill done for the drawing room, three transparencies made in a rage for transparencies, for the three lower panes of one window, where Tintern Abbey held its station between a cave in Italy and a moonlit lake in Cumberland; a collection of family profiles, though unworthy of being anywhere else, over the mantelpiece, and by their side, and pinned against the wall, a small sketch of a ship sent a few years ago from the Mediterranean by William ...[31]

Transparencies of Tintern Abbey; family silhouettes; the needlework for a footstool; these three sets of artefacts are a microcosm of women's leisure practices.

Transparencies formed the basis for many subsequent optical recreations. Their influence upon the phantasmagoria, diorama and cosmorama, explains the new found prominence of the screen. It is no coincidence that the phantasmagoria appeared at the same time as the fashion for transparencies – for its unique feature was its appropriation of the screen used for painted transparencies. The phantasmagoria extended the stained-glass imitation of the transparency into a much more recognisable form of screen for receiving projected images. As is well known, the phantasmagoria employed a magic lantern placed at a distance behind a screen to conjure up ghosts and the dead figures of notorious individuals. The lantern was mounted on rails and, by moving it backwards and forwards, the spectral figures could be made to increase and decrease in size, and move towards the audience. It was first exhibited by Paul Philidor in Paris in 1792. Philidor's show conjured up the devil, along with figures from the Terror of the French Revolution like Marat and Darnton.[32] The figure who nevertheless did most to achieve the success of the phantasmagoria was Étienne Gaspard Robert, a Belgian scientist and skilled projectionist, who opened his 'Fantasamgorie' in Paris in 1798. Robertson's shows, like Philidor's, conjured up phantoms and the spectres of famous figures.

The mobile back-projection of the phantasmagoria set it apart from other magic lantern shows. Yet its ghostly drama was equally reliant on its use of translucent cloth. The screen hid the projection apparatus so that the ghosts appeared out of thin air. The audience had no means of seeing the way the spectral figures were able to dissolve, move, or pass through each other. William Nicolson's review of the phantasmagoria show in Edinburgh, mentioned earlier, describes how he entered a darkened room with skeletons and other ghouls painted on the walls. The screen itself was only let down after the room was submerged in total darkness. It was, to quote Nicolson, 'consequently unknown to most of the spectators'.[33] More important than the shielding effect of the screen though, was its permeable nature. Robertson's memoirs reveal that he was well aware of the added benefits of the screen used for painting transparencies:

> I have acquired a sheet of three *aunes* in width, such that it does not require a seam, and to render it translucent, I have melted very white pure wax into which I have immersed it while it was boiling; I nailed it immediately into the opening formed in the wall and, passing a well-lit burner over it gradually, I spread the wax which gave my sheet the diaphanous quality I have sought for so long.[34]

The impact of the phantasmagoria depended on the projection being seen through the screen. Transparency was vital for removing the boundary between the audience and the spectral figures. Its mixture of the material and the insubstantial was perfectly keyed into the ghostly nature of the show. Dead figures were able to materialise through the solidity of the screen. At the same time, its permeability suggested the insubstantiality of matter itself. The phantasmagoria combined magic lantern projection with the fashion for transparencies.

Instructional articles on the phantasmagoria in the periodical press were careful to emphasise the importance of its screen and the way it differed from the standard magic lantern performance.[35] In 1839, the *Magazine of Science* recommended either tissue paper or waxed muslin as appropriate materials.[36] With magic lantern shows, the light was normally reflected back to the audience from the surface of the solid white wall or sheet. The screen was more receptive than expressive. In contrast, the phantasmagoria image was literally projected out of the screen towards the spectator. Numerous reviews emphasise that it was the movement of the ghosts that gave the shows much of their effect. The audience was drawn into a spectral world that also came out to meet them. The phantasmagoria was a gothic show, where the permeability of the screen helped to create a space that was imbued with a psychological dimension.

The phantasmagoria was premised on a screen practice that broke down boundaries between internal/external, between the material and the spectral, between illusion and reality, between this world and the next. Terry Castle has argued that, for Romanticism, the phantasmagoria was a dominant trope for an excessive reverie of thought.[37] It connoted a condition where consciousness had been overcome by its spectral world, where the imagination was swallowed up by its own virtual space. Thomas De Quincey, in *Confessions of an English Opium Eater*, described the multifarious 'phantasmagoria' playing in the brain of the opium-addict.[38] Such usage marks an extension of earlier Renaissance uses of optical artefacts as a trope. Descartes was one of many to compare the functioning of the eye to a camera obscura.[39] However, when the phantasmagoria quickly became part of common word usage, it suggested a far more ambiguous state of being-in-the-world. In *The Vision of Judgement*, Byron used it to connote a spectral flatness when describing the ghost of George III:

> … the wight
> Mysterious changed his countenance at least
> As oft as they their minds: though in full sight
> He stood, the puzzle was only increased;
> The man was a phantasmagoria in
> Himself – he was so volatile and thin.[40]

George III lacks the solidity of selfhood because of his volatility and his thinness. It is this flatness in particular that reveals the way Byron's troping on the phantasmagoria is keyed into the operation of its screen. Edgar Allen Poe also frequently used the term in his gothic tales. In *The Fall of the House of Usher*, the narrator describes being disturbed by the atmosphere of the decaying stately home, 'the carvings of the ceilings, the sombre tapestries of the wall, the ebon blackness of the floors, and the phantasmagoric armorial trophies which rattled as I strode'.[41] The house itself functions as both an ancestral gothic setting and a symbol for the psychological condition of Roderick Usher. *The Fall of the House of Usher* uses the phantasmagoria to destabilise the boundary between the internal working of the mind and an external corporeal reality. As Castle demonstrates, Poe's story takes it as a trope for the porous membrane that exists between self and world.

The diorama, like the phantasmagoria, exploited the screen technology developed for the painting of transparencies. It is impossible to understand the success of Louis Daguerre's diorama without understanding the popularity of transparencies. The subjects shown by the diorama, which included Holyrood Chapel, the Village of Unterseen, and the Environs of St Cloud and Paris, were exactly the same picturesque scenes favoured by transparencies. The magical scene changes of the diorama nevertheless extended the appeal of the transparency by employing a combination of reflected and refracted light in a controlled and successive time-frame. Daguerre first opened his diorama in Paris on 11 July 1822. As is well known, it employed a canvas painted on both sides in exactly that same way that Orme and Ackermann recommended.[42] Daguerre took their methods further, however, in two important ways. By placing the backlit transparency in a darkened auditorium, he added the skills and showmanship of a theatrical scene-painter to a well established process of screen making. It was the exhibition space, as much as Daguerre's skilful painting of his illusory and translucent scenes, which made the diorama a new development within the genealogy of screen entertainment. Indeed, the ceiling of the auditorium of the Regent's Park Diorama was a transparent blind, complete with painted medallion portraits. As the *Mirror of Literature, Amusement and Instruction* noted, 'further to increase the illusion, a transparent blind [is] suspended over the *Arena*, and throwing it into partial obscurity, tends to give full effect to the intensity of light admitted from above on the picture'.[43] Daguerre's clever use of the ceiling transparency underlines the way that the diorama was an enthralling extension of the well-established technique of transparency painting.

The second important feature of the Diorama is the way in which the building itself was purposely designed to function as a giant screen. It acted simultaneously as a

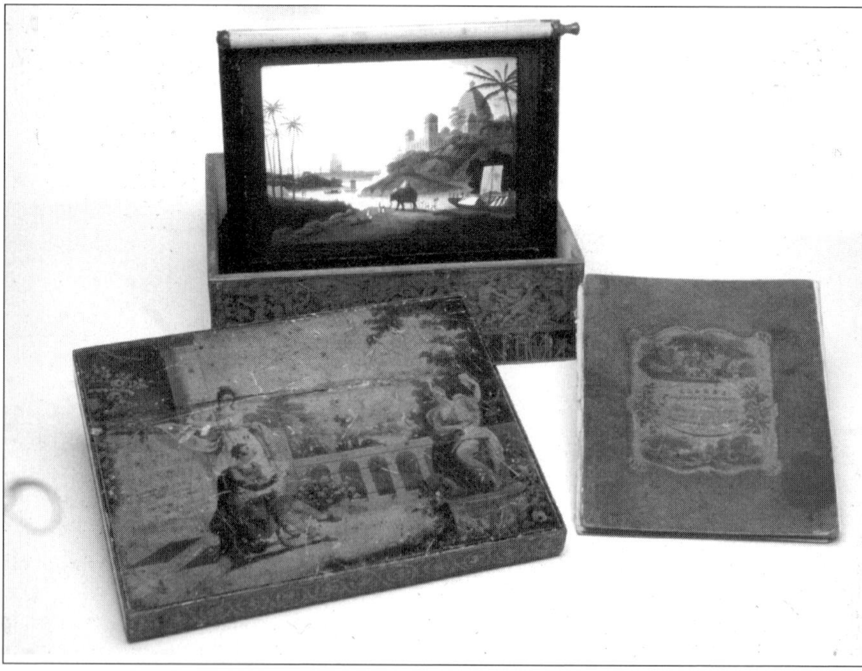

Fig. 3. John Heaviside Clark, Portable Diorama *(London: Samuel Leigh, 1826).*

filter of light and as an architectural creation that literally screened the audience off from the outside world. By varying the play of light, Daguerre was able to transform the appearance of the scene. A review from the *Mirror of Literature, Amusement, and Instruction* describes one typical transformation:

> This fine picture represents a Gothic Gallery falling to decay, situated at the extremity of a narrow valley, beneath barren mountains. All is sombre, desolate, and mournful; the long-drawn aisles, at a first glance, are alone perceived, for a thick fog reigns without, and such is the illusion of the scene, that you actually fancy yourself chilled by the cold and damp air. By degrees, however, the fog disperses, and through the vast arches are plainly discovered the forest of pine and larch trees that cover the valley. The magic of this effect of light is indeed most extraordinary, and the illusion is complete and enchanting.[44]

The dioramic transformation was achieved by an arrangement of shutters and curtains; these controlled the light that either passed through the backlit transparency or was reflected off its front surface. The top of the building contained a large skylight, while at the end of the room, there was a large window of ground glass. Between each of these windows and the pictures there was a series of coloured transparent blinds. All of these blinds could be moved in order to create different coloured lighting effects. There was also an elaborate system of shades beneath the skylight. The whole building itself functioned as a giant screen; a membrane that let light through but only in a deliberately controlled fashion. The translucent nature of its screen also makes the diorama akin to the phantasmagoria in that it provided a new way for matter to be imagined. The most successful subject matter for its shows: smoke, fire, sunlight, moonlight, fog, are precisely those nebulous elements of the material world that are rendered least successfully by the two-dimensional solidity of painting.

In 1839 Daguerre published a manual on the true principles of the daguerreotype, which also detailed his method of dioramic painting. He was well aware of the importance of the screen to the diorama:

> whether the subjects be illuminated by reflected or refracted light, one indispensable essential is to employ a medium or canvas which is exceedingly transparent, and the texture of which is as equal as can possibly be obtained. Either lawn or calico may be used.[45]

Daguerre was equally precise over the preparation of the screen and the colours to be used. It was to receive two coats of parchment size, a gelatinous solution used for stiffening textiles. The colours themselves were ground in oil, but laid on the cloth in a turpentine mix to add to their reflective quality. This method is exactly the same as that used for creating transparencies. When Daguerre invented his double effect diorama, which used a second screen placed behind the first, he extended the layering technique recommended by Orme for the creation of transparent effects upon windows.

The diorama, like transparencies, soon became accessible in several different small-scale versions. The most notable of these is John Heaviside Clark's portable diorama, which was first produced in 1826. It is an artefact that demonstrates the extent to which the amateur production of screen media was an extension of the taste for picturesque sketching. The portable diorama was, in part, the continuation of the tradition of devices, such as camera lucida and Claude Glass, which were used by artists to aid their drawing. Clark was a well-known landscape painter whose guides to picturesque sketching acquired a canonical status. His diverse activities are a microcosm of the way optical media could converge with artistic practice. Significantly, his *Practical Essay on the Art of Colouring and Painting Landscapes* (1807) was published by Edward Orme. In the early 1820s, he also executed two panoramas of London and was responsible for the *Myriorama*, a game imitating the panorama.[46]

The elaborate design of Clark's portable diorama is wholly in keeping with the aristocratic milieu of *Mansfield Park*. It consists of two removable screens, behind which an Argand lamp could be placed to create a translucent backlit scene. The performative aspect of the diorama is emphasised by the proscenium-like frame in which the top screen sits. It was originally accompanied by twelve scenes, six front transparencies of picturesque scenes and six rear transparencies with aerial effects such as a rainbow and moonlight.[47] A rolled shade running across the top of the main frame connects to the rear screen and prevents any shadow interfering with the show. The shade, when fully unrolled, leaves the rear screen at a wide angle from the front screen. As the shade is rolled up, the two screens become closer together and the rear screen is viewed through the first. The movement creates a transformation similar to that of Daguerre's institution in Regent's Park.

The screens for Clark's diorama were prepared in exactly the same way as transparencies. They have the same combination of varnish, glazed coloured paper, and picturesque subjects. Although it included pre-painted screens, the accompanying guide to the portable diorama provided all the necessary instructions for turning a page from a sketchbook into a finished transparency, which could then be used in a domestic show. According to Clark, the portable diorama was intended to 'increase the desire of the amateur and the tourist to retain remembrance of the spots they have visited'.[48] It was not only as an aide for the tourist though, or even through its typical subject matter, that the portable diorama was part of the taste for the picturesque. It aimed at 'the promotion of that knowledge by which an increased pleasure may be experienced, either in witnessing the admiral productions of pictorial representation, or in beholding the beautiful scenes of animative nature'.[49] Animative nature was more than an early form of the moving image. To an even greater degree than transparencies, the diorama was a picturesque homage to the ability of light to create the variousness of landscape.

Through his promotion of sketching from nature, Clark was a strong advocate of the picturesque. In 1811 he wrote *A Practical Illustration of Gilpin's Day, Describing the Various Effects of Landscape Scenery from Morning till night, in Thirty Designs from Nature*. It was a guide that illustrated the effect of different forms of light upon a landscape, wherein Clark provided sketches of a single landscape taken at different times of the day. Yet the portable diorama could embody the changing illumination of a landscape far better than a series of consecutive watercolours. The guide to the portable diorama quoted approvingly a definition of the picturesque from Uvedale Price: 'Intricacy in the disposition, and variety in the forms and lights and shadows of objects, are the great characteristics of the picturesque in scenery'.[50] Variousness was a key element of the picturesque for both William Gilpin and Uvedale Price. It could be created by gothic ruins and rugged natural features breaking up the play of the eye over a landscape. However, striking contrasts of light and shade were an equally important means of achieving variety. The diorama fulfilled a picturesque aesthetic far more than a static print could ever do because its performances were able to embody the changefulness of the landscape. Gilpin in particular believed that the play of light off different surfaces was key to achieving a picturesque landscape. The materiality of the diorama screen literally consisted of different types of surfaces. Light was reflected off the screen as well as refracted through it; its contrast of brilliancy and shade, its luminous and ethereal scenes, made the diorama the culmination of a picturesque aesthetic.

The ongoing nature of the permeable boundaries between screen entertainment and domestic decorative screens is exemplified by the success of the cosmorama. A cosmorama was a miniature peepshow-cum-diorama; it usually employed a translucent scene viewed through a convex lens. The most well known Cosmorama Rooms opened at 207–209 Regent St in May 1821, and the institution functioned as a highly fashionable space for lounging and *conversazione*. Cosmoramas were nevertheless also standard entertainments at fairs, pleasure gardens, and bazaars. They were one of the most ubiquitous forms of public screen entertainment. At the back of most exhibition guides for the Regent Street Cosmorama was an advertisement addressed 'To the Nobility and Gentry'.[51] It noted that many people had enquired whether it was possible to fit up their houses 'with one or more Windows and views similar to those of this Exhibition'.[52] Cosmoramic views

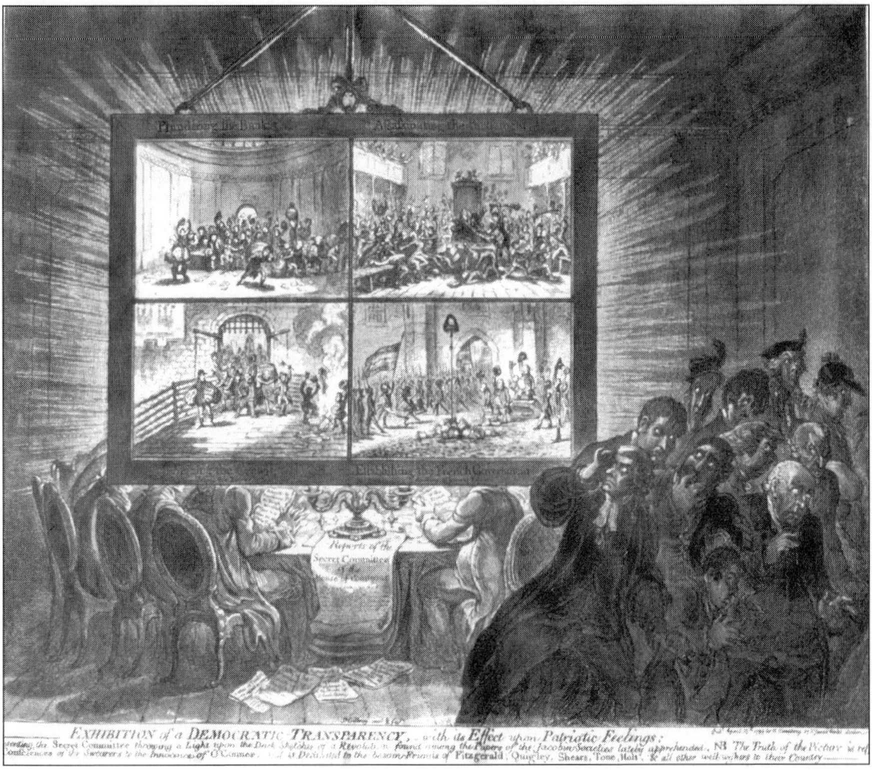

Fig. 4. James Gillray, Exhibition of a democratic transparency, with its effect upon patriotic feelings *(London: H. Humphrey, 1799).*

installed in the 1820s and 1830s extended the fashion for both the homemade transparencies described in *Mansfield Park* and the window-screens illustrated by Whittock. Although decorative transparencies were at their most fashionable during the first decades of the nineteenth century, as late as 1856 an instruction manual was published detailing the painting of transparencies for ornamental blinds and dioramas.

One telling index to the prominence of the screen is the way it functioned in numerous early nineteenth-century caricatures. Optical tropes recur frequently in satires by Gillray and Rowlandson for example. At one level, their use is premised upon the satirist's desire to make their audience see clearly. It was the satirist's role to pull aside the screen that separated the viewer from the true meaning of political events. In so doing though, satirists implicitly treat the screen as a boundary. They connect screen practice with the layering of reality, that it is made up of a series of surfaces that have to be peeled away. Figure 4 is a 1799 satire by James Gillray that was produced in response to the revolutionary threat that the British Jacobin Societies were believed to pose in the aftermath the French Revolution. The print is entitled *Exhibition of a Democratic Transparency, with its effects upon Patriotic Feelings*. Politically, the print takes a conservative standpoint. It shows the people

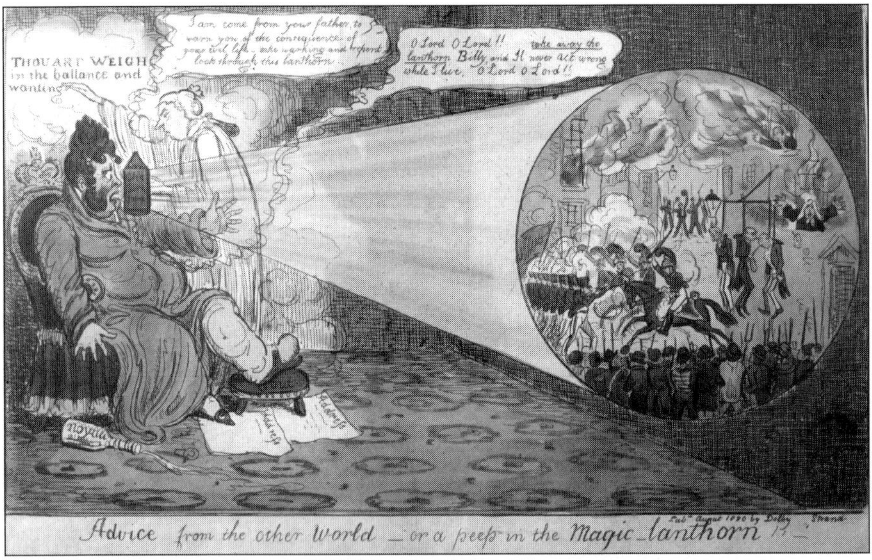

Fig. 5. Advice from the other world: or a peep in the magic lanthorn *(London: Dolby, 1820)*.

being turned away by the revolutionary scenes in the transparency. The four transparencies show the British parliament and the Crown, along with the Bank of England, being overthrown by the Jacobins. The bottom right hand scene shows a French government being established, with a cockade hat prominently displayed. The revolutionary intentions of the Jacobin Societies were supposedly uncovered by Reports from a Secret Committee of the House of Commons. It is this anonymous committee that is hidden behind the transparency. The type of information they were receiving is shown by texts on the floor, which have titles such as 'Names of Traitors at large' and 'Oaths of members of the Society of United Irishmen in London'.

The screen has a number of functions in Gillray's caricature. First of all, it is the members of the committee themselves who are the source of light for the transparency. The text at the bottom of the print notes that the work of the committee threw 'a Light upon the Dark Sketches of a Revolution found among the Papers of the Jacobin Societies'. It is the committee that is literally bringing to light the undercover activities of the various revolutionary societies. The committee members make the sketches not only visible but transparent: they allow the people to metaphorically see through the supposedly democratic aims of the Jacobins. Yet, at the same time, the screen has a solidity that separates the viewer from the identities of those who belonged to the secret parliamentary committee. In Gillray's print, the screen consequently has a double function. It is a boundary that cannot be penetrated and at the same time a surface that has been illuminated. Political intentions that had previously been cordoned off are shown up.

A similar type of screen practice is evident in a satirical print from 1822 that uses the magic lantern. The print is an attack upon the excesses of George IV, especially his love of expensive ceremony.[53] It portrays a magic lantern projecting an image of George IV and his court onto a screen. George IV is shown as a fat Chinese Mandarin surrounded by his elaborately dressed courtiers and the Duke of Wellington. George IV was often cast as a Chinese mandarin because of the Oriental excesses of the Brighton Pavilion, and the monarchy itself was often seen as being shrouded by expensive ceremony. Thomas Paine, in *The Rights of Man*, for example, compared the monarchy to something kept behind a curtain about which there was a wonderful air of seeming solemnity; but when, 'by any accident, the curtain happens to be open, and the company see what it is, they burst into laughter'.[54] Here the magic lantern literally and figuratively shines a light through the veil that shrouds the court. Instead of the court's dissolute activities remaining hidden to anybody but itself, the magic lantern reveals its true nature to a collective audience. The magic lantern looks through the screen between George IV and his subjects.

The multiple character of the screen is evident in a print published in 1820, wherein it functions as a boundary and crossing point into both a spectral other-world and the virtual world of the imagination. The print itself is a critique of the reckless life of George IV. George is confined to his chair, burdened down with gout and riotous living. The ghost of William Pitt has been sent by his father to warn him of the consequences of his behaviour. Pitt uses a magic lantern to show George scenes of devastation and revolution unless he mends his debauched ways. As in the phantasmagoria, the screen helps to remove the boundary between this world and the next. Significantly, the ghost of Pitt exhorts George to actually look through the magic lantern in order to see his potential future. In technical terms, the print is obviously incorrect. However, such a model of spectatorship is suggestive in terms of the way screen practice was conceptualised. The screen on the wall does not simply receive the otherworldly image projected by the magic lantern. It is also what the Prince sees by looking through it. His mind's eye is directly plugged into the screen; even more importantly, his imagination is itself figured as a screen-image. The image is both an internal vision and an external projection. The print is not using the magic lantern simply as a symbol for consciousness, but for a type of virtual space that interweaves thought and the image.

The function and figuring of the nineteenth century screen reveals that it was an essential part of the fascination exerted by optical media. Its appeal stemmed from the fact that it was the crossing and the limit point of so many boundaries. Moreover, the screens employed by the diorama and transparencies continued to play an important role in a variety of subsequent optical recreations, notably protean view prints, toy theatres, and polyorama panoptiques. The use of optical artefacts for their decorative appeal similarly continued with lithophane frames, dioramic lampshades and drawing-room paintings. It is therefore unsurprising that tropes concerning our contemporary relationship with the screen are heavily influenced by the contrary yet seductive mixture of surface and depth, reflection and refraction, which characterised its nineteenth century precursors. There are also potential continuities this essay has not touched upon, such as the impact that the idea of screen-as-veil might have upon theories of spectatorship, voyeurism, and the male cinematic gaze. Thus, when discussing the visual delights of the nineteenth century, as well as thinking through a glass darkly, we should think through a screen, bright, luminous, and translucent.

Notes

1. William Nicolson, 'Narrative and Explanation of the Appearance of Phantoms and other Figures in the Exhibition of the Phantasmagoria', *Journal of Natural Philosophy, Chemistry and the Arts* 1 (February 1802) 148.
2. Steve Connor, 'Flat Life', http://www.bbk.ac.uk/eh/skc/flat/
3. Steve Connor, 'Screens' http://www.bbk.ac.uk/eh/eng/skc/magic/screens.htm
4. Isobel Armstrong, 'Transparency: Towards a Poetics of Glass in the Nineteenth Century', *Cultural Babbage: technology, time and invention* ed. Francis Spufford and Jenny Uglow (London: Faber and Faber, 1996) 125.
5. Richard Altick has noted that transparencies were employed in the theatre as early as the masques of Inigo Jones in the first half of the seventeenth century, although they subsequently lost their popularity. Richard Altick, *The Shows of London* (Cambridge, MA: Belknapp Press of Harvard University Press, 1978) 119.
6. Guildhall Library *Exhibition of Mechanical and Other Ingenuities* C.26.53.T1780 .
7. See Altick, 120–121.
8. Louis Carmontelle, *Figure Walking*(1780) 18 $^{5}/_{8}$ x 148 $^{7}/_{16}$ in. Getty Institute, 96.GC.20. Birgit Verwiebe, 'Transparent Painting and the Romantic Spirit', *The Romantic Spirit in German Art* ed. Keith Hartlet, Henry Meyric Hughes, Peter-Klaus Schuster and William Vaughan (London: South Bank Centre, National Galleries of Scotland, and Oktagon Veralg, 1994) 173.
9. See *Leigh's New Pictures of London* (London: Samuel Leigh, 1830) 350. E. Beresford Chancellor, *The Pleasure Haunts of London* (London: Constable, 1925) 223.
10. *A short Account of the Amusements preparing in St James's Park; With a Description of the Allegorical Transparent Paintings, &c. &c.* (London: J Whiting, 1814) (EXEBD78052).
11. Edgell Rickword, *Radical squibs and loyal ripostes: Satirical pamphlets of the Regency period, 1819–1821* (Bath: Adams and Dart, 1971) 278.
12. Verwiebe, 171.
13. W. Williams, *Transparency Painting on Linen. For Decorative Purposes, Panoramic and Dioramic Effects, Ornamental Blinds, &c.* (London: Windsor and Newton, 1856) 13.
14. Edward Orme, *Subjects for Transparencies* (London: Edward Orme, 1799).
15. Rowlandson's transparencies were published as part of a series of seven. Only 'The Visit' and 'The Incantation' were signed by Rowlandson. These transparencies are less effective than Orme's in that there is much less use of varnish; the contrast in shades is also less effective. The publication date of 'The Wedding', 1 August 1799, suggests that these were published after Orme.
16. Edward Orme, *An Essay on Transparent Prints, and on Transparencies in General* (London: Edward Orme, 1807) 5.
17. Orme, *Essay* 7.
18. Rudolf Ackermann, advertisement, *Egyptian Transparencies* (London: R. Ackermann, 1806) (EXEBD70407)
19. Orme, *Essay* 65. See also Edward Orme, *An Illumination* (Edward Orme, 1806), held by Guildhall Library, Prints and Drawings, and EXEBD70310.
20. Rudolf Ackermann, *Introduction for Painting on Transparencies* (London: R. Ackermann, 1800) 12.
21. See Rudolf Ackermann, *A Catalogue of Various Prints, Adapted for Furniture, Ornaments etc* (London: Rudolf Ackermann, 1802) 21,. Copy bound into back of Beinecke Library's Rudolf Ackermann, *Introduction for Painting on Transparencies* (London: R. Ackermann, 1802).
22. Orme, *Essay* 25.
23. Ackermann, 9.
24. *Illustrations of Her Majesty's Palace at Brighton; formerly the Pavilion executed under the command of George IV* (London: J.B. Nichols and Son, 1838).
25. Ackermann, 15.
26. Quoted in Ian Gow, 'Scottish Luminaries', *Country Life* CLXXXIII (8 June 1989): 300.

27. Nathaniel Whittock, *Decorative Painters' and Glaziers' Guide* (London: Isaac Taylor Hinton, 1827) 200.
28. See Rudolf Ackermann, *A Catalogue of Various Prints, Adapted for Furniture, Ornaments etc* (1802).
29. Orme, *Essay* 43.
30. Ackermann, 14.
31. Jane Austen, *Mansfield Park* ed. Claudia Johnson (New York: W.W. Norton, 1998) 106–107.
32. For a full history, see Laurent Mannoni, *The Great Art of Light and Shadow: An Archaeology of the Cinema* trans. Richard Crangle (Exeter: Exeter University Press, 2000) 136–175.
33. Nicolson, 140.
34. Quoted in Mannoni, 155.
35. See Francis West, *Fun for Winter's Evenings: containing Descriptive Dialogues for the Slides and full Directions for exhibiting the Phantasmagoria* (London: J. Harris and C. Chapple, 1833) 8.
36. 'Magic Lantern and Phantasmagoria', *Magazine of Science* 3 (20 April 1839) 18–19.
37. Terry Castle, 'Phantasmagoria: Spectral technology and the Metaphorics of Modern Reverie', *Critical Inquiry* 15.1 (1988) 26–61.
38. Thomas De Quincey, *Confessions of an English Opium-Eater* ed. Edward Sackville-West (1822: London, 1850) 257.
39. See Jonathan Crary, *Techniques of the Observer: On Vision and Modernity* (Cambridge, MA: MIT Press, 1992) 40–43.
40. George Gordon, Lord Byron, *Byron* ed. Jerome J McGann (Oxford: Oxford University Press, 1986) 961.
41. Edgar Allan Poe, *Tales of Mystery and the Imagination* (London: Ward, Lock, 1891) 215.
42. See Helmut and Alison Gernscheim, *L.J.M. Daguerre, The History of the Diorama and the Daguerreotype* (London: Secker and Warburg, 1956).
43. 'The Diorama. A New Exhibition', *Mirror of Literature, Amusement and Instruction* 2 (1824) 425–426.
44. 'The Diorama – Ruins in a Fog', *A History of Pre-Cinema* ed. Stephen Herbert, vol 2. (London: Routledge, 2000) 95.
45. Louis Daguerre, *History and Practice of Photogenic Drawing on the true principles of the Daguerreotype. With a new method of Dioramic Painting* (London: Smith Elder, 1839) 69.
46. John Heaviside Clark, *Panorama of the Thames from London to Richmond* (London: Samuel Leigh, c1825). Copy in Abbey Collection, YCBA. John Heaviside Clark, *Views of London from the Adelphi* (London: Samuel Leigh, c1824). *Myriorama* (London: Samuel Leigh, 1824). At least two series of cards were published, the first showing British rural scenes and the second Italian scenes.
47. YCBA has a number of screens on wooden frames that were obviously made for use with a Portable Diorama. YCBA B1977.14.22092-22095.
48. John Heaviside Clark, *The Amateur's Assistant: or, A Series of Instructions in Sketching from Nature, the Application of Perspective, Tinting of Sketches, Drawing in Watercolours, Transparent Painting, &c, &c. To accompany the subjects which form The Portable Diorama* (London: Samuel Leigh, 1826) 12.
49. Clark, *Amateur's Assistant* vi.
50. Clark, *Amateur's Assistant* 36.
51. *Descriptive Catalogue of the Cosmorama, Dioramic and Panoramic Exhibition* (London: Crozier & Mullin, 1845) n.p.
52. *Descriptive Catalogue of the Cosmorama, Dioramic and Panoramic Exhibition* (London: Crozier & Mullin, 1845) n.p.
53. Reproduced in Altick, 118.
54. Thomas Paine, *The Thomas Paine Reader* ed. Michael Foot and Isaac Kramnick (Harmondsworth: Penguin, 1987) 283.

15

Biologiska Museet: a Habitat Panorama in Late Nineteenth-century Stockholm

John Fullerton and Elaine King

This essay characterises the Biologiska museet in Stockholm, a habitat panorama established by Gustaf Kolthoff in 1893, and compares the architecture of the museum with national pavilions built for international expositions in the latter part of the nineteenth century, and for the 1897 International Art and Industry Exhibition in Stockholm. Brief consideration is also given to three other habitat displays established by Gustaf Kolthoff in Sweden: a habitat panorama in Uppsala in 1889 (no longer extant), and two surviving habitat dioramas in, respectively, Uppsala (opened in 1910) and Södertälje (opened in 1913).[1]

Departing from the tradition of natural history museum display in late nineteenth-century Sweden, Gustaf Kolthoff sought to exhibit natural history specimens in environments that simulated their natural habitat. Rather than arrange specimens in the taxonomic, classificatory system typical of museums in the nineteenth century, an approach familiar to visitors at the Natural History Museum in Drottninggatan, Stockholm,[2] Kolthoff sought to present the flora and fauna of Sweden in displays that we would now characterise as biotopes, i.e., specimens were shown in an environment representing a typical habitat and regional geomorphology. Primarily interested in arranging specimens naturalistically, Kolthoff sought to educate the general public by showing specimens in their typical *levnadssätt* (life situation), to employ the term used in one of the contemporary reviews of the opening of the museum.[3]

Brought up in rural Sweden in the second half of the nineteenth century and largely self-educated, Kolthoff was renowned as a hunter-collector and supplier of exhibits for private collectors before being appointed, in 1879, as a curator-taxidermist (*konservator*) in the zoology department of Uppsala University.[4] Although the research agenda of the department was primarily concerned with animal anatomy and embryology, Kolthoff was given the opportunity in 1889 of establishing a habitat panorama in the former seventeenth-century anatomy theatre of the University. Housed in the magnificent cupola of the Gustavianum, which had been used as a store for a large natural history cabinet, Kolthoff saw the potential the cupola offered for displaying natural history specimens in an environment lit by daylight from windows in the cupola and the upper walls of the anatomy theatre. Thus, in the same year in which a large panorama building was opened in Stockholm, Kolthoff established a habitat panorama in Uppsala. He installed an artificial floor on the uppermost level of the anatomy theatre, and in accordance with the illusionistic principles of the panorama, constructed a glass-enclosed viewing platform approached by means of a dark corridor. On entering the exhibition space, the viewer was confronted with two large ornithological biotopes (a forest habitat and a marshland habitat with specimens from Kolthoff's personal collection), the background landscapes of which were painted by Bruno Liljefors, a local artist and hunter with a growing reputation as a landscape painter, who volunteered to paint the landscape panorama in the anatomy theatre.[5] As is evident from a surviving photograph,[6] a structural feature of the anatomy theatre – a capital of a column – was incorporated in the panorama. The habitat panorama was displayed until 1902 when it was dismantled.[7] One surviving panel is housed in the zoology department at Uppsala University where it can be seen, framed as a conventional painting, on the main staircase of the department at Villavägen 9. In the attention paid to light reflected on the surface of the lake, and in the depiction of a reedy and boulder-strewn shore of a woodland lake typical of the Uppland countryside which Liljefors knew well, the surviving panel is reminiscent of contemporary landscape paintings by Liljefors such as *Uppländskt landskap* (1882).[8]

Kolthoff's second habitat panorama – Biologiska museet, in Stockholm – was a much more ambitious venture than the panorama in Uppsala. A private company was formed in 1892 by the wealthy businessman, Carl Fredrik Liljevalch, to create a habitat panorama showing indigenous animals and birds in a series of early spring landscapes. With an administrative board that included the professor of zoology at Uppsala University, Tycho Tullberg, a former minister and sometime county administrator, Robert Themptander, the arctic explorer, Adolf Erik Nordenskiöld, consul Frans Kempe, the royal game warden, Tage Thott, the director of the Royal Institute of Forestry, C.G. Holmerz, the editor of *Svenska Jägareförbundets Tidskrift* (the journal of the Swedish Hunting Association), J.W. Lindblad, a reader in zoology at Uppsala University, Carl Bowallius, and the editor of the newspaper, *Nya Dagligt Allehanda*, J.A. Björklund, the board raised approximately 130,000 kronor as capital for the project.[9] The King of Sweden, Oscar II, gave crown land for the site where the museum was built in Djurgården which, a royal park east of the city centre, had been used, among other things, for the recreation of well-to-do Stockholmers for much of the nineteenth century: a diorama building, for example, had been established in the park in 1842, and as recently as 1889, a large-scale panorama of the last day of the Paris Commune – *The Struggle for the Buttes-Chaumont*, painted by the Dutch artist, C. Martens – had opened to considerable acclaim.[10] Amidst much pomp, and as one further instance of the flowering of panoramas in late nineteenth-century Europe, Biologiska museet was inaugurated by the King and Queen of Sweden with other members of the royal family and with Themptander, Bowallius, and Kolthoff in attendance on Saturday, 11 Novem-

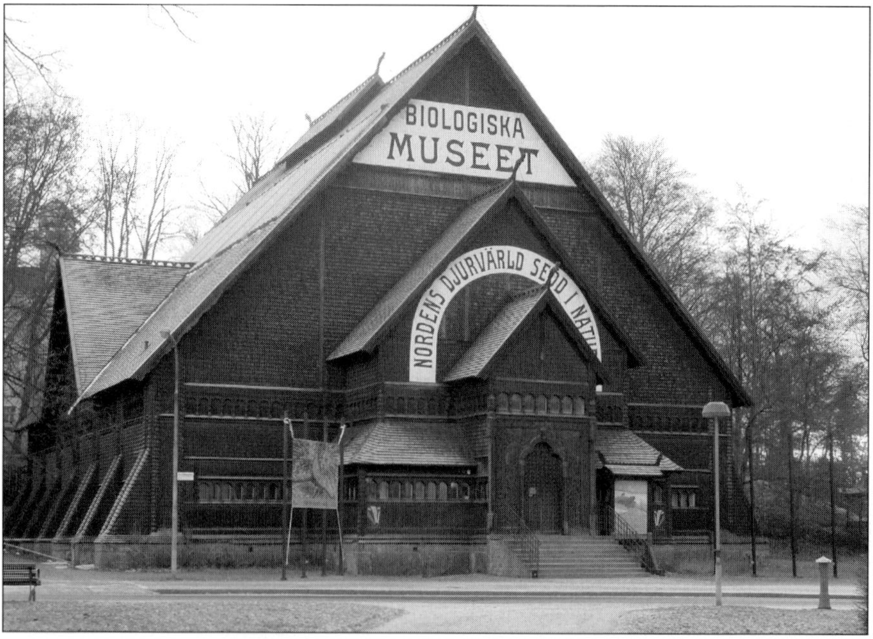

Fig. 1. Biologiska museet, Stockholm.

ber 1893.[11] The following day, the press were invited to a private view, and after reviews were published in the national press on Monday, 13 November, Stockholm's latest panorama opened to the general public two days later.

Agi Lindegren, the architect who had been responsible for designing the exterior decoration of the Paris Commune panorama building, was commissioned to design the structure for Biologiska museet, which he completed in the *fornnordisk* (early Nordic) style freely modelled on the Norwegian stave-church (Fig. 1). On entering the museum, the visitor is led by a double-spiral staircase from the entrance hall to two glass-enclosed oval viewing platforms (Fig. 2) which, placed one above the other, are shielded from the source of overhead natural illumination by a canopy. Although the exhibition is housed in a rectangular building measuring 140 feet by 89 feet and with a height of 72 feet (to which shape Liljefors' canvas conforms),[12] the museum was described as an animal-life panorama (*djurlivs panorama*) in all the newspapers that reviewed the opening of the museum.[13] In spite of the shape of the building, therefore, we can be certain that Biologiska museet was regarded as a panorama since contemporary reviewers described the painting as a *rundmålning*,[14] a term which, literally translated, denotes a circular painting.

Kolthoff constructed the cliff scene on the south-east wall of the museum, and was assisted by five curator-taxidermists who prepared approximately 4,000 specimens for the habitat display. Bruno Liljefors, assisted by Gustaf Fjaestad, was commissioned to paint the panorama. Two principal biotopes are presented: a seascape which includes a section representing the coast of Sweden and the rugged cliffs of northern Sweden (Figs. 3 and 4), and a landscape representing Norrland and central

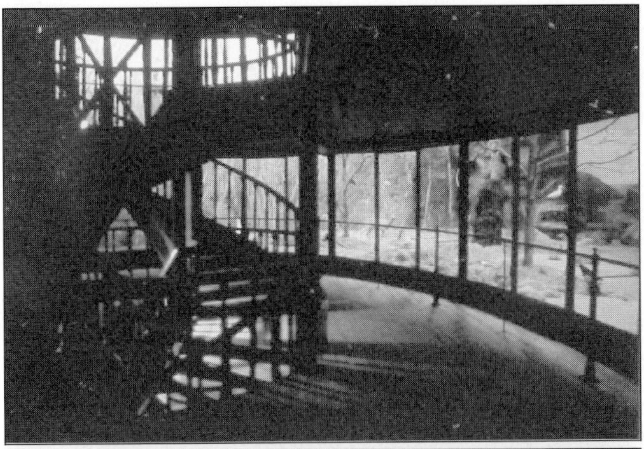

Fig. 2. Double-spiral staircase and viewing platforms, Biologiska museet, Stockholm.

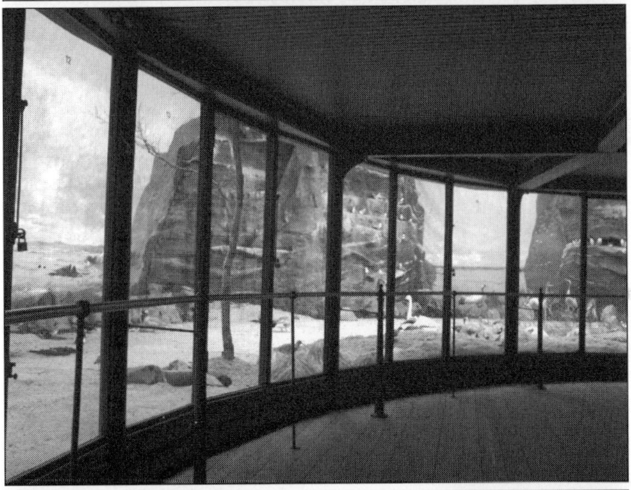

Fig. 3. Bruno Liljefors, assisted by Gustaf Fjaestad, detail of the panorama painting and habitat display representing the coast and cliffs of northern Sweden, Biologiska museet, Stockholm, 1893.

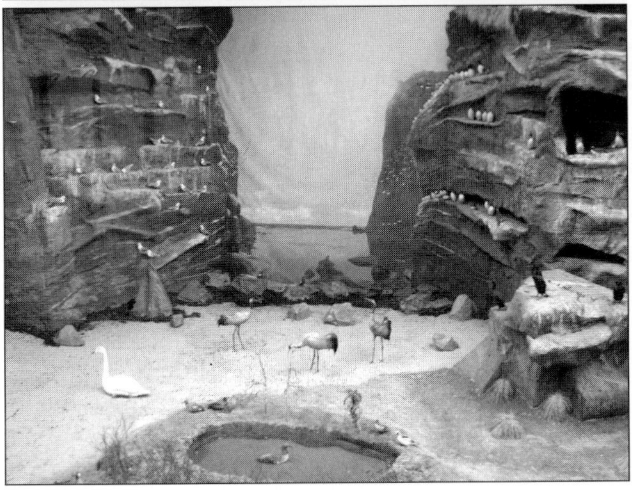

Fig. 4. Bruno Liljefors, assisted by Gustaf Fjaestad, detail of the panorama painting and habitat display representing the coast and cliffs of northern Sweden, Biologiska museet, Stockholm, 1893.

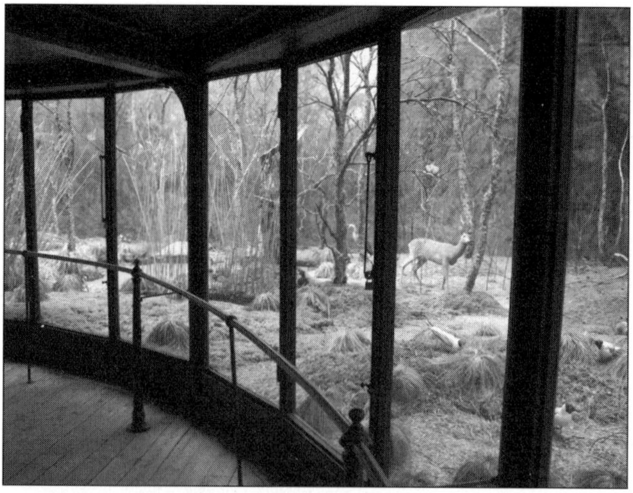

Fig. 5. Bruno Liljefors, assisted by Gustaf Fjaestad, detail of the panorama painting and habitat display representing the deciduous woodland of southern Sweden, Biologiska museet, Stockholm, 1893.

southern Sweden (Fig. 5). These occupy, respectively, the north-east/south-east walls and the south-west/north-west walls of the museum, and merge seamlessly at the corners of the building. Although, therefore, the panorama does not represent a topographically accurate location, it does nonetheless constitute a continuous 360° view of a series of typical natural habitats.

The principles employed in the earlier habitat display at Uppsala were elaborated in the new museum. As one national newspaper noted:

> The ambition of the new museum is that through self-sufficient pictures, the general public is provided with an exhibition of Sweden's fauna presented in a more realistic manner than is possible in a zoo where animals certainly are alive, but only exceptionally represent the characteristics of their lives in the wild.[15]

In this respect, Kolthoff's display dramatised moments typical of an animal's interaction with a given habitat, an understanding of nature that Kolthoff had acquired through many years of field observation as a hunter-collector. While the Linnaean tradition outside Sweden is commonly regarded as privileging the taxonomic concerns of natural history, such a characterisation overlooks the importance Linnaeus also attached to understanding specific regional habitats through field observation,[16] which knowledge the naturalist primarily obtained from nature rambles (*strövtåg*), an activity in which Kolthoff and Liljefors were well practised. The ability to depict a regional landscape intimately may be instanced in Liljefors' previously mentioned *Uppländskt landskap* which presents a recognisable regional topos. Similarly, the trees represented in the Norrland landscape at Biologiska museet evidence a familiarity with depicting this more northerly region. Paintings such as those of the courtship display of wood grouse by Liljefors in the late 1880s – *Tjäderlek* (1888)[17] and *Tjäderlek* (1889)[18] – dramatise moments in the birds' courtship display, and in the close delineation of the woodland habitat, anticipate the type of display seen in Biologiska museet.

The growth of interest in Sweden's regional landscape and natural habitat was not

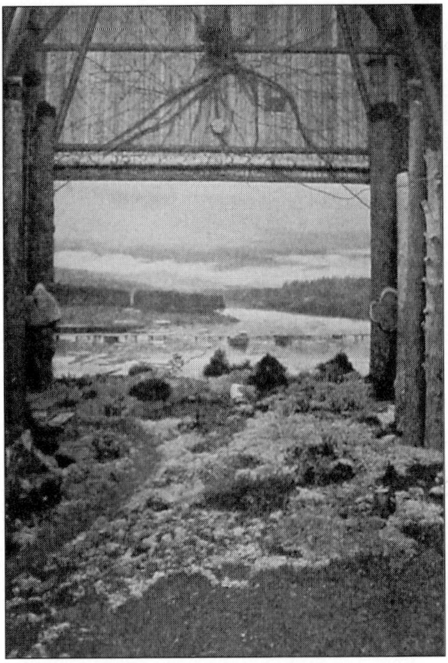

Fig. 6. Ferdinand Boberg and Johan Tirén, interior of the Forest Products Pavilion reproduced in A. Hasselgren, Utställningen i Stockholm 1897. Beskrifning i ord och bild öfver Allmänna Konst- och Industriutställningen *(Stockholm: Fröléen + Comp., 1897): 933.*

only a feature of Biologiska museet but was also reflected in the development of tourism and in other forms of popular entertainment in the late nineteenth century. Stockholm's Panorama International, for instance, a Kaiser panorama established in Hamngatan in 1889, presented 'A tourist trip through Sweden' (*En turistrip genom Sverige*) in the week prior to the opening of Biologiska museet.[19] Interest in Sweden's regional cultural heritage may also be evidenced in the work of Artur Hazelius who, a collector of Scandinavian ethnographic artefacts, opened Skansen in 1891, an open-air folk museum which was devoted to exhibiting Sweden's rural past. In this context, Biologiska museet, a short distance from the main entrance to Skansen, is but one example of a more general movement to present Sweden's regional cultural heritage to an urban audience, which trend ensured that Biologiska museet, in its early years, proved to be one of Stockholm's biggest attractions with over 30,000 visitors attending the museum in its first year of operation.[20] So popular was the museum that the guidebook which accompanied the display not only reached its seventh edition by 1896, but was expanded to include 67 pages of text describing the display. In the following year, when the museum was included in the International Art and Industry Exhibition (*Allmänna Konst- och Industriutställningen*, which ran from 15 May to 1 October), attendance reached an all-time high of 106,490 visitors.[21]

Fig. 7. General view from Strandvägen of the main administrative building, main entrance and Industry Hall (centre) of the 1897 Stockholm Exhibition reproduced in A. Hasselgren, Utställningen i Stockholm 1897. Beskrifning i ord och bild öfver Allmänna Konst- och Industriutställningen *(Stockholm: Fröléen + Comp., 1897): 163.*

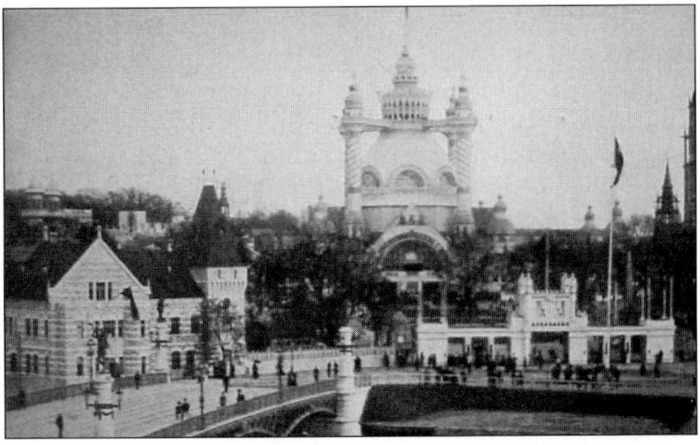

The nation's cultural heritage was also brought to international attention through world fairs. The Swedish pavilion built for the Paris Exhibition of 1867, for example, replicated the ancient timber building in which Gustav Vasa had allegedly escaped from the Danes in 1521,[22] and the Weltausstellung held in Vienna in 1873 and the Philadelphia World's Fair of 1879 both adopted the *fornnordisk* style of architecture employed in Biologiska museet for the design of Sweden's pavilions at these expositions. The exhibition of items from Hazelius' collection of Scandinavian ethnographic artefacts also brought international attention to the regional cultural heritage of Sweden, particularly at the 1878 exhibition in Paris. For the 1889 Paris Exhibition, the Swedish pavilion incorporated a vernacular form of ornamentation, *snickarglädja* (carpenters' joy), to decorate the gables of the pavilion located near the newly-completed Eiffel Tower. Although this style of ornamentation was frequently adopted in upper middle-class villas built for the growing number of city-dwellers in late nineteenth-century Stockholm, *snickarglädja* also represented a broader, pan-Baltic movement wherein vernacular features were used to impart a sense of tradition for city-dwellers (similar decoration, for example, may be seen in the Latvian coastal resort of Jurmala where the wealthy citizens of Riga built their villas). The Swedish pavilion for the 1893 Columbian Exposition in Chicago, designed by Gustaf Wickman, combined elements from the American tradition of shingle construction with the Nordic tradition.[23] Pyramidal in structure, two cylindrical brick towers directed the eye towards the entrance to the pavilion while the structures at its corners were strongly reminiscent of Uppland bell towers (*klockstapel*), traditionally built on ground adjacent to the parish church.

The conjunction of the secular tradition associated with Sweden's cultural heritage with the vernacular tradition of church architecture thematised in the Chicago pavilion and Biologiska museet, was widely evident in the design of pavilions for the 1897 Stockholm Exhibition. Although Kolthoff was responsible for installing a modest habitat diorama in the entrance hall to the Swedish Association of Hunters Pavilion, which building is one of the few to have survived to the present day, many of the larger pavilions celebrated the conjunction of religious with secular motifs. For example, the clerestory windows in the Forest Products Pavilion, designed by Ferdinand Boberg, enhanced the building's religious associations where its rich nave-like interior, carpeted with a three-dimensional floral diorama, was set against a landscape of northern woods painted by Johan Tirén (Fig. 6). Piers within the pavilion demarcated side bays in which, in the manner of side chapels, further forestry exhibits were displayed. The secular associations of the building are evident in the may-pole decoration of the minarets that flanked its entrance and in the garland wheel which crowned the front facade, a conjunction of secular and religious motifs that may be seen at its most spectacular in Boberg's Industry Hall, where a flamboyant extemporisation of the may-pole motif is set against a mix of minarets, elevated walkways and external elevated viewing platforms that housed this temple to industry (Fig. 7).

Following the closure of the Stockholm Exhibition, many of the pavilions were dismantled, including the 1889 panorama building which had been converted to house the Chemical and Technology Pavilion and the main restaurant (Fig. 8). In an increasingly competitive environment (Skansen, for instance, opened a small zoo in 1900), and reliant on the sale of comparatively expensive admission tickets,

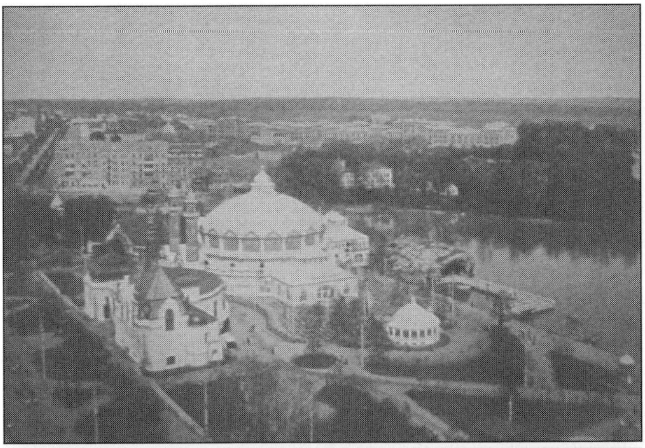

Fig. 8. View of the Chemical and Technology Pavilion and main restaurant (the former Paris Commune panorama building) reproduced in A. Hasselgren, Utställningen i Stockholm 1897. Beskrifning i ord och bild öfver Allmänna Konst- och Industriutställningen *(Stockholm: Fröléen + Comp., 1897): 220.*

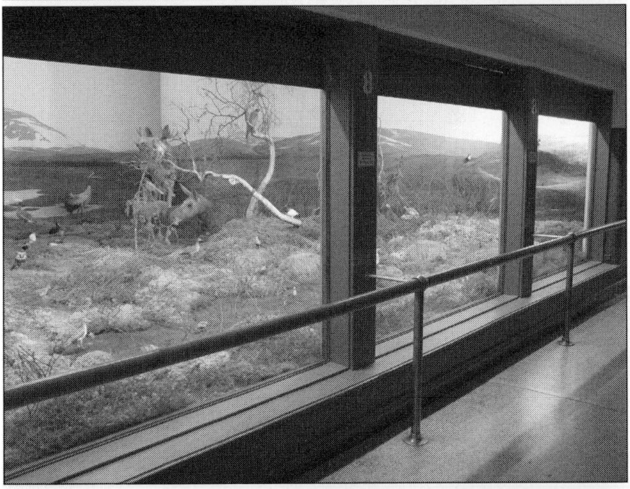

Fig. 9. Kjell Kolthoff, detail of the diorama painting and habitat display representing the mountainous landscape of Lappland, Biologiska museet, Uppsala, 1910.

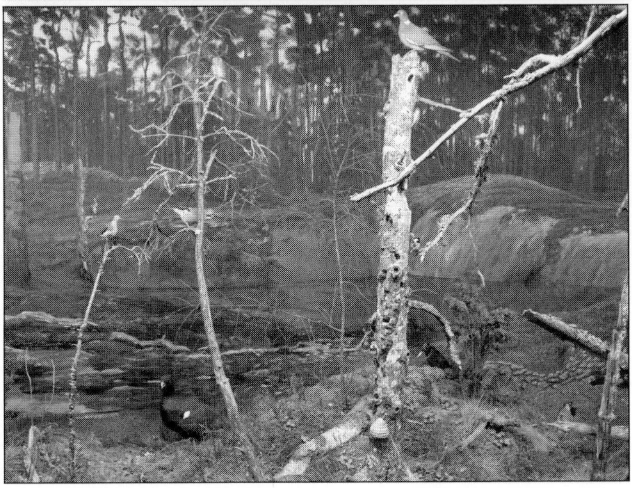

Fig. 10. Kjell Kolthoff, detail of the diorama painting and habitat display representing a coniferous woodland scene, Biologiska museet, Uppsala, 1910.

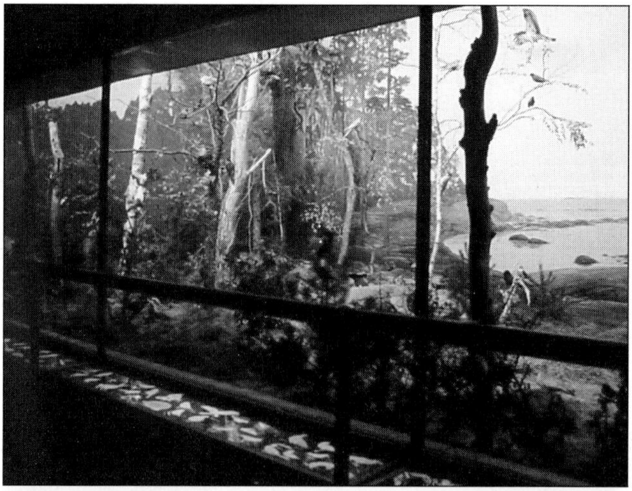

Fig. 11. Kjell Kolthoff, detail of the diorama painting and habitat display representing a west coastal scene, Biologiska museet, Södertälje, 1913.

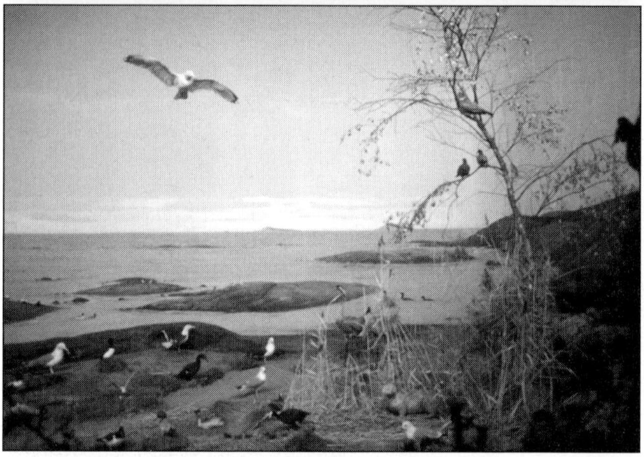

Fig. 12. Kjell Kolthoff, detail of the diorama painting and habitat display representing a west coastal scene, Biologiska museet, Södertälje, 1913.

the future of Biologiska museet was far from assured. Although the price of admission to Biologiska museet (1 krona for adults and 50 öre for children, i.e., half price) was the same as that for admission to the Paris Commune panorama,[24] this price was relatively high when compared with the cost of admission to the Panorama International which, in the heart of the city's commercial district, charged 30 öre for adults and 20 öre for children during the week, and 25 öre for adults and 20 öre for children on Sundays and public holidays,[25] and included a weekly change of programme in the exhibition of stereoscopic slides. Against this competition, it is hardly surprising that Biologiska museet proved to be a short-term attraction for a city of only 250,000 inhabitants.

Nonetheless, the academic establishment acknowledged the significance of Kolthoff's work by awarding him an honorary doctorate in 1907, and in the following year, a national newspaper, *Svenska Dagbladet*, published a lengthy letter by Kolthoff in which he explained the exhibition policy of the museum and argued for its continued support since it would have been impossible to relocate the canvas.[26] Noting that even well-educated Swedes had a poor knowledge of natural history, Kolthoff reaffirmed his belief in the museum by quoting Richard Bowdler Sharpe, of the Natural History Museum in Kensington, London, who had visited Biologiska museet: 'Here one can learn in a short while that which cannot be learned from many years of studying text books'.[27] Had it not been for Carl Fredrik Liljevalch's continued financial support, and growing regard for Liljefors' work as an artist, the museum may well have been forced to close.

The subsequent development of habitat dioramas in Åbo (Finland, 1907), Uppsala (1910) and Södertälje (1913) continued to rely on private funding, the latter two being financed from Liljevalch's estate. The museum in Uppsala contained eight autonomous habitat dioramas painted by Gustaf Kolthoff's son, Kjell. Five of these have survived to the present-day including a fascinating representation of the Swedish landscape at night. The other dioramas represent a deciduous wood- and lakeland biotope in southern Sweden, a mountainous landscape from Lappland (Fig. 9), a similar terrain in winter, and a coniferous woodland biotope (Fig. 10) which, highly naturalistic in its rendering, makes the distinction between canvas and habitat display almost impossible to perceive. When the museum was restored in the early 1960s, three further dioramas were repainted, two by Lindorm Liljefors (an Uppland lakeland biotope and a coastal biotope) and one by Birger Nordahl (a sandbank habitat).

The museum in Södertälje (Liljevalch's home town) was built next to the secondary school, and like the other Kolthoff museums, was intended to function as a teaching and study collection. Kjell Kolthoff assisted his father in mounting the displays, and painted the background landscape for this habitat diorama (Fig. 11 and Fig. 12). In a better state of preservation than the Bruno Liljefors panorama in Stockholm, Kjell Kolthoff's painting of a west coastal scene is strongly illusionistic. There can be little doubt that Kjell Kolthoff was an extremely talented painter of habitat dioramas who has for too long been overlooked.

It is probable that the continued popularity of Bruno Liljefors' work helped the Stockholm Biologiska museet survive to the present day. Apart from his work as an animal and landscape painter, Liljefors illustrated some of Kolthoff's books which continued to have a popular readership long after Kolthoff's death in 1913. Future discussion of Kolthoff's work, therefore, could usefully relate the discourse of his natural history writing to the natural history displays considered in this essay. These displays could also be appraised in a more general history of the development of natural history education in Sweden in the late nineteenth century. In this context, all three Swedish museums not only represent a physical embodiment of Kolthoff's educational philosophy, but as a habitat panorama, the Stockholm Biologiska museet survives as a unique elaboration of the tradition of the nineteenth-century panorama in Europe.

Acknowledgements: We would like to thank Kerstin Bergdahl (Torrekällbergets museum), Mats Bloch (Uppsala University), and Lars Erik Larsson (Biologiska museet, Stockholm) for their assistance in researching this essay.

Notes

1. A further habitat diorama, established by Gustaf Kolthoff in Åbo (Turku), Finland in 1907, is not considered in this essay.

2. For an illustration of this type of display, see the drawing by O. A. Mankell of the main gallery of the Natural History Museum, Drottninggatan reproduced in *Ny illustrerad tidskrift*, 1871, and reprinted in Jenny Beckman, *Naturens palats. Nybyggnad, vetenskap och utställning vid Naturhistoriska riksmuseet 1866–1925* (Stockholm: Atlantis, 1999): 221.
3. See 'Ett nytt museum i Stockholm', *Dagens Nyheter*, 13 November 1893.
4. Gunnar Brusewitz (ed.), *Natur och illusion. Biologiska museet* (Stockholm: Informationsförlaget, 1993): 36.
5. Olaus Rudbeck's famous anatomy theatre was reconstructed in the Gustavianum in the 1950s.
6. See the photograph reproduced in Allan Ellenius, *Bruno Liljefors. Naturen som livsrum* (Stockholm: Bonnier Alba, 1997): 114.
7. The above discussion of the 1889 Uppsala habitat panorama also draws on Karen Wonders' account in Karen Wonders, *Habitat Dioramas. Illusions of Wilderness in Museums of Natural History*, Acta Universitatis Upsaliensis, Figura Nova Series 25 (Uppsala and Stockholm: Almqvist & Wiksell, 1993): 52–55.
8. Oil on canvas, 73cm x 59cm, private collection. For illustration, see Ellenius, *Bruno Liljefors*: 36.
9. Wonders, *Habitat Dioramas*: 55.
10. 'Rundmålningsbyggnaden på Djurgården', *Aftonbladet*, 28 August 1889, 'Rundmålningsbyggnaden', *Dagens Nyheter*, 28 August 1889, 'Rundmålningsbyggnaden på Djurgården', *Svenska Dagbladet*, 29 August 1889. According to all three newspaper reviews, the panorama was 16.2 metres high and had a circumference of 116 metres.
11. 'Ett nytt museum i Stockholm', *Dagens Nyheter*, 13 November 1893, 'Biologiska museet', *Svenska Dagbladet*, 13 November 1893.
12. 'Biologiska museet', *Nya Dagligt Allehanda*, 31 October 1893.
13. See also the exterior photograph of the museum taken in 1908 that clearly shows the museum described as a 'djurlivs panorama' in Gunnar Brusewitz (ed.), *Natur och illusion: Biologiska museet* (Stockholm: Informationsförlaget, 1993): 21.
14. See 'Biologiska museet', *Dagens Nyheter*, 13 November 1893 and 'Biologiska museet', *Svenska Dagbladet*, 13 November 1893.
15. 'Meningen med det nya museet är att genom fristående bilder gifva allmänheten en föreställning om Sverges [sic] fauna, framställd på ett mera lefvande och instruktivt sätt, än hvad som är möjligt ens i en zoologisk trädgård, der djuren visserligen ha den fördelen att vara lefvande, men der man dock endast undantagsvis kan få en föreställning om deras egendomligheter och lif ute i det fria tillståndet', 'Ett nytt museum i Stockholm', *Dagens Nyheter*, 13 November 1893.
16. For consideration of this tradition and its influence in nineteenth-century Sweden, see Wonders: 83–96.
17. Oil on canvas, 143cm x 199cm, Göteborgs Konst Museum. For an illustration, see Ellenius, *Bruno Liljefors*: 96.
18. Oil on canvas, 186cm x 275cm, Bayerische Staatsgemäldesammlungen, Munich. For an illustration, see Ellenius, *Bruno Liljefors*: 97.
19. Pelle Snickars, *Svensk film och visuell masskultur 1900* (Stockholm: Aura förlag, 2001): 83.
20. Wonders, *Habitat Dioramas*: 60.
21. Ibid.: 60.
22. For an illustration of this pavilion, see Ann Thorson Walton, *Ferdinand Boberg – Architect: The Complete Work* (Cambridge, MA: MIT Press, 1994): 30.
23. For illustration, see Walton, *Ferdinand Boberg*: 33.
24. 'Rundmålningsbyggnaden på Djurgården', *Svenska Dagbladet*, 29 August 1889.
25. See the display advertisement for the Panorama International in *Dagens Nyheter*, 8 October 1889.
26. See 'Biologiska museets betydelse', *Svenska Dagbladet*, 27 May 1908.
27. 'Här lär man sig på en liten stund hvad man under åratals studier ej kan lära sig af litteraturen', 'Biologiska museets betydelse', *Svenska Dagbladet*, 27 May 1908.

16

The Brighton School and the Quest for Natural Colour

Luke McKernan

In 1948 the film historian Georges Sadoul identified a group of British film pioneers as being the 'Brighton School'. By this Sadoul meant G.A. Smith and James Williamson, whose creative films of fifty years before, with their use of multiple shots, dissolves, close-ups and the like were attracting the interest of film historians. It was known that Smith and Williamson had both lived in the Brighton area; the further names of Esmé Collings, a filmmaker none of whose work was then known to survive, and the presence locally of engineer Alfred Darling, all gave rise to the catchy concept of a 'Brighton School'.[1]

The idea of a 'school' proved to be a useful critical short-cut, but has been seldom subjected to any sort of further analysis, accepted as simply a slight geographical coincidence. It is the contention of this paper, however, that there was such a thing as a 'Brighton School', if not literally then virtually so, and that while it involved all of those names traditionally associated with Sadoul's school, it embraced a wider group, all active in the Brighton and Hove area in the early 1900s, many of whose names have been largely lost to film history. For the goal that they were seeking was not innovation in cinematic form, but a far more obviously lucrative goal, that of natural colour cinematography. To the names of G.A. Smith, James Williamson, Esme Collings and Alfred Darling, let us add those of Edward Turner, Captain William Norman Lascelles Davidson, Dr Benjamin Jumeaux, Dr Edward Grün, Otto Pfenninger, William Friese Greene and Charles Urban. Their particular history now follows.

The three-colour principle

Firstly, it is necessary to know something of the history of colour photography, especially the principles upon which such colour reproduction is based.

In 1855 the physicist James Clerk Maxwell gave a lecture to the Royal Society, where he argued how the three-colour principle of colour vision might be applied to create colour photography. Using colour filters in combination with monochrome photography to create a red, green and blue record would result in a full

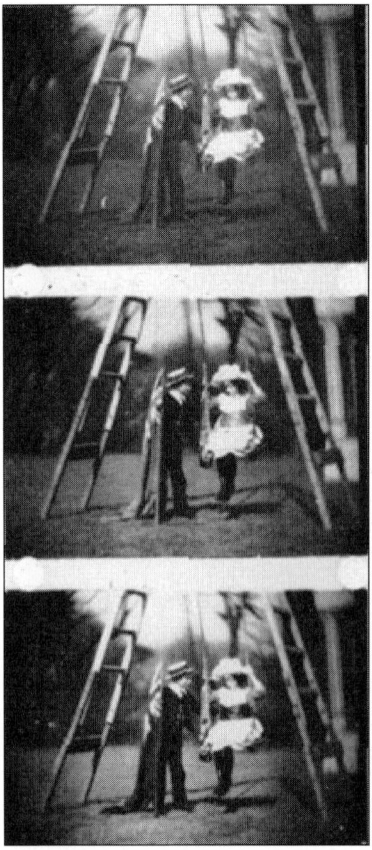

Fig. 1. Lee and Turner three-colour film strip, c.1901. [NMPFT Collection.]

colour reproduction when those three versions of the same image were brought together. In 1861 at the Royal Institution Maxwell demonstrated the practical results of his theory, photographing a tartan ribbon in colour, after a very long exposure. This was before sensitizing emulsions had been discovered, and Maxwell was using photographic plates that were insensitive to red light, so he achieved his results somewhat by accident.[2]

Many took up the challenge of creating an effective colour photographic system from here on, but most significant for our purposes was the work of the American Frederic Eugene Ives. Ives had been working since 1877 on ways of taking and viewing three-colour images with a camera known as a Photochromoscope. The result of this experimentation resulted in the Kromskop, a stereoscopic viewer which combined the Photochromoscope images from six monochrome transparencies through colour filters to created a stereoscopic colour image called a Kromogram. This was first marketed in Britain in 1898. The Kromskop itself, by an arrangement of mirrors, coloured glass screens, red, green and blue filters, and a light source, produced a full colour and stereoscopic image.

The Kromskop was ingenious, and beautiful in its effects, but as Ives admitted, 'this is not the kind of color photography that the world has been looking for … because it does not produce fixed color images which can be framed and hung upon the wall'.[3] Additive synthesis was fundamentally impractical as a means of securing photographic still images, and would be completely abandoned once Lumière Autochromes appeared on the market in 1907. However, it was to be pursued as a means of creating colour motion pictures into the 1930s, before subtractive colour, notably in the form of Technicolor, conquered all before it.[4] It was the pursuit of additive natural colour systems that came to characterise the work of the 'Brighton School'.

Working as assistant to Ives in his development of the Kromskop in London for two years had been Edward Raymond Turner. In 1898, while he was with Ives, Turner teamed up with financier Frederick Marshall Lee to develop a three-colour motion picture system, along the additive principles set down by Maxwell. Ives knew of Turner's experimentation with colour cinematography, and sanctioned work which clearly owed ideas to his Photochromoscope camera and Kromskop viewer.

The result of Turner and Lee's collaboration was British Patent (B.P.) no. 6,202 of 22 March 1899, 'Means for taking and exhibiting cinematographic pictures'. A conventional cine camera had its shutter replaced by a rotating wheel with red, green and blue filters, interspersed with opaque sections, in synchronisation with the movement of the film through the camera. The 38mm film passing through the camera would therefore record in succession a red, green and blue record. The film was to be shown through a three-lens projector of some complexity, with each frame projected through each lens in turn, and again a rotating shutter was used to reintroduce the colour.[5] The results, however, were practically unwatchable. There is an eye-witness account:

> It was when we came to superimpose the pictures on the sheet through three-coloured glasses that we found the process unworkable. As soon as the handle of the projecting machine was worked the three pictures refused to remain in register, and no knowledge that any of us could bring to bear upon the matter could even begin to cure the trouble. The difficulty is mainly due to the fact that cinematograph pictures are small to begin with, and they have to be enormously magnified in exhibiting, as you all know. The slightest defect in registration it pitilessly magnified, and when the minute defects of registration in the first three pictures are followed by minute defects of another sort in the next three, and by yet another sort in the succeeding three, and so on throughout the length of a film, the effect on the observer is almost unbearable.[6]

The eye-witness is George Albert Smith. Smith, a Brighton resident, became involved with Turner's work because when Turner and Lee in 1899 required further finance, they turned to the premier film company of the period, the Warwick Trading Company, whose film processor was then G.A. Smith. Warwick as a company soon lost interest in what seemed a lost cause, but its manager Charles Urban took on the development of the system personally. The camera and projector were constructed by an engineer chiefly employed by Warwick, namely Alfred Darling, another Brighton resident. The film tests moved from Turner's premises in London to Brighton, and it may even be Smith's own children who feature in a sample strip of the Lee and Turner colour system from circa 1901, held in the National Museum of Photography, Film and Television.

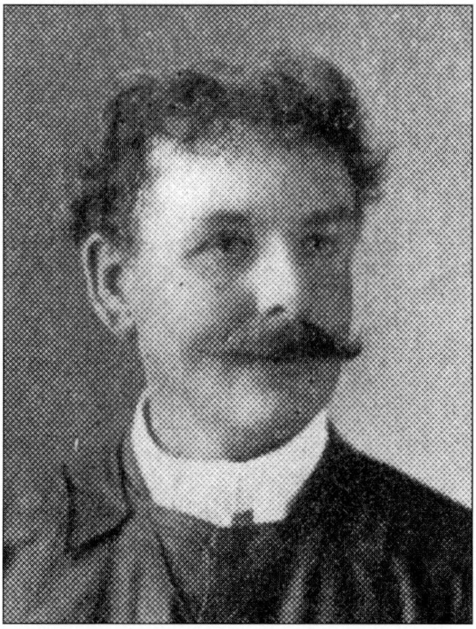

Fig. 2. George Albert Smith. [Note: A rare image of Smith taken from Penrose's Pictorial Annual 1908–09.*]*

Lee lost interest in supporting the system in 1902; then, on 9 March 1903, while working in his workshop, Turner fell dead of a heart attack.[7] Urban turned to Smith to continue the experi-

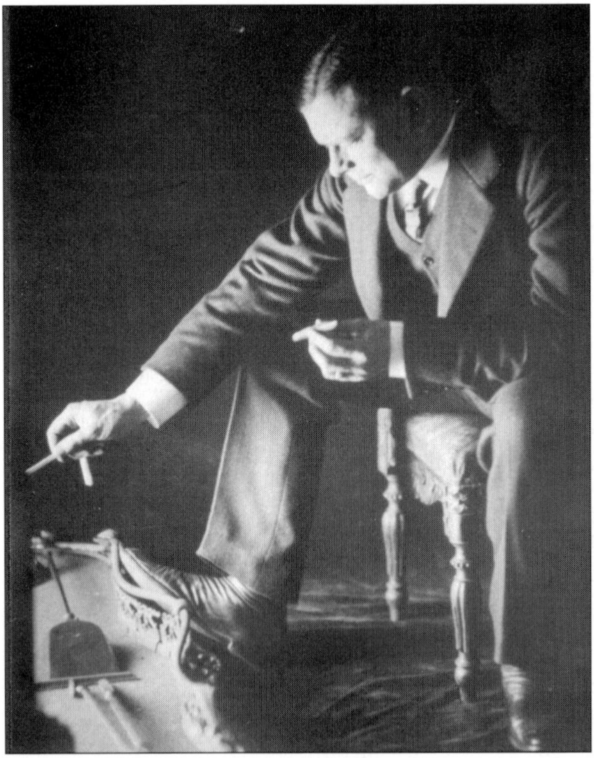

Fig. 3. Charles Urban. [Author's personal collection.]

mental work, though Smith was never paid by Urban at any time on his development of what would become Kinemacolor. Smith effectively abandoned his filmmaking and film processing activities, and devoted himself chiefly to invention, and in particular to discovering a practical means of effecting natural colour cinematography.

There is a simple historical account of how Smith discovered what eventually came to be known as Kinemacolor. It was based on the psychological process whereby our brain compensates for the colours that should be but are not there. Smith described it thus:

> One has a very curious illustration about that with flags. I very often amuse myself about it, because this matter of blue has been on my mind a good deal, and I have discussed it a good deal. There is a rather curious thing that crops up in everyday life about blue, and that is in the Union Jack. You will find a Union Jack is very often indeed in a shocking state; it is a sort of dull grey, red and black almost, and yet if you were to say to anybody, What colour is that? he would say, Red and blue; but when you took it down you would find there was no blue in it, it is red and black and dark grey, but no blue at all. I do not deny that you do get blue in Union Jacks, but it is called blue often when it is not; it is described as the good old blue and red Union Jack.[8]

The question of the missing blue would later be fatal to Kinemacolor. Urban, meanwhile, wrote romantically of the day when they first experimented with the system, in July 1906:

> One Sunday – we were ready for the first real two-colour test. It was beautiful sunshiny day. Smith dressed his little boy and girl in a variety of colors, the girl was in white with a pink sash, the boy in sailor blue waving a Union Jack; we had the green grass and the red brick house for a setting. This was in July 1906. It took about thirty seconds to make the exposures on a specially prepared negative film after which we went into Smith's small dark room to develop the results in absolute darkness. Within two hours we had dried the

> negative, made a positive print of the 50 feet length, developed and dried it – and then for the grand test. Even today – after seventeen years, I can feel the thrill of that moment, when I saw the first result of the two-colour process – I yelled like a drunken cowboy – 'We've got it – We've got it'.[9]

This is a suspect account. The description of the girl with a pink sash and the boy with a Union Jack is clearly the film taken in 1901 with the Lee and Turner process. The 'eureka' moment is almost invariably a romantic fiction, the process of invention being far more gradual than simple accounts will allow.

The reality behind Smith's discovery was, inevitably, rather more complex, and brings in the Brighton School.

The Brighton School

In 1903 Smith moved to Southwick, a small town to the west of Brighton, where he worked on his colour experiments at his home 'Laboratory Lodge' in Roman Crescent.[10] Close by lived his good friend Dr Edward F. Grün, whom Smith had known since 1901, and whose hobby was experimenting in colour photography. Smith soon made the acquaintance of Captain William Norman Lascelles Davidson of the 4th Battalion The Kings (Liverpool) Regiment. Davidson was a wealthy man who had been experimenting in colour photography as a hobby for some years, and had several patents to his name. He would spend some £3,000 between 1898 and 1906 in what would an unsuccessful search for a workable motion picture colour system. His close associate in his experiments was a surgeon and experimenter himself in various aspects of colour photography, Dr Benjamin Jumeaux, who became another friend of Smith's.[11] Charles Urban lived in London, but made weekly visits to Brighton to follow Smith's progress.

In Hove, meanwhile, along Western Road lived professional photographer and dabbler in cinematography Esme Collings (at no. 120), and a chemist and keen amateur photographer James Williamson (no. 55), who became a noted producer of cinematograph films and later film equipment.[12] Williamson supplied photographic materials, and became friends with Collings and G.A. Smith, like them benefiting from the expertise of local engineer Alfred Darling, who lived at 25 Ditchling Rise, and who manufactured most of the cinematographic equipment used locally.[13] Williamson, who began making films in 1897, also knew Grün and Davidson. Another customer of Darling's was William Friese Greene, who lived in Dovercourt in Essex but who was the business associate of Collings and visited Brighton regularly on photographic trips, eventually moving to 203 Western Road in 1905.[14]

Friese Greene is one of the more exasperating characters in early film history, whose romanticised biography and the film made out of it, *The Magic Box* (1951), have confused the historical record for decades. Recent critical activity has done something to revive his reputation of late, but essentially Friese Greene was a man of scant technical genius, an opportunist, fantasist, and an incorrigible borrower of others' ideas.

Having seen his efforts to invent motion pictures in the late 1880s and early 1890s overtaken by others better capitalised and far more technically adept than he, Friese Greene turned his attention to motion pictures in colour. His is the first British patent for a system of colour cinematography. B.P. 21,649 of 1898 described a method by which a disc, or shutter, with red, green and blue sectors would be rotated rapidly in front of the lens, recording a single image, and projecting this by a like process. It failed totally when put to practical use.[15] It would be a notable feature of the considerable activity in colour cinematography at this period that so many rushed to the patent office before having a working system to support such claims. The riches that colour cinematography seemed certain to bring made it seem worthwhile to hazard the expense of a speculative patent, as these inventors repeatedly made premature attempts to establish a 'master' patent. Even G.A. Smith submitted a provisional patent for colour cinematography in 1905, one year before he successfully patented what would become Kinemacolor.

Later in 1898, still a year before Lee and Turner's three colour patent, Davidson patented a triple-lens motion picture camera (B.P. 23,863). Davidson's patent proposed a camera with three lenses with the three colour filters behind each of the lenses.[16] Again, it was accompanied by no practical working model. The Lee and Turner patent followed in 1899, in which year Davidson patented a three-colour still photography system (B.P. 3,560). On 27 February 1900 William Friese Greene gave a demonstration of his colour system at the Royal Photographic Society. The system was manifestly unready to be presented before an audience, the colour manifestly unnatural, and the thick-skinned Friese Greene was subjected to a substantial amount of heckling.[17]

In 1901, the year that Lee and Turner approached Urban about their three-colour system, activity in Brighton in the field of colour cinematography was on the increase. In May 1901 Captain Davidson purchased a Kammatograph from its inventor Leonard Kamm.[18] The Kammatograph was designed for amateur use and made no use of film at all; instead it recorded its images as a series of tiny photographs in a spiral on a twelve-inch diameter glass disc.[19] Davidson was to employ the Kammatograph in his colour experiments, but he was also experimenting with celluloid. In November 1901 Davidson and his Southwick neighbour Benjamin Jumeaux made a provisional patent for a three-colour camera and projector which was improved upon by their later patents of 1903–04.[20] Also at this time, Edward Grün first approached his friend G.A. Smith with his new invention, a fluid lens.[21] Grün was a doctor and an enthusiastic amateur photographer. His lens contained fluid instead of being wholly glass, and excited some attention at the time for its novelty, though the invention was to find no practical use. Grün wanted Smith to test out his lens for cinematographic work, and would later suggest its use with coloured fluids to Smith for colour cinematography, an eccentric idea which was not pursued.

In 1903 Davidson and Jumeaux patented a three-colour projector (B.P. 3,729). It is possible that at this time they were responsible for an unusual strip of film which survives in the Will Day film collection at the Archives du Film du CNC in France. Unique in format, it is 82mm in width, and features three parallel monochrome images, each registering a red, green and blue record. Laurent Mannoni identifies this as being the work of Davidson and Jumeaux, partly through the evidence of perforator for 82mm film held by the Cinémathèque Française, though a film of such description did not feature in any of the public exhibitions of their work.[22]

For practical exhibitions, Davidson was dependent on the Kammatograph, and

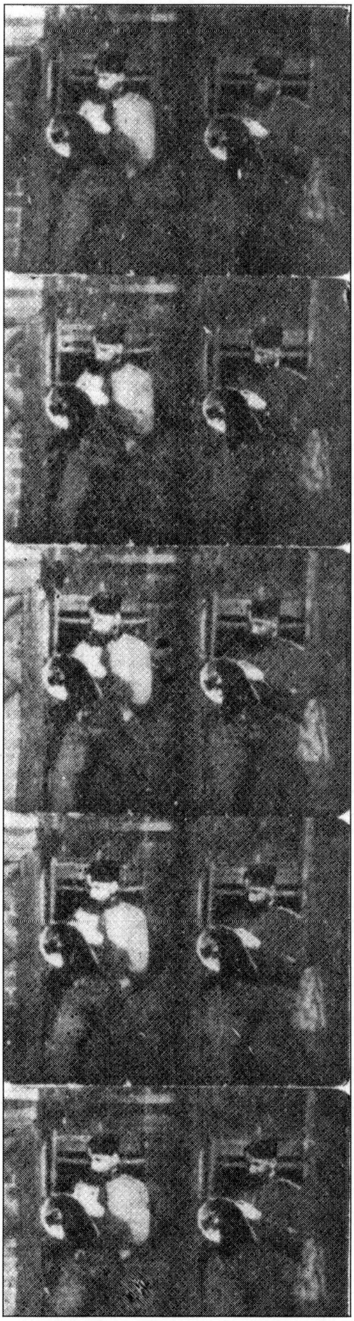

Fig. 4. Davidson-Jumeaux two-colour system, 1904. Byepaths of Colour Photography, *by O. Reg (1921).*

crucially on two-colour work. In this he anticipated Smith's work on Kinemacolor, though it is a moot point whether he influenced it. Davidson's two-colour work was of two kinds. In 1903 at an Inventors' Exhibition in Brighton he employed a Kammatograph, to which was added a revolving disc with red and blue-green sectors.[23] Davidson and Jumeaux also patented a two-colour camera and projection system which employed prisms (B.P. 7,179). For this system two prisms were placed base to base in front of the camera lens, partitioned in front by a shield. Two refracted images were thereby formed side by side on the film. Projecting the results followed a similar arrangement, but the refracted image suffered from a considerable falling off in definition from the one side of the film to the other, and the colour effects were deemed quite unnatural by observers.[24]

Davidson demonstrated this system in Paris in May 1904 and at the Brighton Hippodrome in November of the same year, for which Smith supplied him with film stock and processed the films.[25] Smith by this time had moved to Southwick, becoming Davidson's near neighbour, though Davidson conducted all his experiments in a rented room at 20 Middle Street, Brighton.

In March or April of 1905 William Friese Greene joined Davidson as his paid employee in his experiments at Middle Street.[26] Friese Greene had only recently come from a short period in prison for borrowing money while an undischarged bankrupt, and was struggling to re-establish himself as a photographer. He brought out a patent in April for two or three-colour cinematography that was in essence a simplification of the Davidson-Jumeaux prism idea, using a single prism behind the lens (B.P. 9,465). Colour cinematography historian Adrian Klein dismisses the patent as 'hopeless'.[27] Friese Greene, however, felt that it was 'undoubtedly' the best patent in the field so far, and was advanced £500 on the strength of it by local furniture dealer, Harry Birch.[28] In 1905 another knowledgeable experimenter in colour photography appeared on the Brighton scene,

Otto Pfenninger. Pfenninger assisted Davidson and Jumeaux in their two-colour work, and patented for himself a projection system of a lens and prism variety (1905, B.P. 322). Klein calls it 'of doubtful practicality'.[29]

On 25 January 1906 Davidson and Friese Greene demonstrated their two-colour work at the Royal Institution[30] and in July at the Photographic Convention of Great Britain in Southampton. The *British Journal of Photography* was dismissive, observing that 'The real reds are ignored, and while this may be useful for pure landscape work, it can never be a true scientific record of colour by the aid of cinematography'.[31] July is also given as the month when the first of Smith's successful two-colour tests were made, though there is no primary documentary evidence to back this up. In October Friese Greene left Davidson's employment, and opened a photographic business with Harry Birch at 203A Western Street.[32] His interest in colour cinematography was certainly not over, and he would now take steps to seek out capital on the strength of his 1905 patent.

How Smith's own experimental work may have benefited from this hotbed of experimentation and the ambitious filing of patents is difficult to determine. It would seem inevitable that Smith had to be influenced by such activity, conducted by friends and neighbours, work which he witnessed and about which he was consulted, and for which he was often the processor of the films concerned. In essence, however, Smith had nothing to learn from his less technically-adept neighbours, and he worked alone. He had followed his own route by experimenting first with Ives' Kromskop, then testing out the making of naturally-coloured lantern slides with two colours. He had probably considered the idea of two-colour cinematography by 1902, while Turner was still alive – correspondence exists which suggests that this is so.[33] He worked on three-colour cinematography for a while, because this was held to be the ideal, but once he believed such a system to be impossible, his mind was wholly devoted making a two-colour system with rotating filters work. He probably achieved a working system in July 1906.

Kinemacolor was patented in November 1906 by G.A. Smith, B.P. 26671, 'Improvements in & relating to Kinematography Apparatus for the Production of Coloured Pictures'. It employed a revolving shutter with red and green filters, and a projector similarly set up, projecting red and green records alternately from the monochrome film. Shown at double speed of thirty frames per second, in the words of the patent, 'the two colour records blend & present to the eye a satisfactory rendering of the subject in colours which appear to be natural.'[34] The commercial exploitation of the system was undertaken by Charles Urban, who launched it upon the word in May 1908, and through it gained world-wide fame.

Kinemacolor vs Bioschemes

The history of the further development and the years of triumph for Kinemacolor as the one effective natural colour motion picture system before the First World War, is a history told elsewhere.[35] What follows here is an account of how the 'Brighton School' came together once more in 1913, for a court case which argued just who it was among them who invented natural colour cinematography.

From the very moment that Kinemacolor was launched upon the world in 1908, Urban was dogged by the baleful presence of William Friese Greene. While the

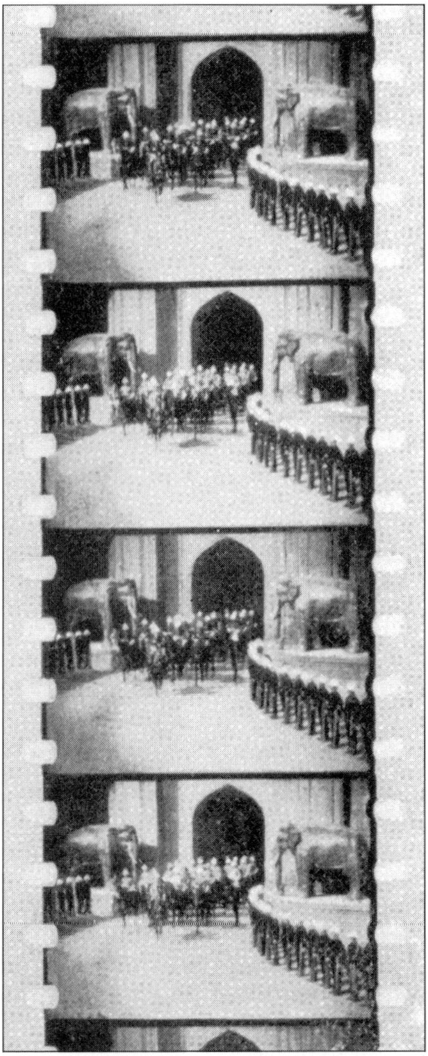

Fig. 5. Film strip from the Kinemacolor film With Our King and Queen through India *(the 'Delhi Durbar'). [Note: Taken from Adrian Klein's* Colour Cinematography *(1936).]*

other experimenters in Brighton and Hove – Davidson, Jumeaux, Grün, Pfenninger – faded from the scene after G.A. Smith's patent of 1906, Friese Greene soldiered on, steadfast in the belief that his own patent of 1905 was the master patent for colour cinematography. This method involved a beam-splitting prism which obtained two pictures of orange-red and blue-green, side by side. The few public exhibitions of this system demonstrated nothing of value, but Friese Greene persisted with it, while simultaneously developing a further system in 1908 which was dependent on successive frames of red, green and blue.

In 1911 a company was registered, Biocolour, by Walter Harold Speer, the manager of a Brighton cinema, the Montpelier Electric Theatre. The intention was to exploit two-colour films made using the prism colour process from Friese Greene's 1905 patent, and the films started to be shown regularly in Brighton.[36] Biocolour started placing advertisements in the trade press declaring itself to be the only perfect natural colour system in the world, claims which led to Urban successfully applying for an injunction to restrain Biocolour from exhibiting its two-colour films, an injunction passed in August 1912. That, however, was not the end of it. Friese Greene had found a wealthy backer to support his claims, Selwyn Francis Edge.

S.F. Edge was a renowned motorist, motor boat racer and cyclist. He belonged to various learned societies, and it was at a meeting of one of these that Friese Greene, an assiduous pursuer of likely investors, told him of the manifest injustice that he was facing. Edge took on the cause with enthusiasm. He formed a new company, Bioschemes, taking over most of the Biocolour shares, with the overall intention of challenging Kinemacolor's perceived monopoly.[37] The fight would go on.

The climax to the years of rivalry, dispute and enmity came in December 1913. Bioschemes petitioned for the revocation of Smith's patent. The validity of the patent was attacked on six grounds: firstly, that Smith was not the 'true and first inventor of the said letters patent'; secondly, that 'the complete specification does not particularly describe and ascertain the nature of the alleged invention nor the manner in which the same is to be performed'; thirdly, that 'the said alleged invention was published within this Realm prior to the date of the said letters patent'; fourthly, that 'the said alleged invention was not new inasmuch as the said alleged invention had been publicly used within this Realm prior to the date of the said letters patent'; fifthly, that 'the said alleged invention was not proper subject-matter of letters patent'; and sixthly, that 'the said alleged invention was not useful'. In short, the patent was not detailed enough, and the invention had been known of and used by others before Smith.[38]

The hearing took place at the Royal Courts of Justice before Mr Justice Warrington on 8–12 December. Urban himself was not called upon to give evidence, but several of those involved in the competition to discover a workable system of colour cinematography prior to 1906 were, most notably Smith, Friese Greene and Grün. Davidson was apparently indisposed, while neither Jumeaux nor Pfenninger were called. Among the witnesses called were James Williamson; Harry Birch, the furniture dealer who had financed Friese Greene on the strength of his 1905 patent; and Leonard Kamm, inventor and vendor of the Kammatograph, the film-less cine camera used by Davidson.

A significant point came early on the second day, when scientists speaking for the Natural Color Kinematograph Company were called upon to give their impressions of Kinemacolor. Professor Sylvanus Thompson said found it 'both wonderful and beautiful'. He nevertheless confessed that he had never seen a satisfactory sky blue.[39] Dr Reginald Clay, however, confessed:

> ... it was not until I actually saw with my own eyes the results that were obtained that I believed it was possible that the eye could be deceived so successfully as this patent shows that it can. I had always been under the impression that you could only distinguish yellow from white when blue was present or absent, and to my surprise I find that undoubtedly one can see both the yellow and the white, and so with other colours, that one had expected three colours to be necessary, for I find that, as far as one can judge in the absence of something to compare them with, one can get a very good deception.

Clay was then asked the question, 'You would not have expected to get blue, but to the ordinary observer, partly because he thinks he is going to see blue or something like it, you get a fair deception?'. He replied, 'I saw an Indian river scene in which the sky was undoubtedly – well, as far as one could judge, blue'.[40] On the judgement of blue, and the understanding of deception, would ultimately rest the whole of Kinemacolor's fortunes.

Friese Greene gave contradictory and sometimes foolish testimony, claiming that his 1905 patent was now worth £50,000. Throughout, the hearing concentrated on the minutiae of who worked for whom, whose ideas influenced the others, and most crucially where did the idea come from that led to Smith's patent. The influence of Grün, and the nexus of activity between Davidson, Jumeaux and Friese Greene was analysed, and a confusing picture arose, as memories played false and wishes turned to certainties. Smith, cool and superior throughout, aimed to appear at a remove from it all.

It was a performance that impressed Justice Warrington. He found Smith to be the true inventor; he found the patent to be sufficiently detailed for the user to put the invention into practice; and other, minor charges similarly failed. The petition for revocation of the patent was therefore dismissed.[41]

Bioschemes appealed, however, and at a hearing in March 1914 Lord Justice Buckley overturned the previous judgement. Buckley found the patent to be imperfectly worded and too imprecise in its language and meaning, and homed in particularly on the concept of a true blue. The patent stated that it would provide 'a practical method by which the well-known animated photographs or bioscope moving picture may be projected in the colours of nature approximately'.[42] Justice Buckley was taxed by the meaning of the word 'approximately', but decided that the patent should mean blue when it meant blue, and not the delusion of blue. He summed up the point ruthlessly:

> The patent is I think invalid because it does not achieve the result which the patentee says it will achieve. The matter may be summarised thus: The patentee says his process will reproduce the natural colours or approximately so. Blue is a colour. He says: Drop the tri-colour blue; do not employ the blue end of the spectrum – blue or approximately blue will still be reproduced. It will not. The patent is consequently invalid.[43]

There is not, and there never could be, a monopoly on colour. This was the assumption that underpinned Kinemacolor, and its arrogance led to the court case that effectively spelled the end of Kinemacolor as a commercial force. Urban appealed against the decision in 1915, and lost, but his Natural Color Kinematograph Company – founded on a worthless patent – had already gone into voluntary liquidation. Friese Greene's victory was short-lived, however, for his Biocolour system was of negligible value, and just one fiction film was made in the process before it became defunct. True, or truer, motion picture colour would emerge elsewhere.

Colour blind

The story of the 'Brighton School' and its quest for natural colour is one of speculation, romanticism, greed, and a lot of blind faith. Adrian Klein writes of the delusions of the pioneers in colour photography:

> It is remarkable how men who have spent a large part of their lives in pioneering colour processes have retained their ability to observe faulty colour reproduction in other processes, but long familiarity with their own process has blinded them to its imperfections; and to sometimes such a degree that they are prepared to swear that brown is green and grey is violet. They are like men in love, who cannot conceive that others may see obvious defects in the supposedly perfect person, or their processes are like old friends whose faults they have long since ceased to be conscious of.[44]

Such blindness is not uncommon in many other fields, of course, but has a particular aptness when considering natural colour and the apprehension of reality. As with Smith's Union Jack of dull greys, they saw the blues that were not there.

The Brighton School existed, therefore, but it was not a school for the discovery of cinematic language. In so far as it was a school, with its pupils learning from each other, sharing, stealing, misreading others' ideas, then its central preoccupation was the perfect apprehension of motion picture reality through colour. It was an idealistic search, and it was a search dominated by the hope of riches. The films that they shot were the antithesis of cinema: static displays of flowers, flags, or children in their Sunday best, displays that hoped to impress the viewer that here was photographic truth at last. And yet there was some connection nevertheless between the cinematic magic of the traditional 'Brighton school', and those that pursued the dream of colour. There was magic in the additive principle itself, creating colour where none would seem to be. Hold up a strip of Kinemacolor film, and all you seen is black and white – run it through the appropriate projector, and the miracle occurs. Klein accuses the inventors of self-delusion, but many ordinary people who saw Kinemacolor believed that it showed that which was natural, the sort of compulsive wish-fulfillment which lies at the heart of cinema.

We who enjoy colour reproduction today so perfect that it has become effectively invisible to us have lost something – that sense of marvel, Charles Urban whooping for joy like a drunken cowboy on a Brighton lawn, when red and green came magically together and brought forth the subject of their quest, natural colour.

Notes

1. Georges Sadoul, *Histoire générale du cinéma: Part 2: Les pionniers du cinéma 1897–1909* (Paris: Denoël, 1948), pp. 155–176.
2. A much later recreation of the experiment (1960) showed that both red filter and ribbon emitted ultraviolet rays, which made an impression on the photographic plate, resulting in an approximately true colour photograph. Jack H. Coote, *The Illustrated History of Colour Photography* (Surbiton: Fountain Press, 1993), pp. 15–16.
3. Frederick Ives, *Handbook to the Photochromoscope* (London: Simpkin Marshall, 1894), quoted in Jack H. Coote, The Illustrated History of Colour Photography (Surbiton: Fountain Press, 1993), p. 29.
4. Colour television, however, is produced additively.
5. British patent no. 6,202 A.D. 1899, 'Means for taking and exhibiting cinematographic pictures', Frederick Marshall Lee and Edward Raymond Turner; D.B. Thomas, *The First Colour Motion Pictures* (London: HMSO, 1969), pp. 4–5, 7; Brian Coe, *The History of Movie Photography* (London: Ash & Grant, 1981), pp. 116–117.
6. G.A. Smith, 'Animated Photographs in Natural Colours', *Journal of the Royal Society of Arts*, no. 2925 vol. LVII, 11 December 1908, pp.70–76.
7. Details of Turner's dealings with Urban can be traced through his papers held as part of the Charles Urban papers, National Museum of Photography, Film and Television, Bradford, URB 6/11.
8. *In the House of Lords, On Appeal, re Letters Patent 26671 of 1906 – Natural Color Kinematograph Company, Limited (in liquidation) v Bioschemes Ltd*, URB 7/2-6, p. 292, cited hereinafter as *Natural Color Kinematograph Company, Limited (in liquidation) v Bioschemes Ltd*. Union Jacks were common subjects for early colour film tests, and Captain Davidson's film of the flag was a key exhibit in the Bioschemes court case.
9. Charles Urban, *Terse History of Natural Colour Kinematography* (New York, 1921), URB 9/1-1, pp. 3–4, now published in *Living Pictures: The Journal of the Popular and Projected Image before 1914*, vol. 2 no. 2 (2003), Special Issue: Colour, pp. 59–68.
10. August 1903 date kindly supplied by Frank Gray.
11. Grün's address is given as Southwick, URB 7/2-2; Davidson lived at 3, White Rock Road, Southwick, and Jumeaux in Colebrook Road, Southwick, URB 7/2-3.

12. Martin Sopocy, *James Williamson: Studies and Documents of a Pioneer of the Film Narrative* (Cranbury, NJ/London: Fairleigh Dickinson University Press, 1998).

13. Frank Gray (ed.), *The Hove Pioneers and the Arrival of Cinema* (Brighton: University of Brighton, 1996), p. 39; John Barnes, *The Rise of the Cinema in Gt. Britain* (London: Bishopsgate Press, 1983), p. 100.

14. Ray Allister, *Friese-Greene: Close-up of an Inventor* (London: Marsland Publications, 1948), pp. 89, 110.

15. Klein, *Colour Cinematography*, pp. 5–6; E.J. Wall, *The History of Three-Color Photography* (Boston: American Photographic Publishing Company, 1925), p. 584; R.B. Foster, *Hopwood's Living Pictures: Their History, Photo-Production, and Practical Working, with Classified Lists of British Patents and Bibliography* (London: The Hatton Press, 1915), p. 262.

16. Klein, *Colour Cinematography*, p. 6.

17. *British Journal of Photography*, 2 March 1900.

18. *Natural Color Kinematograph Company, Limited (in liquidation) v Bioschemes Ltd*, p. 224.

19. John Barnes, *The Beginnings of the Cinema in England 1894–1901: Volume 5: 1900* (Exeter: University of Exeter Press, 1997), p. 125.

20. Laurent Mannoni, 'La Collection des Appareils de Will Day: Machines bizarres et films étrangers, les délices du chercheur', in Michelle Aubert, Laurent Mannoni and David Robinson (eds.), 'The Will Day Historical Collection of Cinematograph & Moving Picture Equipment', *1895* (October 1997), p. 155.

21. *Natural Color Kinematograph Company, Limited (in liquidation) v Bioschemes Ltd*, p. 283. Grün claimed (p. 124) that he first knew Smith around 1894–96, but his vague memory for dates was exposed during the court case. Smith admitted that his memory was dates was equally poor, but he had the documentation of a diary and his cash books to back up his assertions.

22. Mannoni, 'La Collection des Appareils de Will Day', pp. 154–155.

23. *Natural Color Kinematograph Company, Limited (in liquidation) v Bioschemes Ltd*, p. 9. Otto Pfenninger, who assisted Davidson and Jumeaux, says that they first achieved a two-colour record with the Kammatograph in 1902. O. Reg [Otto Pfenninger], *Byepaths of Colour Photography* (London: Percy Lund, Humphries & Co., [1921]), p. 110.

24. [Alfred S. Cory], 'Color Cinematography', *Motion Picture News* vol. 14 no. 18 (4 November 1916), p. 2887, URB 9/4.

25. *Natural Color Kinematograph Company, Limited (in liquidation) v Bioschemes Ltd*, p. 296; Reg, *Byepaths of Colour Photography*, p. 111.

26. Allister, *Friese-Greene*, p. 112; *Natural Color Kinematograph Company, Limited (in liquidation) v Bioschemes Ltd*, p. 177.

27. Klein, *Colour Cinematography*, p. 7.

28. *Natural Color Kinematograph Company, Limited (in liquidation) v Bioschemes Ltd*, p. 174.

29. Reg, *Byepaths of Colour Photography*, p. 111; Brian Coe, *Colour Photography: The First Hundred Years 1840–1940* (London: Ash & Grant, 1978), p. 104; Klein, *Colour Cinematography*, p. 7.

30. *Optical Lantern and Cinematograph Journal*, February 1906, p. 78.

31. *British Journal of Photography*, 27 July 1906.

32. *Natural Color Kinematograph Company, Limited (in liquidation) v Bioschemes Ltd*, pp. 178, 204.

33. In a letter from 1907 to Turner's widow, Smith wrote: 'I often wish that your husband could have lived to take part in the work now it is all so much easier and the German chemists have cleared the way so well by the discovery of sensitising materials. Your husband used to condemn the methods I used to advocate and which I am now making use of – partly I think because they were not in harmony with his patent, but mainly because he knew that the results could never really be true to nature'. G. Albert Smith to Mrs [Edith] Turner, 22 June 1907. Papers of Edward Raymond Turner, URB 6/11.

34. 'Improvements in & relating to Kinematograph Apparatus for the Production of Coloured Pictures', p. 1.

35. The best account remains Thomas, *The First Colour Motion Pictures*. See also Luke McKernan, '"Something More Than a Mere Picture Show": Charles Urban and the Early Non-Fiction Film

in Great Britain and America, 1897–1925', PhD thesis (Birkbeck, University of London: 2003), Chapter 3.

36. Allister, *Friese-Greene*, pp. 137, 144; National Archives BT 31/13680 file 117253, Biocolour Ltd. Speer would later go on to form a film production company in the Brighton and Hove area, Brightonia. Curiously, his other key interest was psychic research, an area in which Smith had considerable experience. Speer wrote two books on the subject, but what he knew of Smith's background in the field is not recorded.

37. Allister, *Friese-Greene*, p. 146; National Archives BT 31/20311 file 118694, Bioschemes Ltd. Bioschemes was short for Bioscope Schemes, and was a nominal holding company only, having paid-up capital of just £31. *The Bioscope*, 18 December 1913, p. 1219.

38. *Natural Color Kinematograph Company, Limited (in liquidation) v Bioschemes Ltd*, p. 346.

39. *Natural Color Kinematograph Company, Limited (in liquidation) v Bioschemes Ltd*, pp. 92–101.

40. *Natural Color Kinematograph Company, Limited (in liquidation) v Bioschemes Ltd*, pp. 104–107.

41. 'In the High Court of Justice, Chancery Division, Royal Courts of Justice 19 December 1913. Before Justice Warrington: In the Matter of Letters Patent No. 26671 of 1906, granted to George Albert Smith, and In the Matter of the Patents and Designs Act, 1907. Petition for Revocation', in *Natural Color Kinematograph Company, Limited (in liquidation) v Bioschemes Ltd*, pp. 345–357; 'An Important Action: Bioscope Schemes, Limited, v. Natural Color Kinematograph Co., Ltd.', *The Bioscope*, 18 December 1913, pp. 1219, 1189; 'Bioscope Schemes, Limited. v. Natural Color Kinematograph Company, Limited: The Petition Dismissed', *The Bioscope*, 25 December 1913, p. 1302.

42. 'Improvements in & Relating to Kinematograph Apparatus for the Production of Coloured Pictures', p. 1.

43. 'In the Supreme Court of Judicature. Court of Appeal, Royal Courts of Justice, Wednesday, 1st April 1914. Before the Master of the Rolls, Lord Justice Buckley, Mr. Justice Channell. In the Matter of G.A. Smith's Letters Patent No. 26671 of 1906 and In the Matter of the Patents and Designs Act 1907', in *Natural Color Kinematograph Company, Limited (in liquidation) v Bioschemes Ltd*, p. 367. An example used by Bioschemes in the appeal was that, if a Kinemacolor film had been taken of a man wearing the blue ribbon of the Order of the Garter, it would have come out green as though he were wearing a decoration of the Hibernian Association. Rachael Low, *The History of the British Film: 1914–1918* (London: George Allen & Unwin, 1950), p. 74.

44. Klein, *Colour Cinematography*, pp. 304–305.

17

The Sensation of the Century: Robert Paul and Film Exhibition in Brighton in 1896/97

Frank Gray

This essay concentrates on film exhibition in Brighton and Hove in 1896–97 and, as such, it only represents the first part of an early film exhibition history of Brighton & Hove that begins with the arrival of the Kinetoscope in 1895 and concludes with the opening of the first purpose-built cinemas in 1909–10. This work has emerged out of my study of film production in these towns in the late Victorian and early Edwardian period (1896–1903) and its examination of the work of the pioneer filmmakers George Albert Smith and James Williamson. My interest in film exhibition is the product of the need to conceptualise the dynamic and holistic relationship between production and exhibition as film culture began to develop in this particular place.[1]

At the end of the Victorian era, Brighton and Hove was a distinctive conurbation of marked social and economic contrasts which hosted a Victorian tourist centre. The twin towns of Brighton and Hove had undergone a radical transformation across the nineteenth century. Brighton began the century with a reputation as a genteel, fashionable royal resort but then it literally exploded after the coming of the railway in the 1840s into a Victorian 'Las Vegas' of hotels, guest houses, theatres, music halls, piers, amusements, an aquarium, restaurants and shops. Over two miles of the seafront was developed to accommodate this 'pleasure world', known as 'London-by-the-sea'. Literally millions of visitors per year visited this centre of amusement and spectacle in the 1890s. In contrast to this familiar identity, Brighton had also developed into a railway town with small-scale manufacturing and a working class community living in densely packed terraced housing in town's centre. Hove was essentially a suburb of Brighton at the end of the century that provided a relatively well designed middle class environment of wide, tree-lined streets and spacious homes. It served as a respite from the energy, diversity and carnival-like environment found next door in Brighton. These towns therefore represent a very useful location for the study of the first years of film exhibition.

1896 was the first year of commercial film projection in Britain and therefore marks the birth of the domestic film industry. It was in this year that Robert Paul demonstrated the commercial viability of the new medium and probably became the most successful British filmmaker and film exhibitor. In Brighton in 1896 his name became synonymous with 'animated photography'. Paul's films were exhibited both here and throughout the country not only by Paul but also by showmen who had either purchased or hired the Paul projector, the 'Theatrograph', and a selection of Paul films. Paul's machine visited over thirty British towns and cities in 1896, often for more than one week and sometimes returning to the same venue for repeat visits. Paul personally supervised many of his London shows (from 25 March 1896 to 28 June, 1897 at the Alhambra and for shorter periods at Olympia and the Canterbury and Paragon Theatres) and the Brighton season (July–November) but the provincial tours were led by independent exhibitors, beginning effectively in July after the London success of his film, *The Derby*.

The film screenings in Brighton in 1896 were mounted by British exhibitors using American, French and British films. Five distinct exhibition contexts have been uncovered in this period: (i) the film programme as a self-contained entertainment; (ii) a film programme within a music hall show; (iii) a film programme as part of a demonstration of photographic and cinematographic apparatus and techniques; (iv) a film programme within a theatrical production; and (v) a film programme attached to a magic lantern show. The remainder of this essay examines these different exhibition practices and positions Robert Paul at the centre of early exhibition in Brighton in 1896/97 due to his film presentations at the Victoria Hall and the Theatre Royal.

The Pandora Gallery

Projection began in Brighton on Wednesday, 25 March 1896 at the Pandora Gallery, two weeks after the initiation of commercial film exhibition in London by the Lumières. This was the first commercial film screening to take place outside of London and it was announced in the press in this confident fashion.

The Talk of London

THE CINÉMATOGRAPH

Opened this day (Wednesday), March 25th

Seances every hour, commencing daily at 11.30am.

Admission 1s; Children Half-price.

Must Be Seen.

The Sensation of the Century'[2]

The Pandora Gallery was in an ideal location for this event. It was located at 132 King's Road, a site directly opposite the entrance of the West Pier and therefore part of the town's tourist centre. The venue had already served as a site for visual spectacle. In 1894, a year when the West Pier had recorded over one million visitors in a twelve month period, it was known as the 'Cyclorama'.[3] Here models and photographs were combined to give a portrait of Palestine and scenes from the life of Christ.[4] By September 1894, the 'sights' of Paris, Switzerland and Italy were added to the Cyclorama.[5] The visitor was encouraged to participate in, 'a trip around the world', by viewing these three dimensional panoramas.[6]

'The Cinématographe' was the name coined by the Lumières for their film camera-printer-projector and used by this French company for its commercial screenings that had begun in London on 9 March 1896. However, the only Brighton newspaper notice and advertisements references found in relation to the Pandora Gallery presentation give no indication that this was a Lumière 'show' and there is also, unfortunately, no mention of either the projectionist or the establishment's Manager. It is however appropriate to suggest that the word, Cinématographe, was used in the Brighton context because it had positive associations with the Lumière machine that had received very enthusiastic reviews in the national media over the previous fortnight.

The only press notice for the Brighton show was equally positive. 'Considering the present scarcity of these machines, Brighton is to be congratulated upon counting the Cinematographe as one of its attractions. The Pandora Gallery, opposite the West Pier, was opened yesterday for the exhibition of this marvellous invention, for the Cinematographe, which is really an improvement on the Kinetoscope, enlarges and projects upon a screen what is, to all appearance, a moving photograph, but, in reality, a series of 'snap-shots' of the same scene passing before the eye at the incredible speed of 900 per minute. The succession of images follow one on the other at such infinitesimal intervals that the effect conveyed to the retina is perfect in its illusion of continuous vitality. The subjects of the pictures, which will be changed weekly, are principally dances, but it is hoped shortly to show the King's-road, the cycle promenade, and other local incidents that will doubtless attract the crowded audience they deserve.'[7]

The words, 'principally dances', are of some significance. Given that Acres, Paul and the Lumières were the only active film producers in Britain in March 1896 and that they had made no notable dance films by this date, it is likely that these were prints from one of the *Annabelle* series, the famous Edison Kinetoscope dance films of 1895 made at West Orange and commissioned by Maguire and Baucus' Continental Commerce Company. This evidence, although slight, suggests that this first film screening in Brighton consisted entirely of Edison films and therefore was American in content and origin.[8] This perception is encouraged by the only other fragment of information on the Pandora film programme. An advertisement for the show from early April 1896 contained the sentence, 'Enormous success of "Trilby". Svengali's Death-Scene to the Life!'[9] This was the Edison film, *Trilby Death Scene*, one of a series of three films produced in May 1895 at the Black Maria and inspired by *Trilby*, George Du Maurier's famous novel of 1894.[10]

There is no evidence that the films of local scenes were made and incorporated into the Pandora programme. However, the statement that such films should be made is of interest. It demonstrates an awareness of the attractiveness to commercial venues of film 'views' relevant to the exhibition site. Here was an understanding that representations of the 'local' could act as a lure to views of the 'other' and the 'foreign', a device not uncommon in magic lantern 'tours' and a future feature of cinema culture. Although not achieved at the Pandora Gallery, local content would play an important role in the other major screenings in Brighton in 1896 and after.

There is continuity between the West Pier's introduction of the Kinetoscope in 1895 and the Pandora Gallery's film screenings of 1896. Both presentations were designed to coincide with the Easter period, and therefore benefit from the Bank Holiday tourism. Like the Kinetoscope, the Pandora show had a run of roughly one month, closing approximately on 21 April 1896.[11] More significantly, it is highly likely that only American Kinetoscope films were also used at the Pandora Gallery. These films were designed to be viewed at approximately forty-six frames per second.[12] However, the Pandora Gallery claimed that its projector operated at a frame rate of 900 frames per minute, a rate of fifteen frames per second. A Kinetoscope film projected at this speed would appear in slow motion. There is no mention of this problem in the press and may easily have not been perceived as one by audiences who were seeing projected films for the very first time. In fact, the use of the word seance in all of the advertisements may have worked to suggest something of the other-worldly nature of this spectacle.

This connotation was emphasised clearly with the addition of X-Rays to the Pandora programme for the Easter weekend of 3–6 April. The new advertisement read as follows.

'SCIENTIFIC SEANCES
Commencing at 3pm and Hourly
THE NEW PHOTOGRAPHY
THE "X" RAYS. THE SURGEON'S SPOTLIGHT
THE CINEMATOGRAPHE
OR VITASCOPE
The latest photo electric sensation.
SEANCES HOURLY, COMMENCING AT 3.
Admission 1s. Children 6d.'[13]

X-Rays, referred to at the time as the 'new photography', had only been announced publicly in January 1896 by Röntgen. He discovered that it was, 'possible to photograph the skeleton of an animal while it is still alive'.[14] From February 1896, advertisements began to appear in the *English Mechanic* for, 'The New Photography – Crookes' Vacuum Tubes for Prof. Röntgen's experiment',[15] and by mid-April the new technology was formally introduced to Brighton by a public presentation described as, 'Professor Röntgen's "X" Rays and Photography of the Invisible. A lecture and a public demonstration of the mysterious powers of the new or invisible light'.[16] To combine X-Rays and film within the same programme was not only an imaginative step but also a recognition that these two 'wonders' represented considerable and significant advances in this new, emerging age of electro-photo-mechanical reproduction.

It is intriguing that the venue was named the Pandora Gallery for the purpose of hosting these, 'scientific seances'. Was this viewing space being likened to Pandora's Box which either contained all the evil or all the good, depending on the interpretation of the tale? How was Pandora, as the first woman in Greek mythology, and meaning 'all giving' in Greek, to be related to this new projection technology? What secrets, mysteries and pleasures would be encountered by purchasing a ticket and entering this dark, interior environment? If there were any contemporary speculations on the meanings of Pandora in this context, they came to an abrupt halt when the Gallery was re-opened for business on 1 July 1896 with a new name – the Victoria Hall. This title provided an unambiguous relationship with the nation's first 'lady' and the corresponding sense of national pride and national achievements. This was very appropriate given that it was to host a new British 'invention' for the next twenty one weeks: Paul's Animatographe.

Paul at the Victoria Hall

For Robert Paul to build upon his London success from March to June 1896 and mount a show in Brighton was a very logical step. As previously stated, Brighton was a thriving Victorian seaside resort and provided varieties and spectacles of a London standard. During the summer and autumn of 1896, hundreds of thousands of visitors passed by Paul's exhibition on Brighton's seafront and could choose to enter as well as bathe in the sea, examine a 'fine specimen of the British shark' at the Aquarium,[17] travel along the seafront on Britain's first electric railway, gaze at the 'Nude Enchantress – the Star Picture of the London Exhibitions',[18] a photographic tableaux of the Matabele War[19] and enjoy Marie Lloyd (the 'Queen of the Music Hall')[20] and the Mohawk Minstrels ('the famous troupe of pseudo-Ethiopians').[21] Paul's 'animated pictures of real life' would appear daily for a season of almost five months in Brighton.[22] The organiser of the first Brighton screening in March had recognised that this venue was an ideal location for this new entertainment and Paul exploited this fact.

R. W. Paul's celebrated
ANIMATOGRAPHE
By Special Permission of Mr Alfred Moul,
General Manager of
The Alhambra Theatre, London.
Exhibition of these Marvellous
ANIMATED PICTURES OF REAL LIFE
Will take place daily at short intervals between
the hours of 11.30am and 10.30pm.
CONSTANT CHANGE OF PICTURES.
Prices – Admission, Sixpence.
Reserved Seats. One Shilling.[23]

This advertisement for Paul's Animatographe, it being an alternate name for his Theatrograph, appeared with little change in the Brighton press from 1 July 1896 to the end of November. For most film audiences, the experience of watching 'moving pictures' in 1896, and for many years to come, took place within the context of an evening of live entertainment. However the Victoria Hall, like the Pandora Gallery, was devoted exclusively to film exhibition. Paul's Brighton programme of at least ten films with musical accompaniment was screened daily, as the press advertisements reveal, 'at short intervals' between the hours of 11.30–10.30, with an admission charge of sixpence and reserved seats at one shilling. The Victoria Hall offered an affordable and unique spectacle. The ticket-holder entered an interior space for the novel and concentrated experience of seeing only projected films. It was very close to what we would call a cinema. Given the sixpence charge to the see the Kinetoscope films on the West Pier in 1895 and the shilling charged to enter the Pandora Gallery at Easter 1896, it can be argued that the sixpence admission for Paul's Animatographe represented an amount which suited the town's tourist economy and enabled this show to be sustained for five months.

For two Brighton newspapers, the *Brighton and Hove Guardian* and the *Brighton Gazette and Sussex Telegraph*, the arrival of the 'Animatographe' was an exciting and magical event and his Derby film was an essential part of the experience.

> Fresh from its triumphs at the London Alhambra, R.W. Paul's marvellous result of the blend of electric force and photography, called the 'Animatographe' has now come to Brighton. [...] We strongly recommend the exhibition to our readers, as upon the whole one of the most surprising ever seen. We presume the word 'Animatographe' means 'animated photographs'. This they are with literal truth, and the verisimilitude with which they reproduce the movement and life of the scenes depicted is nothing less than startling. For instance, there is the famous scene of the Prince's horse Persimmon winning the Derby. When the scene is at first disclosed, all we can see is the clear course, with its vast masses of humanity on either side. But in a moment or two the horses dash into sight and come galloping towards us, Persimmon striding grandly, and St. Frusquin toiling not far behind. In another instant the race is won, and we see crowds surging over the course, men taking off their hats and cheering, and the whole multitude in excitement. Through the throng the last horses in the race make their way as best they can.

The review then paid particular attention to the charms of one of the Brighton 'pictures'. It concluded by saying, 'It is no matter of wonder that this scene used to work up the Alhambra audiences to such a pitch of excitement that it used always to be repeated. [...] our readers must see the show for themselves. They will find it something to talk about for a long while after'.[24]

The bi-weekly newspaper, the *Brighton Gazette and Sussex Telegraph*, also provided a detailed and favourable account of the opening of Paul's show.

> There are few things worth seeing in London which are not, as soon as their success in town is assured, introduced to Brightonians. Reports of the extraordinary effects produced by Mr. R.W. Paul's instrument, the animatographe, now being shown at the London Alhambra, have roused the curiosity of Brightonians to a considerable pitch. [...] A number of ladies and gentlemen accepted invitations to be present at the inaugural exhibition yesterday, when the animatographe was manipulated by the inventor in person. Making allowances for preliminary difficulties, which can easily be met in the future, the performance was remarkably successful. In fact one or two 'scenes' which were put through twice came out much better at the

> second than at the first trial. [...] The entertainment has necessarily to take place in total darkness, but the otherwise weird effect is relieved by music.[25]

Paul's film programmes evolved over 1896 so that each had the potential to contain a mixture of topicalities, general and local actualities, music hall acts, comic scenes and dramas. The current evidence has identified films from all but the last two categories as being part of the screenings at the Victoria Hall in early July. Eight Paul films are clearly identified in these first press reports and the phrase, 'two or three street scenes in London', indicates some of the other films which were used. This would make a programme of at least ten films. The films with specific titles are *The Derby*, *Arrival of the Paris Express*, *The Engineers' Shop at Nelson Dock*, *On Brighton Beach/Party Landing from a Boat on Brighton Beach*, *Entrance to the West Pier*, *Rough Sea at Ramsgate* (either *Rough Sea at Ramsgate (1)* or *(2)*) and 'Conjuring Performance by David Devant' (either *David Devant: The Mysterious Rabbit* or *David Devant: The Egg Laying Man*).[26]

All of the Paul films found in Brighton in early July, with the exception of the Devant film, were produced on location. These exterior subjects reflected Paul's interest in bringing familiar 'views' to the screen, providing audiences with a clear relationship between national content and this new British technology. Here were moving images of work (*The Engineers' Shop at Nelson Dock*), leisure (*On Brighton Beach*, *Entrance to the West Pier*), transportation (*Arrival of the Paris Express*), entertainment (David Devant), a national sporting event (*The Derby*) and aspects of the national visual identity (*Rough Sea at Ramsgate* and the London scenes). The films were back-projected, a common film exhibition mode in 1896, and were not seen in silence as piano accompaniment was an integral part of this show by Paul.[27]

Although we are unaware of the complete programme of Paul films at the Victoria Hall, there were real differences between this work and that seen in all of the previous exhibitions of moving images in Brighton. The Edison films viewed on the Kinetoscopes in Brighton in March and April 1895 and seen at the Pandora Gallery in March and April 1896 were American-made, studio-based and depicted either representations of an everyday working class world, such as *Bar Room Scene*, or performances of popular music hall acts, such as Sandow and Annabelle. Superficially, Paul's scene of labour, *The Engineers' Shop at Nelson Dock*, was similar to the Kinetoscope 'work' films of 1893 but it possessed a crucial difference. Paul's film was shot at the actual Nelson Dock in London and not in a studio. The David Devant film was closest to the Edison concept because it shared the Edison interest in filming popular performers.[28] The Edison programmes in Brighton shared the common and defining theme of the erotic and gendered 'skirt dance'. Such subject matter was not part of Paul's evolving filmic identity either in 1896 or after. Instead, his work reflected his interest in contemporary Britain as represented either through special events or everyday scenes, with *The Derby* of 1896 as his 'signature' text.

Paul and his films contributed to the new and developing European understanding of film production and exhibition. The Cinématographe-Lumière was Paul's great rival in the spring of 1896 and they mirrored each other in terms of both the uses of non-fiction and in the use of a similar film style. For example, Paul's film, *Arrival of the Paris Express*, was clearly inspired by the Lumière work, *Arrivée d'un train à La Ciotat*. Paul's Brighton show followed a programming pattern established in London in March 1896 first by the Cinématographe-Lumière and then followed by David Devant and his own work at the Alhambra Theatre. This French model was a structure of roughly ten to fourteen actualities (everyday scenes) with musical accompaniment. However, there was a major difference between the Lumière and Paul programmes and this was the use of national content. To see a Paul show was to view largely British-made material. With the Lumière presentations, French-made work was predominant until they too realised the importance of producing British content for British audiences. By June 1896, Paul took a further step and begun to place his national 'topicals' into his programmes. These film records of specific and significant national events further emphasised the differences between his work and that of the Lumière's. This was expressed at the Victoria Hall through the use of *The Derby*.

From its British base at the Empire Theatre, London, the Lumière show toured Britain in 1896 but it never visited Brighton. Paul's presence was the likely deterrent. It is likely, however, that at least one Lumière film made its first appearance in Brighton during the brief exhibition of the 'Cinographoscope' in Brighton in September 1896. This was the third exhibition of projected films in Brighton in 1896.[29]

We can safely assume that the general content of Paul's Brighton programme conformed with his other shows across the country in 1896 except in one important detail. To cultivate the Brighton audience, draw attention to the new medium's capabilities and ensure commercial success, Paul made two one-shot local actualities in Brighton to launch his season – a view of the entrance to the West Pier (across the street from the Victoria Hall) and a boat scene filmed on the beach at low tide, some two hundred yards from the Hall. Locally produced films had been promised at the Pandora Gallery but this was never achieved. These two local actualities, *On Brighton Beach* and *Entrance to the West Pier*, provided the visitor to the Animatographe with a clear demonstration of the 'sensational' nature of these animated photographs. These views of the seafront, filmed in close proximity to the front exterior of the Victoria Hall, appear to be the first films made in the town and the first commercially exhibited films of the town. These moving image records of Brighton represented roughly two minutes of familiar activity recognisable to all of the town's visitors and residents. They were the products of a commercial strategy carefully planned and delivered by Paul for the Victoria Hall. It was this showmanship which contributed to Paul's success as an animated photographer in 1896.[30]

Paul would continue to make new films across 1896 and therefore his programme at the Victoria Hall would evolve over its five-month residency. By early August, Paul's films of the Henley Regatta of July 1896 and the music hall performer, G.H. Chirgwin, were noted by the *Brighton Society* as significant additions to this 'wonderful' show.[31]By early November, an article on Paul in the *Brighton Society* was impressed by the international quality of the exhibition as it now included films from the tour of Spain and Portugal as well as *A Comic Costume Race*, *Mr Maskelyne Spinning Plates and Basins*, *Passengers Disembarking from Rothesay Pier*, *Princess Maud's Wedding*, 'a somewhat disastrous *al fresco* tea party (at Shoreham, of all good places in the world)' and the Prince's Derby. Obviously, and like good music hall practice, to incorporate new films into the programme and have them noticed in the press was to encourage the Animatographe's summer audience to make a return visit.[32]

Collings and the Vitagraph

The fourth exhibition of film in Brighton in 1896 opened at the Empire Theatre of Varieties on Monday, 19 October 1896 and continued for three weeks, concluding on Saturday, 7 November 1896.[33] It was called the 'Vitagraph' and this presentation is notable because of three factors: the show was organised and presented by the Brighton photographer Esmé Collings, was part of a music hall programme and featured his first films of Brighton.

Collings was a Hove-based commercial photographer who had been in partnership with William Friese-Greene earlier in the decade. As Barnes has charted, Collings was Brighton's first filmmaker and this show at the Empire was the first public exhibition of his moving pictures.[34]Alfred Darling was a Brighton-based mechanical engineer and his *Work Book* for 1896–97 identifies what probably were his first cinematographic contracts. These all dealt with apparatus he constructed for Collings beginning with a perforator in late September and followed by a printer in early October and a projector in November. Darling provided the technical support which enabled Collings to make, process and exhibit his films.[35]

The Brighton Empire Theatre of Varieties had opened in 1892 with an auditorium in the shape of a horseshoe and seating for 1400. With its decorations, 'in the Louis XV style', and a proscenium, 'ornamented with beautifully wrought trellis-work and picturesque panels, the arms of Brighton surmounting the whole', this was a palace designed to serve popular entertainment.[36]The Empire embodied Brighton's very confident entertainment industry. For this particular show in October 1896, the Vitagraph was the headline act. Films had not been screened at this venue before this occasion but obviously the Empire's management was aware of the medium's successful commercial development across Brighton and Britain since March. Accompanying these animated photographs were ten other acts. The complete programme received this complimentary review from the *Brighton Society*.

'The programme to my mind is a particularly good one. Varied it certainly is, embracing sword swallowing, sensational ladder feats, and the usual variety "turns", to say nothing of the marvellous "Vitagraphe". This was undoubtedly the feature of the evening. You are given pictures with moving figures representing West Street on August Bank Holiday, Hove's Sea Wall during a storm (this was excellent), two pictures representing the Royal Artillery at Aldershot during the late manoeuvres, a Paris Boat scene, showing the boatmen carrying young ladies out to a boat; the Tsar in Paris, Brighton King's Road, boys scrambling for pennies under the West Pier, the Dyke Railway Station, a scene at Gatwick Races, Hyde Park in the morning with the cyclists; and a host of other things.'[37]

One of the Brighton newspapers commented on some of these non-film elements by stating, 'Horace Wheatley was also highly successful with his amusing stories, comic songs, and neat dancing. The Jackson Family repeated their refined musical act and were deservedly applauded. George Mozart, an eccentric comedian, gave an excellent and original turn. [...] The Figaros, International duettists, merit praise.'[38] The complete Vitagraph show was clearly a success, a blend of stage performances with a selection of projected films.

To present a film programme as a self-contained act within a music hall show was the common mode of presentation for film in British towns and cities from March of 1896 to the opening of the first purpose-built cinemas in Britain and Brighton around 1908/09. The Vitagraph show at the Empire initiated this mode of film presentation to Brighton. Film-only presentations, as found at the Pandora Gallery and the Victoria Hall, would continue post-1896 but they would always be the exception to this dominant practice.

This enthusiasm for the Vitagraph at the Empire was shared in early November in a substantial article published by the *Brighton & Hove Guardian*. In it, Collings and Chard, the co-patentee of the Vitagraph, were introduced, the nature of the mechanism was outlined and the author described the pleasure of watching the back-projected images.[39] 'The lights are down ... The linen screen, duly damped, is at the front of the stage, with the green velvet curtains dropped about it; you catch a glimpse of the packed audience, rising in the gallery to a dizzy height; blue tobacco smoke obscures the spectorium, a cork pops in the bar opposite; Mr Trussell (the versatile manager) silk hat in hand, steps back from announcing the picture, and sends a wreath of cigar smoke sailing across the cone of light, and – flick, there is your picture! It is stationary for a second, then – away the people go! Round the corner, up the centre, across the back – the thing lives and almost talks. [...] The shifting, unending rout goes on, and then – flick! away bobs the picture, and an oblong patch of light on the screen faces a house yelling with delight and a gallery whistling like railway engines in a tunnel.'[40]

This advertisement was the key publicity device for the Vitagraph.

EMPIRE THEATRE OF VARIETIES
New Road Brighton
Every Evening at Eight
The Wonder of the Age,
THE VITAGRAPH,
The Talk of the Town.
The most realistic representation of real life and action
Ever yet presented to the Public.
Local Pictures: Train Arriving at Dyke Station;
Boys Scrambling for Pennies Under the Pier;
The Hove Sea Wall in a Gale [41]

The words, 'local pictures', are of particular significance because these films were produced by Collings to appeal to an audience with an existing appreciation and interest in the town. Clearly, Paul and his show at the Victoria Hall had set an important precedent for Collings. By examining the advertisements for and the reviews of the Vitagraph show, eleven films from this programme are named. Barnes identified ten of the eleven as by Collings, with the eleventh, *Cycling in Hyde Park*, as the work of Birt Acres.[42] The five single-shot Brighton films shown at the

Empire (*Train Arriving at Dyke Station*, *Boys Scrambling for Pennies Under the West Pier*, *The Hove Sea Wall in a Gale*, *West Street, Brighton* and *King's Road, Brighton*) were part of a series of eight films of Brighton produced by Collings during the summer of 1896. Although only two films from the Brighton series have survived (*Boys Scrambling for Pennies Under the West Pier* and *Children Paddling*), they possess strong compositions and are engaging examples of how animated photography could be used to represent familiar aspects of the town.[43]

The films of Paris reveal another aspect of Collings' preparations for the Empire. This was his ambition to create 'topicals' which would be as significant as Paul's Derby and the Lumière films of the Tsar Nicholas II's coronation of June 1896. The Collings film, *Tsar in Paris*, was produced during the visit of the Tsar to Paris from 6–8 October and launched in Brighton at the Empire on 19 October.[44] This was a concerted attempt to record this news event for the Vitagraph show. Unfortunately, the Brighton press reports did not emphasise this work and it was not a focus of the Empire's advertising campaign. This suggests that Collings had either misjudged the popular interest in the Russian Tsar or that the film was poor in quality. The focus for the Brighton media, as mentioned, was on the 'local pictures'. Collings and the Vitagraph would return to the Empire for a week in early 1897.[45] After this date, there is no evidence of Collings being active in the advancement of animated photography either in Brighton or elsewhere.

Collings' value to the nascent film culture of Brighton and Hove in 1896 was immense because he was the first active filmmaker and film exhibitor to be a resident. His work, we can argue, built upon Paul's success by making tangible the process of film production in a local context. It's hard to imagine that Collings, as a photographer and a filmmaker, was not involved in some capacity in the inaugural exhibition of the Hove Camera Club at the Hove Town Hall. Here from 19–21 November was a display of lantern slides, 'platinotype developing', X-Rays and the cinematograph.[46] This was the fifth exhibition of film in Brighton & Hove in 1896 and the first in Hove. Information on the films screened has not been found but two facts are significant. James Williamson was the Club's Honorary Treasurer and he is named as responsible for the display of the cinematograph at the Exhibition.[47] This is the earliest published reference to Williamson in relation to film and marks, therefore, the beginning of an interest which would transform his life.

Paul at the Theatre Royal

At the end of 1896, Paul's Theatrograph returned to Brighton and the Christmas season in order to become a part of the Theatre Royal's pantomime, *The Babes in the Wood and Robin Hood*. After the adventures of Robin, Marian, Friar Tuck, the Queen of the Glow-Worms, Father Time, Rustics, the 'electric-eyed frogs and robins' and an aerial ballet, came the penultimate scene.[48] It was called, 'the abode of time'. This was where Paul's projector was introduced and, 'a series of living pictures presented with such realism as to evoke the most enthusiastic of applause'. These included the 1896 Derby and one of the Brighton scenes. To conclude the evening a tribute, with the title 'Victoria's United Empire', was presented. A contemporary review described it as, 'a gorgeous display descriptive of Imperial Federation, and introducing representatives of Australia, Canada, Africa, India, Ireland, Wales, Scotland and Britannia, while, at the rear of the brilliantly lighted scene, sat one representing her Majesty the Queen. A burst of enthusiastic applause rang through the house, the whole audience rising on their feet and applauding again and again ...'.[49] This was a very appropriate finale given that the nation was on the eve of the Queen's Diamond Jubilee of 1897.

The Theatre Royal was Brighton's oldest and most distinguished theatre, specialising in the 1890s in hosting major touring productions of classical and contemporary drama and producing an annual Christmas pantomime. It had opened in 1807 and had undergone major refurbishments in 1894, including the introduction of electric lighting. The Theatre proclaimed in early January 1897 that it was very proud of *The Babes in the Wood and Robin Hood* because of its great popularity with audiences. It described it as a, 'Huge Success: Acknowledged to be the best Pantomime ever seen in Brighton. Playing to Record Houses. Beautiful Scenery. Magnificent Costumes. Extraordinary Dances. Aerial Ballet. Theatrograph. Golden Shower',[50] and, 'Beating all Records for Pantomime Business in the History of the Theatre Royal'.[51] This was a perfect showcase for Paul and his films as it was an opportunity to integrate his 'time machine' into a fairytale world constructed out of traditional and electrical stagecraft and defined by a very particular sense of wonder and spectacle. The Theatrograph's appearance, in this context, emphasised its emergence as a new technology and a new magic and demonstrated that it was robust enough to participate in nine live performances per week for roughly seven weeks (end of December 1896 to mid-February 1897). Its magical nature may well have been enhanced through the use of back projection. Disguising the means of projection from the audience would have created, in this pantomime setting, the illusion of the moving images being conjured out of the ether. In 1896, in Britain, no other instance has been found of film being incorporated into a Christmas pantomime.

Particular attention was placed by the Theatre Royal on the significance of the film programme to the production as advertisements began to detail the precise contents of Paul's contribution.

'The Theatrograph – More realistic
Animated Pictures, carefully selected from Mr R.W. Paul's original series of over sixty subjects.
Constant change. The pictures now being exhibited include:
1. Up the River (July 1896)
2. Children at Play
3. A Brighton Beach Scene
4. Steamship "Columba" Leaving Rothsay Pier
5. Blackfriars Bridge
6. The Gordon Highlanders Leaving Mary Hill Barracks, Glasgow (August 1896)
7. Twin's Tea Party
8. A Fire Brigade Call (London)
9. The Soldier's Courtship

10. Sea Cave on the Coast of Galicia
11. Music Hall Sports (Comic Costume Race)
12. The Prince's Derby, 1896
Lavishly Applauded at Every Performance'[52]

This list is the most comprehensive published record of films screened in a single Paul programme in Brighton in 1896–97. It is significant because all of the other descriptions of Brighton screenings in 1896 offer only a partial list of the presented films. The Paul programme for the Theatre Royal, as advertised, falls into four categories: drama (*Up the River*), actualities shot in Brighton (*A Brighton Beach Scene*), London (*Blackfriars Bridge*, *A Fire Brigade Call*), Scotland (*The Gordon Highlanders Leaving Mary Hill Barracks, Glasgow*, *Steamship 'Columba' Leaving Rothsay Pier*), and Portugal (*Sea Cave on the Coast of Galicia*), comic scenes (*Children at Play*, *Twin's Tea Party*, *The Soldier's Courtship, Music Hall Sports*) and a single topicality (*The Prince's Derby*). This carefully balanced mixture of fiction and non-fiction films reveals a programming sensibility designed to exploit the different uses of film and the corresponding need to appeal to a broad, popular audience. It also marks the fact that Paul had not stood still since his first show in Brighton in July. Paul, by the end of 1896, had developed a very clear understanding of the evolving relationship between film production and film exhibition. The advertisement also suggests that the order in which the films are listed is the order in which they were screened. This positions the 1896 Derby film as the programme's concluding work and confirms not only Paul's sense of its particular cultural and commercial significance but also its continuing allure for contemporary viewers in early 1897. By the end of 1896, Paul's understanding of a film programme was very different from the more parochial strategy employed by Collings in Brighton in October. As examined earlier, Collings had relied almost exclusively on the use of local non-fiction material. This may account, in part, for Collings' short life as a film producer and exhibitor.

Film and the lantern

Although Paul was not a magic lanternist before the emergence of film, he clearly drew upon this earlier screen practice for the design of his film programmes. Contemporary lanternists in a single show, especially for children, would use series of slides drawn from fairy tales, mythology, the Bible, comic stories, travelogues, dissolving views, current conflicts (such as the Boer War from 1899) and personalities. The use by lanternists of such a repertoire of visual narratives drawn from different genres and subjects, with accompanying oral commentaries, provided Paul with an understanding of how to organise a projected entertainment.

George Albert Smith, the mesmerist, lanternist and astronomer, managed a pleasure garden in Hove in mid-1890s. In 1896 and 1897, he presented lantern lectures in Brighton which used travel as their narrative concept. At the Brighton Aquarium for the week starting Monday, 29 March 1897, Smith presented three lantern lectures which were very distinctive because each concluded with a presentation of his own films. This was Smith's first public exhibition of his own 'animated photographs' of local scenes and the first record of film being incorporated into a lantern lecture in Brighton. The *Sussex Daily News* described one of his lectures in this manner.

'Last evening Mr G. Albert Smith, FRAS, gave the first of what will unquestionably prove to be a thoroughly instructive course of lectures, taking a large audience through a charming pictorial tour of "Our Glorious Empire". Mr Smith has a happy way of dealing with his subject, and was a most agreeable and indeed fascinating guide on an imaginary exploration of the Queen's Colonies, possessions, and defences in all quarters of the globe, his remarks being plentifully illustrated by a series of beautifully executed dissolving views. At the close of the lecture there was a realistic display of animated photographs, in which local representations played a prominent part. The pictures opened with a Bank Holiday scene on the lower Esplanade just opposite West Street, and included a capital reproduction of an animated scene on King's Road, while towards the close there was a very true photograph of the arrival of a train at Hove and its departure for Brighton.'[53]

From January 1897 Smith had begun to establish what he called his 'film factory' within the grounds of the pleasure garden in Hove. From this base he created one of the country's first film processing works and began to make his own films. This exhibition in March 1897 marked the first public representation of his interest in cinematography. The exhibition practice of the combined magic lantern–film show would have some success in the early period but it would never have the prominence of the film-only programmes designed for music hall and fairground use.

Paul's vision

Paul's success in 1896 and 1897 was the result of his exploitation of an innovatory medium through the sale of his projector and the exhibition of his pleasing and essentially optimistic films. The publication of Paul's advertisement for the creation of the new company to be known as, 'Paul's Animatographe, Limited', was dramatic evidence of Paul's business confidence. The advertisement, which in fact was the abridged prospectus, was over 1000 words in length and began with the astonishing declaration that from March 1896 to March 1897 his business had, 'yielded a Nett Profit of £12,838 15s. 4d., on a capital of about £1000, or 1,200 per cent'. The prospectus invited potential shareholders to participate in this new company which had the potential, it claimed, to make £30,000 profit in the next financial year through the, 'Manufacture and Sale of Animatographes and Accessories', 'Manufacture and Sale of Animated Portraits of Individuals', 'Animated Advertisements' and, 'Exhibitions of Animatographes and Travelling Shows'. On the same day, 24 April 1897, the advertisement appeared in two national publications, the music hall weekly *The Era*, and the London business weekly *The Economist*, and one local newspaper, the *Brighton Herald*.[54] It dominated this Brighton newspaper's front page and was accompanied by a complimentary article on the new company's favourable prospects on its back page. This was Paul, the inventor and entrepreneur, taking the next public step in the development of his film business and targeting Brighton as a likely source of financial support. Unfortunately, for Paul, this was a premature act. His proposed company never traded because of a poor response to the prospectus. Clearly, his confidence was not shared in the marketplace.

However, the failure of his new company was not an obstruction to Paul's development as a major figure in the British film business over the next decade. The very appearance of the Paul prospectus drew real attention to the viability of film production and exhibition as a profitable capitalist enterprise and must have further inspired the few who were encouraged by Paul's example to enter this new field. Animated photography, as Paul's prospectus asserted, was, 'one of the greatest attractions the world of amusement has ever had and it is enjoying a phenomenal success', it was a medium with, 'great possibilities', and this was the moment, 'to develop the resources of the invention, and to extend its present lucrative field of operation'.[55] For the first generation of British filmmakers and film exhibitors, a group which includes the Hove residents G.A. Smith and James Williamson, Paul in 1896 and 1897 had demonstrated the viability of film as a cultural and commercial form.

Notes

1. The history of film exhibition in Britain before the First World War has still not been systematically mapped and analysed. Low was the first empirical scholar to explore this territory in the late nineteen-forties and in more recent years Barnes, Hiley and Toulmin have made important contributions to this area of study. See: Rachael Low & Roger Manvell, *The History of the British Film 1896–1906* (London: George Allen & Unwin, 1948); John Barnes, *The Beginnings of the Cinema in England 1894–1901, Vols. 1–5* (Exeter: University of Exeter Press, 1996–98); Nicholas Hiley, 'At the Picture Palace: the British Cinema Audience, 1895–1920', in John Fullerton (ed), *Celebrating 1895: The Centenary of Cinema* (Sydney: John Libby, 1998): 96–103; Vanessa Toulmin, 'Local Films for local people: Travelling Showmen and the Commissioning of Local Films in Great Britain, 1900–1902', *Film History*, vol. 13, 2001: 118–137.
2. Advertisement, *Brighton & Hove Guardian*, 25 March 1896: 1.
3. The Brighton West Pier Company announced in October 1894 that, 'the total number of visitors for the year ending on 31 August was 1,021,878'. This was highest figure recorded in twenty two years. ['A Million Visitors to the Brighton West Pier', *Brighton Herald*, 13 October 1894: 3.]
4. 'Palestine at Brighton', *Argus*, 24 July 1894: 2.
5. Advertisement, *Brighton Examiner*, 21 September 1894: 4.
6. Advertisement, *Brighton Examiner*, 9 November 1894: 4.
7. 'A Novelty at Brighton', *Sussex Daily News*, 26 March 1896, p. 6.
8. There was a strong commercial logic in signalling the presence of this particular film genre within the Pandora Gallery's programme as contemporary 'Skirt Dancing', as influenced by Loie Fuller, was already a popular attraction in Brighton's music halls. For example, during the run of the Pandora Gallery show, the Alhambra Music Hall in Brighton featured Jenny Mills and her 'luminous dance'. [Advertisement and notice: 'The Alhambra', *Brighton & Hove Guardian*, 15 April 1896: 1 and 8.]
9. Advertisement, *Sussex Daily News*, 4 April 1896: 1.
10. Charles Musser, *Edison Motion Pictures, 1890–1900: An Annotated Filmography* (Washington DC: Smithsonian Institution Press, 1997): 187–188.
11. This is the last day on which the Pandora advertisement appeared in the *Brighton & Hove Guardian*, having featured continuously on this newspaper's front page since 25 March 1896.
12. William Kennedy Laurie Dickson and Antonia Dickson, 'Edison's Invention of the Kineto-Phonograph', *The Century Magazine*, London, vol. 26, no. 2, June 1894: 208. American films produced for projection at the slower speed of approximately 15–18 frames per second were not available in the UK in March 1896.
13. Advertisement, *Sussex Daily News*, 3 April 1896: 1.
14. Alfred Porter, 'The New Photography', *The Strand*, London, vol. 12, July to December, 1896: 107.
15. Advertisement, *English Mechanic*, vol. 62, no. 1611, 7 February 1896: vi.
16. Advertisement, *Brighton Herald*, 4 April 1896: 4.

17. Advertisement for the Brighton Aquarium, *Brighton Herald*, 18 July 1896: 4.
18. Advertisement, *Brighton & Hove Guardian*, 8 July 1896: 1.
19. Advertisement for the Empire Theatre of Varieties, *Sussex Daily News*, 18 August 1896: 1.
20. Advertisement for the Brighton Alhambra, *Sussex Daily News*, 20 July 1896: 1.
21. 'The Mohawk Minstrels on the West Pier', *Brighton Herald*, 18 July 1896: 5.
22. The Paul show at the Victoria Hall commenced on 1 July 1896 and appears to have concluded in the week of 21 November 1896. ['The Animatographe at Brighton', *Brighton Gazette and Sussex Telegraph*, 2 July 1896: 6; advertisement for the Victoria Hall, Brighton Society, 21 November 1896: 8.]
23. Advertisement for the Victoria Hall, *Brighton & Hove Guardian*, 8 July 1896: 1.
24. 'The Animatographe in Brighton', *Brighton & Hove Guardian*, 8 July 1896: 6.
25. 'The Animatographe at Brighton', *Brighton Gazette and Sussex Telegraph*, 2 July 1896: 6.
26. The 'two or three street scenes in London' could be *Westminster*, *Blackfriars Bridge* and *Hampstead Heath on Bank Holiday*. Barnes lists and describes all of these films at the Victoria Hall except for *Entrance to the West Pier* which is identified in, 'The Animatographe at Brighton', *Brighton Gazette and Sussex Telegraph*, 2 July 1896: 6. [John Barnes, *The Beginnings of the Cinema in England 1894–1901, Vol. 1* (Exeter: University of Exeter Press, 1998): 246–261.]
27. An article on Paul from the *Brighton Society* described the wet, translucent screen. '... and down the vista, in silhouette against the screen (illuminated faintly from the public room beyond) stood a bucket and a syringe with which Mr. Henton presently "damped" the curtain'. It also identified a Miss Kesteven as the pianist for the Paul screenings. The following sentence from the article suggests that her music for the films consisted of complimentary popular melodies. 'A sight of Princess Maud's wedding procession leaving Marlborough House roused the invisible audience to such an unwonted applause that Miss Kesteven's "Wedding March" was nearly drowned'. Paul filmed this wedding on 22 July 1896. ['The Animatrographe', *Brighton Society*, 7 November 1896: 7.]
28. David Devant (1868–1941) was Britain's leading magician in the 1890s, known for his residency at the Egyptian Hall. Devant's first visit to the South East with his show of magic and Paul's films was staged in Folkestone in July 1896. His first visit to Brighton & Hove, with a version of this production, followed in October 1897. [Advertisement for the Town Hall, Folkestone, *Folkestone Herald*, 11 July 1896: 8; advertisement for the Town Hall, Hove, *Brighton & Hove Guardian*, 10 November 1897: 1.]
29. The exhibition of the 'Cinographoscope' opened around 19 September 1896 at the Imperial Hotel, Queens Road, Brighton, and continued until the end of that month. The *Brighton Gazette and Sussex Telegraph* described it in this manner. 'It has been brought from Paris to this country, and Brighton has been selected as the first town in which to exhibit the new discovery. The advantage of the Cinographoscope is that it works the pictures not only forwards but backwards. . . . Among the list of pictures shown may be mentioned the 'Palace d'Opera, Paris', 'The Sea and the Rocks', 'A Gay Spark Coming Home Vexed' and a 'Pantomime by the Clowns Haydon Bros'. Backwards projection was a feature common to most projectors in 1896. Rittaud-Hutinet lists a Lumière film with the title, *Paris, place de l'Opéra*. This may well be the same film as presented on the Cinographoscope. ['The Cinographoscope', *Brighton Gazette and Sussex Telegraph*, 19 September 1896: 5; Jacques Rittaud-Hutinet, *Auguste et Louis Lumière: Les 1000 premieres films* (Paris: Philippe Sers Editeur, 1990): 159 (film no. 154).]
30. These first films of Brighton are 'missing, presumed lost'. The Paul film, *On Brighton Beach*, is listed by Barnes and is described by the *Brighton & Hove Guardian* as, 'The scene is the beach, and we see a small boat coming in to land at rather low water and with evidently a high wind blowing, judging from the tension of the flag, which floats in the stern of the little craft. The boat cannot be hauled quite out of the water, and boatmen go down and haul the passengers to dry land on their shoulders. First the ladies are brought to shore amid great laughter; then the gentlemen, and as one of them is borne towards us we see him laughing and waving his walking stick triumphantly.' Unfortunately, the film which is in the NFTVA and is named as Paul's *Scene on Brighton Beach* is not this work. This preserved film is of 1896/97, may be by Paul, was filmed in roughly the same location and features an incoming pleasure boat but it lacks all of the action described in the newspaper account. [John Barnes, *The Beginnings of the Cinema in England*

1894–1901, Vol. 1 (Exeter: University of Exeter Press, 1998): 253; 'The Animatographe in Brighton', *Brighton & Hove Guardian*, 8 July 1896: 6.]

31. 'There are some new features in connection with the Animatographe ... The whole exhibition, however, is a wonderful one', [*Brighton Society*, 1 August 1896: 9.] Barnes lists two films shot at Henley from 7–9 July and two films of Chirgwin. [Barnes, vol. 1 (1998): 248, 251–253.]
32. 'The Animatrographe', *Brighton Society*, 7 November 1896: 7.
33. 'Brighton Empire', *Evening Argus*, 20 October 1896: 2; 'last day', advertisement for the Empire, *Brighton Gazette & Sussex Telegraph*, 7 November 1896: 1.
34. We still know very little about Collings' life and career both before and after 1896. In the Barnes Collection at Hove Museum & Art Gallery there are studio and landscape photographs by Collings and studio portraits from the Collings & Friese-Greene Studio. Barnes' research into his filmmaking activities in the 1890s is very valuable and the *High Society* exhibition at the National Portrait Gallery of 1998 indicated Collings' place within Edwardian photography. [Barnes, vol. 1 (1996) and vol. 2, (1998); Terence Pepper, *High Society: Photographs 1897–1914* (London: National Portrait Gallery, 1998: 72–73, 90.]
35. The Darling *Work Book* (in the collection of Hove Museum & Art Gallery) is unpaginated.
36. David Adland, *Brighton's Music Halls* (UK: Baron Birch for Quotes, 1994): 33–34.
37. 'The Man About Town', *Brighton Society*, 31 October 1896: 17.
38. 'Brighton Empire', *Evening Argus*, 20 October 1896: 2.
39. Barnes identifies George Henry Chard and Julius Peschek of London as the patentees of the projector used at the Empire and known as Chard's Vitagraph. This Brighton show initiated an English tour of the Vitagraph in late 1896. [Barnes, vol. 1 (1998): 183–190.]
40. 'Out with the Vitagraph Man. On the Prowl for Pictures', *Brighton & Hove Guardian*, 4 November 1896, p. 2.
41. Advertisement for the Empire Theatre of Varieties, *Brighton Society*, 24 October 1896, p. 8.
42. Barnes, vol. 1 (1998), pp. 261–265.
43. *Boys Scrambling for Pennies Under the West Pier* (NFTVA); *Children Paddling* (Will Day Collection at the Centre National de la Cinématographie, Paris). *Scene on Brighton Beach* (see note 31) may be the work of Collings as its composition and location are very similar to *Children Paddling*.
44. Five Lumière films of the Parisian elements of the Russian royal tour of France are listed by Rittaud-Hutinet as nos. 163–167. [Jacques Rittaud-Hutinet, *Auguste et Louis Lumière: Les 1000 premieres films* (Paris: Philippe Sers Editeur, 1990): 159.]
45. Advertisement for the Empire Theatre of Varieties, *Sussex Daily News*, 11 January. 1897: 1.
46. Advertisement, *Sussex Daily News*, 20 November 1896: 1.
47. 'The Hove Camera Club', *Brighton & Hove Guardian*, 25 November 1896: 7.
48. Advertisement for the Theatre Royal, *Sussex Daily News*, 9 January 1897: 1.
49. 'Brighton Theatre Royal. The Christmas Pantomime', *Argus*, 28 December 1896: 8. In this review, the Argus identified ten films in this presentation: 'The pictures given were "Brighton Beach", "The steamship *Columbia* leaving the Harbour", Blackfriars Bridge", "Sea Bathing", "The Twins' Tea Party", "Fire Brigade Call", "The Soldier's Courtship", "Sea Cave", "Music Hall Sports" and the "Derby of 1896"'.
50. Advertisement for the Theatre Royal, *Brighton Herald*, 2 January 1897: 3.
51. Advertisement for the Theatre Royal, *Sussex Daily News*, 9 January 1897: 1.
52. Advertisement for the Theatre Royal, *Sussex Daily News*, 9 January 1897: 1.
53. 'Brighton Aquarium', *Sussex Daily News*, 30 March 1897: 2
54. The advertisements for the Paul prospectus: *The Era*, 24 April 1897: 8; *The Economist*, 24 April 1897, in; 'Public Notice. Paul's Animatographe Limited', *Brighton Herald*, 24 April 1897: 1. Article on the Paul prospectus: 'The Development of the Animatographe', *Brighton Herald*, 24 April 1897: 8.
55. 'Public Notice. Paul's Animatographe Limited', *Brighton Herald*, 24 April 1897: 1.

18

Film and Postcards – Cross Media Symbiosis in Early Bamforth Films

Richard Brown

Historians of early cinema have traditionally linked communication in late Victorian films with the development of narrative construction, in particular, shot-placement, and have seen the advance of both in purely linear terms. Similarly, film length, especially in the case of fiction film has usually been correlated to the relative effectiveness of early film to communicate a theme or story-line.[1] Neither of these approaches are incorrect, but they are rather simplistic and one dimensional, for in choosing to focus on one area only, the possibility of parallel communicative developments occurring independently of narrative film construction has not been explored.[2]

The Bamforth company's preference for featuring 'well known local characters' in their lantern slide sequences, films and postcards, must be regarded as a significant factor resulting in their work being produced not just for, but in active co-operation with their local community. It is indeed possible that the community as much as the filmmaker influenced both the choice and the treatment of some fictional subjects. In these circumstances 'narrative' between filmmaker and audience must be considered in a multi-dimensional sense, and for this reason the selected titles chosen for analysis in this account have been examined from a number of different perspectives in order to test their relative effectiveness. In addition, since early Bamforth audiences should be regarded as participatory in the exhibition process rather than merely passive, their social class, group values and political and religious beliefs are important in any reception study.

Such a highly personalised relationship inevitably affected contemporary perceptions. A particularly illuminating comment, published in March 1899, noted of local audiences that:

> These critics are strong realists. They at once recognise a 'real policemen' and like him much better than the policeman of the opera stage or artists studio... Policeman can always be borrowed in their own uniforms, by arrangement.[3]

Effective communication, based directly on an intimate knowledge of their audience enabled Bamforth's to introduce both social comment and moralistic messages into their films, and it is the recovery of some at least of these elusive communicative processes that is the purpose of the present account. An important resource, are the postcards the company produced, which, in a number of cases, can inform our understanding of the films in ways which are not otherwise accessible.[4]

Historical background

Despite a relatively late arrival to filmmaking and an output that was modest even by late 1890s standards, the collection of early Bamforth films now preserved in the National Film and Television Archive represent a most interesting example of late 19th century British regional film production. A number of the films made in the small West Yorkshire town of Holmfirth have been recognised for some time as internationally important landmarks in the development of film technique. Moreover, this closely integrated group of films is surrounded and contextualised by an exceptional and perhaps unique set of characteristics. Unlike the usual heterogeneous collection of inventors, showmen, and 'get-rich-quick' adventurers who were attracted into the British Victorian film business, Bamforth's brought to film production many years experience in staging 'live model' work for magic lantern slides, and in developing connected narratives for these performances.[5]

As an example of provincial filmmaking rather than the more usual London based production, it will be suggested that a number of the films contain an identifiable and specific regional perspective, and that this was, intentionally, a centrally important feature in the filmmakers objective of communicating effectively with his audience. The collection has a known provenance, being an example of a group of films commissioned by one company from another. Furthermore the emphasis on fictional subjects found in this group of films is most unusual for the period, when non-fiction or actuality subjects predominated. Perhaps most importantly – due to family preservation – the survival rate for prints measured against contemporary references is extremely high, thus enabling inter-group comparisons and conclusions to be more confidently suggested than would normally be the case with films of this period.

Cecil Wray, an electrical engineer from Bradford was a central figure in the introduction of the Edison Kinetoscope, (and R.W. Paul's copies of it), to the West Yorkshire area during late 1894/early 1895.[6] Wray immediately recognised the commercial advantage that projected film offered to the exhibitor and initially tried to adapt a Kinetoscope for this purpose.[7] This was no doubt an unsuccessful experiment, but when projected film became common in 1896, Wray soon developed his own 'Kineoptoscope' projector, which, as John Barnes has noted was 'designed to fit into the slide stage of a standard optical lantern in the same manner as a mechanical lantern slide'[8] The patent that Wray took out on this machine was sold late in the same year to Riley Brothers, another Bradford based company specialising as lantern suppliers and outfitters. They are known to have marketed a Kineoptoscope camera from June 1897, and to have taken a number of local films during 1897 and 1898. By 1898 they were offering either to sell or rent – (the date is significant in the latter case) – films to purchasers of their projectors,[9] and it was no doubt their wish to build an exclusive range of films which they could offer to their customers that led them into film production.

Due to the nature of their business, Riley's would undoubtedly have known of, and quite possibly traded with, the Bamforth company for the supply of glass slides long before either company had developed a connection with cinematography. It seems that Riley's recognised Bamforth's superiority in staging sequences and as far as is known they never produced any fiction films themselves. They appointed the London-based Warwick Trading Company as their distributors, and Warwick included a selection of their actuality subjects, together with at least one Bamforth film – *Weary Willie in the Park* in a catalogue supplement they issued in December 1898. In 1903, under a 'RAB' (Riley and Bamforth) heading, a selection of films was included in a Hepworth catalogue. When this rather involved background history is considered, it can be seen that for various historical reasons – some planned and some accidental – Bamforth films today present a researcher with dauntingly complex problems of source identification, nomenclature, and dating.

Dating problems and the role of the postcards

The production of Bamforth postcards related to the films was perhaps originally simply an economical business strategy designed to repackage the same product in order to reach another market. It should be noted that Bamforth's were not the only Victorian film producing company to run a postcard business in conjunction with their film production activities. The British Mutoscope and Biograph company also had a studio which produced a large number of cards mainly of theatrical celebrities. However, the vast majority of the Biograph cards are unrelated to the films the company produced, and even those that are connected are of no assistance in analysing the films. By contrast, Bamforth film-related cards are few in number, but it will be suggested, of very considerable importance in facilitating an understanding of the social context within which the films were made. Related cards have been found for *The Kiss in the Tunnel, Women's Rights*, *Wet Paint*, and *The Tramp and the Baby's Bottle*; and there may be of course be further examples where the link has not yet been recognised.

The postcards relating to *Women's Rights* and *Wet Paint* are the most interesting and important, since they not only illustrate a sequence of six photographs presenting the thematic development of the films concerned, but also contain a contemporary text designed to personalise the images, and to explain the situation comedies being presented. This is a unique feature of Bamforth cards/films predating the widespread use of inter-titles, and providing an authentic contemporary epitome of the commentary that a 'lecturer' would have used. In these few cases, Bamforth postcards can provide an important key to the elusive communicative process operating between the filmmaker and his audience. Because virtually nothing was written down about this subject at the time, it is today perhaps the least understood area of all in the study of early film history. In fulfilling this function the cards open up further areas for film historians to explore.

Due to the absence of primary production documentation, there has been considerable uncertainty for many years in establishing accurate dating for the early Bamforth films, with 1898, 1899 and 1900, all being suggested as correct by various film historians. Utilising evidence contained within the films, on the postcards, and in contemporary published accounts, it is hoped that a more accurate schedule can now be attempted. On the subject of dating in general it should be

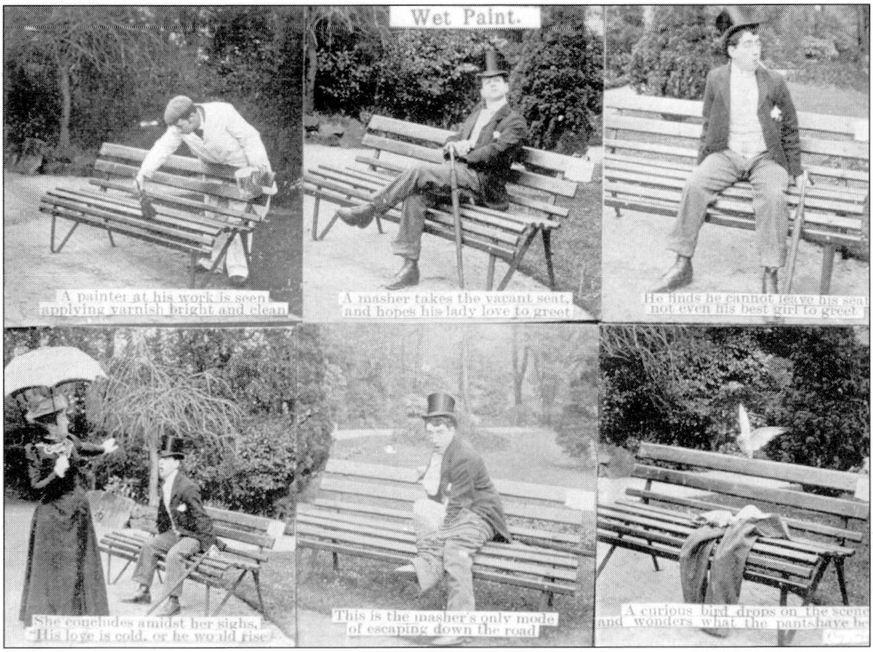

Fig. 1. 'Wet Paint' – photographic postcard, c.1898.
[All photographs are from the Bamforth Company, Holmfirth, from the Collection of Kirklees Community History Service.]

noted that on the basis of research independently carried out by both John Barnes and the author, there is no contemporary evidence to be found for any Bamforth fiction films being taken in either 1899 or 1900.[10] On the contrary, at least one film previously assigned to the latter date can now be proved to have been made much earlier. It is unfortunate, and rather surprising, that although Holmfirth had its own weekly paper by the late 1890s, very few references can found to film despite the fact that several long and very interesting accounts of the company were published during 1899.[11] This directs attention to 1898, and there would seem to be a good factual and circumstantial case for suggesting that, with one exception, all the Bamforth fiction output was taken during that year, as one would indeed expect to have been the case if commissioned as a group by Riley's. It is the postcard record of a now 'lost' film, *Wet Paint*, which pro-

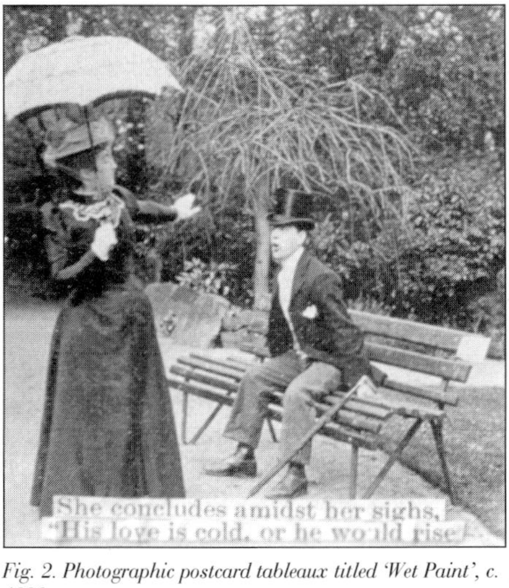

Fig. 2. Photographic postcard tableaux titled 'Wet Paint', c. 1898.

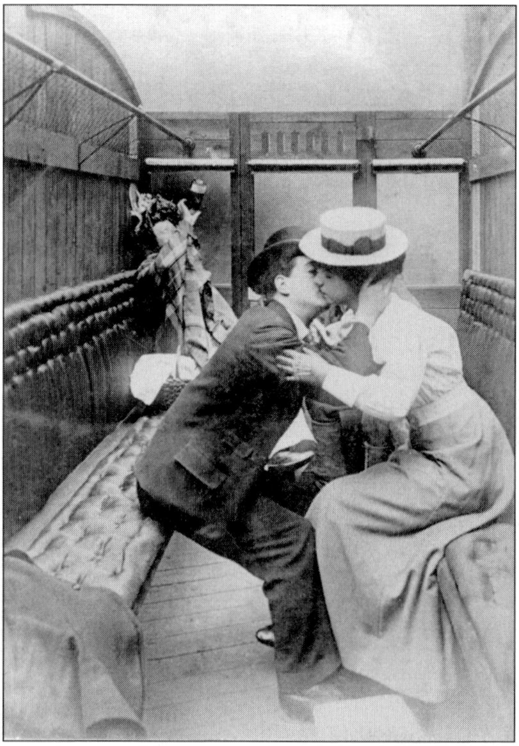

Fig. 3. Photographic postcard titled 'In the Tunnel', c. 1898.

vides a useful starting point in removing some of this doubt. *Wet Paint* is confirmed as a Bamforth film through the postcard connection, and because it is listed together with *Frog Leaping*, *Women's Rights, Snow Scenes at Holme Bank*, and *Railway Scene*, (otherwise known as the *Kiss in the Tunnel*) in a film performance given at the Drill Hall in Holmfirth by Harry Bamforth in March 1900. This group of films was described in a newspaper review as 'of great interest, being Bamforth scenes and local characters'.[12] A close examination of the fourth illustration on the *Wet Paint* card – 'she concludes amidst her sighs/his love is cold, or he would rise' – with a frame enlargement from the film of *Weary Willie in the Park – Or the Overfull Seat*; proves that both films were taken at precisely the same location and very possibly on the same day. John Barnes has been able to confirm from a contemporary reference, (which includes a frame illustration of *Weary Willie*), that this particular film must have been in existence by December 1898, although it was then believed to have been made by Riley Brothers rather than Bamforth's.[13] The distinctive bare weeping willow seen in the background suggests a late autumn date for the production of both films. Furthermore, since *Wet Paint* is indisputably Bamforth's, *Weary Willie* must also be, and previous attributions of it to Riley's are incorrect. Location similarities, and the fact that the baby featured in *The Tramp and the Baby's Bottle* is warmly wrapped up, suggest that this film also belongs to a late 1898 filming date.

There are however, at least two Bamforth films which do not fit into this pattern of production. These are *A Kiss in the Tunnel*, and *Women's Rights*, (known for many years as *Ladies Skirts Nailed to a Fence*). Neither film could have been taken in the late autumn of 1898 – one probably belongs to the summer of that year, and parts of the other may even date back to 1896, and have originally come from another source altogether. A cursory glance at the background shown in both the film and the associated postcard for *Women's Rights*, shows that it was taken at a time when the foliage was fully out. In addition the characters featured are using parasols as protection against the hot sun. Barry Salt has suggested 1900 as the date for its production,[14] but in view of the summer filming this is clearly impossible,

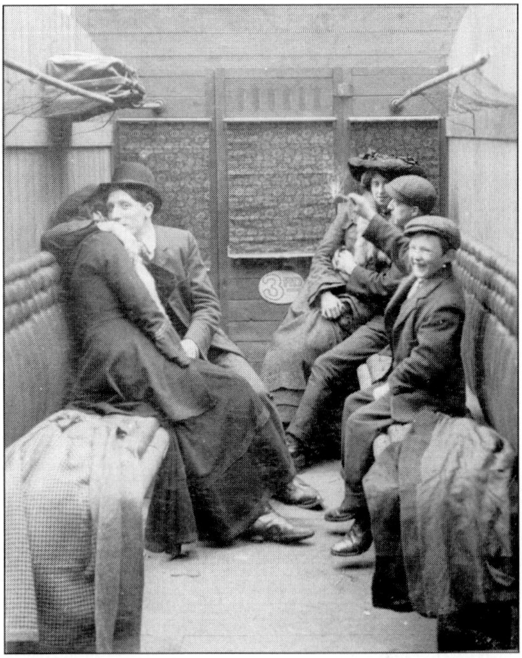

Fig. 4. Photographic postcard titled 'Youthful Impudence', c. 1898.

since the title, as has just been noted was included in the March 1900 Holmfirth programme. However, John Barnes has drawn attention to a brief reference published in August 1898 to a release of films by Riley brothers.[15] If we may assume that these films were in fact Bamforth productions marketed under Riley's name as seems highly probable, it can be suggested that *Women's Rights* is a survivor from this earlier group, which may also have originally included *Rustic Cricketeers* and *The Biter Bit*.

In the case of Bamforth's *Kiss in the Tunnel,* it has been assumed for some years that the film is a composite, with the two flanking actuality sequences of a train entering and leaving a tunnel originating with Riley brothers, and the central sequence of the couple kissing in the suggested darkness of a tunnel being produced by Bamforth's. The existence of a closely related postcard – 'In the Tunnel' – satisfactorily establishes that the central staged sequence is indeed theirs, but the origin of the other shots is more doubtful. Bamforth's re-used the same theme and same 'set' to produce 'Youthful Impudence', a 'naughty boy' genre study in which a boy strikes a match in the tunnel and lights up the couple kissing. Salt suggests a production date of December 1900 for *The Kiss in the Tunnel*,[16] but this can be dismissed without much hesitation. Not only is there no contemporary documentation for any Bamforth film production during 1900 – and none cited by Salt – circumstantial evidence within the film makes it highly likely that, in common with *Women's Rights*, it belongs to a pre-August 1898 release date. The carriage scene must have been taken when the light was good and December would seem a most unlikely choice in this respect. An even more cogent reason for assigning a summer date is that the girl featured is wearing a light summer dress and straw boater hat. To have dressed an actress for a summer scene whilst filming in winter was a concept of time manipulation by film quite alien at this date.

But do the outer sequences of *A Kiss in the Tunnel* belong to 1898, or an earlier period? During 1896, Cecil Wray's Kineoptoscope, exhibited under the title of the 'Cinetograph'; gave a series of shows in Bradford. The company organising these performances was named in associated newspaper advertising as the 'Scientific Entertainment Company' of Matlock Bath in Derbyshire.[17] This becomes relevant when it is noted that film and railway historian John Huntley has identified the location for the second tunnel sequence in the Bamforth film as Monsal Dale, which is not far from Matlock Bath.[18]

There seems to be no good reason why Bradford based Riley's would have selected a distant Derbyshire location to produce a simple, non specific location shot of this nature, especially when there were so many suitable locations available in their own area. It is far more likely that these tunnel shots were originally taken by or for the Scientific Entertainment Company in mid-1896, and then passed, with other material acquired by Riley's, from Wray when they bought the rights to his 'Kineoptoscope'. This would suggest that there may have been a more complex relationship existing between Bamforth, Riley's, and other local filmmakers than has been hitherto suspected; with Riley brothers themselves filming some subjects, acquiring others, and commissioning further titles. In the case of *The Kiss in the Tunnel* these various strands of commercial development came together. A somewhat similar situation exists in the case of G. A. Smith's version of *The Kiss in the Tunnel.* While the central portion was made by Smith, and features himself and his wife, the outer sequences in the copy preserved in the NFTVA were taken by Cecil Hepworth.

Thematic and narrative originality and derivations

Although several Bamforth films pioneer what are now considered to have been important advances in film narrative construction technique, the company's originality did not usually extend to choice of subject, and in a number of cases they remade already well known recent films; no doubt in order to take full advantage of good-will and free publicity. This type of appropriation of films of proven commercial success was seen as a problem at the time, but in the absence of effective copyright protection, was both a legitimate commercial strategy, and an understandable course of action to take, at a time when films were still widely regarded as no more than an ephemeral novelty.[19] The characters that appeared in Bamforth's films such as the couple seeking seclusion, the comic 'stage' tramp, the upper-class fool, the termagant women, and the stupid policeman, were all stock late nineteenth century theatrical or music hall figures emblematic of innocence and experience, and vice and virtue, and instantly recognisable to audiences everywhere.

The Tramp and the Baby's Bottle is a good example of this type of wholesale 'borrowing', for a studio-based version with exactly the same theme had been filmed by American Biograph as *A Tramp's Dinner*, and was available in England as a Mutoscope reel. Also borrowed from Biograph was *Pillow Fight*, an extremely popular subject which had been featured in the Biograph programme at the Palace Theatre in London during 1897 and early 1898. Bamforth's *The Biter Bit* was a straight copy of the Lumiere's *A Practical Joke on the Gardener,* and *The Schoolmaster's Portrait* a copy of a R.W. Paul film of April 1898, *When the Cat's Away.* On the contrary, if Bamforth's *Kiss in the Tunnel* was made, (or at least released) during 1898, the G.A. Smith film of the same title, produced in September 1899 post dates it, and is an example of Bamforth's own work being imitated. It is noticeable that the 'pathetic' type of subject so prevalent in Bamforth's lantern slide output and seen in some early films such as Paul's *Arrest of a Deserter (1898),* does not appear in their early films. Perhaps since this was commissioned work, subject selection was made by Riley's. Plot development can be integrally linked to cutting technique or shot placement as it is in the case of *Women's Rights* and *The Kiss in the Tunnel*, or be cinematically effective without it, as in *The Tramp and the Baby's Bottle*.

In this connection, while there may be some uncertainty about the dating of *The Kiss in the Tunnel*, there can be none with regard to its seminal importance in the development of film continuity. Salt terms it, 'the earliest important example of the use of simple cuts to join shots'[20] and Barnes is even more enthusiastic, stating, 'with this film, film narrative is born!'[21] It is certainly an exceptionally interesting film, but does the present three-shot sequence represent the way in which it was originally presented? In the Hepworth 1903 film catalogue in which this film appears, it is preceded by a (now lost) film of 62 feet entitled *The Honeymoon*, which shows a newly married couple boarding a train at a country station. Given the mundane subject matter, it is difficult to see any point in this film being shown on its own or indeed why – despite a misleadingly provocative title – anyone should wish to see it, for by the late 1890s audiences were used to viewing far more sophisticated and interesting subjects. But suppose that is conjectured that *The Honeymoon* was originally intended to form the opening sequence to *The Kiss in the Tunnel*, (a total length of 140 feet would not have been too unusual to be credible by this date). Then a more balanced and comprehensive structure could be suggested, as the synopsis for both films suggests.

> ***The Honeymoon***
> A newly-married couple are seen entering a railway carriage at a country station. They are surrounded by numerous friends and relatives, who have come to wish the happy pair 'good luck' The handshaking and kissing process occupies a considerable amount of time, and handfulls of confetti are showered upon them and the peculiar custom of tying an old shoe on the handle of the door is also carried out. The train moves out of the station, the friends cheering heartily, which the young couple seem to much appreciate (62 feet).

> ***Kiss in the Tunnel***
> A deep railway cutting is seen, with a train entering the tunnel at full speed. Next there is a view of the interior of a railway compartment, where a young couple are seated at opposite corners of the carriage. Upon entering the tunnel, the young man, who has previously been smoking a cigarette, throws it away and seats himself beside his sweetheart; and the loving embraces with which they greet each other are very amusing. The train is then seen emerging from the tunnel, passing along a very pretty bit of railway scenery and finally drawing up at the railway station where the passengers alight. This is a very good subject, and absolutely free from any suggestion of vulgarity (78 feet).

It will be noted that as the film is understood and viewed, only the continuity of the action in *The Kiss in the Tunnel* is explicit, for the story-line is unknown. Incorporation of *The Honeymoon,* with *The Kiss in the Tunnel* would provide for that need, as well as – crucially- establishing for the viewer the causal relationship between the couple, their presence on the train, and the central action of the kiss. One could then postulate a structurally connected 'circular' sequence of action. Was this film originally even more innovative than it is currently considered to be?

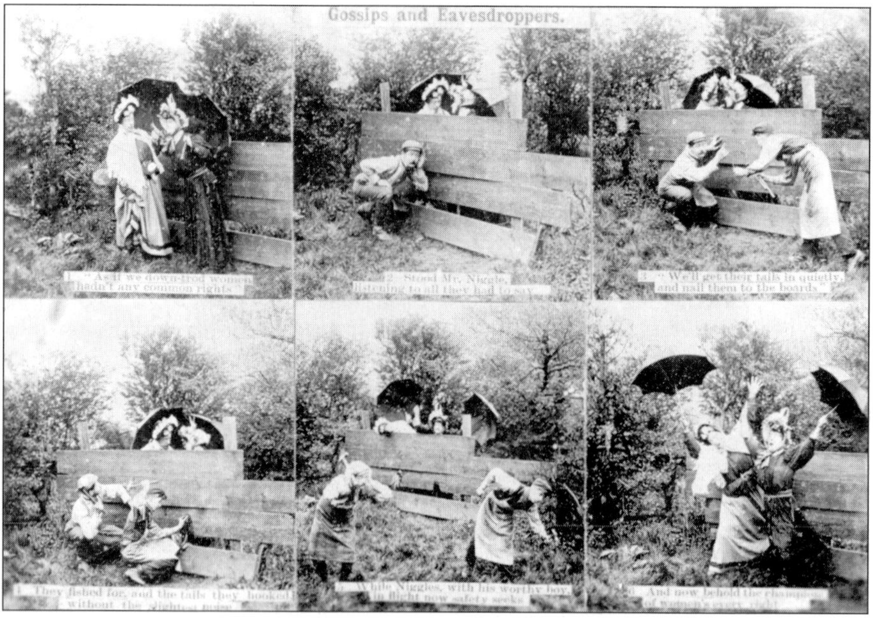

Fig. 5. Photographic postcard tableaux titled 'Gossips and Eavesdroppers', c. 1898.

> **Shot one**: The establishment of the story-line. A Honeymoon couple board a train at a country station. The train is shown leaving. (Away from camera?)
>
> **Shot two**: The development of the narrative sequence journey and anticipation of future action. The train is seen entering a tunnel (Away from camera)
>
> **Shot three**: The climactic sequence. The couple kiss in the tunnel. Scene 'held' by the camera.
>
> **Shot four**: Completion of the circularity of the action, and a 'joining' to the last action of shot one. The train emerges from the tunnel moving towards the camera. The train is shown arriving at the station.

Even in its possibly truncated present form, *The Kiss in the Tunnel* has an understandable narrative, but the narrative intention in *Women's Rights* is obscure to the point of incomprehension. It is however well worth attempting to clarify a meaning in this case for, like *The Kiss in the Tunnel*, this film is regarded as of considerable importance in the development of film production technique in England. Dr Salt for example, claims that it embodies:

> The earliest cut to another direction within a scene … in which the second shot is taken at 180 degrees to the first from the other side of the fence with time continuity. This was obviously done to make the action of the film clear. Interestingly, this cut is achieved by an ingenious cheat, which depends on moving the action to the other side of the same symmetrical fence, without moving the camera for the second shot.[22]

In *Women's Rights* we can see a further development towards a reliance on the unique qualities of film not present in the central sequence of *The Kiss in the Tunnel*.

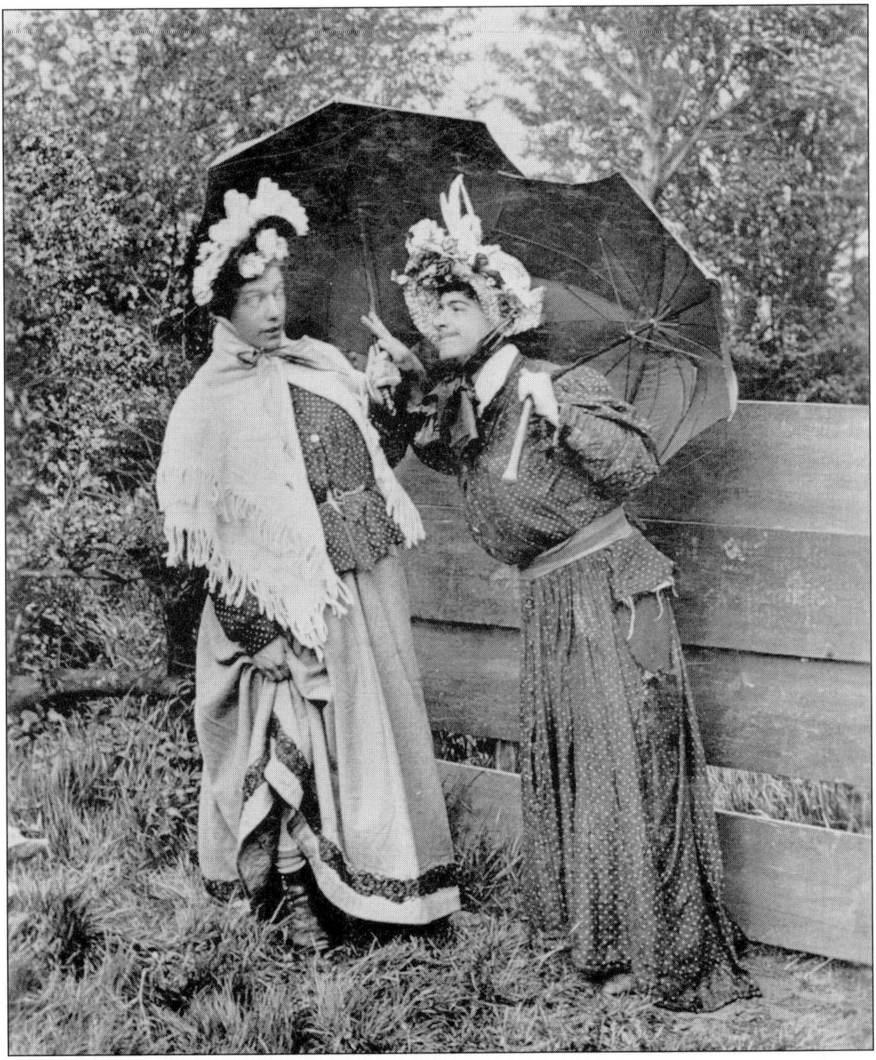

Fig. 6. Photographic postcard 'Don't Talk about your neighbours: If your tongue needs exercise chew Gum', taken from the previous card 'Gossips and Eavesdroppers', c. 1898.

Although sequential shots from both sides of the fence, introduced to aid plot development were included in both the slide and the postcard presentation of this subject, time continuity, which Salt rightly highlights could not be achieved in any other medium but film. But although it may be true that the continuity of the film is clarified by innovative cutting, the meaning of that action still remains unclear. Why are two adults engaged in the odd action of nailing women's skirts to a fence? Clearly there must have been both a meaning to, and a cause for, the action, which the filmmaker expected would be immediately apparent to a contemporary audience but which has since been lost. Fortunately it is the existence of a related

Bamforth postcard which enables the meaning behind this particular film to be recovered, and also establishes that the theme is one of social comment sweetened with humour; a categorisation which applies to a number of other Bamforth subjects, and is especially notable in many of their lantern-slide sequences. The action in the film is now quite clear, and is to be understood as retribution against two foolish women for gossiping about 'Women's Rights'. The commentary included on the card offers a progression and explanation of the scenes, following a straightforward linear time development.

1. 'As if we downtrod (sic) women/hadn't any common rights'.
2. Stood Mr Niggle/listening to all they had to say.
3. 'We'll get their tails in quietly/ and nail them to the boards'.
4. They fished for, and their tails they hooked/without the slightest noise.
5. While Niggle with his worthy boy/ in flight now safety seeks.
6. And now behold the champions/ of women's every right.

Women's Rights at the time were of course primarily concerned with the suffrage question, and the card/film with its final note of triumph, is clearly poking fun at the pretensions of two ridiculous and unfeminine women. (To accentuate this aspect, the parts are played by men) If women waste their time in idle gossip about things they cannot possibly have the intellect to understand, do they deserve to be taken seriously and given the vote? It is possible that the women represented were based on actual known 'local characters' as the March 1900 *Holmfirth Express* reports; so confident are the characterisations in this case.[23]

In attempting to establish the reception of a film such as *Women's Rights* the relevance of socio-economic homogeneity present in a small, self-contained town as Holmfirth at the end of the nineteenth century is key to establishing pre-formed value judgements, and understanding the attitudes formed from them. Nor is this simply a case of considering a working class perspective. Audience attitudes, especially when directed specifically towards a social or moral position that characters assumed, are likely to have been influenced as least as much by shared community religious beliefs, than by purely political questions of the franchise.

From a non-conformist – especially strongly Methodist and patriarchal – perspective, (predominant in Holmfirth in this period) the women's behaviour in *Women's Rights* is doubly offensive. Scriptural authority allotted women a separate and complementary role in society to that of men, whose temporal authority – when for example entering into marriage – women had agreed to obey. To do otherwise was therefore to be interpreted as directly challenging God's word. Equally, idleness was sinful, for, since no one knew how long they were to live, to waste time in idle talk, or action was, in effect, to devalue God's gift of life. We are thus reminded that the innovative internal structure introduced into *Women's Rights* to aid narrative continuity, and which is now the primary interest to film historians, was not the only, nor by any means the most important way in which the filmmaker communicated with his audience. Instead the relationship was far more complex, requiring not just technical ability but social knowledge and empathy to succeed.

Communicating individuality within a local context

If we next examine the characteristics of plot development in Bamforth films independently of cutting technique, it can be suggested that the potential that film offers to construct a narrative is, in fact, better realised in *The Tramp and the Baby's Bottle*, (which includes no innovative shot placement) than it is in the traditionally more famous example of *Women's Rights.* The probable American origin of Bamforth's tramp film has already been noted. In American Biograph's *A Tramp's Dinner*, the device adopted to allow the tramp to steal the baby's milk unseen, is to have the couple engage in prolong kissing. This format could have been – and perhaps originally was – presented as a sketch on stage. The Bamforth film could not. The later Hepworth 1903 catalogue describes the film as follows:

> ***The Tramp and the Baby's Bottle***
> This is a scene is a public park in which a nursemaid is seen wheeling her charge in a mailcart. Coming to a seat she places the mailcart beside it, and sits down and begins to read her Society paper. She is so interested in the contents that she does not notice the approach of [PC] B441, who greets her with a kiss, and seats himself beside her. They afterwards stroll away arm in arm. The Tramp, who had been watching his opportunity, now springs from his hiding place and makes a dash towards the mail cart, and seizing the bottle from the baby, squats down and enjoys the liquid refreshment, much to the baby's alarm. The nursemaid and policeman suddenly return, and while the girl rushes for the baby, the policeman makes for the tramp, and after a severe tussle succeeds in capturing him, and takes him off to the police station (72 feet).

As the catalogue entry notes, in the Bamforth film the policeman initially sits on the park bench with the nursemaid, but, in a far more attractive device for emphasizing the baby's abandonment, and consequent isolation and danger, the couple then stroll arm-in-arm from the foreground through the middle distance to the background. The use of perspective is very effective in this case. As the couple move away from the camera, their size, and hence the importance of their protective role, diminish in parallel.

Moreover a basic personalisation is achieved. The American couple suggest no individuality through their actions. They are simply careless – lost in their own pleasure, they have forgotten about the welfare of the baby. But Bamforth's couple walk past the baby and then turn their backs to the camera symbolically rejecting their responsibility for the infant. The audience can see that they are both stupid and selfish rather than simply forgetful. Their physical separation from the baby introduces an element of tension, noticeably lacking in the American film, in which the cop, only has to turn his head, and rise from the bench in order to chase the tramp away. In the Bamforth film elemental 'bonding' with the audience is achieved through presenting the couple's physical separation from the baby, and reinforced through the fictional representation of a universal shared fear – the danger to infants from strangers. Can the policeman return in time from the distance he has put between himself and the baby? Will the baby come to any further harm in the meantime? Film narrative in this case is effective through scenario and suggestion, rather than any overt demonstration of shot placement. Can there be any doubt

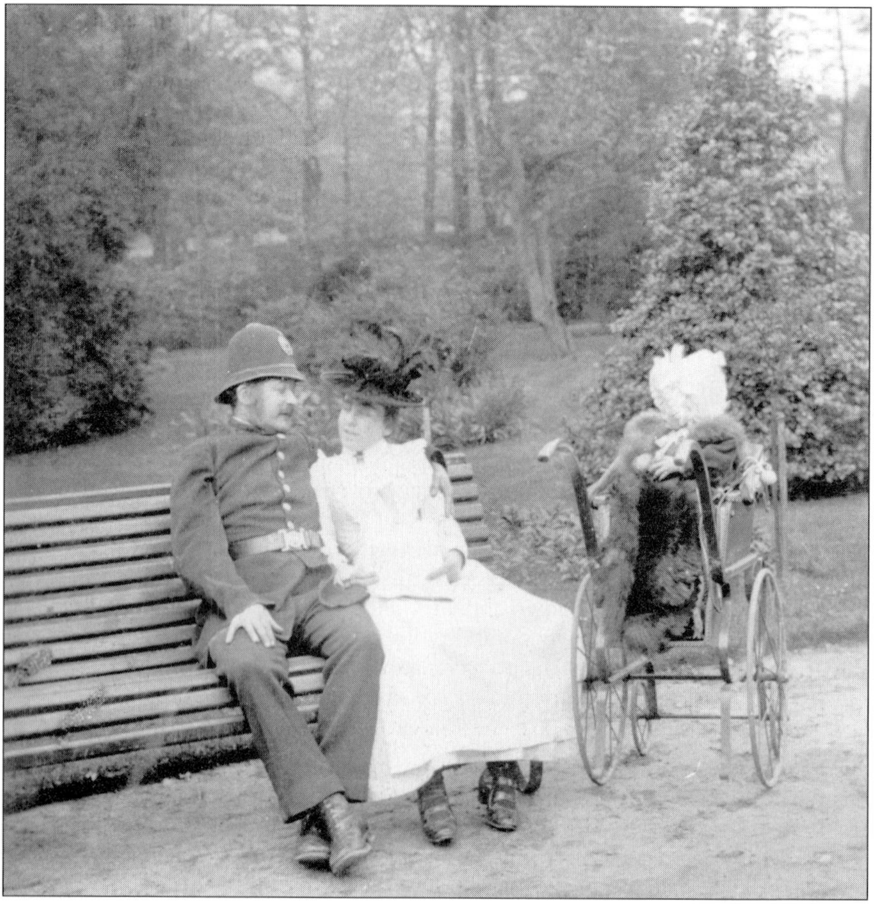

Fig. 7. Photographic postcard 'Robert on Duty', 1898.

that this parallel and concurrent development was effective with contemporary audiences? As in *Women's Rights* there is a possibility that the central figure of the policeman was based on, (and perhaps even played by) a local officer.

The film related postcards – 'Robert on Duty' and 'A Cop's Flirtation' leave no doubt that Bamforth's intended the central character in this case to be the policeman. Thus the source material – the postcards, and the Hepworth 1903 catalogue title to the film – are thematically at variance with each other. Because of this flaw it is possible to demonstrate more easily than would have been the case, that the relationship in this film between theme development and dramatic and humorous content was intended to function within a local context. Lacking such a local reference one would probably make the tramp the central character. And indeed the title given to the film (by Hepworth?) in 1903 makes just this assumption. But the confrontation in the film is between a dull, rather than a comic policeman, interacting with an intelligent and resourceful tramp. The stupidity of the nursemaid's boyfriend is emphasised by the fact that he is not simply an ordinary member

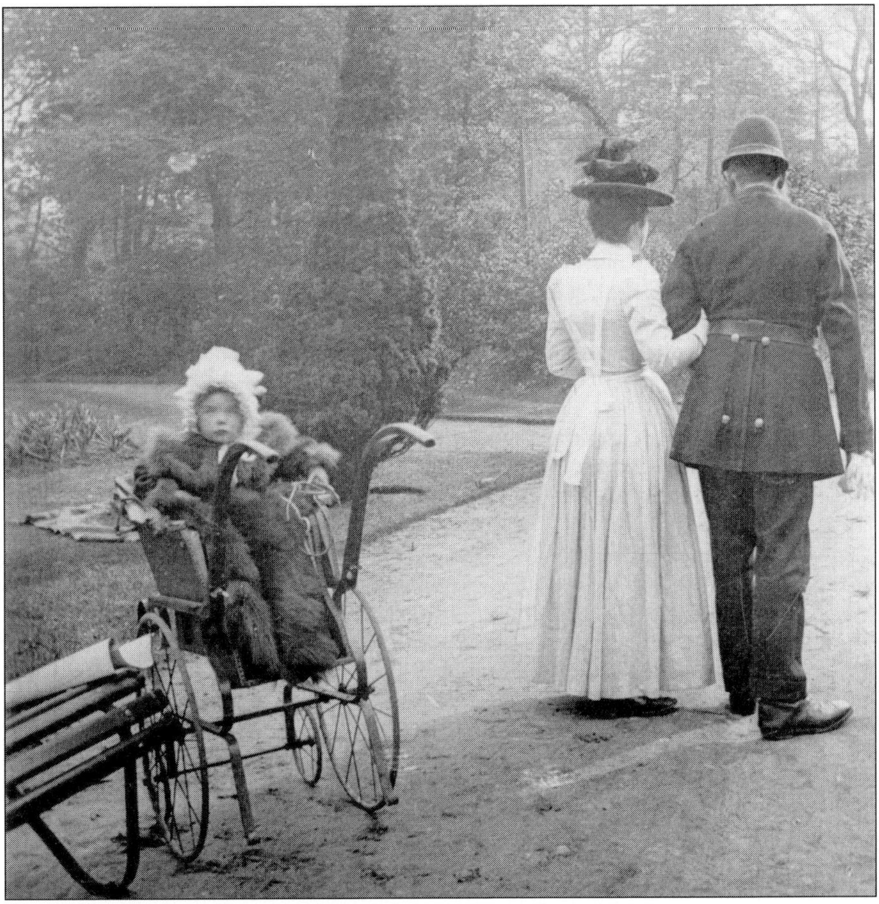

Fig. 8. Photographic postcard 'A Cop's Flirtation', 1898.

of the public, but a policeman supposedly trained to be watchful and observant. In a neat reversal of roles, it is the tramp rather than the policeman who is observant and clever. Naturally in order for this scenario to work, both the filmmaker and his audience must already share a collective perception about the local Holmfirth police. Were they perhaps regarded as stupid and ineffective in the 1890s? Under the heading of 'A Holmfirth man's mistake' we find the local newspaper writing in November 1898:

> making allowances for the dull perception of policeman (and Holmfirth policeman in particular ...)[24]

It would certainly not have been difficult in this case for contemporary local audiences to 'decode' specific references which informed the film for them, and established a bonding of shared knowledge between themselves and the filmmaker.

While *The Tramp and the Baby's Bottle* uses shared experience to create tension through anticipation, *Wet Paint* connects with the audience by exploiting shared perceptions and prejudices. The contemporary context and primary source of information in this case – once again, the text on a Bamforth postcard – carefully defines the young man featured as a 'masher'.[25] This characterisation would have had both a specific meaning and cultural contextualisation for local audiences. It is yet another example in Bamforth's films of the successful communication of a character's individuality. To a working class audience in late nineteenth century Holmfirth, a 'masher' would have been regarded as a symbolic representation of an effete, work shy, 'aristocrat' of independent means.

To a casual viewer, or an uninformed audience, the humour of the film is centred in the chance situation of a man sitting on a park bench which has just been painted; but, as in the case of *The Tramp and the Baby's Bottle*, a contemporary local Holmfirth audience would have decoded this film in a far more subtle and multi-layered way. The reason why the young man is in this predicament is not purely accidental – it relates to his established character. As a 'masher' he has led a drunken and dissolute life; the opposite to that lived by the 'honest working man' in the audience. He is in the park for a specific reason – he is trying to recover from the previous nights debauch and he is pursuing one of the main interests of his life, for he 'hopes his lady love to meet'. We may assume that is it because he is still under the influence of alcohol that he has failed to notice that the bench has just been painted. Unlike *Weary Willie*, the park in this case is deserted. The audience would know from their local knowledge why this was so. A park bench would have been painted on a weekday, when respectable, productive members of society were at work. Thus it is specificity of location, as well as dress, that establishes the 'masher's' individuality and effectively communicates his character.

Like the women in *Women's Rights* he wastes his time in idle and disreputable activity. Moreover, his 'lady love' appears to be considerably older than he is. It is quite possible that this is a deliberate, rather than a chance circumstance, and that the filmmaker intended to communicate a further layer of characterisation. Rather than working honestly to support himself, is the 'masher' instead hoping to live off a wealthy older woman? The masher's character has no real worth; instead he relies on an outward show of dress to impress others. His subsequent punishment – embarrassment, desertion by his 'lady love', and loss of dignity in having to run out of the park without his trousers, is therefore biblically appropriate, retribution.

When considered as social/historical documents, selected Bamforth films can be seen to contain very clear moral debates. Centred on personal behaviour, and the consequences of 'pride before a fall'; these were themes which original audiences would have already been familiar with from the pulpit. Some films clearly reflect tensions present in the small insular community that created and viewed them. As the 20th century drew near, challenges to once accepted social values; and the changing role of men and women in society, were particularly disturbing issues for a provincial, rather than a metropolitan community to confront.

In the three films which have been discussed – *Women's Rights, The Tramp and the Baby's Bottle* and *Wet Paint* - the filmmakers position is conservative. It is not the social order within which the characters exist which is being attacked, but rather the behaviour of the individuals within it. It is improvement rather than radical overthrow which is required. The 'victims' featured in the films have all forfeited their right to sympathy because their behaviour has been inconsistent with their status. Symbolically, it is sometimes articles of their clothing – that highly visible and reliable indicator of social position in the late Victorian period – that are targeted, and damaged or destroyed, as in *Women's Rights* or *Wet Paint.* Bamforth films of 'farcical scenes' often express a reactionary fear of change and of the consequences of a breakdown in the established order of society, but in the resolution of their scenarios they invariably offer comforting reassurance and confirmation to the audience of the validity of working class social values. The sermon may now be delivered from the new 'living picture' cinematograph screen, rather than the old pulpit, and be visual rather than oral, but the message that retribution will certainly overtake those who defy convention is a traditional one. It gains credibility and impact from the filmmaker achieving a high level of specificity in his use of 'local characters' who enable a bond of shared experience, recognition and interpretation to be achieved with the audience by utilising stereotypical characterisation as explanatory vehicles.

The well dressed man in *Wet Paint* is a fool rather than a worthy representative of the privileged class to which he obviously belongs. The occupants of the park bench in *Weary Willie* are snobbish and self centred, assuming a false dignity which deserves to be deflated. The women in *Women's Rights* have lost their femininity, and consequently both their role in society and the respect to which they would have been entitled. They have become inappropriately involved in matters such as politics and the vote, which are exclusively the concern of men. The nursemaid in *The Tramp and the Baby's Bottle* has ideas above her station in life; reading a 'society paper' rather than attending to the baby satisfactorily, and thus discharging the trust that her social and economic superiors have placed in her.

But men have responsibilities too. They may enjoy positions of prestige which are denied to women, but in return for this conferred group status they must earn the respect of society by demonstrating their ability in these roles. The assumption of privilege by the 'masher' is not sufficient to gain him respect and is negated by his behaviour. The policeman in *The Tramp and the Baby's Bottle* is an object of sarcasm and disrespect because he is stupid and unobservant, both qualities that destroy effectiveness in his particular role. Members of society who are ineffective not only damage their own reputation, but endanger the structure of society by betraying the role it has given them. The quick-witted tramp, who outsmarts both his social superiors in *Weary Willie*, and the figure of law and order in *The Tramp and the Baby's Bottle,* also; significantly – refuses to conform to his assigned caste status, by being aggressive, rather than deferential, towards them. He thus represents a real threat to the stability of society; but so to does the policeman whose own failure is responsible for allowing some of this potentially dangerous deviation to occur.

Notes

1. I have previously referred to some of these issues in a longer work, see Richard. Brown and Barry Anthony, *A Victorian Film Enterprise: The History of the British Mutoscope and Biograph Company 1897–1915* (Trowbridge: Flicks Books, 1999): 51–54).
2. For a recent example see 'Cecil Hepworth, Alice in Wonderland, and the development of the narrative film' by Andrew Higson in (ed) *Young and Innocent? The Cinema in Britain 1896–1930* (Exeter: University of Exeter Press, 2002): 42–64. Adopting a film centred definition of 'narrative' allows the author to suggest linear development, which the present account will suggest is both a partial and incorrect assumption of actual early practice.

3. *The Photogram* (March 1899), Vol. 6. No. 63, pp. 76 and 78.
4. The largest collection of 20,000 Bamforth postcards can be found at Huddersfield Library owned by Kirklees Community History Service.
5. According to G. A. Household , *To Catch a Sunbeam* (London: Michael Joseph, 1979): 8, Bamforth's worked to a script when preparing their lantern slide sequences. If this practice was carried over to film – as it may well have been – they could be credited with another remarkable innovation in cinematography.
6. See Richard Brown, 'The Kinetoscope in Yorkshire: Exploitation and Innovation', in Simon Popple and Vanessa Toulmin (eds) *Visual Delight. Essays in the Popular and Projected Image in the 19th Century*, (Trowbridge: Flicks Books, 2000): 105–115.
7. British Patent No. 182 of January 1895.
8. John Barnes, *The Beginnings of the Cinema in England, 1894 –1901, Volume 1: 1894–1896* (revised and enlarged edition, Exeter: University of Exeter Press, 1998): 165.
9. *Catalogue of Magic Lantern and Lantern Accessories manufactured and sold by Riley Brothers Ltd.* (1898): 16. London: British Film Institute.
10. Dennis Gifford in *The British Film Catalogue Vol. 1. Fiction Films 1895–1994* (London and Chicago: Fitzroy, Dearborn, 2001), arranges Bamforth output into two groups (often confusing Bamforth's and Riley Brothers), September 1898 and October/December 1899. Since the author provides no contemporary citations for any of these dates, their authenticity is impossible to verify.
11. See *Holmfirth Express*, (4 March 1899): 8.col. 6, (11 March 1899): 6, Col. 6 (4 November 1899): 6, col. 5 and 6, (2 December 1899): 6, col. 5 and 6. For an illustrated account of Bamforth's slide production see Philip Reynolds, 'Sentiment to Order', *Harmsworth Magazine* (November 1900): 337–334. The first reference to a local series of films (none named) occurs on 31 December 1898, when it was noted that Harry Bamforth gave a show at St. John's Church Upperthong.
12. Entertainment in the Drill Hall, *Holmfirth Express* (17 March 1900).
13. John Barnes, *Pioneers of the British Film, Volume 3: The Rise of the Photoplay* (London: Bishopsgate Press, 1988): 55 illust 28a. Geoff Mellor in *Movie Makers and Picture Palaces, A Century of Cinema in Yorkshire 1896–1996* (Bradford: Bradford Libraries, 1997): 41, has noted that the location used for Bamforth films was Victoria Park, Holmfirth.
14. Barry Salt, *Film Style and Technology: History and Analysis*, (London: Starword, 1983): 65.
15. John Barnes, *The Beginnings of the Cinema in England, 1894–1901. Volume 5*: 1900 (Exeter: University of Exeter Press, 1997): 271.
16. Salt, loc. sit., p. 53.
17. *Bradford Observer* (11–29 June 1896), cited in (Barnes, Vol. 1): 165.
18. John Huntley, *Railways on the Screen* (London: Ian Allen, 1993): 88.
19. See for example a letter from a 'film maker' under Copyright in Cinematograph Films' *The British Journal of Photography*, 52 (15 December 1905), p. 998.
20. Salt, p. 53 loc. cit.
21. John Barnes, *The Beginnings of the Cinema in England, 1894–1901. Volume 4: Filming the Boer War* (London: Bishopsgate Press, 1992): 48.
22. Salt, p. 65, loc. cit.
23. The advertisement for this exhibition, *Holmfirth Express* (10 March 1900): 5, refers to 'A large number of farcical scenes, all of which are acted by well known local characters'. James Bamforth was proud of his ability to effectively use amateurs in his slide and postcard scenarios, see Reynolds op. cit. 340/341.
24. *Holmfirth Express* (26 November 1898): 7. col. 1.
25. A name applied to a fop of affected manners and exaggerated style of dress who frequented music-halls and fashionable promenades and who posed as a 'lady-killer'. The word was common in 1882 and for a few years after. It is said to have been introduced from the U.S. Masher[2]. *Oxford English Dictionary*, 2nd edn. A contemporary who knew the type well, noted that a 'Masher's' slogan for life was 'old wine and young women'. 'Of brains they had few of proffesions as a rule none.' Sir Seymour Hicks, *Vintage Years* (1943, p. 30).

Notes on the Contributors

Richard Brown is an independent film historian and the author with Barry Anthony, of *A Victorian Film Enterprise: The History of the British Mutoscope and Biograph Company, 1897–1915* published in 1999. He has published widely on all aspects of early film and photographic history with particular interest to business and economic practice.

Alan Burton is Senior Lecturer in Film at De Montfort University, Leicester. He has published widely on political and documentary cinema, and his major new study, *The British Consumer Co-operative Movement and Film, 1890s–1960s*, is published by MUP in 2005.

Patrizia Di Bello lectures on the History and Theory of Photography at the School of History of Art, Film and Visual Media, Birkbeck College, University of London. She is working on a book on Victorian women's albums, considering them in the context of the tactile, as well as visual, culture of the time.

John Fullerton is an Associate Professor in the Department of Cinema Studies at Stockholm University, and has published widely on early Scandinavian cinema and early mass visual culture. Recent publications include *Screen Culture: History and Textuality* (ed. Fullerton, 2004) and *Allegories of Communication: Intermedial Concerns from Cinema to the Digital* (co-ed. Jan Olsson, 2004). He and Elaine King are currently researching representations of Mexico by nineteenth-century and early twentieth-century European and North American travellers.

André Gaudreault (1952) is full professor of film studies at the Université de Montréal, in the Département d'histoire de l'art et d'études cinématographiques. There, he heads CRI (Centre de recherche sur l'intermédialité) and the research group GRAFICS (Groupe de recherche sur l'avènement et la formation des institutions cinématographique et scénique). He has presented numerous scholarly papers and published extensively on film narration and/or early cinema. He is also director of the scholarly film journal *Cinémas*.

Frank Gray is the Director of the South East Film & Video Archive at the University of Brighton and a specialist in early English cinema. He has written widely on the work of the Sussex film pioneers George Albert Smith and James Williamson and curated museum exhibitions on early and regional film history.

Ann Hartley trained as a geneticist and had a career in teaching, educational administration and epidemiological research. After retirement she returned to her interest in local and family history. *Joseph Burton Wallett: The Life of a Travelling Photographic Artist* is the story of her husband's great, great grandfather. She is continuing to research the itinerant photographers, actors in portable theatre, and showmen in the family.

Joe Kember is a lecturer in Film studies at the University of Exeter. Most of his research and publication has concerned nineteenth century popular culture and early film.

Elaine King is an independent researcher currently researching representations of Mexico by nineteenth-century and early twentieth-century European and North American travellers.

Philippe Marion is Professor in the Département de Communication (Faculté des sciences économiques, politiques et sociales) at the Université catholique de Louvain, where he is a member of the *Unité de recherche en « journalisme et récit médiatique »*. He is a co-founder of the *Observatoire du récit médiatique* and has published a wide range of articles on film and technology in French and English.

Luke McKernan is Head of Information at the British Universities Film & Video Council. He has written books on newsreels, Shakespeare and the moving image, and Victorian cinema. His doctoral thesis was on Charles Urban and the early non-fiction film, and he recently completed a research fellowship with the AHRB Centre for British Film and Television Studies, investigating the film business and cinema audiences in London 1894–1914.

Charles Musser is Professor of American Studies and Film Studies and co-chair and Director of Undergraduate Studies for the Film Studies Program. His books include *The Emergence of Cinema: The American Screen to 1907* (1990), *Before the Nickelodeon: Edwin S. Porter and the Edison Manufacturing Company* (1991), *High-Class Moving Pictures: Lyman H. Howe and the Forgotten Era of Traveling Exhibition*, 1880–1920 (with Carol Nelson, 1991), and *Edison Motion Pictures, 1890–1900: An Annotated Filmography* (1997). Charlie is completing a book entitled *May Irwin's Kiss*, about the interplay between live performance and theatrical film entertainment during the mid-1890s.

John Plunkett is lecturer in Victorian Literature and Culture at the University of Exeter. He is the author of *Queen Victoria – First Media Monarch* (OUP, 2003), and co-editor of *Popular Print Media 1820–1900* (Routledge, 2004) and *Victorian Print Media: A Reader* (forthcoming OUP, 2005). His long term project is a book provisionally entitled 'Optical Recreations: A History of Screen Practice 1780–1900'.

Simon Popple is Senior Lecturer in Cinema at the Louis Le Prince Research Centre at the University of Leeds. He has published widely in the areas of early cinema, photography and popular culture. He is joint editor of *Early Popular Visual Culture* and is currently writing a book on popular cultural representations of the Anglo-Boer War.

Amy Sargeant is lecturer in the History of Film and Visual Media, Birkbeck College, University of London. She has published widely on British silent and sound film and is co-editor of *British Historical Cinema* (Routledge, 2002) and author of *British Historical Cinema: A Critical History* (BFI, 2005).

Peta Tait is Professor of Theatre and Drama at La Trobe University, Melbourne, Australia and researches in Physical theatre and performance, gender identity and Australian theatre. Recent publications in Australian studies are an edited volume: *Body Show/s: Australian Viewings of Live Performances*, *Amsterdam: Rodopi*, 2000; co-edited with Elizabeth Schafer *Australian Women's Drama: Texts and Feminisms*, Sydney: Currency Press, 1997/2000, and authored *Converging Realities: Feminism in Australian Theatre*, Sydney: Currency Press, 1994.

Vanessa Toulmin is Research Director of the National Fairground Archive at the University of Sheffield Library. Joint Editor of *Early Popular Visual Culture* and co-founder with Simon Popple of both the journal and the Visual Delights conferences. She has published widely on all aspects of popular entertainment and has just completed a four year AHRB project with the British Film Institute on the Mitchell & Kenyon Collection which formed the basis for the bfi publication *The Lost World of Mitchell & Kenyon*, co-edited with Simon Popple and the BBC 2 Series of the same name.

Gerry Turvey is Field Leader in Film Studies at Kingston University and a director of the Phoenix Cinema in London. He is currently researching the films, personalities, and organisational arrangements of the British and Colonial Kinematograph Company (1908–1924) and their relationship to both popular culture and 'respectable culture'. He has published widely on this company and contributed to the *Proceedings of the British Silent Film Festival* edited by Alan Burton and Laraine Porter.

Ine Van Dureen, Dutch in origin, but since 1995 lives and works in the UK as the Moving Image Archivist for the South East Film & Video Archive at the University of Brighton. She has a special interest in domestic film, family lantern slide collections and the Life Model Slide genre; from screen imagery to screen resources; archival concerns moving between the personal and the public domain. Presently Research Officer of the Magic Lantern Society.

Helen Walasek was curator of the *Punch* Archives and Collection from 1998 until its sale to the British Library in 2004. She continues to work as a consultant to Punch Cartoon Library.

William Merrin is a Lecturer in Media and Communications at the University of Wales, Swansea, specialising in media theory, media history and new media. He is the author of *Baudrillard and the Media,* (forthcoming, Polity, 2005), and *New Media: Key Thinkers* (with N. Gane, forthcoming, Berg, 2006), and a member of the editorial board of the on-line *International Journal of Baudrillard Studies.*

Index